IMPRISONING OUR SISTERS

Imprisoning Our Sisters

The New Federal Women's Prisons in Canada

STEPHANIE HAYMAN

McGill-Queen's University Press
Montreal & Kingston · London · Ithaca

© McGill-Queen's University Press 2006

ISBN-13: 978-0-7735-3078-2   ISBN-10: 0-7735-3078-9 (cloth)
ISBN-13: 978-0-7735-3079-9   ISBN-10: 0-7735-3079-7 (paper)

Legal deposit third quarter 2006
Bibliothèque nationale du Québec

Printed in Canada on acid-free paper that is 100% ancient forest free
(100% post-consumer recycled), processed chlorine free

This book has been published with the help of a grant from the
Canadian Federation for the Humanities and Social Sciences, through
the Aid to Scholarly Publications Programme, using funds provided
by the Social Sciences and Humanities Research Council of Canada.
Funding has also been received from the International Council for
Canadian Studies through its Publishing Fund.

McGill-Queen's University Press acknowledges the support of the
Canada Council for the Arts for our publishing program. We also
acknowledge the financial support of the Government of Canada
through the Book Publishing Industry Development Program (BPIDP)
for our publishing activities.

Library and Archives Canada Cataloguing in Publication

Hayman, Stephanie
  Imprisoning our sisters : the new federal women's prisons in
Canada / Stephanie Hayman.

Includes bibliographical references and index.
ISBN-13: 978-0-7735-3078-2   ISBN-10: 0-7735-3078-9 (bnd)
ISBN-13: 978-0-7735-3079-9   ISBN-10: 0-7735-3079-7 (pbk)

  1. Reformatories for women – Canada.   2. Women prisoners –
Canada.   3. Correctional Service Canada. Task Force on Federally
Sentenced Women.   I. Title.

HV9507.H39 2006   365'.43'0971   C2006–900767-5

Typeset in 10/12 Sabon by True to Type

Contents

Acknowledgments

Imprisoning Our Sisters emerged from a thesis I completed at the London School of Economics and Political Science. Paul Rock and David Downes were supportive and wise supervisors, who provided encouragement when it was needed and the stability essential for the completion of the work. No PhD candidate could have received more help and I am deeply grateful to them both. I also valued the comments made by other members of the academic staff, and my fellow doctoral candidates, at various stages of my research. Frances Heidensohn and Kathleen Kendall examined the thesis and subsequently offered very helpful critiques. Tim Newburn encouraged me to continue when other commitments encroached and Elaine Player helped from the beginning. Members of the MLSG offered valued, alternative perspectives on writing a thesis (in ways they will remember). I am pleased to acknowledge the financial assistance of the Economic and Social Research Council (award number R004204284) and the grant from the Central Research Fund of the University of London, which helped fund the initial visit to Canada. This financial support facilitated more extensive fieldwork than I previously envisaged.

I am grateful to the Correctional Service of Canada for allowing me consistent and unfettered access to the new prisons and, later, to the archives relating to the work of the Task Force on Federally Sentenced Women. It should be emphasised that the views expressed in *Imprisoning Our Sisters* are mine and do not necessarily reflect the views of the Correctional Service of Canada, or its employees. The research underpinning this book would not have begun had Hilda Vanneste, Correctional Service of Canada, not opened the initial doors and provided consistent support and encouragement as the project continued. Her extensive knowledge of the Task Force, and the prisons which emerged from its deliberations, provided a constant reference point and

I am indebted to her. Lisa Watson was another helpful and informed guide to many of the processes which this book describes.

In all of the prisons I visited I was given considerable and unreserved help by their respective Wardens, the two Kikawinaw and their staff. Many often went out of their way to ensure that I met other people involved with the project in their provinces and their assistance and welcome was much appreciated.

Assessing the work of the Task Force on Federally Sentenced Women has involved meeting and interviewing many committed and thoughtful people. As is apparent throughout *Imprisoning Our Sisters*, I guaranteed all of those whom I interviewed that their anonymity would be respected. Therefore, I cannot name many of those who are most deserving of my thanks, so I collectively thank those on the Task Force and the Healing Lodge Planning Circle who met with me. I have many warm memories of their individual kindnesses and the way in which they guided me towards those whom I might not otherwise have been able to meet. I am conscious that this is also their story being recounted.

I wish particularly to acknowledge my debt to the Aboriginal women who assisted me. Aboriginal history is replete with examples of European interpretations of Aboriginal stories, but the importance of the Aboriginal contribution to the Task Force, and beyond, meant that their work had to be considered in this book. I hope the analysis is done with sufficient respect for those cultural and spiritual practices which are generally conveyed in oral form.

The Canadian Association of Elizabeth Fry Societies (CAEFS) played a very significant role during the life of the Task Force and the association continues to be the strongest of advocates for imprisoned Canadian women. It is fortunate indeed to be led by Kim Pate and I was similarly fortunate to have her perceptive assistance on many occasions. I am also very appreciative of the help provided by individual CAEFS' members whom, again, I cannot name.

All projects such as the one I recount are watched with critical interest by academics, and I have had the advice and encouragement of a number. Kelly Hannah-Moffat and Margaret Shaw offered calm comment when it was most needed and their eye for detail made their insights invaluable.

I am thankful that Philip Cercone, of McGill-Queen's University Press, supported the publication of this book. Joanne Richardson and Joan McGilvray were keen-eyed and helpful editors. The financial assistance of both the International Association for Canadian Studies and the Aid to Scholarly Publications Program is warmly recognised.

My family bore the brunt of my absences, occasioned both by field-work and the demands of writing. Jessica and Héloïse Hayman were immensely supportive throughout, as was Craig Batty. Edward Hayman ensured that I could begin the task and his unwavering support was, at all times, essential for its completion.

But this is a book about imprisonment and about those federally sentenced women who have the lived experience of that state. I have been fortunate to meet many and they are the ones to whom I am most indebted. Their individual stories, their many kindnesses, their humour and their courage have stayed with me throughout the long process of completing this work. *Imprisoning Our Sisters* is dedicated to them.

Glossary

AWC	Aboriginal Women's Caucus
CAEFS	Canadian Association of Elizabeth Fry Societies
CCRA	Corrections and Conditional Release Act, 1992
CD	Commissioner's Directive
cedar tipi	Spiritual Lodge at the Healing Lodge
CET	cell extraction team
CSC	Correctional Service of Canada
C-SPAC	Corrections – Senior Policy Advisory Committee
EAC	External Advisory Committee
EIFW	Edmonton Institution for Women
EU	Enhanced Unit
ExCom	Executive Committee of the Correctional Service of Canada
HLPC	Healing Lodge Planning Circle
IERT	Institutional Emergency Response Team
IMH	Isabel McNeill House
Ke Kun Wem Kon A Wuk	Keepers of the Vision (at the Healing Lodge)
Kikawinaw	"Our Mother" (in Cree). The director of the Healing Lodge.
Kikawisinaw	"Aunt" (in Cree). A senior member of staff at the Healing Lodge.
Kimisinaw	"Older Sister" (in Cree). The Healing Lodge's equivalent of a primary worker.
LEAF	Women's Legal Education and Action Fund
NIC	National Implementation Committee
Nova	Nova Institution for Women
NWAC	Native Women's Association of Canada

primary worker   guard/correctional officer
RPC/RTC   Regional Psychiatric Centre/Regional Treatment
                 Centre
ranges   a series of tiered, barred cells in the Prison for
                 Women
restraints   handcuffs and/or leg irons
RI   regional instruction
SLE   structured living environment
SLH/SLU   structured living house/unit
SO   standing order
TFFSW   Task Force on Federally Sentenced Women
WICL   Women in Conflict with the Law

IMPRISONING OUR SISTERS

Introduction

Yeah, I'm proud, but not in the sense of the report or the details, just that it bloody well happened. It is a huge achievement to build five new facilities across this country and we should shut up and say, "Hey, we did it!"[1]

Kingston, on the edge of Lake Ontario, has the air of a respectable, almost complacent city, with its brief period as the capital of what was once Upper Canada visibly manifest in its elegant colonial architecture. The city's present reputation as a centre of academic and military excellence, also derived from that civic history, might encourage the assumption that its prime function has always been the nurturing of those destined to play a prominent part in the public affairs of Canada. Such an assumption would be partially correct, yet Kingston has simultaneously had another, less publicized role; it has contributed to the regulation of Canada's more wayward citizens in the prisons found within, or close to, its boundaries. It is Kingston's less-fêted role as a pivotal centre of social control that forms the backdrop to this book, which examines one of its penitentiaries, the Prison for Women – a prison that came to be seen as an excessively oppressive part of Kingston's regulatory network.

Historically, responsibility for Canada's correctional system has been split between the provinces and the federal government, with those sentenced to imprisonment for two years or more being held in a federal penitentiary rather than in a prison. While there are a number of penitentiaries for men in Canada, relatively few women are sentenced to federal terms, and federally sentenced women were generally confined in Kingston's Prison for Women. This prison was located many hundreds, and often thousands, of kilometers from the home communities of the majority of the women that it used to contain. Were Canada smaller, and not a confederation of provinces, there would probably be no story to relate as imprisoned women might conceivably have been subsumed within the traditionally larger project of providing for male prisoners. But geography and federalism have ensured the primacy in penal history of a small group of Canadian prison reformers who saw to it that federally sentenced women could no longer be ignored. Their achievement was initially encapsulated in the 1990 report *Creating Choices: The Report of the Task Force on Federally Sentenced Women.*

The Task Force on Federally Sentenced Women was immediately distinctive in that its work focused entirely on women prisoners. Unusually for its time, the task force involved both civil servants and members of the voluntary sector working together on a government-sponsored penal reform initiative. The task force's report led inexorably to the closure of the infamous Prison for Women and its replacement by five regional prisons, among them an Aboriginal healing lodge. The task force did, indeed, "do it" – and how it managed such an ambitious project, and its subsequent outcome, is the subject of this book.

The Prison for Women's closure finally came about in 2000, yet a powerful memory of the prison continues to exert an influence upon the civil servants responsible for the care of federal women prisoners and upon individuals from the voluntary sector who act as advocates for the women. These two groups are inextricably identified with the planning that led to the publication of *Creating Choices*, in which they both argued forcefully that the Prison for Women was an unsafe and unfair environment for any prisoner. How those two constituencies came to be united in such a venture is a crucial component of the history of Canadian women's imprisonment, and it is also part of the larger, international history of incarcerated women. Until now, this Canadian enterprise has been a partially recounted history, with various commentators focusing on different aspects of the tale (see particularly Hannah-Moffat 2001; Hannah-Moffat and Shaw 2000). *Imprisoning Our Sisters* supplements others' work by providing a detailed picture of how (and why) the task force undertook its work and the consequences of its reforming venture.

The project of state-sponsored prison reform has frequently centred on improving the physical conditions that covertly continue to reinforce the prison's inherent discipline. It has less frequently questioned the prison's rationale and utility. Moreover, those responsible for prisons, or charged with assessing them, have too often thought of women as peripheral to the larger problem of controlling men and have simply added them on to plans devised for male prisoners (see particularly Woolf and Tumim 1991). The Task Force on Federally Sentenced Women was therefore unique in four ways: (1) it only focused on imprisoned women; (2) it involved both civil servants and representatives from the voluntary sector; (3) it acknowledged the possible contribution of a prisoner's socio-economic status to her offending; and (4) it recognized the importance, and impact, of ethnicity and culture within the sphere of imprisonment. As the task force discovered, its deliberations could not be divorced from Canada's colonial history, with the consequence that *Creating Choices* emerged as an amalgam of penal, feminist, political, and postcolonial theorizing.

Consequently, this book cannot simply recount the story of how a determined group of people (almost entirely women) successfully provided a blueprint for the eventual closure of the distant, unsafe Prison for Women. To reflect the complexity of the situation faced by the task force, *Imprisoning Our Sisters* briefly relates the history of previous attempts to close the prison and sets that discussion within the context of the broader political fight for women's rights in Canada. It also fills in the background to the task force's eventual decisions by examining the reformatory movement, which sprang up in the United States, having built upon Elizabeth Fry's work in England. Those early American reformatories played a significant role in the regulation of offending women, and their influence was also felt in Canada (Freedman 1981; Hannah-Moffat 2001; Rafter 1985; Strange 1985). Using the language of maternalism, women's reformatories relied on the assumption that other women could, through example, assist in the reform of their "fallen sisters." *Creating Choices*, as a woman-centred report, used the more recent language of second-wave feminism to explain its vision of a reformed prison, and it also suggested that other women (i.e., guards) could be role models for imprisoned women. *Imprisoning Our Sisters* notes the parallels to be drawn between the incorporation of both the maternal and feminist discourses into the correctional agenda and the way in which the intentions of the original "maternal" reformers reappeared in Canada at the end of the twentieth century.

While this is interesting in itself, it does not explain the full significance of how *Creating Choices* emerged from the task force's deliberations. Canada embraces three distinct cultures, which coexist within a somewhat uneasy confederation of provinces. It retains many of the institutions set up when Great Britain seized control of the nascent state from the French in 1763, yet the French were not its original peoples. They simply began the process of divesting the First Nations of Canada (the Aboriginal peoples) of their authority over land that had been theirs from time immemorial. The consequence of English authority and laws, imposed upon both Aboriginal nations and the Quebecois, emerged during the life of the task force, even though its few Quebecois members were assumed to be part of the larger Euro-Canadian grouping and had little means of proving otherwise.

The way in which these two groups – the Aboriginal and Euro-Canadian – were represented on the task force is important, because their individual perspectives intersected with the history of Canada and heavily affected the report's outcome. The Euro-Canadian task force members were confronted by their colonial history in a most unexpected way, and they found their work greatly influenced by an articulate and impassioned group of Aboriginal women, who had themselves only been invited to join the task force as an afterthought. The Aboriginal members captured the agenda, politicized the discussion to an extraordinary degree, and finally managed to have "their" language integrated throughout *Creating Choices*. By contrast the Quebecois, with significant issues of their own, exerted very little influence. Unlike the Aboriginal members they largely remained excluded from the venture until the task force's plan was finally implemented in Quebec and they had the chance to fashion a francophone prison. These issues of inclusion and exclusion are a significant aspect of *Imprisoning Our Sisters*.

Canada proved to be the exception to the general rule that the voices of prison reform advocates are sometimes heard yet are infrequently acted upon: the task force's report *was* implemented, if only partially so. It is also important to acknowledge, when discussing "reformers" in the context of this task force, that most public sector members would have assumed a joint moral ownership of such a label. They shared the commitment to improving the lot of federally sentenced women and were sometimes distressed by the assumption that they did not. But in reaching the conclusion that the prison should close, the task force had to confront their individual differences with regard to viewing imprisonment as a sanction. The dilemma faced by many reform advocates is the extent to which they should press for change to the existing system rather than for its reduced use as a sanction or even its abolition. Some task force representatives from the voluntary sector were prison abolitionists, both by instinct and conviction, who nevertheless recognized that the Correctional Service of Canada (csc) would never countenance abolition but might, in this instance, plan for a less damaging environment for federally sentenced women. Their participation in the task force had been premised on the belief that they could not stand by, on a point of principle, and watch as more women were harmed. Yet, in deciding to collaborate with prison administrators, they limited their independence and contributed to legitimating a system they instinctively distrusted. Individual task force members suspended their scepticism about the wisdom of the joint enterprise because they feared that the price of their failure to participate would ultimately be paid by the federally sentenced women.

The consequence has been that all the task force members from the voluntary sector – and this includes the Aboriginal representatives – now share responsibility for the plan with civil servants, irrespective of whether they individually participated in its eventual implementation or approved of its outcome. (The report was taken over by the civil servants once implementation began, and the voluntary sector, with the exception of the Aboriginal participants, was eventually frozen out of the process.) As will be shown, the voluntary sector members have indeed paid a price for their participation. It might be suggested that CSC used the conscience of the voluntary sector solely to legitimate the joint enterprise and that its participation was for the ultimate convenience of the officials. But this is too simplistic a reading because the civil servants were as concerned as the voluntary sector about conditions in the Prison for Women. As the work progressed relationships changed, and the impact of the Aboriginal members' views altered the balance and focus of the task force's most influential committee. This is an essential backdrop to the story related here.

The effect of these various relationships became apparent in specific areas. Part of the importance of *Creating Choices* lies in the way in which it characterized federally sentenced women as "high needs" but "low risk." The report was heavily influenced by the task force's reluctance – for complex reasons, which *Imprisoning Our Sisters* explores – to label women as potentially violent. Federally sentenced women were seen to be victims as much as victimizers, and this led to the task force's failure to be prescriptive about the type of accommodation that should be provided for the 5 percent of women it unwillingly decided might need higher levels of security. This failure left *Creating Choices* with a potentially fatal flaw at its heart because the absence of such decisions subsequently allowed CSC, rather than the task force, to decide what type of secure accommodation should be provided. The report's underlying assumption was that the great majority of federally sentenced women could live with relatively low levels of security and that this security should be "dynamic" rather than "static." Subsequent provision for the "high-risk" women has departed from the task force's original vision and emerges as an unintended consequence of its work, even if, as is later argued, it should have been foreseen.

The themes of *Imprisoning Our Sisters* are: women as prisoners; inclusion and exclusion; the legitimizing of reform and its conse-

quences; and culture, ethnicity, and spirituality within the context of
imprisonment. These themes are illustrated in two ways. I first discuss
the reasons for striking a task force on federally sentenced women, the
way in which it was assembled, and what it eventually planned. I then
examine three of the five prisons that subsequently opened: the
Edmonton Institution for Women, the Nova Institution for Women,
and the Okimaw Ohci Healing Lodge. This is not because the other
two prisons – Établissement Joliette and Grand Valley Institution for
Women – were less important but, rather, because of the scale of
Imprisoning Our Sisters. Indeed, in light of the book's focus on the
impact of Canada's colonial past on the task force itself, a very good
case could have been made for considering the Quebec prison as well.
However, events at the first two prisons so profoundly affected all the
others that they were almost self-selecting.

The concept of the Healing Lodge was a complete departure from
any other Canadian correctional norm, and CSC allowed some Aboriginal people considerable input into the lodge's post-report planning.
The Healing Lodge's significance as a national venture should not be
underestimated. It conveyed a message to the wider Canadian public
that the Aboriginal nations, for so long disproportionately represented within the prison population, could no longer be provided for
without consultation. This was an outcome attributable almost solely
to the political skills of some of the Aboriginal task force members.
Whether the Healing Lodge was indeed the right arena for such a
political intervention is a contentious issue, particularly as prisons are
not an Aboriginal concept. The building of the Healing Lodge itself
raises the possibility that Aboriginal peoples might find themselves
incorporated into a state structure that they have never formally
acknowledged. With the immediate caveat that Aboriginal peoples
rightly question a non-Aboriginal person's understanding of their
issues, within the context of what *Creating Choices* attempted to do I
simply could not ignore the Healing Lodge: to do so would have been
to marginalize the importance of the Aboriginal members' contribution to the task force and to distort any conclusions reached. In
addressing the issues of culture and spirituality within the context of
imprisonment, I also explore historic questions of colonialism as well
as the related question of whether Aboriginal peoples have themselves
been compromised by agreeing to work with those previously seen as
their oppressors.

The first half of *Imprisoning Our Sisters* discusses the historical
context to the task force, and then the actual work of the task force
itself, within the framework of the wider literature of prison reform
and the colonial history of Canada. I use these resources as a means of

commenting upon the signal achievement of the task force, which was the publication of *Creating Choices* and the eventual closure of Kingston's Prison for Women. The second half sets out to achieve something different. In describing the planning and opening of three specific prisons, the narrative contributes to a future history. It is essential that what happened at each of these prisons should be recorded accurately and within the context of what the task force had hoped for each of them. Even at this early stage public and bureaucratic recollection of events at the Prison for Women, and the new prisons, is receding, and *Imprisoning Our Sisters* attempts to clarify the record. As a consequence, the histories of these prisons are straightforwardly related, with comment on events from those who experienced them first-hand. There is, however, a separate analysis of what transpired at these three prisons. The final chapter bridges both sections of the book as it enlarges upon the main theme: the unintended consequences of a benevolent enterprise.

The Task Force on Federally Sentenced Women hoped to provide a distinctly *Canadian* solution to the problem of imprisoning *women*, yet its project also sheds great light on the wider enterprise of prison reform. A remarkable aspect of this story is that the task force's work focused upon a relatively small group of prisoners – a little over 200 women at the time the task force was struck – yet its importance far transcends this. Worldwide, women consistently comprise a very small proportion of each country's total prison population, and their relative absence from prison statistics has been prison administrators' historic justification for pursuing the less expensive option of planning for them as though they were men. This Canadian task force challenged that history of neglect and showed, by dint of comprehensive research and consultation, that such an approach could no longer be sustained. Had the task force achieved nothing else, this would have been a singular accomplishment. That it achieved so much more is the reason for this book.

CONDUCTING THE RESEARCH

I undertook this research during four separate trips to Canada. During my initial trip in 1996 I visited all five of the new prisons, but only the three featured in this book had received any prisoners. Other prisons I visited included: the still-functioning Prison for Women; the Burnaby Correctional Centre in British Columbia; the Provincial Correctional Centre in Sackville, Nova Scotia; and the Minnesota Correctional Facility – Shakopee, which influenced the task force's plans for new prisons. In 1998 I revisited all of the new federal prisons, in addition to Maison Tanguay in Montreal, the Regional Psychiatric Centre in Saskatoon, and the Springhill Institution in Nova Scotia, where a unit for maximum security women had been opened, following the withdrawal of all such women from the new prisons. The Healing Lodge was the only prison I visited four times.

While the prisons were the main targets of each journey, I supported my research with many interviews with members of the task force, civil servants, representatives from the voluntary sector, and academics. I also formally interviewed prison wardens and engaged in informal discussions with prisoners and prison staff. CSC made task force papers available in 1998, and I supplemented these with papers provided by the Canadian Association of Elizabeth Fry Societies (CAEFS) and a member of the task force. The government papers illuminated many aspects of my research, but they were also problematic in that some of them were not for public release. It was generally possible to verify information from other sources, and the absence of a very small amount of data has not affected the conclusions reached. There was a network of information providers, many of whom knew each other, and maintaining the previously guaranteed anonymity of all these sources was a constant preoccupation during the writing of *Imprisoning Our Sisters*. Two respondents eventually allowed themselves to be identified, but the others chose to have their anonymity respected. I paraphrase their interviews when directly quoting them might reveal their identity.

As the research progressed I became one of the few people to have seen all of the new prisons. I was working in an arena constructed upon relations of power and depended upon various groups to facilitate my research. I had been granted access to the prisons by civil servants who worked at CSC headquarters, and within each prison I was dependent upon staff to allow me contact with the women. Since I was obliged to carry an alarm, my position vis-à-vis the women prisoners was very clearly marked out as being similar to that of a staff member. The staff members had their own hierarchies and, in interpreting "their" prison, they introduced me to some of the dynamics of each prison's organization. The women themselves had hierarchies, sometimes dependent upon a status they had individually carved out, so it was always necessary for me to negotiate separately my own association with each group. The fundamental inequality of my relationship with the women was underscored by my ability to leave a prison at will and the fact that I continued to see some of the same women at different prisons during the period of research. Yet those same women had an invaluable knowledge of the developing prisons – a knowledge upon which I relied – so the power was not as one-sided as one might suppose. Their changing perspectives often mirrored those of staff and became less optimistic as time passed.

The Healing Lodge presented particular difficulties. The fact that I chose to visit it four times reflected my ambivalence about assessing the venture, knowing the pain that had led to its creation. I was yet another "Euro," if not a Euro-Canadian, venturing into Aboriginal territory. As will become apparent, there has been a long and dishonourable history of non-Aboriginal people doing just that. The "rules" of the lodge, both disciplinary and cultural, were not always clear to me, and to ask what they were was to highlight my outsider status. I accepted an initial invitation to attend the morning Spiritual Circle and subsequently attended each day I was at the lodge. I also participated in a sweatlodge, while worrying that I might be viewed as a cultural tourist. Both experiences were valuable and illuminating, yet this combination of culture and spirituality, within the confines of a prison that did not look like a prison, was a perplexing one. Indeed, the messages conveyed by all the new prisons were altogether confusing, especially during my first visit. They did not look like prisons; they did not smell like prisons; the staff members were not dressed like guards; there was an absence of noise. Yet at Edmonton the tannoy system routinely referred to the women as "offenders," and they were frisked whenever they moved between buildings. The juxtaposition was bewildering.

A researcher hopes to be able to blend into the scenery, to be almost forgotten, so that observation can be less contrived. I simply had to speak in order for people to know that I was not a Canadian. But there are also advantages to being an outsider because you can ask the question "why?" rather more often. Strategies and plans, which perhaps seem logical in the local context, might not seem quite so obvious to others. My being a non-Canadian was mostly an advantage, primarily because I was distanced from events. However, the longer I stayed with the research the more this objectivity was strained, and that was entirely due to the fact that I had come to know the participants. I wanted them to succeed because I could imagine the bitter cost of their not doing so. I wanted the civil servants to improve the lot of federally sentenced women because I had seen Kingston's Prison for Women. I wanted the members of the voluntary sector to feel that they had succeeded as I knew the painful compromises they had made in order to join the task force. I did not want to see hope die in the imprisoned women themselves. Because I accepted the integrity that had brought the task force members together, I frequently did not want to be in the position of examining their project critically and sceptically. However, research is a fluid and flawed process, with no absolute "truth" awaiting discovery. The "truth" of *Imprisoning Our Sisters* is a mediated truth, relying on factual evidence, observation, discussion, and instinct. Such "truth" requires justification and context, and the following chapter begins that task.

CHAPTER ONE

Prelude to a Task Force

Because of its resolute focus on women, *Creating Choices: The Report of the Task Force on Federally Sentenced Women* has achieved a significance and importance beyond Canada. This raises questions about why Canada should have been able to produce such a woman-centred document long before other jurisdictions. Viewed from an entirely Canadian perspective, *Creating Choices* needs to be understood in terms of its genesis. Why was it so important that Kingston's Prison for Women should be closed? How was it possible for such a combination of reformers to be brought together for the task? Why did questions of history, culture, and ethnicity come to affect the final report so heavily? To begin answering some of these questions it is necessary to know more about the old prison itself and about events in Canada that made possible the formation of such an historically unique task force.

A VERY BRIEF HISTORY

The city of Kingston stands on the edge of Lake Ontario, and its strategic position at the mouth of the St Lawrence River ensured it an early importance among the first colonial towns of Ontario. Kingston houses a number of penal establishments, but none is more prominent than Kingston Penitentiary, which was built between 1833 and 1835, its design influenced by the "silent," or "congregate," system then practised at New York's Auburn Penitentiary.

Although built to incarcerate men, women were imprisoned in the penitentiary almost as soon as it opened. As Cooper (1993, 35) observed, "the historical record of corrections tells us that the small female population has always been housed wherever and in whatever manner best suited the interests of the larger male population," and Kingston Penitentiary illustrated that point well. In 1848, what became known as the Brown Commission[1] was appointed by the Reform government to investigate Warden Henry Smith's administration of Kingston Penitentiary. Brown recommended that women should be kept entirely apart from men and that a separate prison should be provided for them; yet the women continued to be housed in various cramped locations within the penitentiary, being moved as the needs of the men altered. The women were well-nigh invisible within the infinitely larger male group, as was evident when a lengthy report from the New York Prison Association, on American and Canadian prisons and reformatories, was submitted to the speaker of the State Assembly of New York in 1867. Kingston Penitentiary's "female ward" was simply mentioned in passing (Wines and Dwight 1867, 102–3).

The British North America Act, 1867, specifically Section 91, conferred authority over criminal law and the "Establishment, Maintenance and Management of Penitentiaries" upon the new Dominion (federal) government. At that stage, not only Kingston but also smaller penitentiaries in Halifax, Nova Scotia, and Saint John, New Brunswick, came under the federal umbrella and, in the following decade, a further ten joined them. The provinces became responsible for "Public and Reformatory Prisons." According to Oliver (1998, 303): "This division of authority excited much later comment ... it led, together with the 1868 statute [the Penitentiary Act] that defined a gaol term as two years less a day ... to a division of authority in correctional matters which would be condemned by every twentieth century commission on correctional practices, from Archambault in 1938, through Fauteux in 1956, to Ouimet in 1969, and frequently thereafter."

The acceptance of the two years plus a day provincial-federal divide recognized the function of gaols as local institutions, whereas the penitentiaries became part of the social control network (as exemplified by the criminal law) of the Dominion. Ekstedt and Griffiths (1988, 46) contended that "federal correctional policy was designed to establish the dominance of the federal government and to create a system of penitentiaries that would assist in the task of building a nation," a perspective that arguably continues to apply to present-day Canada. They also cited a Task Force on Corrections' report (1976, 8): "the federal government may have been considered the only government with the resources available to establish long-term institutions, *or there may have been insufficient numbers of long-term offenders in some regions of the country to justify an institution for them in each province*" (cited in Ekstedt and Griffiths 1988, 47, emphasis added). This argument could easily have been used for the federally sentenced women's population.

The Brown Commission's wish for a separate women's prison, based on Brown's knowledge of "inadequate living conditions, the extreme punitiveness, the absence of penitentiary discipline and the inability to occupy women with profitable labour" (Hannah-Moffat 2001, 80), was not fulfilled until 1913, when such accommodation was made available for thirty-four women. Yet the new quarters still remained within the walls of Kingston Penitentiary. The provision of this accommodation directly contributed to what some would later consider to be the missed opportunity provided by the recommendations of the *Report of the Royal Commission on Penitentiaries* (Macdonnell Commission), in 1914.[2] This suggested that female federal prisoners should be placed in the care of their home provinces; however, the costs so recently incurred by the building of the new women's quarters in Kingston were a powerful disincentive for change. The persuasiveness of the provincial-incarceration option for federal offenders continued (and continues) to be debated decades later.

The 1921 Nickle Commission, notable for being the first to consider federal women prisoners separately from male prisoners, emphasized what it regarded as the inappropriateness and vulnerability of the women's situation within Kingston Penitentiary. Nickle believed that there should be "adequate segregation of female convicts from male convicts and male staff," citing his concern that "the disclosures of the past year have shown how unscrupulous officers have taken unfair advantage of the opportunities for flirtations, improprieties and indecencies that presented themselves" (Nickle 1921a, 4–5, cited in Hannah-Moffat 2001, 83). Nickle's argument for closure led directly to the beginning of construction, in 1925, of what is now known as the Prison for Women. When this was finally completed in 1932 100 men, rather than women, were its first occupants. Rioting within nearby Kingston Penitentiary had damaged the men's accommodation, with the result that the women were kept waiting for the move to their new prison (87). The rioting had been widespread and had not been confined to Kingston. Between 1932 and 1935 there were outbreaks at other penitentiaries across the Dominion, and, for the first time, the public began to hear informed critical comment on penal affairs, with the riots providing "a sort of climax in the efforts of prison and penal reform bodies to obtain light upon conditions in the penitentiaries" (Kidman 1947, 41).

An inadequate prison for women

The Prison for Women formally opened to women in 1934. What was it like? The four-storey stone building, crowned by a copper-wrapped

Prison for Women, Kingston

cupola, had the appearance of a civic building rather than a penitentiary. The prison was a bewildering mixture of narrow passages,
myriad stairs, and inadequate communal spaces; for many it engendered a feeling of claustrophobia, heightened by the inadequacy of its
living accommodation. The Prison for Women became infamous for its
double-tiered A and B "ranges," which consisted of small cells fronted
by bars stretching from floor to ceiling, affording the women no
privacy and even less quiet. The cells looked like – and were – cages.
"A" Range contained fifty cells, half at floor level and half arranged
above at mezzanine level. "B" Range, while identical to "A," was split
in two, with half used for protective custody and dissociation, and the
remainder used for accommodating women whose institutional
(mis)behaviour had led to their being assigned there. Some women
remained on these ranges for years, never qualifying for the next step,
which was the "wing." This provided accommodation for the rest of
the women and contained fifty non-barred, largely single cells that
offered the women a modicum of privacy and the possibility of creating a space that was more distinctly their own. As Arbour (1996, 9)
was to comment, the prison was "inadequate for living, working,

eating, programming, recreation and administration." The prison was eventually enclosed by a huge wall, "half a mile long ... bolted into solid bedrock," erected at a cost of $1.4 million in 1980 when the previous wall was replaced (Johnson, cited in Cooper 1987, 140; TFFSW 1990, 63). This wall was the hallmark of a maximum security prison, although the prison was actually multilevel.[3] The only respite from this level of security was provided by Isabel McNeill House, directly across the road from the prison, which provided minimum security accommodation for just ten women.

In 1932, for reasons of economy, the authorities had built a "congregate-style prison, as opposed to a cottage-style [prison] (more associated with maternal discipline)" (Hannah-Moffat 2001, 86). But even so, and presaging what happened in England when Holloway Prison was being redeveloped (see Rock 1996), the building of the Prison for Women was delayed by architectural changes that added considerably to its cost. The prison contained neither an exercise yard nor educational facilities. Although there was a "supervising matron," the prison was administered jointly by the Kingston and Collin's Bay Penitentiaries (for men), and it was not until 1960 that this link was severed and a separate warden, Isabel McNeill, appointed (Hannah-Moffat 2001, 99).

The Prison for Women was administered by the Correctional Service of Canada (css), which is part of the Ministry of the Solicitor General. As a federal facility it received women sentenced to two years or more in custody. The prison took federally sentenced women from across Canada, but the development of exchange of service agreements (ESAS) meant that, by December 1988, 40 percent of federal women remained in their own provinces, although largely in Quebec and British Columbia (Shaw 1991, 4).[4] While provincial incarceration allowed these women to remain closer to their home communities, it also meant that they were disadvantaged in other ways, particularly with regard to the paucity of available programs. Provincially sentenced women could be transferred to the Prison for Women when their behaviour became, in provincial corrections' eyes, difficult to manage. Because the prison was the only federal facility for women, those who were sent there could be thousands of kilometres from their homes. A woman from Edmonton, for example, would be 2,898 kilometres from her home, and a woman from Vancouver would be 3,542 kilometres from hers. This geographic dislocation generally only applied to women. The far larger number of federally sentenced men had a greater number of penitentiaries to which they could be sent, and these were not all at the same security level. Men had the possibility of "cascading" through the system, whereas federal women had no such choice and could spend

their entire sentence in conditions of security entirely disproportionate
to the risk they posed.

A continuing history

The general description of the Prison for Women includes changes that
took place over the years; however, as soon as the prison opened, it
was the focus of criticism. Within the short space of four years the
Archambault Commission (1938) had recommended that the prison
be closed and the women transferred to the provincial authorities:
"Your Commissioners are strongly of the opinion that the number of
female prisoners confined in Kingston Penitentiary did not justify the
erection of the new women's prison and the further continuance is
unjustified" (forty were initially transferred to the prison). The
Archambault Commission was one of the first "to acknowledge the
rights of women prisoners to equal treatment" (Archambault, cited in
Cooper 1993, 43). Archambault had been prompted by revelations
during the trials of the men who had rioted in Kingston and elsewhere
as well as by the subsequent fierce parliamentary debates led by the
redoubtable parliamentarian, Agnes Macphail.[5] Women were not, as
a rule, permitted to visit the penitentiaries, but legislators – irrespective of their sex – were. Macphail made it her business to inspect them
"from dome to dungeon," leading Kidman (1947, 48) to suggest that
"on visitation committees of prisons there should be a woman [as
they] invariably see something that mere man overlooks." Archambault's implementation was derailed by the intervention of war, but
Kidman still felt able to hail it "as the most challenging document that
has been put forth on Canada's penal problems. Some commissions
deal with grain, harbours, fisheries, forestry and minerals, but this
deals with human beings, not all of whom are inhuman because they
are found in prisons" (51). Archambault's closure recommendation
could not withstand the fiscal reality of the recent building of the
Prison for Women, but in 1938 the provinces were at last prepared to
consider the idea of assuming responsibility for federally sentenced
women. By 1946, however, when the commissioner of penitentiaries
and the minister of justice finally decided to ask the provinces if they
would house federal women, it was made clear that, without heavy
financial assistance, they would be unable to do so. Federal assistance
was not forthcoming.

The question of what should be done with the Prison for Women
continued to occupy various committees in successive years, with the
Fauteux Committee (1956) recommending that a central facility
should be retained, and the Ouimet Committee (1969) suggesting a

unified prison service. The Royal Commission on the Status of Women (1970) returned to the theme of equality and was the first such body to make specific "recommendations for the provision of appropriate and relevant services and programs for Aboriginal and Francophone women" (Arbour 1996, 243).

The 1977 MacGuigan Report was a major government report and, like others, focused on male federal offenders; however, it also roundly damned conditions at the Prison for Women. It is now largely remembered for the aptness of one of its phrases, that the prison was "unfit for bears, much less women" (MacGuigan 1977, 135, cited in Shaw 1991, 17; Cooper 1993, 45). The National Advisory Committee on the Female Offender (Clark Report 1977), was "only the second major committee set up specifically to consider the future of the federal female offender" (Shaw 1991, 16). It took three years to produce its report, and it also recommended the closure of the Prison for Women, citing specific inequities experienced by female federal offenders, such as: geographic dislocation, the lack of adequate programs and services, and undue classification. Unusually for the time, this committee included three members from the voluntary sector. The Clark Report prompted the formation of the National Planning Committee on the Female Offender, which was asked to respond to the points raised by Clark, particularly the two alternative plans the report had formulated. These had suggested that the federal government should continue to be responsible for federal women but should house them in small regional facilities and/or that the provinces should take charge of these women. The Needham Report (1978) was the result of the National Planning Committee's deliberations, and it opted for the closure of the Prison for Women and the building of two replacement facilities in the east and west of Canada, which would remain in federal control. As with the two previous committees, Needham supported the idea of more community-based facilities and raised the possibility of a "co-correctional" institution (Ekstedt and Griffiths 1988, 337). The Chinnery Committee had simultaneously been charged with assessing the viability of the regional facilities and, in its report, also rejected the notion of keeping the Prison for Women open. By 1981 the Canadian Association of Elizabeth Fry Societies (CAEFS) had presented a brief to the solicitor-general advocating closure and suggesting that a Sixth (administrative) Region, responsible for federal women, should be created within corrections.[6] This last point was echoed by the Canadian Bar Association, which produced *Justice behind the Walls* (Jackson 1988). While this largely dealt with male prisoners, it bluntly stated that legislation should be introduced to compel closure of the prison. This overwhelming pressure for change culminated in the Daubney Committee recommending that the Prison for Women should close within five years and that a Task Force should be instituted to decide on the best way of facilitating this. The task force that finally emerged insisted that it "was not a government response to the *Daubney Report*" and was "not premised on the closure of the Prison for Women" (TFFSW 1990, 70). While it should be recognized that "every major correctional inquiry in Canada [at least until 1988] has commented on the Prison for Women" (Ekstedt and Griffiths 1988, 336), it should also be acknowledged that almost all did so within the context of discussing federal imprisonment as a whole rather than focusing solely on women.

The unifying theme of these reports was the inequity of a system that imprisoned most federally sentenced women far from their families and home communities, confined them in conditions of security disproportionate to their needs, allowed no possibility of transfer to a less secure environment during the course of their sentence, offered relatively few program opportunities, and operated within a building totally inadequate for its purpose. Some provincial inquiries, such as the *Report of the British Columbia Royal Commission on the Incarceration of Female Offenders* (Proudfoot 1978), further echoed concerns about imprisoned women. Yet, as each report was published, there was little political will to implement them.

The influence of the reformatory

The reformatory movement, and the legacy of the Andrew Mercer Reformatory in Toronto, which was the first separate prison for women in Canada, is the backdrop to women's imprisonment in Canada (see Strange 1995). As Hannah-Moffat (2001, 52) makes clear, it played a crucial, if largely unacknowledged, part in the history of the governance of imprisoned women in Canada, primarily through its use of "maternal discipline [of the sort] most often associated with middle-class nuclear families." In North America it was in the United States, rather than in Canada, that "middle class women who had been abolitionists and health care workers during the Civil War" in the late 1860s first began to take an interest in penal affairs and, specifically, in the situation of imprisoned women (Rafter 1985, xxi). They concluded that conventional, congregate prison design was inappropriate for women, "whose milder, more passive nature required a gentler environment," and their preference was for "cottages" in rural settings that would house relatively small groups of women (Rafter 1985, xxi). (As Rafter [1985, 33] made clear, these "cottages" were not on the small scale associated with the common usage of the word; rather, they duplicated the "cottages" of wealthy Americans and were "large, substantial houses" wherein the women would live under the guidance of a matron.)[7] The initial vision of these reformatories was predicated on the ideal of the "reformable" woman and "common womanhood" (Freedman 1981, 63), whereby "virtuous women could uplift their fallen sisters" (Hannah-Moffat 2001, 56). But not all "fallen sisters" were included because the original reformatory ideal was selective in its range and excluded those most commonly confined in custodial prisons. The first American reformatories concentrated on a group not previously brought within reach of "state punishment – vagrants, unwed mothers, prostitutes and other 'fallen' women who seemed more promising material for their attempts to uplift and train" (Rafter 1985, xxi). Freedman (1981, 47) contended that these first, visionary female reformers, while attempting to further the *rights* of women prisoners, believed in an "innate sexual difference" that enabled women to "control women's prisons"; the reformers were not attempting to press for "sexual equality." Moreover, the reformers' femininity enabled them to encourage similar feminine behaviour in imprisoned women, simultaneously transferring their own middle-class values on to women who had not previously experienced them (54). Zedner (1991), in chronicling Victorian attitudes to women's criminality in England, offered rich parallels with the North American reformatories and present-day attitudes to offending women, particularly in relation to their socio-economic status, their mental health, and their addictions. Even then, female prisoners were subjected to closer surveillance than were males, leading to heightened tensions and, unsurprisingly, the emergence of a determined few whose "discipline ... subjected the whole female convict population to increasingly rigid regulation" (213).

The Andrew Mercer Reformatory was the direct result of energetic lobbying by J.W. Langmuir, an Ontario prison inspector, who was also convinced of the need to imprison women separately from men. A timely legacy of $100,000 to the Province of Ontario secured the possibility of Langmuir's dream being realized, and he encouraged the province's premier to allow construction by telling him that "women's prisons, both in construction and administration, were 'of a far less costly character' than men's prisons" (Oliver 1998, 428). Canada's first reformatory differed from the first American reformatories in that the Mercer had to take "frequent offenders" and had "very modest expectations as to rehabilitation" (459). Further, at Langmuir's instigation the Mercer was based on the congregate system, yet its design allowed for "distinct and separate accommodation for four grades of prisoners" (429) – a hoped-for system of classification that does not appear to have survived the Mercer's opening in 1874. The logic and means of maternal governance applied at the Mercer outlasted its closure and, as has been contended by Hannah-Moffat (2001) and others, reappeared in the 1990s as the discourse again moved towards "women-centred" prisons. In a curious twist, the influence of the original American reformatory movement again became manifest in Canada during the 1990s, when the Minnesota State Reformatory, now known as the Minnesota Correctional Facility – Shakopee emerged as the exemplar for Canadian planners.

The growing influence of feminism

It was not only the various commissions of inquiry that suggested change at the Prison for Women. Legal challenges were mounted, one of the most important being a charge of sexual discrimination that Women for Justice filed in 1981 with the Canadian Human Rights Commission against the federal government. The commission found for Women for Justice, who alleged "discrimination in the provision of goods, services and facilities" (for federally sentenced women), and it upheld nine of their eleven complaints (see Berzins and Hayes 1987).[8] The founding of Women for Justice was a "turning point in Canadian women's prison reform [being] the first time that women outside the field of corrections came together to fight for the rights of federally sentenced women ... [seeking] to politicise and contextualise the discrimination faced by women" (Hannah-Moffat 2001, 135).

The patriation of the Constitution had united women across the country in their efforts to ensure that the equality provisions in the Charter of Rights and Freedoms (which is Part 1 of the Constitution Act, 1982) differed from those in the Canadian Bill of Rights. It is debatable whether the women's efforts would have been quite so vociferous had the government not urged the cancellation of a conference planned by the Canadian Advisory Council on the Status of Women (CACSW), scheduled for February 1981, which was to be the culmination of CACSW's campaign to ensure that women's rights would be protected under the proposed Charter (Razack 1991, 33–4). The conference was to coincide with parliamentary debates over the Charter, a clash that the government wished to avoid (Geller-Schwartz 1995, 53). Members of CACSW were government appointees and all, with the exception of the president, caved in to the government. As Brodsky and Day (1989, 17) noted, "men were negotiating a new Constitution, which would be very difficult to amend. It contained entrenched rights clauses that would affect women in Canada for decades to come ... Though outsiders to the process, women injected themselves forcefully into the constitutional debates, arguing with one voice for ... guarantees that could bring real change to the lives of women in Canada." The CACSW conference would have highlighted those sections of the proposed Charter that the government wished to deal with in its own way. This heavy-handed approach inspired women from across the country to attend an alternative conference in Ottawa and to continue campaigning until their message had been heard and was reflected in the Charter (Geller-Schwartz 1995).

Section 15 of the Charter of Rights and Freedoms covers equality, thus:

1. Every individual is equal before and under the law and has the right to the equal protection and equal benefit of the law without discrimination and, in particular, without discrimination based on race, national or ethnic origin, colour, religion, sex, age or mental or physical disability.
2. Subsection (1) does not preclude any law, program or activity that has as its object the amelioration of conditions of disadvantaged individuals or groups including those that are disadvantaged because of race ... [as above]

Section 28 continues: "Notwithstanding anything in this Charter, the rights and freedoms referred to in it are guaranteed equally to male and female persons."[9]

These powerful sections were to have been the basis of a class action by the Women's Legal Education and Action Fund (LEAF) under the Canadian Charter of Rights and Freedoms (1982).[10] LEAF intended to challenge CSC to prove that federal women were *not* actively discriminated against by the location of the Prison for Women. It intended to show that having just one federal facility for women precluded their moving to less secure accommodation as their security classification changed and that they were disadvantaged by the programs offered to them. This action was not pursued once the government committed itself, in 1990, to the closure of the Prison for Women. Earlier, it had been argued, in *Horii v. Canada Commissioner of Corrections (1987) 17 F.T.R. 190*, that women were discriminated against by being forced to serve a federal sentence in Kingston rather than in their home province. Although "Horii was unsuccessful in the first stage of her challenge to sex discrimination in the federal penitentiary system" (Brodsky and Day 1989),[11] her case helped underpin the ongoing construction of an argument that forced CSC to rethink its policy for federally sentenced women.

All of these latter actions had been taking place against a backdrop of increasing feminist interventions in the criminal justice arena, and, as Shaw (1996a, 179) suggested, "nowhere else had feminism made such marked inroads into official discourse than Canada." While imprisonment was not at the top of the agenda, considerable progress had been made in recognizing the prevalence of violence against women. The victims' movement was becoming entrenched, and, in 1983, changing attitudes towards sexual mores had led to the wider definition of sexual assault replacing rape on the statute book. Within government there had been a women's bureau since 1954, but it took a larger "coalition of 32 women's organisations, calling themselves the Committee for the Equality of Women in Canada (CEWC)" (Geller-Schwartz 1995, 43), to persuade the Canadian government to appoint a Royal Commission on the Status of Women. This commission led directly to the appointment of an eponymous minister in 1971, but there was no specific department for which this person was responsible, and the position continues to be that of a junior minister within the Cabinet. A further coalition of women's groups, the National Advisory Committee (NAC), campaigned specifically for the full implementation of the royal commission recommendations, and the Canadian Advisory Council on the Status of Women finally emerged in 1973. While this was mandated to highlight the interests of women, it was not independent of the executive, as the royal commission had recommended, and women's groups eventually shunned it (Geller-Schwartz 1995). Encouraged by the United Nations' declaration of International Women's Year, in 1976 the government established Status of Women Canada, which had specific responsibilities for scrutinizing legislation and policies for their impact upon women. As Geller-Schwartz (1995, 48) observes, "once established, women's policy agencies in Canada do not fade away. Successive Governments may reorganise structures ... but the institutions themselves seldom disappear." This institutionalization of women's influence paralleled the growing influence of a number of non-state women's organizations, many of which were represented in NAC, which was at the height of its influence in the mid-1980s.

This by no means exhaustive examination of inquiries, commissions, submissions, and legal challenges provides some explanation of why CSC was under such pressure to do something about the Prison for Women. But it would be wrong to suggest that much importance was attached to the Prison for Women by other government departments, let alone by the public at large. Employment, education, and adequate health care were of far greater public concern than was the welfare of a tiny group of women incarcerated in Kingston. So what made *this* prison such an icon for campaigning groups? And why did campaigners think it so particularly unsuitable for imprisoned women? To be, in MacGuigan's phrase, "unfit for bears, much less women"?

The answer to this lies in the Prison for Women's design and location. But there was also, increasingly, a feminist questioning of the subordinate role of women within Canadian society, which became centred on the fight to amend the wording of the Charter of Rights and Freedoms. The Prison for Women represented many of the larger inequities against which women were campaigning; on every score the prison failed the equality-with-men test. It was a microcosm of the wider discrimination women faced within Canadian society, as had been made so abundantly clear during the 1970s, with the wide publicity accorded both the *Lavell* and *Bedard* cases (see chapter 2) and the *Bliss* case (see Krosenbrink-Gelissen 1993; Brodsky and Day 1989; Razack 1991). These legal challenges had separately highlighted the ways in which the law discriminated against women on the basis of their sex. As is later made clear, women's expertise was co-opted for a variety of purposes by individual groups, and there was a nationwide network of women who were familiar with each other's interests and prepared to campaign on specific issues. Together, these women were able to reach key civil service personnel and to focus on the inequities faced by federally sentenced women.

Upon reading this list of inquiries and commissions it might be assumed that CSC relied on successive, conflicting reports as a means of avoiding action. Such assumptions would ignore the scale of the problems to be surmounted in a country the size of Canada and, in particular, the complexities of federal-provincial relationships. Rock's (1986, 169) comments relating to the Ministry of the Solicitor General are also applicable here: "On occasion it is as if ... dealings with the provinces map out a Balkans of the Canadian criminal justice system: one maladroit move always promising to lead to a much wider disturbance." Indeed, one senior official, interviewed during the course of this research, was asked whether there had been any consideration of the federal-provincial responsibilities being merged for imprisoned women. He responded: "the task was onerous enough, so to start the Third World War by discussing provincial-federal jurisdiction just wasn't an option."[12] As Rock went on to say, "in every (official) paper will be found a routine reference to the preservation of amicable federal-provincial relations" (ibid.), and this delicate partnership frequently leads to a proliferation of committees. Provincial sensibilities may never be ignored.

Within the context of what could be achieved federally, tackling the Prison for Women was finally something the civil service could do as the end of the 1980s approached. Imprisoned women were a less contentious group than were imprisoned men, and CSC believed that it could deal with the Prison for Women without attracting huge public debate. As a senior civil servant noted, "if you looked at treating men and women equally, this was not equal ... How long can you continue such unequal treatment of people before the public becomes sympathetic and begins to demand action?"[13]

The history of penal reform tells us that change is often achieved at a cost. As Cohen (1983, 115) warns us, "we must be wary of good intentions [as] benevolence might do more harm than good." A closer examination of the history of women's reformatories in the United States demonstrates that, once women were engaged in the management of separate female prisons, "power triumphed over sisterhood not because these were single-sex institutions, *but because they were prisons*" (Freedman 1981, 105, emphasis added). The innate discipline attached to any prison ensured that the initial benevolence was absorbed and subverted, simply because the prison could never be anything other than a place of involuntary confinement; prisoners could not see their imprisonment as a benevolent act, executed by a benevolent state. Similar good intentions failed spectacularly and tragically in the rebuilt HMP Holloway (see Rock 1996). The Prison for Women itself had originally been built as an act of benevolence towards women who were, rightly, seen to be disadvantaged compared to male federal prisoners. Yet it, too, had failed. However, it can equally be said that history should not be the reason for refusing to contemplate change; rather, we should learn its lessons, act upon them, and accept that benevolence can play a crucial role in effecting change. Canada was faced with a uniquely Canadian problem, occasioned by the federal-provincial split in jurisdiction and the vast scale of the country itself. While the protagonists were also aware of the lessons of history, they felt that their circumstances impelled them towards doing something distinctively Canadian rather than simply replicating the solutions found in other jurisdictions. They needed a catalyst, and the appointment of a new commissioner of corrections proved to be just that.

PREPARING FOR A TASK FORCE

Throughout its colonial history Canada relied on imported skills to develop its vast hinterland, pursuing expansionist policies despite the initial presence of large numbers of Aboriginal nations. Varying migratory patterns are evident in the very diverse nature of its present population, reflecting the results of social and economic upheavals throughout the world. Canada has also resorted to soliciting the help of specific individuals as needs have arisen both within and without government. The appointment in 1988 of a new commissioner of corrections, Ole Ingstrup, proved crucial to the continuing endeavour of

closing the Prison for Women. While much of his correctional background lay in his native Denmark, he came to Canada in 1983 as
special adviser to the then commissioner of corrections. Following
that appointment he was briefly chair of the National Parole Board,
so he was not unknown to corrections, nor seen as a complete outsider, by the time he assumed the role of commissioner himself. He
brought with him a Scandinavian perspective on prisons and punishment and was known as someone with a specific interest in programming, wanting to focus on the prisoners themselves rather than strictly
on their security management, as had generally been the case. He
wanted change throughout CSC, and within a very short time had
established a number of task forces and had brought in a new Mission
Statement for CSC. As Adelburgh and Currie (1993, 19) observed,
when reflecting upon his rethinking of the Mission Statement: "for
those of us who had worked with women in the federal correctional
system before Ingstrup's appointment, this sort of commitment from
the commissioner represented a radical departure from that of his
predecessors – who generally dismissed female offenders as insignifi-
cant or beyond rehabilitation."

Involving the voluntary sector: A partnership with CAEFS

On 1 September 1988 Ole Ingstrup distributed to the members of Corrections – Senior Policy Advisory Committee (C-SPAC) an outline proposal for the creation of a task force on female offenders. This proposal had already been discussed, informally, during an August
meeting with the Canadian Association of Elizabeth Fry Societies
(CAEFS), recognized within Canada as the foremost advocacy organization for imprisoned women. As CAEFS' Mission Statement notes, its
individual societies are "community based agencies dedicated to offering services and programs to marginalised women, advocating for legislative and administrative reform," with "volunteerism ... [being] an
essential part of [their] work." (CAEFS is the umbrella group for the
local societies and the national agenda is determined following intensive consultations with all its members.) On 16 September C-SPAC
agreed that a task force should proceed, and soon afterwards a formal
approach was made to CAEFS, inviting their participation. CAEFS' executive director, Bonnie Diamond, told CAEFS members in November that
she had already met with the deputy commissioner of corrections,
James Phelps, and the director of Native and Female Offender Programs, Jane Miller-Ashton, to discuss the proposals.[14] (It is noteworthy that CSC did not have separate directors for women and Aboriginal
peoples in 1989. Both were seen as "minorities," despite incarceration

rates for Aboriginal males, and particularly Aboriginal females, being entirely disproportionate to their numbers in the larger Canadian population.)[15] Diamond wrote: "I really want us to work quickly in having the task force up and moving. Time goes so quickly and I do think that Ole Ingstrup is very open to alternative ideas. The average term for a Commissioner of Corrections is three years and he has already been in the position for six months."[16] (Diamond was correct: Ingstrup was to move to another federal position in 1992.)

This willingness to consider a task force represented a compromise on the part of CAEFS as, for some time, it had been pushing for a royal commission on female offenders. As has been noted, "a favourite way in Canada to induce legislative change is through a more elaborate form of research and education, namely the public commission of enquiry. Governments find commissions a handy response to pressure from women's groups to do something" (Geller-Schwartz 1995, 51). Or, as Bruckert (1993, 4) wrote more bluntly, "establishing a Task Force or special committee to examine an issue that has successfully been defined in the public forum as a social problem has historically been a common strategy by the state to quiet the voices of opposition." Such commissions or task forces are seen "as an instrument of policy making, combining intellectuals, aware of the practical constraints of government, with civil servants and other knowledgeable private citizens" and are used to "facilitate both long-range planning and the control of government by the political executive" (Wilson 1971, 122, 123). Royal commissions are struck under the Inquiries Act, 1985, and are established by the "Governor [General] in Council." Such Commissions "have the power of summoning before them any witnesses, and of requiring them to: (a) give evidence, orally or in writing ... and (b) produce such documents ... as Commissioners deem requisite" (Section 4). Royal commissions are independent of government, with members being appointed from outside the sphere to be investigated. Task forces, by contrast, are "informal administrative aids to the executive" (Wilson 1971, 124) and for Ingstrup's purposes it was important that civil servants from CSC should be included as they would enable him to maintain control of both the time-scale and the personnel involved. He could also incorporate others from the various criminal justice departments, such as the Office of the Solicitor General and the National Parole Board, whose support would be needed should a workable solution be provided by the task force. CAEFS recognized that Ingstrup's preferred way of focusing on various issues was through such task forces and pragmatically accepted that this was the only means of change available to them. In her December 1988 executive report Bonnie Diamond wrote: "It looks like the task force will be a go but CSC is quite nervous entering into such an undertaking with us. If we can pull it off it will be a new model in co-operation."

The means of "pulling it off" required protracted negotiations between CSC and CAEFS. The CAEFS' Executive Committee met at the beginning of December to discuss the basis of a partnership with CSC and shortly afterwards formally sent its proposals to Deputy Commissioner James Phelps, who was then to negotiate the various points personally with Bonnie Diamond. CAEFS' view of the purpose of the task force was that it should "comprehensively study the circumstances of federally sentenced women and ... recommend an integrated national system of services that is based on meeting the needs of these women. The task force will produce a blueprint for action *complete with an implementation schedule*" (emphasis added). CAEFS outlined nineteen "important elements" and at that meeting Bonnie Diamond was able to obtain agreement on all but three: the financing of CAEFS' task force representatives, co-chairmanship, and the financing of the regional consultations. The gist of these discussions was conveyed to Ingstrup, who expressed reservations about some of the conclusions reached. Co-chairmanship was an essential prerequisite to CAEFS' participation and Phelps was able to point out to the commissioner that there had been a precedent set when the secretariat worked jointly with the private sector during the Women in Conflict with the Law initiative. There were concerns that the "co-chairmanship would make accountability for the Task Force unclear and would be inconsistent with the development of a policy framework for the Correctional Service of Canada,"[17] but CSC remained committed to involving the voluntary sector.

Canada was adopting an unusual approach. At that time most jurisdictions jealously guarded the right to produce their own reports and, while they might have consulted outside agencies, did not share the writing of the final report with them, nor did they necessarily disclose the consultations. A rare European exception was the Dutch initiative, *Women in Detention* (Ministry of Justice 1992), which involved external specialists in the working group. Stern, commenting on the role of the voluntary sector and pressure groups working in the criminal justice arena in the United Kingdom, cited their importance in being "free to argue for a better and more humane [penal] system" in that "they do not have the dual, and sometimes conflicting, responsibilities of many of the statutory bodies." She then highlighted the difficulties such groups face when dependent upon government for some of their funding and the fact that "grants are given ... on condition they are used to meet needs as defined by the Government or by statutory bodies. The effect of this is to erode the independence of voluntary organisations"

(Stern 1994, 244; see also Ryan 1983). When there is a financial relationship between an organization and government, there is an inevitable dulling of the critical edge, with "consensual limits and both sides know[ing] the boundaries" (Ryan 1983, 109). Independence is an ever-present worry for most campaigning groups and there is often little incentive for government departments and voluntary organizations to view each other as partners. Indeed, the voluntary sector has cherished its independence, largely (in the penal sphere) because of fears of incorporation and being used to legitimate government policies.

This Canadian decision to opt for joint participation in such an important policy venture had wide ramifications because the involvement of a national umbrella organization, CAEFS, and eventually the Native Women's Association of Canada (NWAC), signalled to the provinces that women's imprisonment was firmly on the national correctional agenda. What was being undertaken by the federal authorities could not fail to have an impact upon the provinces, which in turn might conceivably find it harder to ignore the regional branches of the national voluntary organizations. But there was also an underlying pragmatism in CSC's approach, as acknowledged by a senior civil servant: "it was better that they [voluntary-sector groups] participate because then you have a solution that satisfied them as well as the government – and, ideally, they would stop criticizing the minister at every turn!"[18] Such pragmatism, if indeed it was that, could also be viewed as a means of neutralizing and incorporating the voluntary sector. To have both CAEFS and NWAC involved made it harder for each organization to exercise its more usual function of informed, and often critical, commentator. CAEFS, in particular, was such a consistent and vocal critic of CSC that some federal officials thought the organization compromised its effectiveness because of its ubiquity, whereas some outside observers thought that CAEFS' prime function was "to be the burr in the government saddle."[19]

For CAEFS, the larger unresolved question was that of funding. CAEFS received sustaining funding from the Secretariat "to ensure the maintenance of the Association's national structure and to cover the core operating expenses necessary to fulfil their objectives,"[20] but it was insufficient to cover the additional cost of participating in the task force. CAEFS relied heavily on volunteers to pursue its work and it was felt that those asked to join the task force could not be expected to do so without recompense for the time involved, particularly as the civil servants would continue to be paid by their individual departments. Pressure to conclude the negotiations was compounded by the need to satisfy the Treasury Board, which, during the negotiations to finalize the Burnaby Agreement,[21] had made it clear that the ad hoc agreements for federally sentenced women were unsatisfactory and unlikely to be financed in the future. The commissioner finally met with Bonnie Diamond and Felicity Hawthorne, the president of CAEFS, in February. The meeting was an uncomfortable one ("in retrospect, we find the tenor of the meeting was disturbing"),[22] and the CAEFS' representatives failed to resolve the three outstanding matters. An angry CAEFS board, upon hearing that the commissioner considered the proposed task force an "internal operational review," passed the following resolution: "whereas CAEFS is a member of the voluntary sector it has no part to play in an internal CSC review of the Federal Female Offender except in an advisory capacity as consultants."[23]

The impasse was eventually resolved and agreement reached on the outstanding issues including, crucially, co-chairmanship of the task force's working group and steering committee. The working group was to carry out the bulk of the work, while the steering committee would "monitor, review and approve the activities and output of the Working Group"[24] and offer a "broad context for the work of the Task Force."[25] CAEFS formally agreed to participate in the task force on 14 March and, at the same time, nominated its members of the working croup. CAEFS' March Executive Report commented on recent developments and the board's action in reversing its earlier decision, saying: "Most of us approach such a joint venture with healthy awareness but also with optimism that any system reform will be better for our participation. *We will however have to remain very alert*" (emphasis added). Commissioner Ingstrup's retention of certain "accountabilities" because of the "government structure within which the Task Force [would] operate," was an indication to the voluntary-sector members of the structural reality of the enterprise they were joining.[26]

The constraints of co-operation

CSC's wish to work in partnership with CAEFS amounted to its recognition of the latter's pre-eminence as an advocacy organization for imprisoned women and partially explains why the service went to such lengths to accommodate the association's various demands. However, CSC's tactic was a particularly *Canadian* approach, rather than one that might be replicated within other correctional services, and a possible explanation for this can be found in the complex relationship between provincial and federal sensibilities and the curious dance in which each side engages while delineating the boundaries that each may not exceed. The consequence of this sometimes fraught relationship is the need to consult widely before decisions are reached. Every avenue must be explored, and in Canada these avenues frequently lead to the voluntary sector, whose alternative voices add legitimacy to the public debate. With respect to CAEFS, such a joint initiative also had the effect, as has earlier been suggested, of neutralizing it for the period of the task force and beyond because CAEFS would be intimately linked to, and sharing responsibility for, the eventual report. The risk of incorporation by government is a constant one for voluntary-sector organizations, and CAEFS understood the twin possibilities of both compromising its reputation as an independent organization and alienating its own membership. As a CAEFS' representative, looking back, said: "We had to accept one really difficult thing, which was that we had to operate within the law as it was then, because we thought it [the situation at the Prison for Women] was urgent enough to have to do that, so we knew that whatever we recommended would be prison of some sort ... and we had to know that we could live with that bottom line."[27]

The urgency of the need to do something about the Prison for Women underpinned CAEFS' decision to enter into partnership with CSC, but the relationship with CSC was never clear-cut. As well as the sustaining funding received by CAEFS, which enabled it to carry out its advocacy work, CAEFS also received government funding for the many community programs it managed across the country under the auspices of its various branches. CAEFS was involved in supervising women in the community on behalf of corrections,[28] and this reliance on government money led to tension between its independence as an advocacy organization and its status as a paid agent of the state. As Rock (1996, 23) wrote: "private bodies cherish their privacy. A paradoxical consequence has been that the private sector periodically petitions federal departments for money to support its independence." This paradox lay at the heart of CAEFS' relationship with government. At the time of the task force CAEFS would have been astonished had CSC considered any organization other than itself as the major partner. (When the Corrections and Conditional Release Act [CCRA] was subsequently passed in 1992, CAEFS interpreted Section 77: "the Service shall ... (b) consult regularly about programs for female offenders with (i) appropriate women's groups" as applying particularly to it.) However, many of its members questioned the wisdom of being involved in a government project that might conceivably lead to the building of new prisons, making CAEFS' negotiations with CSC particularly delicate. It tends to be forgotten that CAEFS' members, while then displaying many of the sensibilities of prison abolitionists, did not formally adopt an abolitionist stance until June 1993.[29]

In many voluntary groups, there is often a considerable overlapping of key personnel, and, although Canada is a vast country, the need for provincial branches of national organizations frequently means that those operating in specific spheres are in close contact with representatives many thousands of kilometres away. The pool in which they are operating is often quite small. As Shaw (1998, 108) wrote, in connection with groups operating in Nova Scotia, women frequently "sat on each other's boards [and] made representations to authorities in support of member organisations in trouble." There was a thread uniting women's groups with other women's groups: violence, victimization, and inequality before the law. It was not surprising that the boundaries should have been permeable and that a woman's expertise in a specific area was valuable to more than one group. CAEFS was no exception, in that its members often had broad connections.

Helping each other campaign, often against government agencies, was not uncommon amongst these various organizations, but there was a fundamental dilemma as to how far women in the voluntary sector should cooperate with government in order to achieve change. There was a history of government involvement with women's umbrella groups and their subsequent neutralization or marginalization. For example, the high profile of the government-funded NAC during the 1970s diminished following the 1984 election of a Conservative government, at which time individual women's groups were sidelined because they did not reflect the prevailing political ideology. Some women's groups were no longer always national in scope, as in Quebec, where the women's movement became identified with the independence movement and was reluctant to be linked publicly to pan-Canada women's organizations (see Geller-Schwartz 1995). CAEFS knew of this collective history – because some of its members were personally involved – and a number within the organization, fearing similar incorporation by government, remained sceptical of any requests to advance specific causes collectively.

There were those whose pragmatism regarding the means was largely occasioned by the worsening situation at the Prison for Women. Carlen (1998, 167), with respect to prisons, has long advocated that "campaigners [should] continue to engage in democratic discussion and co-operative enterprise with prisoners, prison staff, prison administrators and opinion leaders ... [because] it is essential to keep open to public view the inner workings of the whole carceral machinery so that its endemic secrecy can be held in check." How far this cooperation should be extended was the crux of the problem for many within CAEFS. Its members were aware of the historic failure of many benevolent penal enterprises, the record being characterized as one of "not just good intentions going wrong now and then, but of continued and disastrous failure" (Cohen 1985, 19). However, the plight of women at

the Prison for Women convinced the board of the need to risk the possibility of further failure.

Their ambivalence would have been shared, in a different fashion, by
some of the civil servants. They, privately, would also have thought of
themselves as feminists, but this was an uncomfortable label to wear
while employed by the state. Some were already ghettoized by virtue of
working in fields focused on women, and their future careers were
dependent upon not being seen as devoted to one particular area.
Geller-Schwartz (1995) noted that, as "femocrats,"[30] they were
"suspect" within the wider bureaucracy. Increasingly, the term "feminism" came to be used derogatively, and supposedly neutral civil servants would have been wary of being too closely identified with
women's issues.

The emphasis in this chapter on the role of CAEFS is necessary
because the association, mainly through its executive director Bonnie
Diamond, played a fundamental role in shaping the task force and in
suggesting who the various non-government members might be. CAEFS'
success in securing voluntary-sector parity with CSC representatives
ensured that neither faction was publicly paramount during the life of
the task force (although there were undoubted power differentials
between individuals behind the scenes). The composition of the
working group, which was to undertake the bulk of the work, illustrates the balance achieved, even though a look at the names published
in the task force's report, where there are four government appointees
alongside six voluntary-sector ones, would indicate an imbalance in
favour of the voluntary sector. (There were actually five civil servants,
but one withheld her name from the final report, as will be discussed
in chapter 5.) This unanticipated imbalance finally derived, not from
the withdrawal of a civil servant, but from the addition of two Aboriginal members. How this was achieved, and the consequences, will
now be explored.

CHAPTER TWO

A Journey Begins

Initially, the Task Force on Federally Sentenced Women's working group was to have equal government and CAEFS representation. During preliminary discussions within corrections, at the time when C-SPAC approved the launch of a task force, it was suggested by the chairman of the parole board, Fred Gibson, that a "*Native* [Aboriginal] *person should be on the task force*", as well as "*two provincial representatives*" (emphasis added). That decision was made in September 1988 and the wording of the minutes suggests that both these constituencies, possibly through oversight, had been omitted from Ole Ingstrup's original proposal. By the end of September it was already clear that the preferred format of the task force was for it to consist of a working group and a steering committee and, following Gibson's suggestion, it was then assumed that an Aboriginal representative would sit on the (less influential) steering committee. Even CAEFS, when suggesting in its December letter to James Phelps that the "particular needs of native women must be highlighted," initially only requested Aboriginal representation on the steering committee (a position it later amended, when Bonnie Diamond also suggested an Aboriginal Working Group member).[1]

What significance did Gibson's suggestion have? And what was its importance to the task force? The answers lie in the history of Canada as a colonized country – a country that eventually came to be a confederation of provinces. The provincial aspect of this story is important and will shortly be explored more fully. For the moment, it is important to reflect upon the history of the First Nations of Canada, those Aboriginal nations that were displaced and dispossessed by waves of European immigration. This knowledge is needed in order to understand why Aboriginal peoples came to be so disproportionately represented in Canadian prisons – and why their eventual participation in the task force came to be so important.

DISPOSSESSION AND ATTEMPTED ASSIMILATION:
THE FIRST NATIONS OF CANADA

The first peoples of Canada were the Aboriginal peoples. They were there, in their many nations, at the time of Canada's "discovery" by Europeans. The nations were self-governing and did not acknowledge the European concept of "ownership." This is best summarized by the Royal Commission on Aboriginal Peoples (RCAP):

In general, the European understanding – or at least the one that was committed to paper – was that the monarch had, or acquired through treaty or alliance, sovereignty over the land and the people on it. The Aboriginal understanding, however, recognized neither European title to the land nor Aboriginal submission to a European monarch ... the Aboriginal concept of land and its relationship with human beings was based on the concept of communal ownership of land and ... while people could control and exercise stewardship over a territory, ultimately the land belonged to the Creator. (RCAP 1996, 1:5, 3.3)

The term "Aboriginal" is often used loosely. In Canada there are three distinct groups that can accurately claim to be part of this larger group: those known as First Nations, those known as Métis, and those known as Inuit. In reality, the groups are distinct, even if it has sometimes been politically expedient for them to be seen as homogeneous. These groups were further divided by whether or not their members were considered to be "status" (registered) or "non-status" Indians; the legislative aegis of the original British North America Act, 1867, only included registered Indians. The relatively recent Constitution Act, 1982, defines Aboriginal peoples, in Section 35(2), as including "the Indian, Inuit and Métis people of Canada." This was the first time that the Métis had been officially recognized as a distinct group (see Frideres 1993).[2] The Métis emerged as a separate entity following the first contact with Europeans and share a mixed heritage in that they are Aboriginal – or Inuit in the case of the Labrador Métis – and European. Following the example of the Constitution, and that of RCAP itself, this book generally uses the term "Aboriginal" and only uses the term "Indian" when it is being quoted from another source. In correctional terms, however, Aboriginal peoples are not treated as three separate groups but, rather, as a single entity.

The very first contact between Aboriginal nations and Europeans was mutually beneficial: trading links were established and there was little encroachment on the land. Indeed, without Aboriginal assistance the first European settlers would have found it difficult to survive.

However, as Europeans arrived in increasing numbers, assuming that they had found a land to which they could freely lay claim, the situation quickly changed – and it was not just the question of land occupation that was to have an impact. A devastating consequence of contact with Europeans was the exposure of Aboriginal communities to foreign diseases and illnesses that they could not withstand. Consequently, during the first 300 years of European immigration the Aboriginal population declined by 50 percent, and towards the end of the eighteenth century it was estimated that the numbers of Aboriginal and non-Aboriginal peoples had become, in an astonishingly short period, approximately equal (RCAP 1996). Another consequence of contact with Europeans was Aboriginal exposure to the proselytizing of missionaries, which undermined the belief systems underpinning the social organization of Aboriginal nations, caused divisions among these nations, and encouraged the adoption of a way of life far removed from traditional ones. These missionaries later became highly involved in the education of Aboriginal children.

Loss of land and sovereignty is the continuous thread of Aboriginal history. As we shall see, the Royal Proclamation of 1763 had a particular application to Quebec, but it was also a statement of intent towards Aboriginal nations living within the newly conquered land. Those nations were seen to be autonomous and ones with whom treaties could be concluded, but, as RCAP earlier indicated, the Aboriginal peoples' understanding of what these treaties meant was fundamentally different from that of the Europeans (see also Miller 2000). As European immigration increased and, with it, the illegal occupation of Aboriginal land (and its clearing for European-style agriculture), Aboriginal communities were further displaced and left without a traditional means of supporting themselves. They then became increasingly reliant on the state for treaty payments as a means of survival.[3] The notion of Aboriginal peoples as autonomous nations abated as immigration increased, and the treaties became "little more than real estate transactions designed to free Aboriginal lands for settlement and resource development" (RCAP 1996, 1:6). Moreover, there was a concerted effort to increase the conversion of Aboriginal peoples and thus "civilize" them through the added benefits of European-style education, while ceremonies such as the potlatch and the Sun Dance, which were of spiritual significance to various nations, were proscribed. Such proscriptions were "analogous to passing a Catholic Act to regulate the lives of Canadian Catholics that prohibits them from attending mass" (Morrison and Wilson 1995, 608).

The Gradual Civilization Act, 1857, first introduced the idea of voluntary enfranchisement as a means of assimilating Aboriginal nations into European Canada, but the consequence of enfranchisement was the loss of legal Indian "status."[4] Providing that Aboriginal peoples could prove they "were debt-free and of good moral character" they could apply for enfranchisement and become citizens of the country that was already theirs. The bait used was land. Any Aboriginal male accepted for enfranchisement would receive twenty hectares of land; and this would be taken by the colonial government from reserve lands, which, under the Royal Proclamation, the government had no power to touch. Land that had previously been held in common ownership by nations could, by this means, be subdivided and held in private ownership by a man who was no longer legally Aboriginal (Miller 2000). By this means Aboriginal claim to land would be weakened. (It was only in 1960 that unqualified enfranchisement was extended to all Aboriginal peoples.)

The policy initially failed – only one Indian asked to be enfranchised – but the idea re-emerged in the Gradual Enfranchisement Act, 1869, and women were singularly targeted by many of its provisions. Those who married non-Aboriginal men lost their Indian status, as did their children. Conversely, if a woman married an Aboriginal man who elected to be franchised she also lost status as a consequence of his decision.

The main means of regulating Aboriginal nations was, however, the Indian Act, 1876, and, although amended at regular intervals, this continued to be the pre-eminent legislation concerning Aboriginal peoples until the Constitution Act, 1982. Under the 1876 act Aboriginal peoples were seen as being in a state of "wardship" in relation to the state, no longer competent to administer their own affairs.

Women were particularly disadvantaged by the Indian Act, 1876, specifically by Sections 12(1)(a) and 12(1)(b), as amended in 1951. Any Aboriginal woman who "married out": "lost any claim to Indian status ... [and] was not entitled to registration. Like generations of women ... who had married out, loss of status meant loss of the right under Canadian law to hold land on the reserve and loss of status for any children of the marriage. With the loss of status and membership came the forced sale or disposal of any reserve lands she may have held ... [and] she was also struck off the band list and was no longer entitled to distributions of band moneys" (RCAP 1996, 4:2, 3.1).

This inability to return to reserves should a marriage fail, and to protect the status of their children, contributed to the growing number of Aboriginal women in the urban Diaspora, where, despite having marginally better education than Aboriginal males, they found it harder to gain work. They were disadvantaged relative both to Aboriginal men and to other Canadian women. In 1970 the Royal Commission on the Status of Women recommended that "the [Indian] act be amended 'to allow an Indian woman upon marriage to a non-Indian to (a) retain her Indian status and (b) transmit her status to her children'" (RCAP 1996, 4:2, 3.1). The 1985 Bill C-31 partially restored women's rights in this regard, but anomalies remained and are a continuing source of concern and grievance.

Federal control of Aboriginal governance, land, resources, and education ensured the subjugation of once-independent nations, but land loss did not only occur as a result of failure to honour treaties. In the twentieth century there were enforced relocations of whole Aboriginal communities. Some, such as the Mi'kmaq in Nova Scotia, were moved because it was administratively easier to have them in one area rather than scattered across various reserves, and others were moved because their land was needed for development purposes. Many of the relocations were undertaken without adequate consultation, and informed consent did not appear to have been obtained from those moved. Removal was often to areas with which these people had no previous links and where the host communities had not been consulted to determine whether or not they were agreeable to an influx of newcomers. The new accommodation was usually inadequate, and sometimes nonexistent, and there were insufficient jobs to provide an income for all families. RCAP details the case of the Gwa'Sala and 'Nakwaxda'xw, two fishing communities on Vancouver Island, who were forced to move in 1964 when the government threatened to withdraw all funding for housing, school, and services if they refused. Promised moorings for their boats never materialized, and new houses were not ready:

When boats were used for homes because the promised houses were not built, fishing licences were revoked because the boats were no longer defined as fishing vessels. Most of these boats, as well as others used for fishing, had to be moored in the river or on the beach, where they were eventually destroyed by high winds, waves and rain. This deprived the bands of access to marine resources, formerly a mainstay of their economy. (RCAP 1996, 1:11, 4.2)

Their old homes were often burned to discourage any possibility of return, and the consequence was a drift to the cities, where paid employment was possibly more likely. In turn, this drift led to increased social and economic problems and an increasing dependence on state welfare. The end result of these enforced relocations was the further destruction of the Aboriginal peoples' relationship with the land and their cultural identity.[5]

While Aboriginal peoples were being displaced from their communities, yet another piece of the grand project to "civilize and assimilate" them was undermining their social cohesion. Education was the means. Early on it had been recognized that, through education, the colonial government would be able to reach the most easily influenced group of Aboriginal peoples – the children. Their parents were believed to be beyond reach because they had already been exposed to the traditions and beliefs that were so inimical to the tenets of Christianity. Although some Aboriginal communities had requested that education be provided for their children, this was due to the belief that they needed the skills of the dominant culture, such as literacy and numeracy, in order to be able to compete with Europeans in the workplace. At no stage in those early years of colonization did the majority of Aboriginal peoples wish this new knowledge to replace traditional skills; rather, it was to complement them. The state thought otherwise and, in collaboration with the four main churches – Anglican, Roman Catholic, Methodist, and Presbyterian – established, in the nineteenth century, a mix of industrial and boarding schools. As RCAP (1996, 1:10, 2) shows, the system was driven by "missionary efforts" and the "considerable force of the churches' political influence in Ottawa by which they secured funds to operate the schools." Over time the schools came to be known simply as residential schools, but, whatever their original name, the intention behind each was identical: the obliteration of all that made the children self-identify as Aboriginal and the creation of new Canadians who reflected a Euro-Canadian image. In this scheme parents had no part to play because they were considered to be part of the perceived problem. As RCAP (1996, 1:10, 1.1) said, "while they [parents] could not learn, they could, as parents, teach their children. Through them to their children and on through successive generations ran the influence of the 'wigwam.'[6] If the children's potential was to be realised, it could only be outside the family ... A wedge had to be driven not only physically between parent and child but also culturally and spiritually." As the system developed it was hoped that the children would act as civilizing forces in their own right by returning to the reserves to influence others.

The schools, where the children were forbidden to speak their own languages, were under-resourced, with poorly paid and often ill-trained teachers. The children were used as unpaid labour to offset the cost of their care and they worked long hours, with no more than half of each day actually being spent doing school work – a situation that prevailed until the end of the Second World War. The emphasis was on their acquiring practical skills, which would enable them to find employment in manual occupations. The children were inadequately clothed and fed, and the physical conditions in which they lived were particularly bad, with the insanitary conditions leading to high incidences of disease, particularly tuberculosis, as was well known to the Department of Indian Affairs and the churches (see RCAP 1996; Miller 1996). Indeed, in the early 1900s the deputy superintendent general of Indian affairs, Duncan Campbell Scott, freely admitted that "it is quite within the mark to say that fifty percent of the children who passed through these schools did not live to benefit from the education which they had received therein" (Miller 1996, 133). Many children ran away from the schools and some died while attempting to find their way home in the depths of winter.

Although Miller (1996) estimates that no more than one-third of Aboriginal children attended such schools, RCAP suggests that, because of the extent of the schools' reach, any figures should be treated cautiously. It was not only the children attending the schools who suffered; the impact of their absence, and eventual return, was felt by their extended families and communities. The children found themselves straddling two cultures, being neither traditionally Aboriginal nor recognizably Euro-Canadian, and this dislocation from their roots affected all who were linked to them. In this sense, the residential schools had an impact upon generations of Aboriginal families and communities. The ravaging effects of alcohol, and attendant violence, filled the vacuum left by the children, and, more recently, drug addiction has contributed further to the destruction of these communities, both on and off reserve (see Maracle 1993). The pattern of failure was perpetuated in successive generations: in attempting to create their own family units, the "graduates" replicated what they experienced in the schools, having seen no other consistent models. The extreme abuse that the residential school children experienced was often meted out to their own offspring. It was not until the 1980s that any serious attention was paid to the way in which many of the children were subjected to widespread physical and sexual abuse. Again, the churches and government were privately aware of what had happened but denied the extent of their knowledge before finally accepting public responsibility for the systematic degradation of the children (see RCAP 1996).[7]

The relationship between churches and state, and the governance of these schools, ended in 1969. Government policy was eventually pushed in the direction of "Indian control of Indian Education" by the National Indian Brotherhood, which led to some of the original schools being transferred to the control of Aboriginal organizations (Miller 1996, 405). However, the demise of residential schools did not lead to less intervention in the lives of Aboriginal children. The policy was replaced by the "Sixties' Scoop,"[8] whereby children avoided residential school but were instead taken into care and fostered by non-Aboriginal families (see Fournier and Crey 1997).

Aboriginal history cannot be covered in a few short paragraphs, and the foregoing has given the barest glimpse of a colonial process that began with the intention of offering protection and ended in coercion. While enforced relocations for purposes of economic development may now largely have ceased, the consequences of those policies remain apparent, with many Aboriginal communities having found it impossible to recover their previous independence. The results of Euro-Canadian policies of colonialism and assimilation can be found within Canada's prisons in the disproportionate numbers of incarcerated Aboriginal peoples. While the residential schools may have closed thirty years ago, the generations of lost parenting are manifest in Canada's Aboriginal prisoners. Chapter 9 explores the way in which the TFFSW provided for Aboriginal federally sentenced women.

THE PROVINCIAL DIMENSION: QUEBEC

These Aboriginal nations were not, however, the only culturally distinct group deserving of inclusion in – or at least consideration by – the Task Force on Federally Sentenced Women, and it is at this point that we need to reflect on the first colonizers of Canada, the Quebecois.

The original C-SPAC recommendation that two provincial representatives should be on the task force was reconfirmed on 6 February 1989, but the decision created problems. There were "difficulties involved in selecting two individuals to represent *all* provincial and territorial governments" (emphasis added).[9] Eventually, there were to be representatives on the steering committee from all five *correctional* regions.[10] However, the decision to opt for the correctional regions – as a means of avoiding offending provinces that might otherwise have been omitted – has subsequently been cited by CSC as the original reason for being unable to include Quebec in the working group as it would have been impolitic to include one province, ahead of others, on the most important of the task force's two committees. Yet during those first discussions about forming a task force that concern did not appear to be an issue.

As has already been shown, assembling the task force was no easy matter. CSC had taken great pains to ensure that CAEFS was highly involved in the project and had made considerable concessions, such as joint chairing, in order to ensure its participation. On that point alone the task force was already breaking new ground, but corrections went further when it belatedly invited the Native Women's Association of Canada (NWAC) to join the deliberations and to speak for Aboriginal women, as will be discussed shortly. Federally sentenced women, as personified by their "representatives" on the task force, immediately became two distinct groups: Euro-Canadian women and Aboriginal women. The addition of the Aboriginal members also meant that the composition of the most influential part of the task force, the working group, was then balanced in favour of the voluntary sector. As we already know, the commissioner preferred a task force because this allowed him to exercise some control over its direction, precisely because civil servants could be appointed to it. The addition of NWAC meant that the civil servants ended up as an unexpected minority on the very group they were unofficially expected to guide through force of administrative expertise.

In Canada, however, there are other considerations when creating representative bodies, and the reasons for these are firmly bedded in the political structure of the country itself. The federal government can never assume that provinces will share the same perspectives; they are as much formed by their individual histories as is the single entity of Canada. Nowhere is this more apparent than in the French-founded province of Quebec, where the question of political and cultural identity has been of profound importance since it was "conquered" by the English and incorporated into an anglophone Canada in 1763.

Why should this be important within the context of a task force on federally sentenced women? Looking at the composition of the working group it is already known that six of the members were non-civil servants. What has not been made clear is that all of these lived and worked outside Ottawa, coming from as far as British Columbia and the Maritimes, whereas the five civil servants were all then based in the capital city and were not Quebecois. Of course it is scarcely surprising that civil servants, working largely at corrections' headquarters, should be selected for a task force related to their areas of expertise, but there is a further dimension to all of this. CSC had recognized the need to involve the voluntary sector and saw that, realistically, its primary partner within the context of federally sentenced women could only be CAEFS. CSC then had to accept the need to involve Aboriginal peoples as a separate group and, as we will see, eventually involved many more than first anticipated. This resulted in a distinction being made between federally sentenced women – a distinction based on ethnicity and culture. Aboriginal women were only 2.5 percent of the total Canadian population yet were then 23 percent of the federally sentenced women's population. At the time of the 1991 census French-speaking Canadians formed roughly 25 percent of the country's population, and the majority of these lived in Quebec (Bothwell 1998, 234). Federally sentenced women from Quebec comprised 21 percent of the sentenced population at the time of the task force, and those Quebecois could correctly have claimed to be a distinct ethnic and cultural group in their own right. Yet they were not represented separately on the most influential of the groups comprising the task force. It is now important to look at what had been happening in Quebec prior to the formation of the task force to see whether or not it might be justifiable to ask why the Quebecois were not also separately represented.

RETURNING TO HISTORY

It is not necessary to delve too far back into Quebec history to establish that the province had experienced immense political and social change during the two decades prior to the task force, but knowledge of Quebec's history provides a broad context for what will shortly be discussed. As far as Europeans were concerned, Jacques Cartier "discovered" Canada in 1534 (although there is evidence of much earlier European contact on the eastern seaboard), and the French were the first colonizers of Canada, or New France (as it became known). In turn, the French were colonized by the British in 1760 – a time known as the Conquest – and New France was ceded to Britain. This was made formal by the Royal Proclamation of 1763, through which Quebec became a British province, English law was imposed, the Church of England became the established church, English became the official language in any representative assembly, and any Quebecois wishing to sit in such an assembly had to renounce his (Roman Catholic) faith. Such a strategy proved impossible to implement, and the Quebec Act, 1774, reimposed French civil law, leaving the Roman Catholic Church again ascendant (McRoberts 1993, 44–5).

In 1791 Quebec was divided into two separate areas known as Lower Canada and Upper Canada, with the French-speaking former Quebecois comprising the majority in Lower Canada. It was always an uneasy division, exacerbated by increasing numbers of English-speaking immigrants into Lower Canada, and in 1837 the francophone nationalists, led by Louis-Josèph Papineau, rebelled. They were defeated, and in 1838 the newly arrived governor general, Lord Durham, was charged with recommending "how further disturbances might be avoided" (Bothwell 1998, 34). His solution was to propose that both Upper and Lower Canada should be united into one Province of Canada, with a legislature that would entrench the hegemony of the anglophones. An associate of Papineau's, Louis-Hippolyte LaFontaine, pragmatically recognized that, irrespective of Durham's dismissal of the francophones as "a people with neither history nor literature," the French-speaking majority could use Parliament to their advantage (McRoberts 1993, 51). That pragmatism and astuteness was to translate into adept political manoeuvring by various francophone politicians in the following decades; however, by the 1860s, the political structures were once again at breaking point. A solution was found in the concept of Confederation, and with the British North American Act, 1867, the Dominion of Canada emerged. Quebec was once again a separate province, with the francophones overwhelmingly in the majority. While French-speaking Canadians at last had a political structure that enabled them to dominate provincial matters, a more powerful federal government was at the same time created – and in this the Quebecois would be a minority (Bothwell 1998, 39).

Quebec was a largely Roman Catholic province, as distinct from the Protestant-dominated provinces in the rest of the Confederation, and the church had played a considerable role in encouraging Quebecois to believe that they were an agrarian society, a society "with a special mission" and "a society where the government did not play a significant role, thereby leaving the leadership of the society to the church" (Cook, cited in Bothwell 1998, 42; see also Cook 1986). Although it is simplistic to characterize Quebec as a nationalist province defined by its history, language, and religion – together with the implicit underlying issue of ethnicity – the twin questions of faith and language have resonated throughout the province's history. Moreover, they have been viewed by other Canadians with a great deal of distrust and have sometimes been seen as an excuse for Quebec's having remained aloof from the rest of Canada, while continuing to reap the benefits of being within the Confederation. The view that Quebec benefited from being part of the larger Canada was not shared by many Quebecois. As the major means of Quebec employment moved from agriculture to industry, with the consequent drift towards conurbations, the bedrock of the francophone society also changed and the old certainties came to be questioned. More Quebecois began to be educated outside the province, and those who returned saw their society with new, and frequently non-religious, eyes. As the 1960s progressed, what became known as the "Quiet Revolution" unfolded, with the province assuming responsibility for functions that had previously been very much the domain of the church, particularly those of education and social welfare (see Cook 1995). The result of this was that Quebec frequently opted out of federal programs, choosing to implement its own plans, thus emphasizing its distinctiveness. Meanwhile, the 1965 Royal Commission on Bilingualism and Biculturalism had declared that "Canada, without recognising it, was passing through the greatest crisis in its history," and this became evident at the same time as the country was celebrating its centenary as a Confederation. The president of France, Charles de Gaulle, came to Montreal in 1967, declaimed "vive le Quebec libre!" and was promptly asked to leave the country. In the same year René Lévesque founded the Mouvement Souveraineté-asso-ciation, which was to become the Parti Quebecois in 1968 (Bothwell 1998, 121–3).

Just two years earlier Pierre Elliott Trudeau had been elected to the federal Parliament as a Liberal representing a Montreal riding, and within less than three years he was to be prime minister of Canada. Although the Liberal party within Quebec had become identified with nationalism and nationalists, Trudeau himself had not, and he and a group of like-minded friends believed that the previous federal govern-ment, led by then Prime Minister Lester Pearson, had not done enough to promote the case for a united Canada. Within weeks of becoming prime minister, Trudeau had laid the groundwork for the Official Lan-guages Act, 1969, which declared that both English and French were the official languages of Canada, much to the dismay of many Cana-dians living far from Quebec.

Despite Trudeau's leadership, nationalism continued to flourish within Quebec. Even as the Quiet Revolution had been unfolding a small group of nationalists resorted to bombing in and around Mon-treal, and in October 1970 the Front de Libération du Quebec kid-napped the British trade commissioner, James Cross. Five days after that they kidnapped, and later murdered, the Quebec minister of labour, Pierre Laporte. Trudeau's response was to proclaim the War Measures Act, 1970, which suspended all civil liberties and allowed for government by decree. While most Canadians supported his actions, many in Quebec never forgave him for supposedly crushing part of the separatist movement (remarkably small, as this branch of it turned out to be). The move towards separatism had not, however, died.

Language continued to be a potent issue in Quebec, partly because the changing patterns of immigration meant that new ethnic groups were asking to be educated in English rather than in French. The declining birth rate within the francophone community suggested that the supremacy of French would relatively soon be seriously challenged, and in 1974 Quebec's Premier Bourassa brought in Bill 22, which gave priority to the use of French in both education and business. (Bill 101 further strengthened the position of French three years later, making it the official language of the province.) By 1976 René Lévesque had led the Parti Quebecois to victory in the Quebec elections, and in 1980 he sought a mandate from the Quebecois, by means of a referendum, simply to start talking to the federal government about sovereignty-association.[11] Trudeau, who was again prime minister after a brief period out of office, was appalled by the possibility of a "yes" vote to the proposition and actively campaigned against it. In the event, the referendum was lost, but Trudeau wasted no time in setting out his own constitutional stall: he would seek the patriation of the Constitution from Great Britain, and this would be supported by a charter of rights and freedoms. After hard bargaining with the provincial premiers Trudeau achieved his objective in 1982, but René Lévesque, still premier of Quebec, refused to sign the newly patriated Constitution.

SIMILAR ASPIRATIONS?

While the foregoing has done little but skim the surface of very complex issues, it is clear that Quebec was not a province that any federal government could afford to ignore. Many of the major federal initiatives had been designed either to placate or thwart Quebec's wish to be recognized as an historically, linguistically, and culturally distinct society within the larger Confederation of Canada. The reason, here, for examining the situation in Quebec prior to the creation of the Task Force on Federally Sentenced Women is to demonstrate that Quebec was rarely out of the headlines. The patriation of the Constitution did not end that situation. Indeed, it increased Quebec's high profile and the federal government then attempted, through the Meech Lake Accord, to entice the province back into the constitutional fold.

At this point, however, the interests of both women and Aboriginal peoples – ignored during the constitutional debate – need to be considered as they were both absent from the provincial–federal negotiating table. Chapter 1 shows how women from across the country were united in their opposition to the inadequate equality clauses in the Charter of Rights and Freedoms. The remarkable parallels between Aboriginal and Quebecois reactions to those events in the 1980s should be examined. All of these should be viewed in the knowledge that Aboriginal peoples have always been the First Nations of Canada, notwithstanding the fact that the French were the original colonizers of those nations and that the French were themselves conquered by the British. The British North American Act, 1867, had formalized this colonization, characterizing both the French and the British as "founding nations" of Canada while ignoring the Aboriginal nations. The Royal Commission on Aboriginal Peoples (RCAP) put it succinctly:

Equating Aboriginal peoples with racial and cultural minorities is a fundamentally flawed conception. People came to Canada from other countries in large numbers, over a period of several hundred years, and they came as immigrants – that is, for the most part they chose to leave their homelands as individuals and families and to settle in an already established country. Aboriginal people are not immigrants. They are the original inhabitants of the land and have lived here from time immemorial. (RCAP 1996, 1:14)

While it is known that Aboriginal peoples had generally been excluded from the negotiating table on all major constitutional matters, it was Trudeau's decision to introduce the 1969 White Paper, entitled *Statement of the Government of Canada on Indian Policy*, proposing the ending of the Indian Act and the assimilation of Aboriginal nations into the "dominant" culture of the larger European Canadian society, which proved to be a catalyst for Aboriginal protest and activism. "They were to be allowed to keep their cultures, much as other Canadians do in a multi-cultural society, but they were to give up the other features that make them distinct – elements such as treaties, Aboriginal rights, exclusive federal responsibility and the department of Indian affairs" (RCAP 1996 1:6, 9). An immediate consequence of the paper was the founding of the first pan-Canada political Indian (Aboriginal) organization, the National Indian Brotherhood. Although the Indian Act had been responsible for many of the ills visited upon Aboriginal peoples, it also represented a link to the promises made when the First Nations were afforded the protection of the Crown in 1763, irrespective of how these promises might have subsequently been interpreted by the dominant culture. When Trudeau later decided that the Constitution should be patriated Aboriginal nations responded by actively lobbying the British government because they feared that patriation would lead to a loss of their treaty rights as guaranteed by the Crown. The three major Aboriginal men's organizations were only permitted to be observers at the first of the constitutional conferences preceding patriation, and NWAC was totally excluded. The original draft legislation included three sections specifically providing for Aboriginal rights; however, by the time the actual November Accord was published in 1982, these had been removed as a direct consequence of horse-trading on the part of some of the provincial premiers. The outcry was vociferous, and, at this point, Aboriginal peoples had the added support of Canadian women's organizations, who were protesting about threats to equality posed by the Charter of Rights and Freedoms that accompanied the Constitution Act, 1982. An amended reference to Aboriginal rights was eventually inserted in the legislation, together with the promise of a subsequent first ministers (provincial premiers) conference, which would focus on Aboriginal affairs. The issues of Aboriginal sovereignty and self-government were finally to be discussed at the first minister level (Chodos, Murphy, and Hamovitch 1991; Cook 1995). In the event, four first ministers conferences took place between March 1983 and March 1987, but they eventually failed because of an inability to agree on "whether the right of Aboriginal self-government flowed from inherent and unextinguished Aboriginal sovereignty ... or whether it was to be delegated from provincial and federal governments" (RCAP 1996, 1:7).

There was therefore outrage among Aboriginal peoples when the Meech Lake Accord was announced only one month after the ending of the last of these first ministers conferences. Meech Lake was intended to persuade Quebec to accede to the Constitution, and it offered the province recognition as a "distinct society." Zachary wrote: "from the federal point of view, spending the political capital required for a native agreement would have left little in the bank for the constitutional negotiations that really mattered electorally – the talks that took place in April on Quebec's status within Confederation" (Zachary, cited in Chodos, Murphy, and Hamovitch 1991). As Hall (1989, 434) described it, "Aboriginal leaders had faced consistent resistance to the assertion that there must be constitutional reform to enable Aboriginal governments to preserve and promote the distinct identity of Aboriginal peoples. Within a few weeks of the termination of this process Native people learned that the kind of recognition denied to them was to be extended to the provincial citizens of Quebec" (see also Monture-Angus 1995, 158; RCAP 1996, 1:7). Ovide Mercredi, former grand chief of the Assembly of First Nations, dealt with Meech Lake trenchantly, observing that "many people think Quebec has the market cornered, so to speak, on the phrase 'distinct society' and that even using the expression 'distinct peoples' in reference to the First Nations is unacceptable." He continued, "the concept of 'distinct society' is as real for us as it is for you [Quebecois]" (Mercredi and Turpel 1994, 167 and 175). Another Aboriginal leader, Louis Bruyere, said that "Aboriginal people's views of the *Accord* can be summarised in four words: It abandons Aboriginal peoples. It does this by being silent about the uniqueness and distinctiveness of Aboriginal peoples" (cited in RCAP 1996, 1:7). (See Mercredi and Turpel 1994; Frideres 1993; RCAP 1996; Krosenbrink 1993, for a fuller discussion of these issues.)

The Meech Lake Accord was later to fail, when Aboriginal parliamentarian Elijah Harper stood up in the Manitoba Legislative Assembly in June 1990 and said "no."[12] The collapse of the Meech Lake Accord had as much to do with the federal government's failure to allow for "the highly volatile nature of provincial politics" as with anything else, and, during the 1980s, Quebec was believed by many to be acting against the best interests of confederal Canada (Behiels 1989, 475). From all of this, it is evident that the whole issue of Quebec and its place within Canada was much debated during the period. As has also been seen, many of the issues seemingly exclusively linked to Quebec were also Aboriginal issues; for example, sovereignty, culture, distinctiveness as separate nations. As RCAP (1996, 1: 7,1) itself summarized: "Meech was meant to heal the wounds created by the patriation and amendment of the Constitution in 1982 over Quebec's objection. For years, Quebecois were seeking recognition of their historical rights – the reality of deux [two] nations – in the Constitution. Aboriginal peoples were unable to have their nation-to-nation relationship recognized, and Quebec was unable to have its distinctiveness as a society recognized. The fate of these two Canadian dilemmas had become inexorably linked."

The Quebecois had the overwhelming advantage of being entrenched within their own province – and of being recognized as an ethnic group reflecting the traditions and European sensibilities so familiar to their Anglophone counterparts, even while these same traditions appeared to divide them. Aboriginal nations had no specific homeland and, therefore, no bargaining position. They were vastly outnumbered, thanks to the ravages of colonization, and their traditions were not readily understood by the dominant culture. Aboriginal peoples were very easy to ignore and, if they chose to organize themselves into protest groups, it was easy to label them as militants rather than to see them as a people responding to injustice. Yet Aboriginal concerns were never far from the public gaze during the 1980s: the carrying of the Olympic flame across the country was politicized by Aboriginal groups; a number of inquiries highlighted the grossly inequitable treatment of Aboriginal peoples by the justice system.[13] And, it should not be forgotten, the 1985 amendment of the Indian Act, Bill C-31, had specifically focused attention on Aboriginal women.

It was Quebec, however, that continued to be of major concern to the federal government, and, as has been seen, every effort was made during that decade to tempt the province into a closer federal embrace, while Aboriginal aspirations appeared to be expendable. Quebecois nationalism had not died with the failure of the referendum, and the place of the province within Confederation was an issue of concern to the Canadian public as well as to the federal government. It is therefore right to ask why astute civil servants, charged with putting together a task force, failed to include a representative from Quebec on the working group, while eventually accommodating another distinct ethnic group, as represented by NWAC. It is also right to ask why Aboriginal women were initially not included in the task force at all, bearing in mind the high public profile they had recently enjoyed. Both these questions are considered in chapter 5, where their importance should be apparent.

For the moment the relative impact of both these distinct groups on the work of the Task Force on Federally Sentenced Women must be considered, and the initial focus is on the role of NWAC.

NWAC JOINS THE TASK FORCE

Although Aboriginal participation in the task force had been suggested in September 1989, it took until early January 1989 for NWAC to be asked if it would nominate a representative.[14] NWAC was already the national voice for Aboriginal women. Although well aware of the disproportionate number of federally sentenced Aboriginal women,[15] NWAC was involved in other grassroots issues; there were simply too many areas demanding its attention at the time. The heavy rates of Aboriginal offending were not necessarily felt to be shameful; rather, they caused anger, and this was directed at the dominant culture responsible, so it was felt, for the socio-economic inequities contributing to Aboriginal peoples' disproportionate rate of offending.[16] NWAC also had the recent memory of the failure of the 1984 Women in Conflict with the Law (WICL) initiative, when it had been excluded from the "ministerial committee ... which possessed the authority for final approval on proposals" (AWC Submission, 29.8.-2.9.1989). Even more recent had been the publication of the report of the Task Force on Aboriginal Peoples in Federal Corrections, which had devoted two and a half out of 109 pages to women. This report was viewed by most Aboriginal commentators as a *government* report, and great offence had been caused by the task force's original title – Task Force on the Reintegration of Aboriginal Offenders as Law-Abiding Citizens. It raised questions such as "Whose laws?" and "If a group has never been integrated, how can it be reintegrated?"

NWAC was among those Aboriginal groups campaigning for legislative, social, and economic change. It also had to fight its own battle to establish its right to represent Aboriginal women independently of other Aboriginal organizations, such as the National Indian Brotherhood and the Native Council of Canada. Unlike NWAC, these last two groups determined their membership "in accordance with the status regulations of the *Indian Act*" and were fearful that any attempt to achieve sexual equality for Aboriginal women might lead to the repeal of the Indian Act and the loss of Indian rights (Krosenbrink 1993, 341). In essence, Aboriginal women were being "requested to subordinate their goal – Indian rights for Indian women – to that of Indian men; they were used as a political vehicle to pursue an *Indian Act* revision the way status Indian males saw fit" (342).

The process of patriating the Constitution also involved NWAC but, strikingly, not as formal participants sitting at the conference table. Attempts to achieve parity (with, among others, male Aboriginal organizations) were to occupy NWAC in the late 1980s and early 1990s, which partially explains why NWAC did not immediately accede to CSC's invitation to join the Task Force on Federally Sentenced Women. But there were also other reasons. Like CAEFS, NWAC is an organization based on volunteers, and no one on the executive committee felt able to commit herself to the amount of time that the task force would require. Additionally, Aboriginal women's voluntary organizations operated under greater constraints than did many other women's groups, not least of which were their relative financial positions and levels of education. Although its membership was large, NWAC did not have a big pool of women it could call upon to participate in government initiatives. Nevertheless, the request that they should be on the task force was discussed by the executive council and was supported by the Elders, who felt that it was important that an Aboriginal voice should be heard during the task force's deliberations. These women knew that they were after-thoughts to the original proposals, but for them this was not an uncommon experience. Eventually, Sharon McIvor, an Aboriginal lawyer from British Columbia, agreed to be nominated, but the question of how many Aboriginal women should be on the task force remained. CSC's assumption that one would be sufficient was "totally, flatly unacceptable to us because when you put one Aboriginal woman on a committee like that you're just so alone and so marginalized and you've got no support."[17]

The question took some time to resolve. The Ontario branch of NWAC suggested that Patricia Monture, another Aboriginal lawyer and academic, should also be on the working group, and this request was relayed to corrections and eventually accepted. At the same time NWAC wanted Aboriginal women who had served federal time to be on the task force, and two names were put forward for consideration by the Prison for Women's Aboriginal Sisterhood.[18]

Thanks to persistent lobbying, by the time of the first steering committee meeting its Aboriginal representation had been increased to two. Those Aboriginal members then persuaded the committee that the two federally sentenced women should be included in its already large list of representatives, alongside two other members of the Aboriginal Women's Caucus. The working group's balance was also altered by the addition of two Aboriginal members, leaving voluntary-sector representatives outnumbering the civil servants. Thus the eleven-strong working group – five civil servants, four CAEFS and two NWAC representatives – ended up looking rather more like the tripartite group it later proclaimed itself to be. The thirty-one-member steering committee had representatives from a much wider field, and the civil service members were again outnumbered by one voluntary-sector member. Whether this lack of absolute balance might possibly undermine the commissioner's grasp on the task force remained to be seen. That NWAC managed to have Aboriginal federally sentenced women included on the task force raises interesting questions about CAEFS' failure to press for federally sentenced women, of whatever ethnic identity, to be included. Perhaps more importantly, it raises questions about why NWAC's proposals were so readily acceded to, and that is something that will be considered later. The striking fact is that federally sentenced women were considered to be legitimate members of such an enterprise. What this means is open to interpretation. It could have been a simple recognition of their inherent expertise – and certainly it was for that reason that NWAC insisted they should be included. But their inclusion also added further legitimacy to CSC's venture, in the manner of both CAEFS' and NWAC's participation, and the civil servants would have been well aware of that.

The Terms of Reference for the task force had already been worked out between CSC and CAEFS, with no contribution from NWAC. Among other issues, the terms documented some of the "unresolved, long-standing issues pertaining to the management of federally sentenced women," including those of geographic dislocation, the inflexibility of the Prison for Women regarding classification and security levels, and the difficulty in providing programs comparable to the range available in male institutions. The terms outlined the mandate governing these objectives: "the mandate of the task force will be to examine the correctional management of federally sentenced women *from the commencement of sentence to the date of warrant expiry*, and to develop a policy and plan which will guide and direct this process in a manner that is responsive to the unique and special needs of this group" (emphasis added).

The Terms of Reference were later presented to the working group at its first meeting, and Patricia Monture pointed out that "it contained no mention of the particular oppression experienced by First Nations Women in prison."[19] Professor Monture agreed to draft an amendment, and she added to the list of "unresolved problems": "the over-representation of Aboriginal people in the criminal justice systems of Canada. This over-representation is also evidenced among federally sentenced women. The unique and valued cultural, historic, and spiritual aspects of the experience of Aboriginal women has an additional significant impact on the ... areas of concern" [centred on accommodation, programming and community release services which left federally sentenced women disadvantaged, compared to men].

But the "unique ... cultural, historic and spiritual aspects of ... Aboriginal women" had, for the most part, not been valued by other Canadians. Aboriginal peoples had consistently been overwhelmed by the dominant culture, with its different historical perspectives and understanding, and were increasingly marginalized within a society that both rejected and, as many saw it, criminalized them through its unaccepted laws. (Aboriginal nations have never formally accepted the authority of the Canadian justice system.) Monture's amendment could be seen as political as much as anything else, and it prefigured subsequent attempts to broaden the task force's agenda when considering Aboriginal issues. (It also marked the beginning of the task force's characterization of Aboriginal women as victims.) For the Aboriginal members of the task force the narrowness of the mandate meant that they could only focus on issues arising from the passing of a sentence, leaving them potentially unable to examine the sentence itself and its legitimacy for Aboriginal women. This initial awareness failure on the part of both csc and caefs with regard to the broader Aboriginal perspective was to be a continuing thread throughout the task force's deliberations.

Both sections of the task force were to work to a set of nine working principles previously agreed upon by csc and caefs, as well as the Mandate, and one of these stipulated that the task force would not be "premised on the closure of the Prison for Women."[20] Nevertheless, a senior civil servant, looking back, said: "I thought the most important thing would be to find an alternative to that one national institution in Kingston – and certainly to that particular national institution. I thought that a national institution in any event was a bad idea. These women were so far away from their relatives and their support communities, and I thought that no one around that table would suggest that we keep the Prison for Women and that nobody would suggest that we replace it by another national institution."[21]

That belief was about to be tested. As a member of the task force was later to remark: "so much of what happened is like a magical period of time, with a constellation of people and a series of events that created a very unique opportunity or problem, depending on how you wanted to look at it."[22] All were about to discover the extent of their individual contributions – and what the opportunities or problems might be.

CHAPTER THREE

Struggling for Consensus

The first meeting of the Task Force on Federally Sentenced Women Steering Committee was held on 3 April 1989, under the co-chairship of CSC's James Phelps and CAEFS' Bonnie Diamond. The task force was expected to present its completed report to the commissioner by 15 December 1989, and the steering committee's prime function was to provide direction for the whole of the task force rather than do the bulk of the work, with the four co-chairs liaising with each other. Commissioner Ingstrup made his only formal appearance before the task force at that first meeting, challenging the members to "think broadly" and stressing that there were "no limits or conditions on the task force work within the confines of the Mandate."[1] Yet there *were* limits and possible impediments to change, and these were already implicit in the commissioner's retention of financial accountability and the government structure within which the task force would operate.

The working group, co-chaired by CSC's director of Native and Female Offender Programs, Jane Miller-Ashton, and CAEFS' past president, Felicity Hawthorn, met for the first time ten days later. (Unlike the steering committee, which included four men, the working group had none.) They had to decide upon an operating model and acknowledged that any failure to explain their final recommendations clearly and sufficiently would make it difficult for those outside the task force to "appreciate" and "*implement*" the plan (emphasis added).[2] They were concerned that any shortcomings might allow their work to be shelved, as had been previous commissions and inquiries into the Prison for Women. They immediately decided that the report needed a philosophical basis and were determined to identify early "principles on which the task force might premise its work."[3] From the beginning the group grappled with the concept of "difference": how women differed from each other; how Aboriginal federally sentenced women differed from other federally sentenced women; how women differed from men; how difference in treatment of women and men might be justified, if the end results were comparable.[4] During this meeting the group also arranged its first visit to the Prison for Women to meet the women for whom it was planning and to encourage their participation in the forthcoming consultations.

The working group's members inevitably brought varying perspectives to the deliberations, as well as different ways of working, and, due to the intensity and scale of the work, they recognized the need to be vigilant in acknowledging differences among themselves. One member of the group later remembered that first meeting, when each woman was "doing her 'who-I-am' bit." She was "blown out of the water" by the ferocity of one contribution and eventually returned to her room, asking what on earth she had got herself into, and whether she would "survive" it? Moreover, did she want to?[5] This, of course, was not a problem specific to the working group, as a member of the steering committee recalled: "very much the same thing ... [applied to] the steering committee, because you have to remember the makeup of the steering committee was that there were [almost] equal numbers of private sector and csc reps, so you had these career csc reps ... all of whom had agendas that we knew nothing about, bringing them all into the steering committee."[6]

Members were individually accountable to their own organizations, as well as to the task force, and, as became apparent at various times, their dual responsibilities were not easily reconcilable. Participation in a government-sponsored task force raises questions about to whom members are ultimately accountable and whether they are able to remain independent. It raises further questions concerning whether participants understand the possible limitations of their role and the manner in which official policies are constructed, as well as whether they are creating joint policy or simply contributing to official policy. In this instance, the commissioner's injunction to the steering committee and, by extension, to the working group, to "think broadly" encouraged some non-civil servants to assume that a large degree of change was feasible.

Yet, when dealing with documents that are expected to be turned into policy, there are certain processes that come into play. In relation to another initiative, Rock (1986, 31) quoted an official in the Policy Branch of the Ministry of the Solicitor General, who said: "you have to facilitate the production of the types of paper that make [policy] go through the system." At federal levels of government, especially, the processes of facilitation require a high degree of diplomacy. It was inevitable, but perhaps not always acknowledged by those from the

voluntary sector, that the civil servants were quite frequently constrained by the requirements of officialdom. While being capable of
thinking imaginatively and laterally, the civil servants knew that
certain procedures had to be followed if there were to be any hope of
the task force's planning being officially accepted. Their training
encouraged a pragmatic acceptance of the necessity of working within
existing legislative parameters, so for them the invitation to "think
broadly" was immediately hedged with (anticipated) constraints. For
plans to be implemented it was imperative that they should reflect the
political sensibilities of the relevant minister. As one senior civil servant
reflected on the ethos of civil service neutrality: "They may mean it,
[that they are neutral] but they may not realize that they have a powerful vested interest, and a whole career of culture and education, in
the political environment of working as a civil servant. You're always
aware that the minister has to be protected, taken care of, that you
can't put him in a political situation that he can't handle."[7]

Their restraint, however, may be otherwise interpreted. Cohen
(1983) argued that state-sponsored personnel have a vested interest in
maintaining the system that employs them. While the Canadian civil
servants might have suppressed self-interest, the bureaucratic instinct
would have been deeply instilled: they would have known the ultimate
lines of accountability. Yet they also brought another dimension to
their work, being women who had experienced the rapid social change
of the 1970s and absorbed the language of feminism. While working
as civil servants – indeed, as "femocrats" – within the complex bureaucracy of federal government, most believed they were advancing the
feminist cause and ideals by means of the perspectives they brought to
their work. Stetson and Mazur (1995, 276) suggest that "femocrats"
have a vital role to play in providing access to resources and opportunities for feminist groups wishing "to participate autonomously in
policy formulation and implementation." They also make the point
that femocrats should ensure that such groups are not co-opted or
dominated by the state, yet this is not always easily achieved because
groups funded by the state inevitably have their independence constrained. Thus, in wishing to advance the feminist cause, state feminists
sometimes manage to diminish the autonomy of such groups, and this
can lead to a painful compromise of their own principles.

As the work of the group progressed through the months, the pressure of the huge task, and of the individual histories and loyalties of the
members, led to intense disagreements. A working group member
articulated some of the stress involved when asked why she had
decided to stay on, despite huge personal reservations: "I had thought
quite a few times during the process of pulling out, but I had a lot

invested in it and the reasons for going into it were still there, that I
wanted to influence the outcome. I was distinctly unhappy about the
Civil Service aspect of the working group and didn't want them to be
the ones that wrote the report."[8] She felt she had "been co-opted by
something that was a 'done' deal," implying that the civil servants had
already decided the outcome. She knew the propensity of a larger
organization – in this case, CSC – to retain control and was determined
that the perspectives of those whom she represented would be heard in
the final report.

The civil servants' apparent acceptance of the constraints of the task
force angered some members from the voluntary sector, who were
hoping for collective radicalism and a willingness to question the limitations. Yet, as a member said, reflecting on the role of her organization: "really, we have an easier role. We're on the side of light and
bright ... We don't have to think about the cost because we've
exempted us from all responsibility there, so we can just ask for what
we think we need. We may not get it!"[9] Yet she also faced constraints,
if of a different nature, in that she was ultimately answerable to her
own organization rather than to herself. Not one member of the
working group could say that she was truly independent, and not one
could say that her allegiance was solely to federally sentenced women,
despite trying to effect change on their behalf.

The added dimension to their struggle for consensus was that of
culture. Members were still unaccustomed to working with each other,
to the extent that it was later necessary to include the following statement in the minutes: "everyone who wishes gets to speak before any
one else can speak again; no interruptions; [and] members will be sensitive to the issue of reinterpreting another's points."[10] Although the
minutes do not specify which of the group's members suggested them,
all of these procedural rules were reflective of the Aboriginal Sacred
Circle, where speakers are heard in turn and in silence (see Waldram
1997, 134–6). It is an Aboriginal custom that allows time for thought,
rather than an immediate, perhaps unconsidered, reply. Similarly, the
consensus model adopted by the working group – based on consultation *leading* to consensus – reflected Aboriginal custom. Ross (1992,
21), writing from the perspective of a non-Aboriginal Canadian Crown
Attorney "coming into remote Native communities to conduct criminal courts," discusses Aboriginal consensus in relation to judicial decision making. He describes the "ordering of relevant facts ... [and the]
sifting to shake out the truly significant facts" (ibid.), which precede
the eventual judicial decision. Although this is similar to a conventional court, the crucial difference lies in the fact that the decision is
"communal", and that it is "arrived at without 'losing,' without

anyone having his or her opinion ignored" (23). It is debatable whether the non-Aboriginal participants, due to their own understanding of what consensus means, would initially have recognized it as being an Aboriginal practice. The distinction between the Aboriginal and the European use of the strategy lay in the way in which it was conducted. Inevitably, the challenge for all members of the working group was to achieve change through consensus, while acknowledging varying shades of opinion, even though, as one participant was later to observe: "a benevolent dictatorship might have been easier."[11]

Aboriginal influence was also beginning to be felt in other ways. In May the group adopted the word "Aboriginal," rather than "Indian" or "Native," for their own usage as it was "consistent with the terminology of the *Constitution Act, 1982*" (although an amendment in the July minutes emphasized that this was the "simplest solution" and might not be acceptable to "all Natives"). During the same meeting the draft principles were reviewed, and it was argued that "differences between and within Aboriginal groups had been ignored" and that, too frequently, comparisons were being made between men and women.[12] A political note was being added to the debate in an effort to force the realization that Aboriginal women came from backgrounds as diverse as those of their Euro-Canadian counterparts and that it could not be assumed that all Aboriginal women would have the same needs.

RESEARCH:
IDENTIFYING THE FEDERALLY SENTENCED WOMAN

Due to the extremely tight timetable for production of the final report, the working group knew that a research strategy had to be formulated quickly. A discussion paper suggested that there had "been a serious gap in previous work in this area, and [this had] contributed in some cases to the failure to implement recommendations of previous work groups and committees. In today's environment, it is even more imperative that any recommendations of the task force, especially if they have resource implications, *have a sound empirical basis*." This was amplified: "while we on the Task Force might be in complete agreement on all major directions in this area, it will still be necessary *to demonstrate objectively* to others that the options we recommend are the best of all available options" (emphasis added). Although it was recognized that a number of constituencies would need to be persuaded, arguably the most important was the Treasury Board Secretariat, which had "in recent years shown an increasing tendency to insist on a thorough analysis of all reasonable options before agreeing to consider a proposal to proceed with any one option."[13] The working group's recommendations were that research should be commissioned on: women's program needs, together with exemplary programs from Canada and abroad; women's risk to themselves and others as well as their security needs (to support accommodation recommendations); a comparative analysis of accommodation options; and the home communities of the women. Not all of the recommended research was undertaken. It was assumed (not altogether correctly) that basic data about the women (such as offence, education, children) could be extracted from official files.

When the task force was first mooted the then deputy solicitor general, John Tait, alerted the commissioner to a study of the "needs and characteristics of female offenders,"[14] which the Secretariat had already begun. This work had been undertaken by Margaret Shaw and was made available to the task force in June 1989. It gave a comprehensive account of the history of imprisoned women in Canada, set this within the context of international practice, asked questions about risks and needs, and frankly stated: "we do not have much idea who [these] women are, why they are there or what are their needs for programs and support" (Shaw 1991, 2).

A further piece of research, also involving Margaret Shaw, attempted to provide some answers. It asked: what are the experiences of federally sentenced women both during imprisonment and prior to their involvement with the law?; and what programs and services did they see as being necessary both in and out of prison? This research was to be based on interviews with all federally sentenced women in the Prison for Women and provincial prisons, and it was accomplished with some difficulty since the Corrections Research Branch of the Ministry of the Solicitor General had earlier decided to undertake interviews with all women in Kingston and had drawn up its own schedule. Its survey was to use the Diagnostic Interview Schedule (DIS), an American instrument developed to measure the prevalence of mental health problems in general populations. It had not been devised for prison populations, yet the Corrections Research Branch had already completed a study using the instrument on a sample of male federal prisoners. In recognition of the task force's interest, the branch suggested that one or two additional questions might be added to its survey. However, because the DIS made no concessions to gender or diversity, this was totally unacceptable to the researcher and to those members of the working group involved in developing an interview survey. Additionally, since its concern was with measures of mental ill-health, it contained little of the broader information the task force sought. The result was that all interviews for the task force had to wait until the DIS interviewer had completed her separate interview schedule. The Corrections Research Branch, as a department within CSC, was firmly psychological in its discipline at that time and had no interest in feminist research or thought, which it regarded as being unscientific.

On another front, having persuaded CSC of the necessity for a separate survey for Aboriginal women, there was intense discussion within the working group about the inadequacy of using even an open-ended interview for gauging Aboriginal women's concerns and experiences. Standard question-and-answer responses would be inappropriate because of cultural differences and different ways of talking. It was agreed, therefore, that Aboriginal women from outside the prison would undertake all interviews with Aboriginal women inside.[15]

THE WIDER SPHERE

During the 1980s it could not be assumed that Canadian knowledge and experience of providing for imprisoned women would be widely disseminated among Canadian practitioners. As Adelburgh and Currie (1987, 13) were to write in the introduction to their ground-breaking book on Canadian women "in conflict with the law,"[16] *Too Few to Count*, "during our years as students of criminology and social work and later while working in the criminal justice field, we scoured libraries and bookstores for literature that would inform and assist us. Little was to be found, at least about Canadian women." In a footnote they wrote that "significant progress has been made in this field in Britain and the United States" (22), citing commentators such as Smart, Carlen, and Klein. But even in England Heidensohn (1987, 26) was writing: "I have already suggested that academic criminology has given some house room to the study of women and crime in recent years, but it tends too often to be the lumber room or attic rather than the visible and visited public rooms. What is still lacking is the integration of all this work into the mainstream." Within Canada, Bertrand had been asking questions about sexual equality and the law, and there had been pieces of unpublished research, which could have added to the understanding of Canadian women and crime had they been more widely available. Adelburgh and Currie (1987, 14) preceded Shaw in observing that there was a "lack of good statistical data on women in conflict with the law," which left the contributors to their book "making tentative, as opposed to written-in-stone conclusions" (15), "relying on their own and others' first hand impressions" (17). The data on Aboriginal women were described as "non-existent."

So the task force – and Shaw – had little option but to look elsewhere for detailed information on imprisoned women, and the review of international practice compiled by Shaw (1991, 33) focused on

England, Wales, Australia, and the United States "because each has certain characteristics of relevance to Canada." Axon (1989) had undertaken a comprehensive review of practice and legislation relating to imprisoned women from fifteen countries for the Secretariat of the Ministry of the Solicitor General, upon which Shaw was also able to draw. Australia, in many respects, was the jurisdiction most closely resembling Canada, in that it had a federal system, a vast geography imposing severe limitations on what could be provided for imprisoned women, a disproportionate number of imprisoned Aboriginal peoples, and a system of justice heavily dependent upon British precedent. Like its neighbour, New Zealand, Australia was only just beginning to assess the problems encountered by Aboriginal prisoners, and the report of the Task Force on Aboriginals and Criminal Justice was yet to be published. The report of the Ministerial Committee of Inquiry into the Prisons System of New Zealand, *Te Ara Hou*, was not published until 1989 and would not have been available as the (limited) resource it might have been (it rejected the concept of differential treatment for women.) Jackson's *The Maori and the Criminal Justice System*, the second of a two-part investigation into Maori offending, had been available since 1988 and its call for a parallel system of Maori justice would have resonated with some of the Aboriginal members of the task force; yet it did not deal with imprisonment. Overall, there was a body of knowledge to be consulted from which many common strands emerged, but the bigger question was whether such knowledge might be translatable between jurisdictions. Such a question becomes particularly difficult to respond to when the "knowledge" is derived from cultural practices specific to indigenous groups.

At the beginning of the task force there was little information readily available, even from CSC, about federally sentenced women, so it was faced with finding solutions for an inadequately defined group even before its commissioned research was completed. In a sense, this left the task force initially free to construct its own vision of the federally sentenced woman. It has since been accused of portraying this "woman" largely as a victim of her economic and social environment, bereft of agency because of her victimization; yet, this initial construction emerged from task force members' individual knowledge of such women. Many on the task force – and, more specifically, those from the voluntary sector on the working group – had worked closely with imprisoned women and knew their collective histories of poverty, abuse, racism, addiction, and educational failure. The civil servants also had this understanding, but it was generally acquired at a remove. They rarely visited the Prison for Women and did not know the women as individuals; rather, they saw the women as the statistics informing

their daily work. As the task force proceeded, the image of the federally sentenced woman assumed some of the characteristics of those
whom the working group began to meet via consultations and prison
visits: "the woman" became more of a physical reality, and, finally, an
event occurred that partially metamorphosed this "woman" into a particular, almost symbolic, woman, as will shortly be seen. Essentially,
however, this "woman" remained shrouded by the status of victim,
and federally sentenced women were "denied even the rhetorical status
of *survivors*" (Bruckert 1993, 11, emphasis in original). The consequences of this may be seen in later chapters.

SPEAKING FOR OTHER WOMEN

Historically, men have always been involved in planning for, and
speaking on behalf of, imprisoned women. The women's reformatory
movement challenged men's right to do this, but, as Chapter 1 outlines,
it has been suggested that the reformers' challenge was premised on
their belief in an innate sexual difference rather than on an attempt to
press for sexual equality (Freedman 1981; see also Rafter 1985;
Hannah-Moffat 2001). In "cross[ing] the boundary between themselves and fallen women" (Freedman 1981, 105) reformers were suggesting a commonality of women's experience and assuming that
women such as themselves had an instinctive, or collective, knowledge
of other women that qualified them to participate in the governance of
women's prisons. Those early reformers accommodated imprisonment
rather than questioned it, and they contributed to its continuing legitimacy as a means of controlling deviant women. In so doing, they
developed a form of maternal governance that was no less controlling
than was the paternalism more commonly found in prisons (see
Hannah-Moffat 2001). While the majority of the members of the 1989
task force were not employed directly by correctional authorities
(although CAEFS had a financial relationship with CSC), and so were
not in a position to exercise maternal authority in a physical sense, they
were nevertheless involved in a project that required them to plan on
behalf of imprisoned women. Once again, women were being asked to
show a collective understanding of other women, yet only two on the
task force had personal experience of actual imprisonment; for the
remainder, their knowledge could be no more than conjecture and
empathy. Additionally, these women exercised their power to plan for
others from various positions of authority, and, most obviously, all
were free (Bruckert 1993; Hannah-Moffat 2001). In no sense could
they be equal to imprisoned women.

Bruckert (1993, 19) has pertinent things to say about the power differentials between "the discourse creators [members of the task force] and subjects [federally sentenced women]," positing that class is a "central [unacknowledged] difference." Irrespective of how each member of the working group might have viewed their own background, the sheer disparity between their economic and social circumstances and those of the vast majority of imprisoned women immediately distanced them from those for whom they were planning. There is often a tendency to assume that it is those working with prisoners who have the greatest understanding of prisons. Indeed, many officers spend longer "inside" than do the prisoners (Faith 1993), but they do not experience the physical loss and pain occasioned by imprisonment. DiIulio (1991, 1) suggests that: "there are no experts on corrections. As near as we come to such experts are the men and women who have spent their adult lives working with criminals: wardens, correctional officers, probation and parole agents." In this analysis the prisoner becomes merely the subject of others' expertise. Indeed, Harding et al. (1985, 171) lamented the loss of prisoners' voices from criminological literature, and then almost immediately discounted prisoners' accounts of their own lives as "not to be greatly relied on for obvious reasons." Within the task force it might have been tempting for some working group members to assume that their somewhat increased contact with individual federally sentenced women, occasioned by visits to the Prison for Women, permitted a closer understanding of their needs. Yet "these [federally sentenced] women ... are one of the most over-studied and over-intervened populations ... As a consequence they are likely [to be] more conscious and articulate about their past experiences" (Bruckert 1993, 33). Many of the women would have been able to convey powerfully the pain of their incarceration, using the "sociological" language of some of the professionals within the prison. This did not necessarily mean, however, that the truth as they experienced it was being fully expressed. Nor did it lessen the power differentials between the two groups. The imprisoned women had few means of expressing their inherent expertise, except through the mouths of intermediaries.

Hannah-Moffat (2001, 43) traced the development of "maternal logics" in the governance of imprisoned women and, in doing so, explored the question of "structural relations of power which are not mediated by gender sameness. Although women reformers, volunteers, matrons and prisoners are of the same sex, relations of power continue to exist between those socio-economically and culturally heterogeneous categories of women." Within the context of the task force, and specifically within the working group, it can be argued that there were also "relations of power" between members. The civil servants on the working group had a power vested in them by virtue of the fact that they were government appointees, with (stratified) access to those who would make the final decision regarding implementation of the final report. With the exception of one member – Mary Cassidy, both a prison warden and a civil servant – their expertise was as government administrators involved in the bureaucracy of corrections rather than in the prisons themselves.[17] The CAEFS' representatives derived their expertise from the specific individual knowledge they had of the imprisoned women whom they represented. The Aboriginal members' knowledge was grounded in their proximity to the disproportionate numbers imprisoned from within their own communities and extended families. Yet the power differentials were remarkably fluid, depending upon the area of expertise being discussed. The civil servants were perhaps politically ascendant, while the voluntary sector often believed itself philosophically ascendant. Moreover, the two federally sentenced women on the steering committee might have been thought, in some ways, to be morally ascendant.

It could possibly be assumed that the Aboriginal representatives were the least advantaged within the formal relationships of power, but this would be to discount the effect of their peoples' history on others in the working group. As the minutes reveal, even while they were failing to document the true extent of Aboriginal contributions to discussions, there was little criticism of Aboriginal perspectives by others on the task force. At times there was a marked deference to the moral authority of the Aboriginal members, indicated not so much by what was said by the rest of the group as by a failure to say anything at all. One Aboriginal member was later to characterize this as "internalised racism," a view also presented by a non-Aboriginal interviewee.[18] By this, they meant that the other working group members' reluctance to criticize and challenge implied that the Aboriginals' perspectives could not withstand critical examination. Some of the non-Aboriginals would have refuted this, as is indicated by this comment from a member of the steering committee: "I would say that at least part of it [the silence] is that the non-Aboriginal members never felt that they were experts on the Aboriginal issues or culture, so when the Aboriginals say they are suffering an injustice, the general attitude of all the people in the room was 'you're right.' No Canadian doubts that they have been treated unjustly ... There is an element of guilt, particularly within government, at having managed it so badly."[19] This might well be interpreted as another means of neutralizing Aboriginal peoples, simply by refusing to engage in debate with them, but interview evidence suggests that there was a genuine acceptance of the strength of the Aboriginal members' case.

POLITICIZING THE AGENDA

The group members knew that they would have to consult across the
breadth of Canada if they were to hear the voices of those most intimately involved with federally sentenced women, and CAEFS had been
given responsibility for organizing the consultations. This strategy was
useful to CSC because provincial correctional officials who contributed
to the regional debate could not subsequently say that they had been
ignored by the task force. Eight consultations were planned for the
months of June and July, and over 500 invitations were extended to
groups and individuals across Canada, leading to over 200 presentations eventually being made to the task force.

In an effort to focus these presentations a sub-committee drafted a
set of guideline questions it wished to have answered. Patricia
Monture's views were subsequently sought "to ensure that First
Nations perspective['s were] included."[20] She added two further questions to the guidelines: "who should have responsibility for women
serving sentences of two years or more?" and "if First Nations had a
self-determined justice system, what would it look like?"[21] The
working group's co-chair, Jane Miller Ashton, provided a written brief
on the matter for James Phelps, in his capacity as deputy commissioner
rather than as co-chair of the steering committee. His response showed
his concern that the task force should not "exceed its authority or
interfere in the jurisdiction of other government departments or other
governments."[22] Some members of the working group would undoubtedly have seen the attempt to broaden the brief, and circumvent the
mandate, as an attempt to politicize their deliberations, and, subsequently, the co-chairs jointly decided to remove the sovereignty question. Yet again, Ole Ingstrup's injunction to "think broadly" was seen
to be circumscribed, and in this case the limitations were reinforced by
a co-chair of the steering committee in his capacity as a corrections'
official and civil servant. James Phelps's response highlighted the dual
roles of some on the task force and raises further questions about their
ultimate accountability. It could be construed that, in attempting to
add a political dimension to their deliberations, some of the Aboriginal
members were showing that they had a wider constituency than just
federally sentenced women.

In June it was the steering committee's turn to meet, and a great deal
of time was spent discussing the draft principles. Although still a distance from the principles that were finally published, certain words of
great importance in the final report made an appearance: "respect,"
"dignity," "self-esteem," and "empowerment." Co-chair Phelps found
the suggested wording altogether "too soft" and suggested that, if the

task force's credibility were not to be undermined, it ought to refer to such things as assisting "offenders to become law-abiding citizens" (a phrase sure to annoy the Aboriginal members). The co-chairs of the working group were indeed "steered" by the committee to reconsider much of the draft.[23]

HISTORY REPEATED: IGNORING QUEBEC

Although Aboriginal perspectives were heard from the outset, an entirely outnumbered francophone Quebecois[24] member of the steering committee had also been trying to raise Quebecois issues. At the first steering committee meeting in April she had expressed concern about the lack of a Quebec representative on the working group, but no response was recorded in the minutes, and the general reaction to her proposal is not known. The question of francophone representation on the group was also raised during the May working group meeting, "given the significant number of federally sentenced women from Quebec," and it was agreed that all four co-chairs would consider the options of either appointing a francophone member to the working group or allowing francophone members of the steering committee to take on a greater role.[25]

The task force's four co-chairs then invited a francophone Quebecois civil servant to join the working group, in recognition of the importance of the Quebecois' perspective, but she was unavailable until August, which was felt to be too late. This is the clearest of indications that Quebec, from the task force's inception, could have been represented on the working group – by a civil servant – without there being undue worries about offence being caused to other provinces. This supposition is supported by the fact that one of the task force's four co-chairs was a deputy commissioner, itself a very senior rank, and that he had acquiesced in the decision to co-opt a civil servant. Twenty-one percent of all federally sentenced women were French-speaking, and, given the fraught history of relations between Quebec and the rest of Canada, it is remarkable that their needs had not assumed an earlier importance. With the signing of the Exchange of Services' Agreement (ESA) – the Tanguay Agreement – 1982, Quebec Corrections had negotiated a considerable amount of autonomy, and most Quebec federally sentenced women were already incarcerated provincially at Maison Tanguay in Montreal. This prison inevitably provided a francophone milieu and resolved some of the issues, but it also led to others. The ESA implicitly accepted the rationale of those agreements negotiated earlier; that is, that provincial imprisonment meant acceptance of provincial standards in programming. And, as these were based on the infinitely more short-term needs of the provincially sentenced woman, the requirements of the long-term prisoner were consistently overlooked. In this regard Quebecois federally sentenced women were actively disadvantaged, while their provincially sentenced peers faced increased levels of security because of the presence of federally sentenced women. (The federal government provided almost a million dollars to upgrade security once federal women were incarcerated at Maison Tanguay.) The inescapable conclusion, sustained by the late invitation extended to the civil servant, is that those responsible for the initial composition of the task force did not, to begin with, see Quebec as a major component in what they were undertaking. They only came to see it as such during the life of the task force and were again faced with the consequences of omission as the task force made its final decisions.

The limitations of ESAs were again highlighted by the Burnaby Correctional Centre for Women (BCCW) in British Columbia, a prison that, once completed, was due to hold both provincially and federally sentenced women under the 1988 Burnaby Agreement. A working group member was particularly alarmed by what she observed during a fact-finding visit: "We had a meeting with the staff who were going to be ... at Burnaby when it opened, and we asked them all sorts of questions about how things would be different when the new institution opened, and of course the answer was 'not at all,' and that was when it really came to me most forcefully – probably half-way through the task force – that we may be on the wrong track. That you can't fix the present system. That you have to have a new system."[26] The prison was later described: "technically, the institution is a medium security facility, but for all practical purposes, due to the architectural design and high-level technological security systems, and because women from every classification are locked up together, they must all abide by the maximum custody rules intended for the control of the few women who are perceived as security risks" (Faith 1993, 146). The BCCW thus replicated the style of Kingston's Prison for Women.[27] The distinction, however, between this new ESA and all its predecessors lay in the fact that federally sentenced women, who both qualified and elected to remain in British Columbia, would be under federal jurisdiction. Others making the same decision in other provinces lost their "federal" status and became provincial prisoners. This generally meant that women from other provinces received the benefit of being held closer to their homes but had significantly fewer programs available to them. Because of the great number of penitentiaries, federally sentenced men did not face the same dilemma.

LISTENING TO OTHER VOICES:
LOOKING AT EXISTING PROVISION

Although members of the steering committee assisted during the regional consultations, those most affected by the scale of the task force's work were on the working group.[28] The task force found itself interviewing its own members, Bonnie Diamond and James Phelps, in their professional capacities. Ole Ingstrup was asked for his personal view "on the issues and possible solutions."[29] The unions were questioned. Extensive meetings took place with provincial heads of corrections and their staff. The National Parole Board, both nationally and regionally, was consulted, as was the noted advocate of prisoners' rights, Claire Culhane.[30] Task force members visited eleven provincial institutions housing federally sentenced women, and they met with federally sentenced women in the Prison for Women and on parole in the community. The task force was determined to show that it had "heard" the various voices, and it also needed to ensure that provincial sensibilities were not offended, as the ESAs had made provincial corrections key partners in the business of housing federal women.

The fourth working group meeting was held in August 1989 in Ottawa. Although they were beginning to receive information and ideas from community, regional, and institutional consultations, the group knew that it still had some time to wait until the bulk of the research material would be available. The minutes stated: "Given the Task Force timeframe, the working group [will] have to move forward using assumptions based on their personal expertise, that of the organizations consulted and the findings of previous studies. The research results, therefore, [will] be used to validate or modify these assumptions."[31] In assuming a collective expertise – and, in this instance, having little choice – the working group was straying into problematic territory. James Phelps had earlier urged the group to validate is work by means of empirical research, whereas the commissioner had imposed an almost draconian timetable for completion. Both stances were determined by the demands of the Treasury Board, and they left the working group in an untenable position. Without research evidence it could not accurately plan, yet if it failed to complete its report on time then the Treasury Board would refuse funds essential for implementation. In relying on its own expertise and its members' shared experience of womanhood, if not imprisonment, the working group was replicating the strategies of the first women prison reformers and planning for only a partially identified group. It was a risky position to be in, yet the working group saw no other option.

At this critical half-way stage the working group also needed to start planning the outline of the final report. There was a diverse public that had to be persuaded of the need for change and, above all, the final document had to open the Treasury Board's purse. The report had to be logical, persuasive, and defensible. In short, its style could not be too different from that of most other government reports, but this could not preclude its language from being radical. Where the working group was ground breaking, at that juncture, was in deciding that the voices of federally sentenced women would open the report; the women would have a chapter to themselves and be recognized as possessing a unique knowledge. As the working group was constrained by a tight budget, and per diem hours were fast being used up by the non-government representatives, it was decided that the civil service members would undertake the writing of the first draft. The wisdom of allowing the civil servants to be the initial drafters of the report was apparently not questioned, but the minutes of all the meetings were at best an approximation of what was said, and we already know of one working group member determined to counterbalance the civil servants' influence.

The commissioned research was under way and the interviews providing the basis for Shaw et al.'s *Survey of Federally Sentenced Women* had commenced at the Prison for Women. A separate piece of research, the Security Needs Assessment, also involving Shaw in the preliminary discussions, was delayed. This was to be based on earlier work that Berzins and Dunn had carried out for the Chinnery Report in 1978 (see chapter 1) and was expected to demonstrate, as it had some ten years earlier, that women were frequently over-classified, with most of them capable of being accommodated in minimum security settings.

ADDING TO THE AGENDA:
ABORIGINAL ISSUES

During the working group's July meeting concerns about the failure to consult with Aboriginal groups in the "more remote northern or rural native communities" had surfaced. Invitations to meet with the working group had been extended, but the response had been discouraging, so in August the working group decided that the final report would document the failure. And, importantly, Aboriginal issues would not be confined to a sole Aboriginal chapter in the final report but, rather, would be raised throughout. The Aboriginal members' success in pressing their case continued, with the question of Aboriginal sovereignty again being raised in the context of a discussion on the "artificiality of the federal-provincial split in jurisdiction." Aboriginal self-determination was considered another "jurisdictional issue." Despite James Phelps's earlier-cited view that this question was outside the mandate of the task force, the working group agreed that the report would acknowledge Aboriginal peoples' wish for self-determination. By then the working group members were largely persuaded of the moral strength of the Aboriginal case (and some had needed no persuading at all), but a minority also conceded certain arguments in order to keep the peace and to ensure a completed task.

Yet Patricia Monture still felt that her attempts to "communicate awareness/sensitivity to the working group [had] not been effective."[32] What she had been trying to convey to the group was perhaps best expressed in the research report accompanying *Creating Choices* and eventually produced by Lana Fox and Fran Sugar, themselves one-time federally sentenced women and members of the steering committee. They discussed other task forces that had requested meetings with the Native Sisterhood inside the Prison for Women: "We always agreed to meet, somehow believing that there was hope for change ... We never said out loud that we were teaching them something about being a people. The circle of chairs we sat in represented the cycle of life from birth to death and that cycle did not exclude anyone ... In our private conversations afterwards, we felt that even though those officials were our enemies, our jailers, our keepers, the all-powerful representatives of white authority and the state, *that they would have heard our truth*" (Sugar and Fox 1990, 15, emphasis added). As has been shown, Aboriginal claims to "truth," or understanding, had historically been swept aside by the dominant culture, and the situation was little different within prisons. In an effort to understand Aboriginal issues more fully, and to show that Aboriginal women came from backgrounds as diverse as those of their Euro-Canadian counterparts, the August working group meeting concluded with a workshop conducted by Elder Joan Lavallee.[33] She reflected upon the impact of residential schools on Aboriginal women and their consequent separation from traditional teachings, yet she warned that Aboriginal spirituality was not a "quick fix" (see chapter 9).

Some Euro-Canadian members of the task force were further exposed to Aboriginal concerns in August, when Jane Miller Ashton and Bonnie Diamond attended the Aboriginal Women's Caucus (AWC) Conference. The opening lines of one of the papers, "dedicated to the memory of all women who have died unnatural deaths as a result of their incarceration," gave some indication of the mood of the meeting: "The relationship of the Aboriginal Women's Caucus and the federal government is not a relationship that is based on trust ... All Aboriginal, First Nations citizens are in conflict with the law. We are First

Peoples with an inherent right to exercise our own systems of justice
and the values these systems represent. The issue of Aboriginal women
and the criminal justice system is merely the most blatant example of
the oppression of First Nations people under a system of laws to which
we have never consented."[34] In considering the task force itself, caucus
members expressed frustration at the failure of the steering committee
to "take account" of their views and questions, and the equal failure
of the minutes to record their contributions. This point was later made
most strikingly by Sugar and Fox (1990, 2): "When our rage became
uncontainable [during task force meetings] we spoke of prison conditions, of the actual experiences of being Aboriginal women in prison ...
Yet our words were met with tense silences and appear nowhere in the
minutes of meetings. Our descriptions of the reality are buried as our
sisters are buried in prison."

Despite the clear concerns, the September minutes followed much
the same format as had previous ones, but in this instance it is possible
to compare them with very detailed notes taken of the same meeting.
In the minutes there was one line that said: "Karen Paul spoke of her
vision for responding to the needs of Aboriginal women." In the notes
this "vision" took half a page to explain. Whether these omissions
were in support of "consensus" or were simply meant to avoid the
appearance of dissent is a debatable point, but their effect was to
heighten distrust at a time when the task force, and the working group
in particular, needed to work cohesively in order to prepare for the
final stage of its work.

The critical role played by the minutes in passing information to
both parts of the task force was also apparent at the September
working group meeting, when Patricia Monture reported that "the
Aboriginal Steering Committee members had [understood] from the
[August] Minutes ... [that she and Sharon McIvor] considered acceptable the fact that the consultations had failed to reach Aboriginal communities."[35] Had the minutes been fuller, this misunderstanding might
not have occurred. But it also reflected the continuing anxiety on the
part of the Aboriginal participants that they were listened to, but not
"heard"; that Euro-Canadians, while appearing to be more deferential
in that they did not interrupt or criticize, were in effect "internalizing"
their unacknowledged racism, as has been discussed earlier.

For some of the Euro-Canadian members of the task force the
emphasis on Aboriginal concerns, while understood, at times occasioned discomfort. Although theoretically familiar with Aboriginal
history, a number had had very little contact with Aboriginal women,
particularly those who were articulate and assertive in the company of
Euro-Canadians, and some found the emotions expressed during meet-

ings very difficult to deal with. One recalled: "You sat there. You listened politely. It was also a period when you were extremely politically correct. There were scenes – I remember waiting for an hour for the representatives to come to the table because they were late and no one mentioned anything, no one said, 'let's start,' we just waited ... There could be all kinds of ... personal histories ... around the table ... with an awful lot of emotion being shared and people just felt very uneasy."[36]

FEDERALLY SENTENCED WOMEN: VICTIMS?

The language used by the AWC, in speaking of the "oppression of First Nations people," is particularly interesting because it continues a theme that has previously emerged: the victimization of Aboriginal women. Although used in the context of *imprisoned* Aboriginal women, it is not entirely about their victimization by the criminal justice system. There is a larger political strand to the discourse encompassing the historic victimization of Aboriginal women by the dominant culture, through the application of unjust laws to which the individual nations had never assented. Had these laws not been enforced, Aboriginal women might not have been dispossessed of their families, communities, and cultures, and they might have avoided the ravages of alcohol. Although imprisoned Aboriginal people were undeniably offenders against Euro-Canadian law, their disproportionate imprisonment was assumed to be almost entirely attributable to their historic victimization and was not necessarily a cause for shame. The AWC's language reflected some Aboriginal people's belief that the only solution to their many problems lay in the adoption of separate strategies and, in this case, one focused on an Aboriginal justice system. To the Aboriginal members of the task force it seemed that some members did not appreciate the scale of past injustices.

However, it was not only Aboriginal women who were seen as victims. Within the context of the task force the theme of victimization had four strands: (1) the victimization of federally sentenced women by CSC's failure to recognize that women have needs distinct from those of men; (2) the victimization experienced by many federally sentenced women, from all ethnic groups, as a consequence of their economic and social positions in Canada; (3) the victimization imposed by the correctional/justice system on federally sentenced women due to there being only one federal facility available to them (while to be held in a provincial prison meant foregoing federal rights, which compounded the injustice); and (4) the victimization experienced specifically by Aboriginal women, exacerbated by racism. As will be seen, the task force was later accused of characterizing all federally sentenced women as victims, rather than as women who had themselves created victims. These various distinctions must be made, if only to avoid perpetuating what some commentators have interpreted as being the *collective* image of a group of women completely without agency. It is apparent that the traditional image of the "victim" as being the innocent bystander to whom something unwarranted has happened was somehow lost. Yet that same description could apply to an Aboriginal woman, should her life be seen within a social context, so the terminology was necessarily imprecise. At this point it is important to be aware of the evolving, undisputed image of the federally sentenced Aboriginal woman as "victim" – a view reinforced by Johnson and Rodgers (1993, 110), who characterized Aboriginal women as suffering from "racial discrimination, gender discrimination ... and legislated discrimination." That image eventually affected how all other federally sentenced women were characterized by the task force.

GLIMPSING THE "DIFFICULT TO MANAGE" WOMAN

Of all the research areas discussed by the steering committee in September, the area that was eventually to have the greatest impact appeared to receive the least debate, according to the minutes, but this was belied by the very full discussion documented in the Detailed Notes.[37] The Security Needs Assessment, to be undertaken at the Prison for Women, was deferred. The main reasons offered for the deferral were the lack of time and recent disturbances at the prison.[38] As the minutes recorded, "while the exercise was not without merit, it was not considered of high priority, and therefore would not be completed as an integral part of task force work."[39] But the Detailed Notes revealed that committee members were worried that the results would be "skewed by recent events" (disturbances and a lockdown at the prison) and that the women would consequently be over-classified. Looking ahead to the possibility that there might be a facility other than the Prison for Women, the exercise provided an important opportunity to ask what kind of "static and dynamic security features [might be] required in alternate (sic) accommodation" and was "critical for long-term accommodation planning."[40] What seemed to sway the committee towards deferment was the worry that the assessment might "falsely suggest the women have become tougher since the last exercise" (carried out for the Chinnery Report in 1978) and, by implication, that this depiction would make it harder to justify a new style of prison. The cancellation of the Security Needs Assessment also worried the working group when it met separately two days later, causing it to specify in the minutes the "recommendation that the exercise should be implemented at the first possible moment." One group member noted that this would leave them unable to make "as precise a recommendation regarding maximum security type accommodation," which eventually proved to be the case.[41] The task force was thus deprived of information crucial to the planning of any new prisons as they had no specific information on the numbers of women requiring higher levels of security, leaving the working group to rely heavily on its own knowledge of the women when proposing its plans.

Meanwhile, those women remained at the Prison for Women. Ingstrup had stressed at the task force's first meeting that "no major decisions regarding federal women would be made during the life of the task force,"[42] but the administration of the Prison for Women remained firmly within the grasp of CSC. The task force worried about its ongoing work being used as an excuse for allowing conditions to stagnate at the Prison for Women, and, although an undertaking had been given that any initiatives being considered would be "brought to the attention of the task force" (TFFSW 1990, 75), this did not mean that the task force could influence day-to-day procedures. Nor did it mean that initiatives always *were* brought to the attention of the task force, as was evident when the working group queried a proposal to establish a mental health unit at the Prison for Women. Mary Cassidy told them that she had not raised "this initiative at the previous meeting since the unit [was] intended to address an acknowledged long-term regional need, whether or not federally sentenced women remain[ed] at the Prison for Women."[43]

This situation highlighted the anomalous position of a member of the working group who was both warden of the prison in question and a government employee. The decisions she needed to make as a warden accountable to CSC would not always be the ones that she could easily convey to her colleagues on the working group. It had been clear at the July working group meeting that the task force was being used as an excuse for inactivity at the prison, with individual members having been told that "the task force will address it" whenever they tried to raise issues.[44] Mary Cassidy's position, on the relatively few occasions when she was able to attend working group meetings (her "unique" position having been noted in the May minutes), was made even more difficult by the fact that she was the public face of the Prison for Women. Irrespective of what she might be attempting to achieve within the Prison for Women, the escalating unrest ensured that she was continually subjected to public criticism and that she also had to face criticism during the group's meetings. One member recalled: "We were all criticizing her." Another remembered: "There's no doubt that they used the meeting as a chance to whip her ... you could see from their criticisms that it was beyond their comprehension that she could have a view ... they were advocating changes to her management, so it wasn't a situation where she was looked upon as part of the team."[45] The sense of being "apart" must have greatly increased any difficulties Mary Cassidy experienced as a member of the working group, but this is conjecture, as she felt unable to discuss this or any other aspect of her work.

HEARING ABORIGINAL VOICES

During the September steering committee meeting there were still concerns that the views of women on release in the community were not being heard. One of the Aboriginal members had highlighted the need to provide empirical information: "Government has historically not funded Native Organisations unless they were willing to provide traditional empirical data to back up their work ... But the data collection must be appropriate for native people."[46] The committee emphasized that "the community-needs personal interviews [were] a critical element in determining what programs/services [for Aboriginal women were] required to support community-based intervention strategies." The committee recognized the extreme workload being carried by the working group and decided that "consultation can be considered a type of research," which meant that "traditional research instruments" need not be used. Thus the committee provided Aboriginal women with a means of undertaking research appropriate to them, irrespective of whether "traditional" researchers would accept the validity of the finished piece. This decision inspired the AWC members, at their separate meeting, to propose that Fran Sugar be sent to "eighteen cities to locate Aboriginal women through names obtained from the Native Sisterhood, CSC databases, word of mouth and consultation with street workers" and their proposal was accepted by the working group. (Lana Fox was to join her in this endeavour.)[47]

The report eventually produced by Sugar and Fox, both of whom were on the steering committee, was a powerful document, as has already been seen. Their own experience of serving federal time enabled them to provide a running commentary on what women individually told them, and they did this with a passion and articulacy that far exceeded the cool prose normally reserved for such research. They did, indeed, produce something that "challenge[d] traditional understandings of effective research methods" (Monture 1989–90, 467). Monture continued: "This report is also important in academic circles and women's circles because it carries a powerful message about research. Research methods to be effective must be culturally relevant. In this case, that meant respecting the traditional way of doing things of First Nations' Peoples." In large part this meant accepting the validity of qualitative information, listening to the voices of those directly affected and not attempting to put them within a quantified context. Yet the fact that the style of Sugar and Fox's report was considered acceptable, alongside the task force's commitment to underpinning their work with rigorous (read "empirical") research, also said something about the dynamics of the task force and its increasing willingness to accommodate Aboriginal members. This is not to imply that Sugar and Fox's report was less worthwhile than traditional research, as their report allowed different voices to be heard in a highly effective manner, but, rather, to emphasize the changes that had taken place within the task force.

The untested question is whether the cultural difference to be found within the francophone community would have been respected had the Quebecois pressed for a similar report, irrespective of the fact that Quebecois culture shared a common European heritage with that of the anglophones. As it happened, Quebec's federally sentenced women were interviewed by francophones, but their voices did not emerge as a distinct faction within the Euro-Canadian group. It might be argued that, as both Euro-Canadian groups shared a history of reliance on the penitentiary as a means of social control, few distinctions needed to be made. Furthermore, most Quebecois federally sentenced women were imprisoned in a francophone milieu, and so were seen to be less disadvantaged than were many other imprisoned women. Yet, to accept these positions is to continue ignoring the importance of culture and the way in which it influences understanding – indeed, the way in which it reflects the "truth" to which Sugar and Fox (1990) alluded. In assuming that the francophones were quite naturally part of the Euro-Canadian plan, the task force – perhaps unwittingly – imposed anglophone understanding upon a province familiar with such treatment since the Conquest. This left a Quebecois member of the steering committee appealing fruitlessly for "the interests and special interests of French women" not to be overlooked.[48] While it is not known what a truly Quebecois plan might have looked like, it can perhaps be safely assumed that it would have been somewhat different from the one that was proposed, precisely because Quebec itself is different from the other provinces.

With three months left until the deadline of 15 December 1989, the working group had reached the point where it needed to start the final planning process and to acknowledge the importance of two strands: community interventions and prison incapacitation. It was suggested that, as long-term federally sentenced women would spend the greatest period in whatever new prisons emerged, their needs should dictate what would be regarded as the "norm" when designing accommodation. Lee Axon, who had been commissioned to look at exemplary programs available outside Canada, had told the group of the adverse effects of visible and intrusive security on inmate participation in programming. She stressed that the greater the security the more likely it was to promote a "them-and-us" culture, adding that it would be difficult to have programs requiring "openness and self-disclosure" if security levels were too overt. The wish to provide an environment that would "reduce institutionalization and support autonomous living" was seen as a short-term objective by the task force, with the longer-term objective being legislative change permitting greater "flexibility in sentence management" and "an Aboriginal Justice System."[49] Once again, the mandate was being exceeded.

The community model was also becoming clearer, and, more importantly, the need to have adequate liaison between the prisons and those supporting the released woman in the community. Thanks to the consultation process, it was already clear to task force members in September that they would *not* be recommending the continuation of the status quo. They were also able to put in the minutes that the "Prison for Women, as it exists now, [should] be closed."[50] But the working group had set itself a problem, which it recognized, in wanting to move towards a community rather than a prison-based solution for these women, and the members referred to it is as the "central conundrum" (TFFSW 1990, 78): "if a capital investment is made in construction (or lease/buy) how will the strategy to replace prisons with community-based interventions be moved forward?"[51]

The working group members understood the risks inherent in providing better prisons and programs. Sentencers would see them as being beneficial to the women, whereas the geographically dislocated Prison for Women had been a disincentive to sentence women to federal terms (see Bruckert 1993). The working group's interim compromise was to take shape in the next three months.

As this chapter chronicles, the task force and, more specifically, the working group were experiencing geographic dislocation of their own. They needed to cross the country both for meetings and consultations and, in between, they had formidable piles of papers to read and analyze, as well as extra papers to prepare themselves; they were under enormous pressure. This and the previous chapter might have suggested that, in the midst of this pressured existence, some members of the working group took a more dominant role than others. On the evidence of the available minutes there is undeniable truth in this, but there is also another consideration, articulated by several of the group in separate interviews. Certain members were extremely influential, if not always publicly so, and one was repeatedly cited by interviewees for her skill in being able to refocus the working group on the reason for its members sharing what at times seemed like an enforced, unwelcome co-existence. Her name features infrequently in the minutes, but the minutes, being an official record, were continually refined before being sent out. Consensus prevailed, even then. (Minutes for the steering committee were much more forthcoming about names.) Although the use and interpretation of the minutes in this book is necessarily selective and, in many respects, gives little idea of the sheer volume of work undertaken by the working group, the process is justified on the grounds that it illuminates a specific strand – one in which a minority group appears to be taking advantage of an unforeseen opportunity and is politicizing the agenda of a government-sponsored initiative. Moreover, those who were unofficially charged with keeping the project on track – the civil servants – appear to have been reluctant, or possibly unable, to prevent this politicization. Much has been written about the risk of benevolent ventures being incorporated by the state (e.g., Rothman 1980; Cohen 1983, 1985; Freedman 1981; Scull 1983; Hannah-Moffat and Shaw 2000; Hannah-Moffat 2001). At this stage, the task force appears to be demonstrating an alternative version of incorporation, wherein the seemingly less powerful Aboriginal participants capture the moral high ground and are actively involving others in the dissemination of their views. Those whom they have not "captured" appear, nevertheless, to have been neutralized by their own knowledge of Canada's colonial history and the terrible consequences for Aboriginal nations.

Why this should have been so is something to be explored, as parallel stories are now emerging. There is one in which the replacement of a prison for federally sentenced women is being planned. Then there is the other, in which the replacement of a prison for federally sentenced women appears to have been overlaid with considerations of women's victimization and, more specifically, Aboriginal women's victimization. This should be borne in mind while the work of the task force, as it determined the content of its report, continues to be examined. The next chapter shows how events at Kingston's Prison for Women influenced the task force, right up until – and beyond – the time when the completed report was handed to the commissioner of corrections.

CHAPTER FOUR

Facing the Central Conundrum

During the August meeting of the Task Force on Federally Sentenced Women's working group a submission had been tabled from Sandy Sayer, who was a prisoner at the Prison for Women. It eloquently urged the task force to remember that, for prisoners, the real experts on imprisoned women were the women themselves. Ms Sayer was a reluctant contributor to the consultations, having seen many people attempt to provide solutions to the intractable problems of the prison, with few positive results. Yet, despite her doubts about the outcome, she wanted to add her voice to this initiative. Sandy Sayer, the mother of two young children, was a twenty-five-year-old provincially sentenced Aboriginal woman who had been involuntarily transferred[1] to Kingston from Saskatchewan. On 7 October 1989 she committed suicide in the Prison for Women. Hers was the third suicide associated with the Prison for Women in less than ten months, and there were to be another four by the end of February 1991.[2]

Her death had a profound impact on all involved with the task force; women such as Sandy Sayer were the ones for whom they were all working. There was immense pain and, for those who knew Ms Sayer personally, a feeling of disbelief. One member of the task force remembered being told and, in distress, conveying the news to a work colleague, who responded: "Jesus, I can't believe you don't understand this one yet. Every suicide in Aboriginal country is painful for us because there isn't an Aboriginal person alive on the planet who hasn't thought of doing it themselves."[3] Another member thought that for those on the task force with the closest links to Kingston, "who worked intimately [with the imprisoned women], there was a level of anger that this had to happen and here [they] were still talking about the same thing, the closure of the Prison for Women." She emphasized the growing sense of connection they were all beginning to have with the confined women: "we visited the prison, we listened to them speak, we had submissions from them – I don't think anyone could have heard the voices and not been touched in a personal way."[4]

In a sense, Sandy Sayer represented all federally sentenced women living in the unsafe environment of the Prison for Women, irrespective of her provincial status. Of the seven suicides at the prison between December 1988 and February 1991, six were by Aboriginal women. Aboriginal women between the ages of "fifteen to twenty-four have a suicide rate almost six times greater than [that] of other Canadian women" (Johnson and Rodgers 1993, 110), but there were also high levels of self-harm among most federally sentenced women. It seemed to many on the task force that the Prison for Women's environment and location imposed excessive hardship upon its inhabitants, and this perception contributed to counter-balancing the task force's knowledge of individual women's offending histories, as will be seen later.

Nine days after Ms Sayer's death the steering committee met and was urged by co-chair James Phelps to "proceed aggressively" with its work "to find a better process for federally sentenced women in the future." Fran Sugar, an Aboriginal member and one-time federally sentenced woman, spoke at some length about the death of her friend. She reminded the committee that she had "raised the concern of [provincial] transfers in a previous meeting as an urgent matter, but no action followed." (The provinces sometimes resorted to transferring "difficult-to-manage" provincially sentenced women to the Prison for Women and a disproportionate number of these were Aboriginal.) Sugar noted "the composition of the Steering Committee, the numerous government and non-government members who represented sufficient political power to affect [sic] change" and "urg[ed] them to use their influence to produce changes needed in the immediate and short term."[5] The committee responded by suggesting that its long-term contribution would be in the form of a completed report recommending an alternative to the Prison for Women. Its short-term response was to produce an immediate formal motion to send to Commissioner Ingstrup, the deputy commissioner responsible for Ontario (wherein lay the Prison for Women) and the warden of the Prison for Women (who was also on the working group). The motion urged that "the existence of the task force [should] not preclude immediate action" at the prison and that "involuntary transfers of provincially sentenced women to Prison for Women [should] cease forthwith."[6]

This decision to send the motion was not easily reached, irrespective of how each member might individually have felt. Almost half the steering committee members were civil servants, with eight working for either provincial or federal corrections, and, for them, the motion was a direct criticism of those to whom they were answerable in corrections. Although drafted by the steering committee, the motion was sent on behalf of the task force, so the same difficulties were faced by the civil servants on the working group. They understood that, while a task force could be an expedient choice because of its relative speed compared with a royal commission, its expedience also rested on its ability to include members able to influence the decision-making process. Signing a motion so critical of the Correctional Service of Canada appeared to some to be "improper";[7] their role as civil servants was discreetly to further the work of government and, above all, to provide the public appearance of impartiality. They also had to protect the commissioner from adverse criticism, even when the criticism was related to what some knew he wanted achieved – the closure of the Prison for Women. Civil servants operating at this level are always aware that their careers are less important than are those of ministers. Their work is carried out with considerable constraints attached to it because policy, especially within the bounds of a federal system of government, can never be seen as an isolated construct. It is always set within the context of other policies, which inevitably reflect the political bias of the party in government – and, in Canada, the political bias of the federal government is not necessarily reflected in each provincial government. This knowledge would have made the civil servants hesitate before signing, yet sign they did. Co-chair James Phelps was later to say that he felt he had to reflect the views of the task force rather than his own: "for the inclusive consultation process to be effective, and to retain the respect and support of the task force, I had to represent accurately the views of the members of the task force, even in the difficult situation where the views were critical of operations of the Correctional Service of Canada and/or its administration."[8]

How much attention would actually be paid to the motion was beyond the control of the steering committee. Fran Sugar's view that some on the task force "represented sufficient political power" to effect change was accurate, but not in the sense that change could be immediate, or was indeed wanted.

EMERGING FROM THE SHADOWS: PROFILING THE FEDERALLY SENTENCED WOMEN

The working group, meeting on 25–27 October, was equally shocked by Sandy Sayer's death, and its immediate concern was to do whatever it could to ameliorate the continuing lockdown within the prison, which at least one member believed had had a direct bearing on Ms

Sayer's death. Peer support[9] was only at the planning stage, so Elder Joan Lavallee was invited into the prison to work with the women.

The October meeting was, arguably, the most important of any undertaken by the task force as the working group was about to decide on how it would replace the Prison for Women. With recent events at the prison preoccupying the members, they still needed to be able to consider the results of the survey of federally sentenced women, which Margaret Shaw was about to present to them. For the first time they were to have properly documented information about those for whom they were planning, and Shaw's evidence was crucial in supporting any decisions they might make. A remarkable aspect of this was that such information had not been gathered before; csc itself did not know its client group in the detail then made available. In common with imprisoned women across the world, imprisoned women in Canada were a tiny part of what was essentially a male phenomenon, and, with so few imprisonment options available for federally sentenced women, it had been easier for csc to justify gathering information about larger groups of individual men, as defined by their offence. Even this was a haphazard enterprise as "during the 1980s Statistics Canada abandoned efforts to collect national court data" (Johnson and Rodgers 1993, 96). Shaw's report to the working group was a preliminary view of the greater detail she was due to provide in December, and the following, derived from the full report, illustrates the scattered nature of the women's population.[10] Eighty-five percent of all federally sentenced women were interviewed.

Table 4.1   Distribution of incarcerated federally sentenced women's population, 1989

Location	Native	French	Other	Total
Prison for Women	25*	14*	87	125
Quebec	1*	26*	6	32
Manitoba	4	–	3	7
Saskatchewan	5	–	–	5
Alberta	6	2	12	20
B.C.	5	1	8	14
Total	46*	43*	116	203
	(23%)	(21%)	(56%)	

* two women were both Native and French-speaking
Source: Shaw et al. 1991b.

From the above it can be seen that seventy-eight federally sentenced women were living in provincial prisons. Ten of those classified as "other" were from outside Canada. It can also be seen that the number of Aboriginal women, although disproportionate to their numbers in Canada as a whole, was roughly equivalent to that of francophone women.

Table 4.2   Average sentence length of federally sentenced women, 1989

Under 5 years	5–9 years	10 years & over
48%	22%	30%

Table 4.3   Distribution of population by offence, 1989

Offence	Numbers	Percentage
Murder	44	22%
Attempted murder	3	1%
Manslaughter	38	19%
Robbery	34	17%
Assaults	21	10%
Theft, fraud etc.	30	15%
Drugs	24	12%
Other	9	4%
Total	203	100%

Adapted from Shaw et al. 1991b.

OTHER RELEVANT INFORMATION

Over 33 percent of the women were first-time offenders and 87 percent of these were first-time *federal* offenders. Fifty percent had never previously received any prison sentence; 64 percent of the women had children; and 48 percent of those interviewed had responsibilities for at least one child of school age or below. Women held provincially had far greater contact with their children than did those at the Prison for Women, and the interviews had revealed an intense wish on the part of most women to maintain contact with their children. Alcohol and drug addiction was, or had been, a problem for almost 75 percent of the women, and 71 percent of women with addiction problems claimed this had contributed to their offence or offending history. For Aboriginal women, problems with and caused by addiction were even more marked; of the thirty-nine interviewed, only three said they were not addicted.

Of those interviewed, 68 percent had experienced physical abuse and 53 percent had experienced (self-identified) sexual abuse. These figures were much higher for Aboriginal women, with 90 percent having experienced physical abuse and 61 percent sexual abuse. The women drew their own parallels between the abuse they had suffered and their subsequent addictions. A little over 50 percent of the women had self-harmed, either by cutting or by attempting suicide, and 20 percent of these had attempted self-harm during their time in prison.[11]

WORKING TOWARDS A SOLUTION

In considering possible options, the working group had to face the previously cited "central conundrum":

If a capital investment is made in construction (or lease/buy), how will the strategy to replace prisons with community alternatives (including Aboriginal community alternatives) be moved forward?[12]

As the task force members later explained, they believed that society had to "move towards the long-term goal of creating and using community-based, restorative justice options, and an alternative Aboriginal justice system." They also thought that "substantial and significant changes [should be] made *immediately* in the environment of federally sentenced women" (TFFSW 1990, 78, emphasis in original).[13] However, legislative constraints meant that, while they could articulate hopes for community and Aboriginal alternatives, members felt they had no option but to plan for further imprisonment. To have planned on the basis that legislation should be enacted in the future seemingly might have fatally compromised the possibility of the report's eventual implementation.[14] It was also essential that their planning should be transparent and, as co-chair Felicity Hawthorne commented, "detailed testing of [the] options [would] minimize the possibility of individual reconsideration after the report [was] delivered."[15]

Before beginning the process, each member of the working group took time to explain her own view of the way forward and it was clear that Sandy Sayer's death was central to their unanimous decision that the Prison for Women should close. They answered the "central conundrum" by accepting that it would be impossible to plan for the longer-term goal of community solutions for federally sentenced women without first providing interim replacement accommodation. This presupposed adopting a dual-track strategy and led to the suggestion that a limit should be placed on the number of new prison beds provided so as to increase the likelihood of returning women to the community. Such a community solution inevitably meant that the new plan would have a regional dimension.

Having decided against the possibility of retaining the status quo –

the Prison for Women, ESAs, and provincial prisons – the working group had to decide how, and with what, these would be replaced. At the same time it also rejected other options, but it needed to demonstrate their unsuitability so that its logic could not later be questioned by those responsible for implementation. Consequently, the working group evaluated each possibility, using a check-list of ten factors. In outlining the reasons for rejecting the Prison for Women each factor was listed, and it can be assumed that these also applied to the other options discussed. This was done in order to augment the public record because, as will become apparent, the reality of the Prison for Women quickly faded in both the public and civil service consciousness. It is important to understand – and remember – just why the prison was thought to be so unfit for federally sentenced women. There was a considerable degree of unanimity amongst the group on the main issues, and this can partly be explained by what was, increasingly, the working group's shared experience of visiting both the Prison for Women and some provincial prisons. These had powerfully illustrated what the group members did *not* want, making it somewhat easier to focus on what they did want. And, undeniably, exhaustion played a part: "we'd talk and talk and talk until we were too exhausted to fight anymore. That's how consensus worked."[16]

(DECIDING AGAINST) RETAINING THE STATUS QUO

Community involvement: The Prison for Women's design physically precluded much community involvement, and Kingston was not the home community of most federally sentenced women. Additionally, federal women electing to be held provincially received variable community access, depending upon their home province.

Existing realities (those facilities across Canada that already held federally sentenced women): The new prison in Burnaby, British Columbia, had to be part of whatever the working group recommended, irrespective of whether it fitted their developing philosophy. There were deep concerns about its design and the ability of its staff to operate within a new philosophy (see chapter 3), so the working group inserted an important proviso: that the existing Burnaby Agreement should be re-examined after seven years to see if it met the federal standards operating elsewhere. Maison Tanguay (see also chapter 3), on the outskirts of Montreal, was subject to the Tanguay Agreement. The working group was deeply critical of Maison Tanguay's design, lack of programs, and correctional philosophy.

Aboriginal needs: Neither the Prison for Women nor any of the provincial facilities provided a "culturally appropriate physical environment," and few of the existing prisons showed any sensitivity towards, or respect for, Aboriginal spirituality and traditions. It was known that Aboriginal people were disinclined to work in traditional prisons, and Kingston was not close to an Aboriginal community.

Proximity to home/cultural environment: Women were disadvantaged by having to choose between a home-province location (under an ESA) and programming (in Kingston, which would assist parole applications). Federally sentenced women, held provincially, always had the threat of a transfer to the Prison for Women hanging over them, and the working group rejected this coercion of "good behaviour."

Access to appropriate programming: Programming at the Prison for Women was limited by the design of the building. Provincial facilities offered fewer programs, and most were ill-suited to the needs of the long-term prisoner.

Ease of addressing language requirements: Neither the needs of the francophone living in the Prison for Women nor of the anglophone residing in Maison Tanguay were adequately met.

Consistent with views of the federally sentenced women: The choice between location and programming was unacceptable to the women and most wanted to be closer to their families and home communities.

Consistent with consultation and research feedback: The Prison for Women's physical environment, lack of programming, and location had been rejected during the consultations. The commissioned research had shown that most women did not require the Prison for Women's high levels of security and that such security militated against effective programming.

Ease of meeting design assumptions: None of the task force's developing design assumptions (which will be discussed elsewhere) could be met.

Ease of facilitating release: Without adequate local community support (unavailable to most women in Kingston), women were ineligible for release at the earliest possible point in their sentence.

Upon reviewing these factors, the direction in which the working group was moving can be seen: the Prison for Women was totally unacceptable; provincial exchange of service agreements were inadequate; access to families, home communities, and culture was essential; and the women's needs had to be allied to choices. Yet in striving to avoid "coercion" of good behaviour, the group perhaps showed unwarranted hope that such behaviour might emerge, without coercion, in a new prison. It was certainly ignoring what was known about the early reformatories, which showed that failure was "the inevitable result of attempting to improve prisoners within coercive settings" (Rafter 1985, 74). Group members were also disregarding the fact that prisons are what Sparks, Bottom, and Hay (1996) call "dominative institutions," in which people are involuntarily confined and deprived of the right to make the most fundamental decisions about their own lives. Under the working group's emerging plans good behaviour might no longer have been coerced by the threat of transfer to another prison, yet to imprison a woman in a furnished "room" in her own province, rather than in a barred cell, did not eliminate the reality that the "room" was still a place of confinement. The group was in the process of moving from "open to hidden discipline" (Mathiesen 1989, 139), with the women's regulation being ultimately undiminished. In planning the prisons the working group appeared to be paying insufficient attention to the possibility that "prison reforms always take place within political conditions which might result in their outcomes being very different to the intentions of those who put the reforms in place" (Carlen 1998, 98). Yet, as has been discussed earlier, most on the working group felt entirely circumscribed by the reality of the unsafe Prison for Women.

THE OTHER OPTIONS

An enhanced status quo?   The working group rejected the possibility of retaining and *renovating* the Prison for Women, and having it operate in conjunction with enhanced EASs. It emphasized the impossibility of transforming the bleak prison, or the shared provincial prisons, into "truly adult environment[s]," side-stepping the reality that an "adult environment" is not consonant with the removal of personal autonomy. (Unless otherwise indicated, quotes are from Working Group, October minutes, 1989.)

A central facility?   The group also decided against a new centrally located prison, largely because of previously rehearsed arguments but also because of the necessary scale of a replacement. The members felt that "its size alone [would] inevitably result in an institutional environment and ... the reappearance of traditional institutional administration." Security would be disproportionate to the needs of most of the women, and it would be difficult to establish "positive and supportive relationships between staff and prisoners." The group did not discuss the possibility that more and better programs could be made available precisely *because* of a central prison's scale as the argument against geographic dislocation had already prevailed.

Co-corrections? The possibility of a co-corrections model,[17] which would mostly have entailed "sharing all facilities apart from living quarters" (Shaw et al. 1991b, 57), was also rejected. Shaw's research showed that nearly 50 percent of the women favoured this as an option (and about 25 percent had actually experienced it), with some citing the "more normal atmosphere" of being alongside males as their reason for approving (59). The prime explanation given for the working group's rejection of co-corrections was that it was "insensitive to the situation of many federally sentenced women who have been abused and exploited by men." The working group felt so strongly about the inappropriateness of co-corrections that it declared this choice to be "as unacceptable as the location/program choice of the status quo." In this the working group seems to have assumed that its own knowledge surpassed that of the women and that it should recognize women's victimization, even if the women refused to recognize it on their own behalf. This was an instance of the working group seeing federally sentenced women as a homogeneous group, not even separated by ethnicity but, rather, defined by its victimhood and supposed inability to act independently of that definition.

Exchange of Service Agreements? The group rejected ESAS as a standalone option because it wanted federal management of any new prisons. This left Quebec effectively grouped with the anglophone majority, with no recognition that the province might wish to act independently, on the basis of its distinct cultural needs, as indeed it considered doing once implementation was under way.

LABELLING THE "DIFFICULT-TO-MANAGE" WOMAN

The working group members had shown why none of the proposed options should be pursued, in the hope that this explicit dialogue would remove any possibility of their decisions being questioned at a later stage. But what would the new prisons be like? Where would they be located? To be able to answer these questions the working group had to focus more intently on the composition of the federal women's population, and, initially, this meant deciding what proportion of them might not easily fit a new model.

The Security Classification Exercise (which would have provided more detailed information on the security needs of the women, as explained in chapter 3) had been cancelled because of the fear that the situation at the Prison for Women might lead to over-classification of the women. A case management review, which might also have given some information about risks posed by individual women, had been rejected as it was "not designed for women offenders,"[18] so that was another closed avenue. In the absence of specific figures the group looked at those women "whose behavioural problems currently result in their removal from the general population at the Prison for Women." Without the guidance of the warden, who could not attend this meeting, and failing details from CSC itself, the group had to rely on advice from its member Sally Wills, the executive director of the Kingston Elizabeth Fry Society. The assumption underlying the focus on these women was that the provinces only held federally sentenced women whose institutional behaviour was unproblematic. In other words, those federal women who were held provincially would be representative of the mass of federally sentenced women because any found to be difficult would already have been transferred to Kingston. Nevertheless, the working group believed that *all* federally sentenced women should be categorized as "high need," requiring "high support" levels – yet another instance of the group emphasizing the women's presumed lack of agency.

It was estimated that of those women "removed from the general population": four were psychiatrically/psychologically ill; ten had serious behavioural problems, making them "a danger to themselves and/or others"; and twelve required protection from other inmates. These comprised a group of twenty-six women. Referring to Shaw et al.'s *Survey of Federally Sentenced Women,* and using the numbers provided therein, during the months of August through to November 1989 there were 203 women serving federal sentences, with 125 being detained in the Prison for Women. So the twenty-six women represented 21 percent of the total population at the Prison for Women and 13 percent of all federally sentenced women. However, the working group considered that "oppressive environments such as the Prison for Women [fed] unacceptable behaviour." It also thought that "a series of regionally-based facilities would assist the re-integration of the twelve 'protective-custody inmates' into the standard living accommodation."[19] Therefore, the number to be considered was reduced to fourteen. Having assessed the ten who were "behaviourally disordered" the group decided that five would "function well in a different environment." The remaining five would require a "therapeutic milieu," as would the four thought to be psychiatrically ill. These nine women represented less than 5 percent of all federally sentenced women.

The conclusions, reached without benefit of any empirical verification, must raise questions about how aware the group was of the evidence that women were being increasingly sentenced, for longer periods, for crimes of violence, even though Shaw's research had alerted them to this in July (see Shaw 1991, 45, 84). Yet, although more federally sentenced women were being sentenced for crimes of violence, their violence was often set within a context of abuse and addiction, and, once imprisoned, they were not necessarily seen as institutional risks by the prison authorities. Although Margaret Shaw herself attended this meeting to present preliminary findings from what was to be the (separate) *Survey of Federally Sentenced Women*, that study was never intended to be an examination of why or how women had become federal prisoners (although informed deductions could certainly have been made from the assembled data); rather, it was designed to show who they were and "to assess the views of the women themselves on the experience of imprisonment" (Shaw et al. 1991b, 1). In the 1980s much of the discussion in Canada about violent women – when, indeed, there was discussion – centred on women as victims of male violence, who reacted to, rather than instigated, violence. But in the late 1970s and early 1980s there had been much debate about Adler's hypothesis that women's liberation, as exemplified by second-wave feminism, would lead to an increase in women's criminal activity and that their behaviour would more closely resemble male patterns of violent offending (see Adler 1975: with commentaries by Box 1983; Heidensohn 1985, 1994; Gavigan 1987). So it could not be said that the spectre of the violent woman was unknown, even if Box (1983, 198), among others, had largely dismissed this view, demonstrating that "the increase in female convictions for *violence* seemed to be explained by changes in social labelling practices" (emphasis in original).

While in Canada it had been important, politically and socially, for the extent of violence against women to be recognized (see Rock 1986), there was also internationally an "underlying predisposition to view criminal women as more victims than aggressors, more sinned against than sinning, more to be pitied than blamed" (Allen 1987, 93). Further, it was generally accepted "that feminist discussions are ready to explain female offending by reference to social or economic forces ... or to [their] oppressive domestic and familial situations" (92). Although Allen was writing within an English context, her words were equally applicable to Canada, where feminists also found it difficult to grapple with the idea that some women could be intentionally violent in situations where they were not themselves under threat.[20] Additionally, as Johnson (1987, 30) noted, in the late 1980s there was "a serious lack of information about women offenders [in Canada and] their role in crimes of violence." She cited statistics showing that "7,000 charges were laid against women in 1985 for acts of violence, up from less than 1,200 in 1965," and suggested that much of this could be explained as women retaliating in abusive domestic situations. (It must be remembered that only a small percentage of these women would receive a federal sentence.) She also cautioned that the base figures for women were very much lower than were those for men, so that any percentage shifts had to be treated with care. This was a position that Johnson and Rodgers (1993, 110) were to adopt again in 1993, when they also had pertinent comments to make about Aboriginal women in conflict with the law, making specific links with their offending and the "near-complete breakdown of the Aboriginal culture and traditional way of life." La Prairie amplified this point when discussing the "role strain" experienced by Aboriginal *men* and how this had frequently manifested itself in violence towards those closest to them – their partners and children. La Prairie (1993, 237) believed that "the importance of links between the victimisation of Aboriginal women as children, youth [sic] or young women due to sexual assault or family violence and future conflict with the law cannot be overemphasised."

All on the working group were aware of the social and economic circumstances of the majority of federally sentenced women. It is therefore too glib to say that the group erred in characterizing these women as victims rather than (some) as simply violent offenders, because the research evidence supported this view, especially regarding Aboriginal women. However, it seemed the group was reluctant to take the next step and see federally sentenced women as both victim *and* victimizer, and this can partly be attributed to its growing familiarity with some of the women themselves. Yet the question of violence and hard-to-manage behaviour was discussed, even if it did not appear in the working group's minutes: "Some of us were saying ... but supposing, once in a blue moon, all that nice stuff doesn't work ... are you going to have solitary confinement ... are you going to have the normal range of punishments available? What are you going to do when it comes down to a really tough situation? [And] certain people were saying 'no, you never have to do that because these new places are going to be so well run.'"[21]

It had already been tacitly accepted that Aboriginal offending women were victims of the "dominant culture." Their actual offence, while not condoned, was assessed in the light of knowing that much of their addiction and experience of abuse could be traced back to the historic dismantling of their families and communities. "Consensus" was relatively easily reached on this group, largely thanks to the powerful influence of the Aboriginal members of the task force. Many of the same arguments could also be applied to the non-Aboriginal women whom they were considering as they often shared a similar socio-economic background. With the working group reluctant to label federally sentenced Aboriginal women as risky or violent offenders (because of its understanding of what might have occasioned their offending), the need to reach "consensus" determined that other federally sentenced women would also not be labelled. It would have been impossible for the group to make distinctions based on ethnicity, and its decision reflected the widespread impact upon them all of having Aboriginal perspectives presented so consistently throughout their work. Instead, in the final report the women were eventually referred to as being "high needs/low risk," with the clear implication being that providing for their needs would lower their risk.

Undoubtedly, there were dissenting voices, and some group members continued to be unhappy with the failure to address one of the "tough" issues. Largely, these were the civil servants, although one member from the voluntary sector also remembered that: "There were those of us who didn't agree, who felt that there were very serious and real problems to be addressed – and that they had to be addressed in a more secure environment ... It was hard to think how we could accommodate them ... without building another prison that looked like a Special Handling Unit. But some of us felt very strongly that there were women in that category ... We finally had to come to something we all could live with, not necessarily comfortably, so we couldn't put the spotlight on them that they probably deserved."[22] A civil servant commented, within the context of the need to complete their task: "The least productive outcome is to have no report, no solutions. E. Fry didn't get everything they wanted, because they wanted to do away with prisons altogether. I guess csc got most of what they wanted, but the solution to the most difficult female offenders they didn't ... The advocate groups had come a long way and they didn't really want to discuss dangerous women and had we tried to push them ... there would have been a big argument leading nowhere and they would have held off as long as they could in agreeing with anything."[23] Pragmatism aided consensus and, as another civil servant added: "I think there was [a feeling of] let's get a consensus now and, on the part of the csc folks, there was a recognition that we would get it done later."[24]

This failure to be prescriptive later allowed csc to determine the

eventual provision for violent and/or disturbed women. Yet group
members from the voluntary sector would have contended that, had
they been prepared to provide definitively for the "difficult-to-
manage" women, csc would then have taken their plan as a justification for expanded provision once implementation began. The upshot
was that the working group continued to plan almost entirely for a
homogeneous "woman" who required support rather than security.
And that "woman" was identified as a "victim."

In the media, and often in the public mind, the violent woman is
sometimes conflated with the mentally disordered woman. Kendall
(2000, 90) shows that "serious anxieties about women's mental
health" did not really emerge until the release of the task force's report
and the separate 1990 Task Force on Mental Health, Special Needs of
Female Offenders. The latter said that *only five per cent of women
prisoners show[ed] no evidence of serious disorder*" (emphasis added),
which makes it especially notable that relatively little attention should
have been paid to them by the task force. Even if the specific information was not available to them at that precise moment, most of it was
certainly available prior to the time the report was completed. Kendall
adopts Rose's terminology in referring to the "psy-sciences," which
had been well and truly entrenched in Canadian prisons for years, and,
with the acceptance of the medical model during the 1960s, the "psy-
experts" had an even higher profile (Kendall 2000, 87), even if "they
were not the primary mechanisms for the governance of women prisoners" (Hannah-Moffat 2001, 105). The medical model was never
entirely displaced, even when other jurisdictions had moved away from
it. Within the Prison for Women, inmates were subjected to some
highly irregular treatments, and during the 1960s LSD was given to at
least twenty-three women and electro-convulsive therapy was administered to others. Although these experiments were conducted "with the
full knowledge of the prison's superintendent and senior corrections
official in Ottawa" and were published in the *Canadian Journal of
Corrections* in 1964, at issue was the question of obtaining informed
consent. It was only in 1998 that an official complaint was made and
an investigation launched (*Kingston Whig-Standard* 1998; see also
Kendall 2000, 87; Hannah-Moffat 2001, 102–4).

By the early 1990s there were a significant number of psycholo-
gists and therapists at the Prison for Women, many of whom used a
feminist model of treatment. Kathleen Kendall was contracted to
evaluate the prison's services in 1992 and, although she found that
inmates supported the provision of counselling, she warned that
prisoners needed "a choice of whether or not to engage in therapy"
and that prisons imposed a degree of control inimical to the exercise

of personal choice (Kendall 1993a, 45, 39; see also Kendall 1993b, 1993c).

The working group had reluctantly identified a small group of "difficult-to-manage" women, but where should they most appropriately be housed? Within Canada there are regional psychiatric centres (RPCs)and regional treatment centres (RTCs), both of which could be used to house women requiring intensive help. This option was unacceptable as the small numbers of women involved would mean their being isolated within a much larger group of men in an environment where the correctional emphasis overwhelmed the therapeutic. Faced with the women's small numbers, would it be better to have a specialized unit attached to one or two of the new regional facilities (with the implication that specialized staff would be better able to provide for their needs)? Again the working group gave a negative response, prompted by the fear that such a resource could be used as a dumping ground for behaviourally problematic women, in the same way that the Prison for Women had been used for some provincially sentenced women. It was therefore decided that each new institution would manage these women using mental health specialists on an "as-needed" basis, assisted by "unobtrusive security measures." An important aspect of this was that federal women, who in the community would have been assessed as requiring hospitalization, were expected to be admitted to provincial psychiatric hospitals rather than to correctional psychiatric facilities. The task force dealt with the lack of concrete evidence about these women in its report, noting that, although it had received "preliminary data on the mental health needs of women ... as assessed by the Diagnostic Interview Schedule Survey (DIS Study) ... more analysis need[ed] to be done." The DIS study "confirmed ... that federally sentenced women ha[d] a high need for mental health related support and intervention" (TFFSW 1990, 86). *Creating Choices* emphasizes that this lack of information means that the task force could not make a "definitive recommendation" as to appropriate accommodation and suggested standard accommodation, with additional small support units. CSC was again provided with the chance to define provision at a later date.

THE HEALING LODGE:
ACCOMMODATING A "DISTINCT" GROUP

The decision that women with mental health needs should be provided for at each new prison left the working group free to concentrate on planning completely new prisons to house all federally sentenced women. But there was one further decision to make before the precise number could be settled upon. Would there be specific provision made for Aboriginal women or would they be integrated into all the new prisons?

It is at this stage that the official strands become confused. The October working group minutes refer to a proposal made during the September meeting, but nothing was actually noted in the group's September minutes.[25] Following the September steering committee meeting the Aboriginal women had all met, and it is likely that they discussed the possibility of a dedicated Aboriginal facility at that time, but there is nothing in the official record to indicate precisely when the idea first emerged. What is clear from interview evidence is that the idea of a healing lodge was first mooted by Alma Brooks, a member of the Aboriginal Women's Caucus and NWAC, and that this concept had been articulated, if not fleshed out, some time prior to when it was first proposed to the working group. The October minutes clearly credit Patricia Monture with articulating the "preliminary conceptualization," which was "based on her discussions with other Aboriginal women."

The preliminary vision, and its transformation into reality, is discussed in greater detail in chapter 9, but it is important to establish here the unique nature of what was eventually proposed: specifically, that *all* Aboriginal women should be able to choose to go to the Healing Lodge irrespective of their security classification. They would not be sent there because a court had stipulated they should be; rather, the choice would be theirs and could be made at any stage of the sentence. The lodge would be situated in open, spacious grounds, and its heart would be a "large round room to be used for ceremonies, teaching ... healing," and an Elder would be essential to its function as a place of healing. Almost as essential was that the lodge should be "affiliated with an Aboriginal community," yet it "would also have to be located near a major urban centre in recognition that Aboriginals live in a dual reality" (Working Group, October minutes, 1989). How this initial vision should be transformed into physical reality was the task awaiting the working group, and it was advised that a lodge would not lessen the need to provide Aboriginal programs and services in the other prisons. Any sense of the punitive aspect of the Healing Lodge was almost completely effaced from the discussions, almost as though the name itself accurately denoted its purpose. It is interesting that this concept should have taken so long to be placed on the working group's table. A civil servant commented: "It didn't come up early on because most of the meetings were about just women and what were we going to do ... recommend new prisons, joint options? ... and all with the understanding that in the meantime the Aboriginal representatives were in discussions with the Elders and that they would

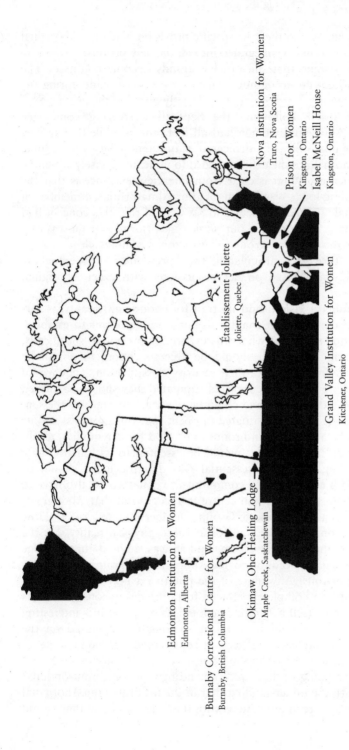

Nova Institution for Women
Truro, Nova Scotia

Prison for Women
Kingston, Ontario

Isabel McNeill House
Kingston, Ontario

Établissement Joliette
Joliette, Quebec

Grand Valley Institution for Women
Kitchener, Ontario

Edmonton Institution for Women
Edmonton, Alberta

Burnaby Correctional Centre for Women
Burnaby, British Columbia

Okimaw Ohci Healing Lodge
Maple Creek, Saskatchewan

Locations of new and existing prisons for federally sentenced women in 1996 bring to the working group the results of those deliberations ... There was also a sense that the Aboriginal members were not prepared to devote the final meetings to fleshing out the Healing Lodge because it was all very new to them as well."[26] This provides another example of the task force declining to be prescriptive about a proposal, but, with the Healing Lodge the outcome did not leave the final definition entirely in the hands of CSC.

The sentenced Aboriginal woman was seen by other Aboriginal people as being almost entirely a victim of colonial oppression, whose personal choices were circumscribed by the larger socio-economic environment in which she lived.[27] It was axiomatic that "healing," or coming to terms with that oppression, had to take precedence over any notions of punishment because the greater harm had been inflicted by the dominant culture, even if its manifestation had been a criminal offence by an Aboriginal woman. Of course, the same argument regarding victimization could be used for many non-Aboriginal federally sentenced women (and the final report perhaps goes some way towards doing this), but it was acknowledged that Aboriginal women experienced double discrimination, or what Monture preferred to call "discrimination within discrimination through the addition of racial stereotypes."[28] For Aboriginal peoples the law remained a dominant society construct, despite the fact that it was also intended to protect them, and their own experience was that justice was not applied equally.

This broad Aboriginal concept of "healing" differed from that of "rehabilitation," which did not attempt to deal with the broader socially based reasons for offending. It was a unique concept and came to be the cornerstone of the task force's report, but it was also an extraordinary venture into the unknown. As *Creating Choices* makes clear, "the [Euro-Canadian] concept of punishment is alien to the Aboriginal culture. The focus on restoration of harm and finding direction through teachings and spirituality in traditional culture is diametrically different from the punitive models that have grown up in non-Aboriginal ... civilizations" (TFFSW 1990, 90). Yet, in an effort to lessen the damaging effects of conventional punishment (imprisonment) on Aboriginal women, here was another group of Aboriginal women proposing that a further prison should be built – and that the building should be done in alliance with the administrators of the old. This was indeed a step born of desperation and recognition of the immediate legislative constraints. Underpinning this decision was CSC's refusal to include consideration of Aboriginal jurisdiction in the task force's remit, and the hope that Aboriginal self-determination would eventually enable such a prison to be administered solely by Aboriginal peoples.[29] But the type of facility they wished to have – where women truly could "heal" as well as restore harm done – was then unattainable, and the first step towards it remained in the gift of csc.

DECIDING THE LOCATIONS

Having accepted the need for a separate Aboriginal prison, where were the other facilities to be placed? The necessity of "a national plan for regional facilities" was already accepted, and narrowing the focus to specific locations was largely determined by existing geographic realities. The working group had to decide which city, in each region, best provided the existing support network required for the community release strategy. It also had to ask whether this targeted city was the most easily accessible to the *majority* of federally sentenced women (and their families) from that region. In reality, the immense size of Canada meant that, wherever the new facilities were eventually sited, some of the women would still be many hundreds of kilometres from their home communities.

The Atlantic Region, covering the Maritimes (Nova Scotia, New Brunswick, and Prince Edward Island), in addition to Newfoundland, presented little difficulty for the working group. The immediate choice was for a prison close to Halifax, the largest of the Maritime cities. Halifax could also be justified on the basis that most federally sentenced women in that region came from Nova Scotia.

Quebec presented larger considerations, partly because of the size of the province (it is the largest in Canada) and the spread of population. A case could have been made for two facilities within the province (and was considered), thus allowing more women to live closer to their homes, but the cost and program disadvantages – and the fact that some Montreal women would be dislocated in order to keep both equally full – persuaded the group that Montreal was the only logical choice.

Ontario is the second largest of the Canadian provinces, and the most heavily populated, with the greatest concentration of people being around Toronto and the adjacent smaller cities. The working group knew that the majority of federally sentenced women from Ontario were from this area, so it might have been assumed that Toronto would be the chosen city. It was felt, nevertheless, that Toronto was simply too large and that there would be "too many competing interests for available resources" (Working Group, October minutes, 1989), so the working group chose the Hamilton-corridor area.

The October minutes record, however, that there was one dissenting voice, that of Sally Wills, the executive director of the Kingston Elizabeth Fry Society, who asked that her "continued support of the Kingston location should be documented in the Minutes." She explained that her support for Kingston (as the site for a *new* Ontario prison) was based not only on her personal knowledge of the "resources available in Kingston" but also on the fact that some of the women had partners in the various Kingston male prisons, which made private family visiting easier.[30] There was a further dimension to her concern, and this is not mentioned in the minutes. Many of the women whom she had met during the course of her work had spoken of the difficulties they faced with the "revolving door," meaning that the Prison for Women continuously had women coming and going. Those serving particularly long sentences found it hard to live with women who would be released long before themselves, and they needed the support of substantial numbers of women experiencing the same difficulties. It was feared that smaller regional prisons, with a proportionately smaller number of women serving lengthy sentences, might make it even harder for those support networks to be developed.

Another factor was the group of women with mental health needs requiring extra support: Wills thought it unlikely that smaller prisons would be able to provide the range of programs and support the women needed. She wanted a new Kingston prison to have two extra functions: to be a national resource to which women could opt to be sent if they were serving longer sentences and to be a national resource for those with mental health needs.

The Prairies – Saskatchewan, Alberta, and Manitoba – are treated by CSC as one administrative area. While CSC is dealing with a smaller client group in the Prairies than in Ontario, it comes from a huge geographic area. The working group had roughly forty-five women from this region to consider, of whom the majority were Aboriginal. As with their deliberations about Quebec, the group was initially inclined towards two prisons, alongside a healing lodge, but acknowledged that the lodge would be likely to "attract a significant number of Prairie women, thereby making two additional facilities unrealistic" (Working Group, October minutes, 1989). With that decision made, the choice of province was largely determined by the higher percentage of women coming from Alberta, and Edmonton was eventually "tentatively" selected as the location. The group did not go so far as to select a site for the Healing Lodge but did conclude that it should be in Saskatchewan.

British Columbia planning was decided by the reality of the new Burnaby Correctional Centre. Accordingly, it was agreed that Burnaby would house federally sentenced women for a "minimum twelve year period" but that, "following this initial period, a new-style federal facility should be available in the Vancouver area if the Burnaby option [had] not been successful in accordance with the principles set out in the task force report." Above all, csc needed to "acknowledge that the task force principles appl[ied] to federally sentenced women housed in Burnaby" (Working Group, October minutes, 1989). The working group had little choice but to accept that Burnaby was a fait accompli, but in doing so, it was consigning women from British Columbia to a style of imprisonment not applicable to other federally sentenced women. In effect, it was allowing two tiers of federal punishment because Burnaby could never hope to replicate the proposed cottage-style living of the new prisons, leaving BC women disadvantaged by comparison.

The Northwest Territories were not considered during the meeting; it was so unusual for a woman from the Territories to be sentenced that the working group felt "innovative alternatives on a case by case ... basis" (Working Group, October minutes, 1989) would be required.

Most on the working group had known instinctively, almost since beginning the task, what their final decision would be. All that they had heard, seen, and discussed in the intervening months had simply led them to concur with MacGuigan's view that the Prison for Women was indeed "unfit for bears, let alone women." Moreover, the dangers inherent in any prison were magnified at Kingston because of its design and its distance from the home communities of most federally sentenced women, as had become devastatingly apparent with the death of Sandy Sayer. The working group had finally declared itself in deciding that the Prison for Women should close.

The proposition was an historic step – yet how the working group's planning should be translated into government action was beyond its authority; they could only hope that the commissioner's public commitment to change would survive the pressures of the inevitable political process to follow. Where the task force departed from other commissions and inquiries was in the way it carefully delineated a style, if not an actual design, for the proposed new prisons, together with a philosophical foundation for their management. The highly visible security of the old prison, manifest in its immense concrete walls, signalled that containment of an apparently dangerous population was its major function, whereas the working group wanted its new, model prisons to relay an equally strong message: that federally sentenced women were yet another part of diverse Canadian communities.

Fundamental to the task force's planning was the belief that the new prisons should be "close to larger cities which offer the desired infrastructure ... and proximity to an Aboriginal community."[31] Each new prison would be placed in no less than ten acres, with "non-obtrusive perimeter security." They would have a "core building," containing a "gym, library, school/program area, administration, health services, cafeteria ... chapel ... inmate committee office, offices for volunteer/community programs." Each would have a "garden; family visiting unit; a dedicated Aboriginal ceremonial/sweat lodge area; occupational buildings." The living units (described as cottages) would be "house-style" and hold "approximately five women." Each cottage would contain "spacious bed-study rooms, living room, study, kitchen, dining room, playroom, telephone corner, staff office/lounge, counselling room." One of the cottages would be "smaller, with more staff space to house trauma cases requiring intensive support."[32] The separate vision of the Healing Lodge has already been outlined.

All the new prisons would be equally provisioned, irrespective of how many women they held; the women were not to be disadvantaged by accident of geography and sentencing trends. The language used reflected a concern with providing care and, by extension, "healing," both of which would be facilitated by the new architectural style of the prisons. In so far as the minutes can be relied upon, staff members do not appear to have been discussed, except in relation to whether they might be stationed within the new houses.[33] The major focus of the group always appeared to be on the women themselves. The task force's report, Creating Choices, expanded upon the staff's role, suggesting that staff members should have wide "life experience" alongside an understanding of women's and cultural issues, yet it was not so prescriptive as to limit the field to specific groups. What was clear was that the military model of staffing, with its emphasis on security and hierarchical relationships, had been rejected. Staff members would play their part in creating "dynamic security" (TFFSW 1990, 116), and this was dependent upon the relationships they would develop with the women. Through the example of staff the women would be encouraged to take responsibility for their own lives. This was a return to staff assuming the position envisaged by Elizabeth Fry, wherein "'respectable' female warders might play a positive role as a 'consistent example of propriety and virtue'" (Fry, cited in Zedner 1995, 301; also, see Dobash et al. 1986), "acting as loving but demanding mothers who forgave past errors but insisted on obedience" (Freedman 1981, 95). Creating Choices specified that males should not be hired as guards (front-line staff, with access to the living units) but that they should be allowed to work in certain educational and vocational roles.[34]

While this brief description conflates the working group minutes and *Creating Choices*, it gives a general idea of how the task force's ideas were built upon and expanded, with the general point being that it provided the foundation for what later followed. The task force suggested the houses/cottages; the home-like regime within the cottages; the "holistic" approach to programming, centred on community standards and community provision; exemplary staff; the mother and child program; and the involvement of volunteers who would provide "important social and intellectual variety" for the women (TFFSW 1990, 123). Yet, irrespective of how any of these concepts might have been redefined as the new prisons took shape, the basic structure was not new, and the task force was not breaking new ground. The women who had been instrumental in founding the first reformatories for women had got there first. Rafter (1995, 35), citing the first annual report of the reformatory at Albion, New York, shows that "the idea of family life, each cottage with its own kitchen, its pleasant dining room adjoining" was reproduced in a custodial setting some hundred years prior to the task force's concept of cottages and exemplary regimes. Freedman (1981, 54, 96) wrote of children being permitted to stay until the age of two in the early reformatories and the way in which the early reformers could influence prisoners through "womanly sympathy." Indeed, as the working group's October minutes noted, the Minnesota Correctional Facility-Shakopee, which had begun as a reformatory for women in 1920, seemed to be "representing the most coherent expression of [a female corrections' model] to date." Canada also had its own earlier model of a reformatory-style prison for women, the Andrew Mercer Reformatory in Toronto (see chapter 1). So in adopting Shakopee as the exemplar, the task force was also returning to its Canadian roots, albeit with an added Aboriginal dimension.

Following their lengthy October meeting, having committed themselves to closure, the working group members revisited the prison in Kingston to thank, by means of a "give-a-way,"[35] the women who had contributed to their work. By then, many of the women were familiar faces and the sense of "them and us" – where it had existed – was becoming blurred. More of the women were coming to be seen as individuals who had experienced adversity rather than simply as offenders. Moreover, they continued to live with adversity because of deteriorating conditions within the Prison for Women, in the aftermath of Sandy Sayer's suicide. In a sense, many on the working group had collectively begun to cross the divide separating empathy from objectivity, but this was scarcely surprising as the fear of another suicide at the Prison for Women was only too real. This degree of consultation with imprisoned women – and, indeed, deference – was remarkable, even within its Canadian context, and without parallel in other jurisdictions.

Another aspect of this "blurring" was the working group's knowledge of feminist research, showing "that women in prison have more in common with *other women* than they do with male inmates" (Shaw 1991, 3, 11, cited in TFFSW 1990, 68, emphasis added). While this is true, from the strict perspective of gender, it is not the whole picture. Hannah-Moffat deconstructed the analogy, stressing that, in denying difference we deny the diversity of women and their unique, individual experience of imprisonment. The most profound difference between the majority of women and imprisoned women is the question of freedom: imprisoned women are not free (Hannah-Moffat 2001, 191). (This is not to ignore another profound difference: that some women offend and that a larger proportion do not.) Yet it is perhaps not too fanciful to say that some within the working group, while aware of these distinctions, had begun to feel as though they might be the "other woman," possessed of an instinctive understanding of federally sentenced women's feelings and needs, as the group had collectively demonstrated in its refusal to countenance co-corrections. While not going as far as English eighteenth-century non-conformist prison reformers, who viewed prisoners as "machines to be tinkered with ... because they had a conscience like everybody else" (Ignatieff 1978, 71), the working group did believe that the provision of exemplary institutions would encourage change in women. The new physical surroundings, allied with the (moral) structure provided by skilled staff, would facilitate these changes.

As previously alluded to, the working group had come to believe strongly in a dual-track approach to providing for federally sentenced women, and this was articulated in the "central conundrum," which asked whether a capital investment in new "residences" might "divert focus and attention from the long-term objective" [of providing community alternatives] (TFFSW 1990, 78). While this strategy might have had something to do with the reluctance of many from the voluntary sector to be associated with building more prisons, it was much more than that. For the working group "community" meant an amalgam of both "culture and geography,"[36] and for a woman to be released successfully into such a community she had to have an easily accessible route, peopled by those whom she had come to trust. Planning for eventual release would start immediately a woman was received into prison, and this would be facilitated by her community worker, who would be from the voluntary sector, but, for unexplained reasons, *Creating Choices* concluded that a team approach was preferable, with a CSC employee being in overall charge. It was envisaged that the com-

munity strategy could be "implemented independently and in advance
of the accommodation model,"[37] and the ultimate failure to do this –
funding was refused by government – was to have repercussions once
the new prisons were opened. Additionally, in wanting to provide new
standards for half-way houses to which the women could be released,
the task force was again faced by legislative impediments that were
beyond the immediate authority of the solicitor general. Once again,
the task force could not think as "broadly" as its members might have
wished.

CONFLICTS OF INTEREST

Work had started some time previously on drafts of the various chapters for the final report, and these were circulated so that all members
of the working group had the opportunity to comment before the next
stage was reached. Most of the group contributed to some of the initial
writing, but some had greater overall responsibilities, and by October
Patricia Monture had completed the fourth draft of what was to
become chapter 2, "The Voices of Aboriginal People." It will be
remembered that the working group had faced problems when formu-
lating the guideline questions to accompany the consultation documents and the difficulties related to whether there should be a question
about Aboriginal self-determination in justice issues. The view formed
then was that the task force had to be careful not to exceed its brief by
venturing into the jurisdiction of other government departments.
Monture's draft chapter ended with a list of nine recommendations,
which elicited a hostile response from some of the civil servants within
the working group, with the sticking point again being the question of
Aboriginal sovereignty. Her first recommendation was a very broad
one: "The Correctional Service of Canada with the Commissioner, the
Ministry of the Solicitor General and the Solicitor General of Canada
must actively lobby the federal legislature to secure future meaningful
negotiations with Aboriginal governments who are now willing to take
over full or limited jurisdiction in the area of criminal justice."

   One of the civil service respondents replied that the task force was
"a very narrow plank upon which to rest such a broad recommendation" and pointed out that the Department of Indian Affairs and
Northern Development (DIAND), rather than the federal legislature,
was responsible for Aboriginal self-government negotiations. She
abruptly dismissed the idea that either CSC, the commissioner, or the
Ministry of the Solicitor General, themselves relatively small cogs in
the larger federal wheel, should be encouraged to "lobby" the federal
legislature.[38] Monture's nine recommendations were subsequently

omitted from the final report, but the debate is included here as further evidence of the difficulties faced by some working group members in attempting to balance their official positions – as government representatives – against the insistence by the Aboriginal members that political considerations should not be ignored. Looking at the civil servant's response to these recommendations it is possible to see how the bureaucratic imperative impinged upon her reply: she knew the impossibility of making recommendations that could not be implemented by the department to which she was answerable.

But her response would have dismayed the Aboriginal members of both the working group and the steering committee, and it emphasized the gulf in understanding still to be bridged. Throughout the work of the task force, Aboriginal members had sought to "educate" the others regarding the reality of Aboriginal peoples' experience of the dominant society. As a group within the task force they knew that they were "an afterthought fighting for meaningful recognition."[39] They had not been part of the discussions about the mandate, and the terms of reference were only amended to reflect the over-representation of Aboriginal women in the criminal justice system at a later stage. It seemed to them that at every point in the deliberations they had to remind the rest of the task force of the Aboriginal perspective. This was encapsulated in the response of an Aboriginal task force member to a draft section, then entitled "The Special Needs of Aboriginal Women Are Not Met." She wrote: "We do not understand what special means. Can someone define it for us? Our needs are culturally unique but they are basic to what every human being needs to survive. Does special mean we are somehow handicapped? or disadvantaged? or perhaps not as 'good' as white people?"

Had Aboriginal peoples been uniformly represented in other government initiatives the dissension regarding the mandate might have been better anticipated by both the Aboriginal members and civil servants, but the Aboriginal women on the task force were mostly newcomers to such a government-sponsored enterprise – and the civil servants were largely unaccustomed to working with them. While some of the Aboriginal members might not necessarily have been aware that the published mandate customarily could not be altered, others simply would not accept the political reality. Therefore, to fight for change seemed logical, whereas the mainly Euro-Canadian CAEFS, with its greater exposure to political stratagems – and having been part of the initial task force discussions – would have recognized the apparent impossibility of changing what had already been agreed upon. Additionally, CAEFS had no accountability to a wider constituency, although it was, of course, indirectly answerable to CSC because of its need for government funding. However, it might also be said that, having recognized the limitations of the mandate early on, the Aboriginal members found it a very convenient political bargaining point and one to which they could turn whenever they thought it necessary. As will be seen, they were ultimately successful in ensuring that self-government was referred to in *Creating Choices*: their perspective again prevailed.

CHAPTER FIVE

Returning to the Cottages: Abandoning the Prison?

The November combined working group and steering committee meeting was held in Ottawa, some two hours drive from what remained a very troubled Prison for Women in Kingston, where the repressive lockdown policy continued.[1] There had been no official response to the committee's motion following the death of Sandy Sayer, which left the question of provincial transfers unresolved and further underlined the impotence of the task force when it came to effecting immediate change. While the working group largely accepted the need for guidance from the steering committee, some members were unhappy about having continually to defend their decisions, and "consensus" ensured that any difficulties in reaching agreement among them were hidden. Yet the steering committee, which did not meet so often, commented freely on work that had been achieved at enormous personal cost. As one group member commented: "how could there be a dialogue with fifty people around the table?"[2] Nevertheless, the steering committee and its joint chairs played an important role in supporting the working group, adding a further perspective to the deliberations, especially with regard to francophone, Aboriginal, and provincial needs. The steering committee was the only means, apart from the public consultations, by which individual interests, such as other minority ethnic groups and religious organizations, could be heard. Yet there was a tension between the roles of both sections of the task force, which undoubtedly added to the burden of the working group.

The final layout of the report had to be decided, and it is noteworthy that James Phelps, co-chair of the steering committee and a deputy commissioner of Corrections, suggested placing the Aboriginal chapter close to the beginning of the report, ensuring it an eventual centrality that, at the outset, no one would have envisaged. From a practical point of view the most important section of the report concerned the proposed new facilities: their siting, their design, and the proposed new style of management. All the careful garnering and presentation of information regarding what had previously existed was crucial, for the foundations of the new would arise from a controlled demolition of old rationales and practices. Most decisions had already been taken regarding the new prisons, so the steering committee was more in the position of fine-tuning than recommending, yet some important points were still raised. Specifically, these were: the need to provide for most women with mental health needs inside the new prisons themselves rather than within existing secure settings; the possible difficulty in providing programs for *all* women in *all* of the prisons; and the need to plan for those behaving aggressively towards other inmates. And, perhaps most importantly in the light of what happened subsequently, that the "areas [of] security and staffing should be clearly discussed [so as] to direct the implementation committee, and to avoid undesirable traditional responses."

One of the meeting's lengthiest discussions focused on what some took to be the draft report's characterization of women offenders as "victims" rather than as women who had also themselves created victims through their offending behaviour.[3] The committee feared the report would be "rejected as fantasy" if it did not address the issue of personal responsibility for offending, yet it also agreed that the social factors behind some offending should be acknowledged. As has already been made clear, the working group was less certain than the task force that this was how the women should be viewed, and the apparent framing of the women as victims themselves is an aspect of the final report for which the task force was later criticized.

The Healing Lodge itself was considered separately, with the steering committee being cautioned that it remained "a concept, an idea to be developed" and that, for the lodge to become a definite option, "the matter of trust, which ha[d] been lacking between the Aboriginal community and parties of the criminal justice system must be addressed." The Aboriginal members of the task force asked for "support and flexibility" while they returned the concept to the Elders and the Aboriginal community at large. It is remarkable how completely the initial planning of this prison was left to these Aboriginal members – and how little the Euro-Canadians felt they could contribute to its development. The task force had been struck on the premise that it would be planning for all federally sentenced women. The terms of reference recognized both the "unique ... aspects of the experience of [federally sentenced] Aboriginal women" and the "unique needs of [all] these women (including, but not limited to, different abilities, race, culture, religion, sexual orientation, language)." Nowhere did the terms stipulate that these different needs could only be addressed by those with specific knowledge, so there has to be another explanation for the reluctance of the non-Aboriginal members of the task force to be directly involved in planning the Healing Lodge. Perhaps the following comment by a civil servant gives some indication of what was happening within the task force: "[it had been made clear to us] you have been speaking for Aboriginal people for some time. It's time to stop and let Aboriginal people speak for themselves. I didn't have a whole lot of difficulty saying 'you know, if we were doing such a good job speaking for Aboriginal people maybe we wouldn't have had all those incidents, all those deaths, all that over-representation, so what do we have to lose by standing back and saying ok, we'll speak for this and we'll let you speak for that and we'll see where it comes together and where it doesn't?'"[4]

As has already been made clear, part of the answer to the profound reluctance to comment on Aboriginal issues may be found in the history of Euro-Canada's relations with Aboriginal nations and the growing understanding within the dominant culture that this engagement had been unjust and oppressive. While most on the task force would have known this Aboriginal reality theoretically, this did not mean that they had individual contact with many Aboriginal peoples or knowledge of Aboriginal communities. Yet during the life of the task force they were all sharing the same table, and the Aboriginal members spoke with a personal authority and experience of living as Aboriginal women within an often hostile dominant society. What can most easily be described as postcolonial guilt precluded any possibility of extensive critical examination of Aboriginal perspectives. Mercredi (1994, 119) referred to the guilt harboured by some Canadians, suggesting that, while it was not the "basis for a future relationship," it was still "quite a powerful force when ... harnessed for changing the socio-economic conditions" of Aboriginal peoples. It can be deduced that this sense of guilt was the main reason for the Euro-Canadian members' reluctance to engage in criticism of Aboriginal perspectives rather than simply the internalized racism suggested, separately, by two members of the task force – although this undoubtedly also existed.

It had long been planned that the writing of the report would be completed by November, and two members of the working group were due to do the work in Ottawa.[5] At the end of November's joint meeting one of the designated writers from the voluntary sector decided that, because of her earlier difficulties when working with a co-writer, she would be better removed from the project. Consequently, another of the civil servants was unexpectedly required to fill the gap, thus leaving the final draft of the report (apart from the Aboriginal chapter) in civil servants' hands, even though members of the group individually provided extensive comments. Drawing all the information together, particularly as some of the research material was still unavailable, presented the writers with enormous challenges, bearing in mind that the task force wished to produce something radical and strikingly different from what had been produced by other task forces. The steering committee received what was termed the "first major draft" prior to their meeting on 18 December 1989, albeit a draft that did not include the Aboriginal chapter. In discussing the report, many of the comments from participants reflected the interests of the organization or department each was representing, but three areas of concern predominated.[6]

FEDERALLY SENTENCED WOMEN AND MENTAL HEALTH

The working group had already spent considerable time debating how best to provide for those needing higher levels of security, as was shown in chapter 4. Lacking details of the number of women in that category, the group had determined its own figures. Within that specific group, there was a subgroup of those termed psychiatrically/psychologically ill; however, looking at the whole federally sentenced population, there was a larger group of women also requiring help with mental health needs. By the time the report was being written the working group had been able to read the preliminary findings of the *Mental Health Survey* (CSC Research Branch 1989), which had been commissioned by the Correctional Service of Canada but was *not* part of the body of research commissioned specifically for the task force. The survey made clear that many of the problems experienced by federally sentenced women could be "linked directly to past experiences of early and/or continued sexual abuse, physical abuse and sexual assault" (TFFSW 1989, 42).

Some on the steering committee were concerned that they had been unable to read the survey themselves, or question its conclusions, and that reference to it in the final task force report might imply agreement with the findings. One member thought it "appropriate to be aware of the findings" that "support[ed] a general impression that there are many women with mental health problems which need to be addressed," and she was backed by another, who suggested that failure to mention the survey might "work against" the task force. It was believed prudent to retain the reference, if only to keep open the programming capacity, which would need to be funded by the Treasury Board.

Nowhere does *Creating Choices* quantify the numbers of women who might be requiring significant help with mental health issues, although it might have been deduced from the figures *Creating Choices* quoted from Jan Heney's research on self-injurious behaviour – 55 percent of a sample of forty-four women self-harmed (TFFSW 1989, 42) – that the numbers would not be small. The actual section on mental health services in *Creating Choices* implied that most women with mental health needs would be able to continue living "in their own cottages" while receiving psychiatric care. Those who were "severely psychotic or certifiable" would be "referred to a local mental health centre" (119). Looking back, a working group member said: "what we missed the boat on was the whole issue of mental health. Are they mental health needs [first] and offenders second – or vice versa? I feel it's very unfair to the general community out there who treat women with mental health needs to say that the women who come to us are just like them. They are not ... they committed a criminal act and I don't think we can get away from that, because there are a whole lot of people out there who have been abused who do not go out and hurt others."[7]

This failure to address the issue fully can partly be linked to the group's reluctance to label federally sentenced women, as was seen in their discussions about women as victims. However, the extraordinarily high number of women identified by the separate 1990 Task Force on Mental Health, Special Needs of Female Offenders as having "serious disorders" – 95 percent – presented the group with yet more difficulties. Having found it impossible to suggest that maximum security women should live in anything other than a conventional cottage, albeit with extra staff in situ, they were unlikely to adopt a different approach for women with mental health needs. The figures provided late in the day by the Task Force on Mental Health would also have appeared suspect because women's problems were frequently pathologized and given a psychiatric label rather than seen as partly resulting from their socio-economic status in the wider community. This failure to address the issue fully – or perhaps an unwillingness further to label an already labelled group – was to have consequences once the new prisons were running, and it left a further area of the report vulnerable to reinterpretation by CSC.

CRIMINALS OR VICTIMS?

Women's "criminality" was also much discussed, as it had been during the November joint meeting, when a member of the task force feared the report would be "rejected as fantasy" if it did not address the issue

of personal responsibility for offending.[8] One member of the committee declared that the draft "read as a victim's (sic) report" and another
said that "if she were 'an outside reader' she would be left with the
impression that all federally sentenced women are victims, that there is
no criminality among women, and that they are there [in prison] only
because of their past experience [of victimization]." She believed that
there was "an element of choice involved in their behaviour." While
one member had understood the report to be writing of women as
"survivors" rather than as victims, it was clear that the committee felt
a need for more clarity on the subject. This, however, was something
the working group had struggled with and related to the difficulty that
all its members had in reconciling differences of opinion. As is by now
very clear, the group's early commitment to a consensus model of operating meant that it was reluctant to identify publicly areas of dissent.
It was impossible for the members to agree on what constituted "the
criminality of federally sentenced women," and they felt that "not
mentioning it was preferable to showing the diversity of views and lack
of resolution on this issue." It is curious that the group members had
felt that their collective expertise was sufficient to allow them to plan
the new facilities but that it was insufficient to allow them to define
this problem.

It is not unreasonable to suggest that the demands of consensus and
the absorption of Aboriginal perspectives had by then coloured the task
force's view of what actually constituted criminality and victimization.
But something else was also going on, as has earlier been suggested: a
crossing of the boundaries that had initially separated members of the
task force from the women at the Prison for Women. Perhaps, for some,
the issues had become more blurred than could ever have been anticipated. A working group member from the voluntary sector attempted
to crystallize her impressions regarding changes wrought in some of the
civil servants during the life of the task force. She had earlier spoken of
the impossibility of hearing the women and not being "touched" by
what was said: "I really think that for the CSC women it was the same
... I think they were seeing it through different eyes. Before, the visits
[to] the institutions had kind of been more in the bureaucratic line. This
time they were coming to really talk to the women ... I think probably
it was very different [for them] and my guess is that it was probably an
eye-opener. I don't think that they had spent any time around the
prisons with the actual inmates. They had been in prisons to go to the
warden's quarters, to go to different meetings, to see the files, but to sit
down in the common rooms with the women and drink their coffee and
listen to their stories, their pain and anger, I would expect that they
were probably pretty touched by that."[9]

The women had stepped off the pages of the files and become women of infinite variety. They had also become more than "offenders": their individual histories now had a familiar face – and any one of them could be at risk the longer she stayed at the Prison for Women, with the memory of Sandy Sayer never being far from anyone's mind. So the language of "victimization" prevailed in a way that would never have been anticipated some months earlier, and the report's eventual language was influenced by Aboriginal people's experience of victimization and racism within the dominant Euro-Canadian society.

QUEBEC

At this very late stage in the task force's deliberations the question of Quebec was again raised. A Quebec regional corrections' representative made it clear that the province did not support the proposals for a new regional facility and hoped for a "modification" of the situation at Maison Tanguay by means of an "enhanced exchange of service agreement." Although the conclusion that none of the existing facilities was adequate had already been reached by the working group, the steering committee debated the possibility of making an exception in the case of Quebec. If the province were exempted from the regional plan, and Maison Tanguay remained in provincial control, jurisdictional issues would have made it almost impossible to enforce "the principles and standards" enshrined in the task force's report (a point already reluctantly conceded with regard to British Columbia). The federal government could not order a provincial government to build a facility, housing both provincial and federal women, to match standards elsewhere, so the federal government had to set the standards itself.[10] Were the provinces to be given the option of individually "modifying" their existing provision the result would be delay and "a nail in the coffin for a truly new future for federally sentenced women." When the committee was asked if it agreed with the idea of an exemption for Quebec, only the Quebec civil servant supported it. Arguably, had a Quebec representative been on the working group, such debates would have been forestalled because the issue would have been discussed at an earlier stage.

PUTTING A WOMAN AT THE TOP TABLE

As *Creating Choices* was later to highlight, the Ouimet Report had suggested as early as 1969 that a woman should be appointed to "a position of senior responsibility and leadership," and CAEFS had sug-

gested in 1981 that a deputy commissioner for women should be.
appointed (Shaw 1991a, 15, 20). This position had been bolstered by
Lee Axon's research, which suggested that "the successful implementation of woman-based corrections is dependent on the appointment of
a woman to a very high level management position" (TFFSW 1989, 95).
How could the task force ensure that women's interests were not again
subordinate to the numerically more pressing interests of men once the
new facilities were built and monies allocated by the federal government were incorporated into the budget of the provincial correctional
authorities? For once the task force acknowledged its lack of consensus. CAEFS still favoured the appointment of a woman deputy commissioner, but the "decentralized, management of CSC was alleged to make
that difficult" (ibid.). CSC was not called to account until 1996.[11]

The report was at last returned to the writers, and the task force was
able to present a draft copy to the commissioner by the due date, with
the steering committee's comments appended in a letter. The Aboriginal chapter was missing, and the crucial Short Term Recommendations
(Emergency Measures), which were intended to provide immediately
for those held at the Prison for Women while CSC considered its
response to the task force's report, were still to be finalized. However,
Ole Ingstrup would have been in no doubt as to the radical nature of
what was being proposed when he read the draft report.

CONSENSUS FOUNDERS

When the Aboriginal chapter was finally completed it was submitted
to the working group for inclusion in the final report. In one crucial
paragraph, when discussing the interlinked nature of being both Aboriginal and a woman, the chapter states: "it is important to understand
that we also share a common Aboriginal history. That common history
is the history of racism, oppression, *genocide* and ethnocide" (TFFSW
1989, 15, emphasis added). One of the working group, Joan Nuffield,
was later to say: "my understanding was and is that while the United
States' government might reasonably be accused of having such a
policy [of genocide], this was never the case in Canada."[12] Further,
Nuffield doubted whether anyone on the task force was qualified to
state definitively whether this had been Canadian policy.[13] There was
some discussion about the options available to her: that she should
simply remove her name from the report; that she should leave it in but
add a footnote indicating that she had withdrawn from the task force
prior to finalization of the report; or that the issue should be treated
with greater clarity in the chapter itself.[14] However, by the time she
received her copy of the draft report it had already been decided that

time constraints made further alterations to the text impossible, and, as a consequence, Nuffield decided that she could not sign the final copy. This decision meant that the report could be published without any hint of dissension attached to it and that, publicly, the goal of consensus had been achieved. The omission of Nuffield's name, however, means that few are now aware of her contribution to the task force.[15]

THE TASK COMPLETED

The final report could not, and did not wish to, avoid the issue of suicide: the death of Sandy Sayer had been fundamental to the working group's unanimous decision that the Prison for Women should be closed. Ms Sayer had become "the" woman for whom they were working. The December draft had opened with almost the complete text of Sandy Sayer's submission, with the added comment that: "her death, her life and her words became a touch-stone ... a reference point whenever we were tempted to put our words and ideas before those of the women living through a federal sentence" (draft, 14 December 1989). After consideration, it was eventually thought "wrong and insulting to use her words [in the report] since she should not even have been at the Prison for Women [as a provincially sentenced, involuntarily transferred prisoner]." An even earlier draft had dwelt in some detail on her death and concluded by saying that such "tragedies ... create profound doubts regarding the humaneness of the current system."[16] The completed report refers to suicide very briefly and contains an unfortunate editing error, which reads: "the questions posed around these tragedies leave *no doubt* about the humaneness of the current system" (TFFSW 1990, 71, emphasis added). Nothing could have been further from what the task force saw as the truth.

Task force members received the final draft of the report just prior to their final, joint meeting on 19 February 1990. All had been invited to submit comments beforehand, and one respondent from the working group wrote to the editors: "I want to say that I have some appreciation for the difficulty you must be having in pulling this together while pleasing us all. In reading it through I see so many points that really didn't get our fullest attention as a group and yet need to be dealt with in this brief. Two or three days with copy in hand and all editing together for consensus sake (not to mention clarification) would have made quite a difference." Indeed it would, but they had not been granted the time, and the report was consequently more open to subsequent reinterpretation than anyone would have wished. There were some members who felt that the report left too much to chance, that it "unfailingly glossed over how the inevitable problems would be addressed once they began appearing" and "that it painted a rather idyllic picture of how smoothly these new institutions would operate."[17] But in producing their report the task force ultimately achieved what had eluded other previous Inquiries: the closure of the Prison for Women. Although it had been a cooperative endeavour between the steering committee and the working group, the key members were the eleven women on the working group. At times uneasily co-existing, they had attempted to cover every conceivable facet of imprisonment for federally sentenced women. By means of commissioned research, public consultations, and their own individual expertise they had assembled a mass of data, which had had to be absorbed, processed, and presented to the commissioner within an extremely short period. It was inevitable that their best endeavours would in some areas be insufficient, given that they had only nine months in which to attempt to repair the damage occasioned by fifty-five years of federal imprisonment at the Prison for Women. It was also inevitable that the differing perspectives they individually brought to the deliberations should impinge on their ability to deal fully with all the issues raised.

On 26 February 1990 *Creating Choices: The Report of the Task Force on Federally Sentenced Women*, as well as the Emergency Measures, was presented to Commissioner Ingstrup. On the same day another Aboriginal woman from Saskatchewan committed suicide in the Prison for Women. The Emergency Measures contained eight recommendations; perhaps the most important one, bearing in mind the suicides that had taken place during the lifetime of the task force – and again directly afterwards – was that transfers from provincial correctional institutions to the Prison for Women should be stopped. That recommendation was implemented almost immediately. *Creating Choices* was officially published on 20 April 1990, and on 30 September 1990 the Government of Canada publicly accepted the report in its entirety. Work on implementation could begin.

CREATING CHOICES

With the publication of *Creating Choices*, the task force's decisions were placed in the public domain and the scope of the report was already clear. It painted a very broad picture of what had led to the formation of the task force, providing an analysis of the history of federal women's imprisonment alongside the voices of imprisoned women themselves. The task force-commissioned research was used to provide a fuller picture of these women, their backgrounds, and their histories, and an entire chapter was entitled, and devoted to, the specific "Voices of Aboriginal Peoples." Voices from the community were added to show that prisoners were the responsibility not only of csc but also of society, while there was less emphasis on the responsibility of the women themselves (for reasons which have already been discussed). It was a carefully developed schema intended to lead logically to the crux of the report, which was that the Prison for Women should be shut and replaced by new regional prisons. The task force wanted to demonstrate that it had covered all possible ground and that its final decisions were cogent and irrefutable, once in the hands of those responsible for implementation.

It is not necessary to cover in great detail what the report recommends as much of this has already been discussed here and elsewhere (see Shaw 1993, 1996a, 1999b; Hannah-Moffat 1994, 1997, 2001; Faith 1993, 1995; Kendall 1999, 2000; Monture 2000; Pate 1999). In summary, the task force recommended five[18] new prisons and a Healing Lodge, all of which should have spacious grounds to which the women would have ready access. There would be cottage-style architecture, allowing the women to live independently in small groups, sometimes accompanied by their younger children. The staff would be carefully selected and trained, and the prisons would offer innovative, holistic programs, appropriate to the needs of the women, while recognizing cultural differences. A complementary package of community-based services, including half-way houses and addiction treatment centres, would facilitate the women's eventual return to the community. The Healing Lodge would be planned and managed by Aboriginal people, with Aboriginal ceremonies and programming being central to its day-to-day running.

Nevertheless, the use of language in *Creating Choices* cannot be ignored. Nor can the way particular perspectives consistently appear throughout the report. It is now time to examine these more closely, while asking how and why they were permitted.

EXPLAINING THE CHOICES

Much of the critical debate about *Creating Choices* has centred on the way in which the language of feminism was incorporated into a penal strategy and subsequently had its original meaning reinterpreted. The principles (TFFSW 1990, 104–12), which have not previously been discussed but have been mentioned at various points, were central to the integrity of the report. The task force always intended that, should questions arise at a later date, the principles would provide a philosophical context for any decision making. Although the minutes do not show that the task force made a decision about this, *Creating Choices* was, apart from one paragraph, remarkably free of references to feminism, choosing instead to describe itself as "women-centred" (perhaps because it knew it would be easier for CSC to adopt the report if it were not seen as polemical). Nonetheless, the writers of *Creating Choices* believed they were espousing a largely feminist vision, even if the language used was not entirely "owned" by feminism, and this was particularly evident in the principles (which are here briefly paraphrased).

1 *Empowerment:* Federally sentenced women had been "dis-empowered" by "inequities" and "reduced life choices." Women were to be empowered through the provision of programs that would help raise self-esteem and enable them to "accept and express responsibility for actions taken and future choices" (TFFSW 1990, 105–7).
2 *Meaningful and responsible choices:* This was linked to the principle of *empowerment,* in that raised self-esteem could be achieved through the availability of "meaningful options" that would "allow them to make responsible choices." The "options" included better programs within the new prisons and better community alternatives post-release. These "choices" were to be relevant to the women's needs, and in learning to make better personal choices they would be better equipped to avoid the cycles of dependency "on men, alcohol or drugs and/or on state financial assistance" once their sentences were completed (107–8).
3 *Respect and dignity* This assumed the need for "mutuality of respect" among "prisoners, among staff and between prisoners and staff"; and that "if people are treated with respect and dignity they [would] be more likely to act responsibly." It also recognized the importance of spirituality and cultural identity (109).
4 *Supportive environment: Empowerment, responsible choices, respect* and *dignity* could only be aspired to, and achieved, in an environment that was positive and conducive to good physical and psychological health. This principle stressed that "equality ... cannot be reduced to equality of treatment in the sense of 'sameness' of treatment, but must be understood as equality of outcome" (110).
5 *Shared responsibility:* This principle acknowledged that none of the others could be achieved without understanding that both corrections and the outside community shared responsibility for federally sentenced women (111).

All of these principles were later reinterpreted by CSC and moved some distance from what the task force, which remained faithful to its largely feminist roots, had intended. Perhaps the most immediately contentious appropriation of language centred on the use of "empowerment" and its relationship with "meaningful and responsible choices." Kendall (1994, 3) writes that she was "concerned that the language of feminism [was] being appropriated and stripped of its subversive potential by corrections in order to facilitate the correctional agenda." Hannah-Moffat (2001) examines the way in which, after the publication of *Creating Choices*, the interpretation of the language changed from the feminist, or women-centred, approach of the task force, which assumed that women's offending could not be divorced from "their life circumstances and the social context of their offences" (175), to one that had been defined anew by CSC, wherein a woman was "responsible for her own self-governance and for minimizing and managing her needs and the risk she posed to herself and the public" (155; see also Balfour 2000). The complexity of Hannah-Moffat's analysis cannot be paraphrased here; however, drawing partly on work by O'Malley (1992), she teases out the connection between what he refers to as "prudentialism" (whereby individuals have responsibility for managing their own risk) and CSC's assumption that, given appropriate options, imprisoned women would be able to make appropriate choices. Not only that, but they would voluntarily choose to make these within the constraints of an environment in which they had been involuntarily confined and where the available options had been determined by CSC. In adopting this "responsibilizing" strategy CSC moved beyond the older "welfare strategies of rehabilitation [wherein] the state is responsible for the offender's reformation" to a position where the woman herself is entirely responsible (Hannah-Moffat 2000, 32).

In the *Creating Choices* model an interesting aspect of taking responsibility is the relationship between Hannah-Moffat's "self-governing" woman and staff, a connection characterized as "dynamic security," which contributes to the smooth running of the prison (TFFSW 1990, 117). Although a member of the steering committee had, at its concluding meeting, urged that the section in the report on staffing should be strengthened, the final version does not dwell at great length on the role of staff members. It recognizes that there have to be changes in the way staff members are both selected and trained, but it does not fully address either the inherent inequality between women and staff or the fact that it was "the authority of the position [of guard] which exact[ed] co-operation" (Faith 1993, 163; see also Kendall 1993). It certainly does not address the possibility that new staff members would require intense support from CSC as they coped with new jobs, in untested prisons, with prisoners also adapting to a new environment. One of the expectations of staff members was that they should "create an environment where relationships based on role-modelling, support, trust and *democratic* decision making" could thrive (TFFSW 1990, 88, emphasis added), ignoring the point that coercive environments could never be democratic environments. The tension between the security and supportive role of a guard would always be resolved in favour of security because the prime function of a guard was to retain control (Liebling and Price 2001). Much of the task force's planning was contingent upon the success of staff/prisoner relationships: the levels of physical security; how many, if any, staff should be in each living unit; and the willingness of the women to respond to a different type of guard.

The self-governing woman became, in effect, an integral part of the governance of the prison because her "responsible" choices – made possible through the benevolence of CSC – contributed to its good order. Her choices could never be made entirely in what she perceived to be her own best interests because the welfare of others also had to be taken into account, as did the probable judgment of staff. Additionally, the final judgment as to what was an appropriate choice was made by others rather than herself, so, in correctional terms, "consequence" appeared to be the obverse of "choice." While this might be said to replicate the choices made on a daily basis by those living outside prison, the crucial difference is the loss of autonomy. This applies to everyday events where, in certain situations, the expression of anger may be construed as an entirely appropriate response, yet in the confines of a prison it may be seen as inappropriate. Within an abnormal environment – and the involuntary discipline attached to prisons means that they can never be anything other than abnormal in comparison with life on the outside – prisoners are expected to behave in an abnormal fashion in order to be seen to be behaving responsibly. For prisoners to resort to usual human behaviour is to risk the possibility of its being interpreted as their failure to address the reason for their imprisonment. To *resist* within an abnormal environment, especially when the resistance is focused on choices that the prisoner might feel are inadequate, is not seen as a positive response. It is again seen as failure, whereas Shaw argues that "in such circumstances, the actions of prisoners should be regarded as rational responses rather than character flaws" (Shaw 1994 cited in Kendall 1998; see also Bosworth 1999). Eaton (1993, 42) suggests that women "preserve something of the self" by "withold[ing] that self from engagement with the world of the prison ... [and that the women's] way to make a choice [is] *to choose not to choose*" (emphasis added). Under the model first presented by the task force, and later defined by CSC, the right to choose could not be declined. To fail to choose was ultimately to act irresponsibly, with consequences that could reverberate as far as Parole Board hearings. Yet choice was the cornerstone of the task force's plan.

As has been earlier suggested, the notion of "responsible choice" was predicated on its interpretation by a largely middle-class task force, whose members assumed that individuals should, and could, make choices that balanced the competing needs of those around them. Such rationality is not always easily achieved, especially among women who have not experienced much order in their own lives, and the rhetoric to which federally sentenced women were exposed prior to being removed to the new prisons did not, generally, touch on the new responsibilities they were to assume. "Choices" were obscured by the larger vision of the new physical style of the prisons, and, as will be seen, some of the women arrived at the prisons with inflated expectations of the degree of freedom to which they would be exposed, largely because of the enthusiasm of those who had discussed the new prisons with them prior to transfer. The question of involving federally sentenced women in responsibility for their own imprisonment is something that will be discussed in a later chapter, particularly in relation to the Healing Lodge, where, due to the added dimension of culture and spirituality, the degree of responsibility and self-governance demanded of the Aboriginal women is potentially greater than that demanded of non-Aboriginals.

HIDING THE REALITY

Such discussions are of particular importance in terms of what emerged following the implementation of the report, but they have also been dealt with by others in some detail (see Shaw 1993, 1996a, 1999b; Hannah-Moffat 1994, 1997, 2001; Bruckert 1993; Faith 1993, 1995; Kendall 1999, 2000; Monture 2000; Pate 1999). Here, the task force's fundamental use of language is examined.

Throughout their work, many on the working group were ambivalent about helping to create new prisons, and this showed in the way they discussed them. In the October minutes, when the working group was in the midst of planning five new prisons, the actual word "prison" was not used at all (apart from the times when the group referred to the Prison for Women); instead, the prisons were transformed into "facilities" or "new accommodation," each having a "milieu" or "environment." One member went so far as to stress that her "support for construction is contingent on not building a bars and cells penitentiary but rather a place where troubled people live while learning to deal with their problems." It was a remarkable linguistic sleight of hand, echoing the language used to justify the rebuilding of Holloway in London (see Rock 1996) and the detention of women at Cornton Vale in Scotland (see Carlen 1983). The eventual report conjured up an image of prisons having the "milieu" of a "facility" run by social workers (as, indeed, many of the new staff members had previously been).

Such circumlocution – or "Controltalk" (see Cohen 1985) – continued with the publication of *Creating Choices* and subsequent CSC policy documents. When the new prisons opened they were named "institutions" and spoken of as "facilities," and the new Aboriginal prison remained a "Healing Lodge," in itself an extraordinary euphemism for a place of confinement. The prisons consisted of "cottages" and the cottages contained "bedrooms" rather than cells. The originally named "assessment cottage" became an "enhanced unit" – and was actually a maximum security complex. When the report portrayed the community aspect of the new plans for federally sentenced women, the accommodation was described as "community release centres," "half-way houses," and "satellite units", avoiding the fact that there remained elements of supervision (or discipline) at each. By the implementation stage, guards or correctional officers had been transformed from "staff" into "primary workers" (see also Bruckert 1993; Faith 1993). The custodial relationship had been made to disappear by a feat of linguistic engineering, and this can be directly related to the task force's and, more specifically, the working group's reluctance to dwell too much on the fact that they were building prisons, thanks to the demands of consensus.

Culhane (1991, 20) refers to such usage as "'system' language which denies prisoners the reality of their own existence [and] also serves to cloud public perception of life behind prison walls." And Faith (1993, 123) comments: "to the women themselves, the euphemisms are offensive. To the person who is forcibly confined within them, these places are prisons and they are prisoners." Ross (1998, 126) adds that such "euphemisms are too gentle and subsequently, misleading in the description of the experience of imprisoned women." Yet such soft language helps legitimate the prison, conferring upon it an apparent normality, while the actual discipline imposed by the prison – assisted, in the Canadian case, by the anticipated self-discipline of the prisoners – is very far from normal. "Controltalk" is not a recent phenomenon (Cohen 1983, 1989): it has a long and dishonourable history in disguising the reality of imprisonment, and, as Bruckert (1993, 17) contends, "obscures the harsh reality of coercive social control allow[ing] middle class reformers and workers to justify (and conceptualise) their roles as benevolent." Yet, in adopting such language, the working group had found a device by which it could disguise, or at least minimize, the reality of its endeavour – and finally produce a plan. The "facilities" and "institutions" were the very end of the road paved by consensus: the prison had disappeared.

DIFFERENT VOICES: ABSENT VOICES

Alongside the language so consistently embraced by the task force there is another highly visible strand. To explore this, the formation of the task force must be remembered, together with the fact that the original vision was of a partnership between CSC and CAEFS. With the addition of the Aboriginal members a "distinct" dimension of culture and ethnicity was added to the profile of federally sentenced women, dividing them into two groups. At the same time another "distinct" society, that of Quebec, was not separately represented on the most influential of the task force's two parties (i.e., the working group), and francophones were eventually planned for as though they had no identity other than that of Euro-Canadian. Despite subsequent CSC protestations that it would have been impolitic to have allowed separate representation, it has been seen that, during the life of the task force itself, an unsuccessful attempt was made to co-opt a Quebecois civil servant on to the working group. Chapter 2 asks if there might be some importance attached to the original suggestion that "a native person [as well as] two provincial representatives"[19] should be on the task force. At the time their inclusion was suggested it was no more than a recognition of the significance of the two constituencies, but how they were both subsequently dealt with raises questions about inclusion and exclusion within Canadian society, as well as the complex nature of ethnic identity in a colonized country. It can now be suggested that *Creating Choices* itself forces us to think anew about the way marginalized groups may capitalize on opportunities presented to them – and that the Aboriginal members exploited the opportunity provided ·by the task force in a manner not previously recognized.

The bare facts speak for themselves. In its 133 pages *Creating Choices* contains a separate Aboriginal chapter, alongside twelve substantial sections addressing Aboriginal issues and perspectives. Additionally, there are innumerable references to Aboriginal concerns throughout the report. *Creating Choices* is quite frank about what it intends: "it was agreed that every effort would be made by the non-Aboriginal members to understand the Aboriginal perspective and to integrate this understanding, with support from Aboriginal members, throughout the report" (TFFSW 1990, 98). Consequently, each new idea introduced by the task force was also examined from an Aboriginal perspective. The principles, with only one exception, also refer to Aboriginal concerns and begin with a preamble that further highlights the specific injustices experienced by Aboriginal women. The Healing Lodge was initially introduced with a caveat not extended to the other proposed new prisons: "it was clear from the outset however, that this

conclusion [that there should be a Healing Lodge] was only the conclusion of this task force. In order to be accepted, this idea must not
only be embraced by the Correctional Service of Canada but must be
developed by and connected to Aboriginal communities" (100).
However, when the task force introduced the "Recommended Plan," it
wrote: "it is a plan which must be seen, assessed and implemented in
its entirety. Isolating parts of the plan, and adopting or rejecting these
parts without seeing their vital interrelationship to the whole, would
destroy the integrity of the plan" (114). Taken to its logical conclusion
such a statement – in association with the previous one – implies that,
should Aboriginal communities refuse to be associated with the
Healing Lodge, the entire plan would be scuppered. This, of course,
was not the task force's intention: it was simply a failure of editing as
the Aboriginal members had already made it clear that the Healing
Lodge, while contingent upon the support of the Elders and Aboriginal
communities, had in principle been backed. But this illustrates the deference accorded Aboriginal participation – a deference not shown to
others.

All of this was in marked contrast to the attention paid to that other
distinct group, the francophones of Quebec, who might have been considered eligible for at least provincial consideration. *Creating Choices*
has no separate chapter devoted to francophone needs and aspirations.
In all, there are eight references to Quebec and only one paragraph
focuses specifically on the province. That, however, is set within the
context of what happened historically rather than what might happen
in the future. Of the sixty quotes that open the report, from women
who had been or were federal prisoners, twenty-six are from women
identified as Aboriginal; there are no quotes recognizably from women
from Quebec. Of the fifty-four quotes used to identify "the voices of
others who care" fourteen come from representatives of Aboriginal
organizations and one comes from Quebec. There is a brief reference
to the need to reduce language and cultural barriers for francophones,
issues that had largely been won in the province during the 1980s, but,
overall, Quebec's needs and aspirations are almost totally ignored. The
francophone women are not seen as a distinct cultural group meriting
separate attention; rather, they are seen as being no different from
other Euro-Canadian federally sentenced women from across the
country.

Does this matter? The most obvious point to make is one provided
by a member of the task force: "there was no doubt. If there was an
institution in Quebec there was no doubt in any of our minds that it
was going to be French ... If you have the institution here, we'll take
care of it, it will be culturally ours. There's no way, because of the

people who will be staffing it, because of the environment, that it will not meet cultural needs."[20] In the event, because of the National Implementation Committee's decision that the new Quebec prison would not be built in Montreal but in the small, almost totally francophone town of Joliette, this was even more true than anticipated, yet it also reflected a characteristically Quebecois pattern of quiet subversion. Quebec might have been omitted from the working group, but the francophones would continue doing what they had been doing for centuries in the face of continued anglophone failure to recognize their distinct culture and status as a nation: they would cultivate their own francophone environment as the new prison emerged from the drawing board.

This was an important lesson to be drawn from the omission of Quebec from the working group, yet it fails to explain either why it should have been neglected in the first place or why the question of Quebecois exclusion has been pursued. Quebec was not a province that the federal government customarily ignored, and, in the decade leading up to the task force, Quebec had seldom been absent from the wider Canadian political debate. A justifiable conclusion is that the civil servants were initially so focused on forging a partnership with CAEFS, partly in order to legitimate the venture, that the broader political perspectives, which generally prevailed whenever task forces were formed, were no longer seen to be pre-eminent. CAEFS was *essential* to the public success of the venture, Quebec was not. What this demonstrates is the way in which political considerations alter over time. Quebec has always been – and will conceivably remain, unless demographic factors affect the province disproportionately – both an integral, yet consciously separate, part of Canada. Its cause has been publicly espoused over centuries of dissension, but, as Canada has become more cosmopolitan, the debate over Canadian identity has had to encompass many diverse groups. As the country has started to come to terms with its changing face, it has also had to confront its engagement with those peoples who were stripped of their heritage by the successive colonization of the French and the English. The civil servants charged with assembling the task force were unexpectedly faced by an able and forceful group of Aboriginal women, and the civil servants' knowledge of Canadian history enabled them to recognize the validity of the Aboriginal members' wish to join. As eventually transpired, Aboriginal participation became essential to the legitimacy of the task force, in the same way that CAEFS had legitimized the venture at the outset. For once, Aboriginal peoples' claims took precedence over those of the colonizers – and the less powerful of the colonizers, the Quebecois, were assumed to be little different from other Euro-Canadians.

When subsequently asked to justify the omission of Quebec from the working group the civil servants' explanation relied on the difficulties associated with acknowledging one province ahead of another, but this was disproved by the attempt to co-opt a Quebec correctional official. When pressed further, it was suggested that conceivably CAEFS should have selected a Quebecois representative for the working group as this would have removed the possibility of a federal department causing offence to the provinces, while still allowing Quebec perspectives to be heard at the most influential table.[21] This was not the function of CAEFS – and it could not be assumed that all their representatives would have been concerned about Quebec, either. As one CAEFS representative said: "From where I sit in the west, Quebec is another province like the rest of us. To me, there is another province that has its idiosyncrasies, as we do here. We struggle with some things, they struggle with others ... It's not like the Aboriginal population who have a separate identity that has really gone unheard – that really matters very, very strongly. In Canadian history we have not heard them, paid attention, and we absolutely were so committed to putting a document together that heard them, that said you are a part of this experience, of what we need to learn, of what we have to do."[22]

The civil servants then became involved in the unanticipated issue of Aboriginal representation and became further distanced from federal–provincial dilemmas. Part of this can best be explained from a francophone perspective: "I'm saying that the Aboriginal question was taken more seriously than the French question because they're [civil servants] used to the French. We've been saying things since day one ... they've heard everything! This body of Aboriginal strength, and what it represented in terms of loss for Canada ... obviously they [Aboriginal nations] are sitting on an awful lot of land, so what I'm talking about is that all this can be lost, the consequences are enormous." And in the midst of this was a particularly important point, that the civil servants were dealing with an unfamiliar group and were not as sure-footed as usual: "Obviously the French are important, but it is more frightening to be confronted by people you are more estranged from. Certainly the English are less estranged from the French than they are from the Aboriginal groups. So the fact that they did not know where they [Aboriginal members] were coming from, what to expect, how organized they were, where they were going, made it much more threatening to the civil servants in Ottawa. And the guilt, also, that has been there forever. They have never felt guilty about the French!"[23]

Remembering the shared aspirations of both the Quebecois and the Aboriginal nations – that they should be recognized as "distinct" societies and have the right to self-determination – it could perhaps be assumed that, together, they might have been effective allies on such a task force. This would be to ignore the legacy of distrust felt by Aboriginal peoples towards the "dominant culture" (of which Quebec was perceived to be a part) and a fundamental linguistic divide between themselves and the Quebecois.[24] Relatively few Aboriginal people speak French: "It's so different because of the language barrier, because most of the Aboriginals are English speaking ... the language barrier is enormous. It was almost felt, from the Quebec point of view, that the Aboriginals were mostly English-speaking – so they were separate in two ways."[25] Moreover, the francophones had always had provincial representation of their perspectives, even if these were not always heard in the federal arena. This sense of Quebecois territoriality was not one permitted Aboriginal peoples who, in many cases, had been removed from their historic homelands. Additionally, these nations had no official parliamentary base to use as a platform for their grievances and were taking advantage of an opportunity – fortuitously provided by the task force – both to work for the good of Aboriginal federally sentenced women and to publicize their wider political aspirations.

So by the time the report was being written there was a group of civil servants, some of whom had been hand-picked because they were there as unofficial representatives of the commissioner, who found themselves unexpectedly outnumbered by those from the voluntary sector. The civil servants early on discovered that the Aboriginal members had an agenda that exceeded the mandate: they wanted to discuss self-government and a system of criminal justice that reflected Aboriginal custom. Above all, they wanted to discuss the issues that contributed to the disproportionate criminalizing of Aboriginal women – and that meant exploring the period before "commencement of sentence," an area specifically excluded by the mandate. Despite being told that this was not part of the task force's remit, the Aboriginal members used every opportunity to pursue these points. Moreover, their insistence that the other members of the task force should be "educated" in an Aboriginal history of racism, abuse, and poverty had the dual effect of simultaneously raising awareness and subduing debate on Aboriginal issues.

It is remarkable just how completely the Aboriginal message permeated *Creating Choices*.[26] What is perhaps even more remarkable is the way that this so influenced the debate on all federally sentenced women. The characterization of federally sentenced women as "victims" provides an illustration of this point. Although the steering committee at its final meeting had urged that greater emphasis should be placed on the part federally sentenced women had played in victim-

izing others – and *Creating Choices* goes some way towards doing this
– the women's offending remained situated in a social context that
somewhat extenuated their behaviour:

The Task Force ... is built on the acceptance of responsibility by the women,
by the justice system, by the government and by communities. But while this
responsibility includes the need to address and repair harm done by federally
sentenced women, *it puts these incidents into the context of social inequalities
and structures which define and lead to crime* (TFFSW 1990, 132, emphasis
added).

As suggested in chapter 4, much of the discourse surrounding "women
as victims" originated from the largely undisputed view that Aboriginal women were indeed victims of an unequal society. There was no
apparent debate of the feminist view that to label women simply as
"victims" was to "perpetuate paternalistic notions and disempower
women prisoners even further" (Kendall 1993, 29). As the task force,
and particularly the working group, came to see the imprisoned
women as individuals who had committed offences in certain circumstances, rather than as an amorphous group of federally sentenced
women, it became harder to categorize them all as women who had
created victims, despite the legal reality that they were. As they were
working within the constraints of "consensus," the working group
could not label just one group of federally sentenced women, the Aboriginal women, "victims." They could not attach a caveat to their work
and did not wish to. Additionally, the working group was determined
that the final report should not be interpreted in a manner that might
lead to groups of women being treated unequally. The acceptance of
the Aboriginal rhetoric spilled over into how they came to view all federally sentenced women and, in the end, the working group found that
they could not differentiate between them.

   In the light of the widespread Aboriginal influence apparent throughout the report, it is reasonable to suggest that *Creating Choices* should
be looked at not just as a document on penal affairs but also as a political document – and a subversive one at that. It is reasonable to say that
Creating Choices is much more of an Aboriginal statement of intent than
has ever been acknowledged. It is a robust riposte to the offensiveness of
the Task Force on the Reintegration of Aboriginal Offenders as Law-
Abiding Citizens and to the failure of the Women in Conflict with the
Law initiative, from which the Aboriginal members had withdrawn.
Aboriginal women were not expected to be part of the task force: two
were then included on the most important of the two parties, the
working group, and a further three were placed on the steering committee. Federally sentenced women were to be consulted but not included

on the task force; the Aboriginal members ensured that two Aboriginal federally sentenced women joined the steering committee. Commissioned research was to "have a sound empirical basis" so at to satisfy the demands of the Treasury Board;[27] the Aboriginal participants were eventually encouraged to undertake their own forms of research. Discussion of an Aboriginal justice system was outside the remit of the mandate; this impossibility was addressed frankly at various points in the report and therefore put the question of Aboriginal government, self-determination, and justice firmly in the public domain.

In short, Aboriginal influences permeated *Creating Choices*, and the reasons for this are made explicit in the report: "just as we cannot tack women on to a men-oriented system of corrections, so we cannot tack Aboriginal women on to any system be it for men or women" (TFFSW 1990, 99). Yet who largely wrote the final draft? With the exception of the chapter entitled "The Voices of Aboriginal People" that final draft was written by the civil servants. While it could be suggested that the civil servants resorted to expediency and incorporated Aboriginal perspectives in order to add political legitimacy to the document, interview evidence makes it clear that most had come to accept the validity of the Aboriginals' case. They had sat through lengthy, often painful, meetings with the working group and were in no doubt that *Creating Choices* "had to reflect/be consistent with working group discussions – and the Aboriginal fact was very strong in these discussions."[28] The civil servants' conversion, bearing in mind the genesis of the whole project and their expected supervisory role, was an extraordinary turn of events.

One of the civil servants was asked if the Aboriginal members viewed the task force as a political opportunity: "It seems to me that [they] would have and [they] would have been foolish not to have seen it as that."[29] Another senior civil servant was asked the same question and the reply was: "Yes, you can see from the results that they brought forward the Aboriginal agenda," adding "the other element was very clearly that we were lucky with the Aboriginal representatives, that they made their points and got their issues on the table. Their agenda was fully understood and if we had more shy people it wouldn't have happened."[30] A member of the steering committee perhaps best encapsulated this when she said: "I would say that those who have gained most out of *Creating Choices* are the Aboriginals. That was not the original intention – the original intention was to have all women gain from *Creating Choices*. When you look back at what has happened I would say that certainly the Aboriginals are the great winners."[31]

Yet all of this still does not answer why the exclusion of Quebec from the working group has been pursued. *Imprisoning Our Sisters* suggests, on the basis of firm evidence, that the civil servants – most probably inadvertently – continued the pattern, begun at the time of the Conquest, of assuming that the Quebecois could be absorbed into the larger anglophone body politic. Although the British North America Act, 1867, had specifically (and erroneously) referred to the British and French as the "founding nations" of Canada, the reality had been that they had not lived as two equal nations within the Confederation. Quebec had consistently needed to assert its unique cultural identity and in the 1980s was finding it increasingly hard to do so, as more anglophones moved into the province. The 1980 referendum on "sovereignty-association" had been lost, but the debate continued (and was to be the subject of another narrowly lost referendum in 1995). Quebec was of paramount importance to the rest of Canada because its departure from Confederation, even with economic ties remaining, might have impelled other provinces to consider similar action in order to safeguard what they saw as "their" resources (e.g., oil). The subject of the task force was of little importance to the vast majority of Canadians, including Quebecois, but it was yet another in a seemingly unending line of government-sponsored initiatives that ignored Quebec's wish to be sovereign. The anglo-Canadians were once again taking charge of matters that, in Quebecois' eyes, were their own. To the civil servants of csc, intent on planning a relatively obscure task force, the participation of caefs appeared to be the main prize. But to those Quebecois aware of the initiative the failure to consider their needs – especially once Aboriginal women had been included in such numbers – was yet another instance of their being sidelined, another instance of their culture being disregarded. In short, the civil servants' political antennae deserted them.

This is not to propose that, had the Quebecois been included on the working group, the final report would have been *significantly* different, but it would have reflected in a distinctive fashion the perspectives of those two groups of original colonizers. The quest for sovereignty, culture, and distinctiveness as separate nations is what binds both the Aboriginal peoples and the Quebecois, even though those Aboriginal nations might dispute the legitimacy of Quebec's claims to sovereignty. The civil servants recognized neither claim in planning the task force and, subsequently, found their carefully balanced enterprise disrupted once the Aboriginal women gained seats at the table. The Aboriginal members took their opportunity and might appear to be "the great winners."

In the light of what has subsequently happened following the implementation of *Creating Choices*, the preceding statement needs to be tested. At this point, the shape of *Imprisoning Our Sisters* alters as the next chapters focus on three of the new prisons. Only upon knowing how these prisons fared during their first years will it be possible to ask whether the Aboriginal peoples were indeed the great winners of the task force's enterprise.

CHAPTER SIX

Edmonton Institution for Women

Having completed its work, the task force was disbanded and its painstakingly prepared plan for closure and replacement of the Prison for Women was returned – to the civil servants, as it transpired – for the next stage: implementation. What happened as all the new prisons emerged from conjecture into physical reality is first examined. Particular attention is then paid to the first three of the new prisons to open. It is important, for the historical record, to document how those three prisons individually fared, because the passage of time inevitably affects and clouds what is remembered of events. Commentators have addressed the initiative, producing compelling assessments of the philosophy underpinning *Creating Choices* and the way in which this was translated into a correctional rationale justifying later amendments by CSC (see Shaw 1993, 1996a, 1999b; Hannah-Moffat 1994, 1997, 2001; Faith 1993, 1995; Kendall 1999, 2000; Monture 2000; Pate 1999). Their analysis has not focused on specific prisons; nor have they compared and contrasted the development of each. Yet it is in such detail that explanations might be found for why things unfolded as they did and, as will be apparent, different stories emerged from each.

In devising its plan to replace the Prison for Women, the task force had to create its own blueprint. No other jurisdiction offered innovation on the scale it was seeking, and those apparent pockets of excellence that did exist were not always fully documented or evaluated.[1] As a task force member later said, "we were desperate to see what was new."[2] This provides another reason for a close scrutiny of *Creating Choices* as its implementation was watched with interest across the world, not least because CSC later went to great lengths to publicize what was being done. The report was potentially a landmark document for imprisoned women, and other jurisdictions were anxious to see what could be learned. But this account remains a Canadian story, and, from it, can be learned the wider lessons of the task force's plan.

To set the scene for what follows it is necessary briefly to return to the history of how the prisons were planned and what happened while they were being constructed. The role the provincial correctional regions played in the planning process is not part of this discussion because, although they were undoubtedly partners in construction, the prisons remained a federal venture.

WITHDRAWING FROM THE PARTNERSHIP

The brief final chapter of *Creating Choices* outlines how the task force's plan should be implemented. It is less than specific about the means, recommending that a "very senior management position" should be created "for the sole purpose of implementing the plan" and that "the Commissioner [should] establish an externally based implementation committee which would report directly to him", and be "comprised of a federally sentenced women as well as representatives from the Canadian Association of Elizabeth Fry Societies, the Aboriginal Women's Caucus and Status of Women Canada" (TFFSW 1990, 130). CSC's response was to establish a national implementation committee (NIC) in November 1990, consisting solely of civil servants and chaired by Jane Miller-Ashton, who was by then the national coordinator for the Federally Sentenced Women Initiative. An external advisory committee (EAC) was later struck, comprising representatives from CAEFS, NWAC, and Status of Women Canada, but no federally sentenced women. EAC was to have a role similar to that of the steering committee on the task force, but with very much less influence. There were no Aboriginal women on the actual NIC, even though Aboriginal women had to be provided for in all the proposed new prisons, but some were involved in a separate NIC subcommittee, responsible for planning the Healing Lodge.

To begin with, the NIC anticipated that all information (apart from Advice to Ministers) would be exchanged with "outside agencies" so as not to undermine those agencies' trust (NIC Minutes January 1991, 11), but within a few short months this position had changed dramatically. This is best illustrated in relation to decisions taken about site location.

At its first meeting the NIC set about deciding the location and selection criteria for the proposed new prisons. As we know, the task force recommended five new prisons, in addition to a Healing Lodge, and had been specific about their locations. By their second meeting, in January 1991, the NIC had largely endorsed the areas chosen by the task force but had identified Toronto as the preferred Ontario site, a city that the working group had already rejected. Other communities were not to be discouraged from submitting proposals but were to be told that the "criteria" pointed to a "location near a major urban centre" (NIC January, 1991). In effect, the decisions of the task force were not considered conclusive by the NIC, which suggests that CSC assumed ownership of the project as soon as the commissioner accepted *Creating Choices.* In March, however, the NIC's minutes became evasive: the "list of communities [to be considered for a prison]" being mailed to members had to be treated as confidential. The April minutes did not mention location at all, and 128 communities across the country had already asked to be considered for the new prisons. By July 1991 corrections' officials, knowing there had been a change in policy, were concerned that any site announcement could leave the minister "open to some embarrassment" if he were to hold a formal news conference. The communities earlier identified by the task force would be expecting confirmation of their selection rather than news that the site radius had been extended. The matter was expected to be of "particular concern to members of the EAC [External Advisory Committee] and the Halifax Elizabeth Fry Society" as those "individuals and their organizations ha[d] been reviewing CSC documents pertaining to the Federally Sentenced Women's Initiative for the past six months [and] none of [those] documents ha[d] given any indication that CSC ... would consider looking outside the vicinity of the recommended communities."[3] A further memorandum spoke of a reluctance to "send out the June and July minutes due to the confidential content, yet we have no explanation to offer the External Advisory Committee [for any delay]" (13 July 1991).[4]

On 31 July 1991 it was announced that communities within 100 kilometres of each of the task force-specified locations (with the exception of the Healing Lodge) – Halifax, Montreal, central/south western Ontario, and Edmonton – could submit bids to have a new prison in their area. In the Prairies, Calgary was added to Edmonton as a possible area for consideration. As is seen in the next chapter, there were immediate protests from organizations that had been closely allied to the task force, particularly regarding the Atlantic region locality.

CAEFS concluded it was being deliberately excluded from the decision-making process, and by the beginning of 1992 its new executive director, Kim Pate, was seeking advice from her board as to whether CAEFS should consider withdrawing its support for implementation.[5] Yet CAEFS' criticism had to be carefully weighed, not least because of ever-present worries about government funding should it be seen as too adversarial. It was suggested by a board member that CAEFS had been "politically naïve in failing to foresee how the site selection process

could become so politicized."[6] Indeed, the signals that CSC would not
share responsibility for the building of the new prisons with CAEFS had
been present throughout the life of the task force, beginning with Ole
Ingstrup's announcement, during initial discussions with CAEFS about
the structure of the task force, that he would be retaining financial
accountability for the venture. There was also the indisputable statutory responsibility held by CSC for the penitentiaries in its care. Once
implementation began, the fact that CAEFS was assigned to the EAC
rather than to the NIC further highlighted CSC's intentions. The task
force's brief attempt to delineate the role of an implementation committee (see TFFSW 1990, 130) could not succeed in the face of the hard
fact that CSC was the paymaster. Yet, as a senior CAEFS' member of the
task force noted, they "were used to CSC having the money and the
power," and CAEFS' initial decision to join the task force had been
made knowing that the extent of its own influence lay in its "ability to
walk away," very publicly, if the initiative appeared to be failing.[7] Its
calculated choice to participate had been based on what it thought was
best for those held in the Prison for Women, and the possible consequence of that choice was the risk of losing credibility should the
venture fail to deliver improvements for these women.

CAEFS continued to debate its response during the months that followed, and on 14 June 1992, at its annual general meeting, carried a
motion: "that following immediate consultation with the women in
P4W [Prison for Women], Burnaby and Tanguay, that CAEFS withdraw
from the External Advisory Committee created to oversee the implementation of the task force Report." Only the Edmonton society
opposed the motion as a decision was still forthcoming regarding the
Alberta location, and it was feared that the prison could be assigned
elsewhere, by way of "revenge."[8] CAEFS' president, Dawn Fleming,
wrote to Solicitor General Doug Lewis, telling him of the organization's immediate withdrawal, partly occasioned by his failure to keep
them "apprised of the progress of the implementation process" and
their belief that "the principles of the task force [had] not been adhered
to." CAEFS had decided to return to its "traditional role as advocates
with and for women who come into conflict with the law."[9]

This decision left the initial planning of four of the new prisons
firmly in the hands of federal civil servants, even though the regions
were later to become involved. Yet even if *Creating Choices* had been
more specific about an implementation strategy it is unlikely that
CAEFS would have remained CSC's partner, not least because CSC's
involvement with the voluntary sector was not statutorily mandated to
continue. CAEFS' ambivalence towards the entire project had shown at
various stages during the task force, to the point where "on more than

one occasion" it came very close to withdrawing.[10] Many CAEFS' members, who had been against the original decision to join the task force, had doubted CSC's motives in encouraging the partnership, and the outcome confirmed their belief that CAEFS had been used to legitimate the venture. Others were less happy with the decision to withdraw because it left CSC free to interpret *Creating Choices* as it wished, yet still able to claim that CAEFS shared responsibility for the document. This nightmarish scenario had been CAEFS' fear, knowing that CAEFS could remain associated in the public mind with a venture whose implementation it might ultimately be unable to influence. In this respect, its calculated gamble had failed, but the outcome was not without precedent in that penal reform initiatives have a history of being incorporated by the state, largely because the state never cedes final control. As a partner in the task force CAEFS challenged the existing system by trying to change its focus rather than fundamentally question its entire rationale. To have done otherwise would have made CAEFS' participation in the task force impossible.

THE APRIL 1994 INCIDENTS

While planning continued for the new prisons the situation at the Prison for Women, which had been volatile throughout the life of the task force, deteriorated. In accepting the recommendations of the task force CSC had committed itself to a new operational philosophy for federally sentenced women, but this – inevitably, given that many of the same staff remained in place – had not been reflected in practice at the Prison for Women, despite the fact that a member of the task force's working group continued to be warden. Planning for the new prisons had the effect of encouraging experienced staff at the Prison for Women to apply for positions in other prisons because, quite early on, it had been made clear to them that they were not considered suited to the new philosophy of *Creating Choices*.[11] The long-term staff members were replaced by employees with relatively little correctional experience, who had no long-term prospects at the Prison for Women and little emotional commitment to it. Budget cutbacks led to the curtailment of psychological services and contributed to tensions among the women, who were themselves worried about the changes they might have to face once the prisons were completed and they were transferred. Additionally, there were a number of "lockdowns"[12] at the prison, which severely restricted the movement of the women on the ranges, particularly those on "B" range.

Events came to a head in April 1994. The following chronology is abbreviated and adapted from the official report of the Royal Commission of Inquiry, which dealt with subsequent events at the prison.[13]

On 22 April 1994 a brief, violent confrontation took place between six women at the Prison for Women and correctional staff. A staff member believed herself to have been stabbed by a syringe, and other staff members were physically threatened. The women prisoners were maced and immediately placed in the segregation unit but were not properly decontaminated (i.e., allowed to bathe, following being sprayed). Tensions were extremely high and the next day three women, who had not been involved in the earlier incident but were in segregation, individually harmed themselves, took a hostage, and attempted suicide. Staff had urine thrown at them and a further macing took place, with the woman involved also not being decontaminated. On 26 April correctional staff demonstrated outside the prison, demanding that the women in the original incident should be transferred. Staff also refused the warden's request that they should unlock the ranges.[14]

On the evening of 26 April a male institutional emergency response team (IERT) conducted a cell extraction[15] and strip search of eight women in the segregation unit. The team wore combat-style protective clothing and carried shields, which were banged against the cell bars to intimidate the women. The extraction took place during the middle of the night, when all the women were securely contained in their cells, and some were asleep. Following the extraction the women either had their clothing cut off them, primarily by males, or removed their own, and were marched, naked, from their cells, which were then cleared of all furniture. The women were eventually returned to their cells and left lying on the concrete floors, wearing paper gowns (which had the effect of a minimal "bib"), leg irons, and body belts. The windows were left open for over three hours, despite the cold temperatures outside, and the women remained in those general conditions until the following day, when they were given a "security" blanket. The entire procedure was videotaped.

The following evening seven of the women were subjected to body cavity searches and these took place on cell floors, while they remained in restraints. There were subsequent doubts as to whether consent to the searches had been freely given by the women. They were then permitted to shower and were returned, naked, to their cells, where the water was turned off and toilets could not be flushed. All of the women involved in the various incidents were denied access to lawyers. On 6 May five women were transferred to a wing of the Regional Treatment Centre within Kingston Penitentiary (for men). An application for habeas corpus eventually allowed them to return to the Prison for Women, where they remained in segregation for up to nine months.

A national board of investigation was convened by CSC to investigate the various events. It comprised four correctional employees, including the warden-designate of the Nova Institution for Women. Madame Justice Arbour strongly suggested, despite the denials of the commissioner and the senior deputy commissioner, that their appointments were compromised by the fact of their all being in the midst of "review and promotion" supervised by those to whom they would ultimately be reporting (Arbour 1996, 110). The board appeared to be confused by the extent of its mandate and had a very short period of time when its members could all be together to conduct the investigation. They did not review all the available evidence and, in particular, only briefly viewed the IERT videotape. Their draft report was then revised and edited at least nine times at national headquarters. The report gave a great deal of detail about all the women involved in the incidents, emphasizing their prolonged records as violent offenders and, in a sense, providing justification for the way in which staff responded to them. The final report made no mention of the videotape, and there were numerous omissions and errors of fact. It specifically stated that the women were stripped by female staff and did not indicate that they were then left without mattresses and blankets (CSC 1994a, 22; Arbour 1996, 116).

In Canada a correctional investigator[16] acts as an "ombudsperson, independent of the Correctional Service of Canada" and "reports directly to the Solicitor General" (Arbour 1996, 20). Soon after the incidents the correctional investigator met with the women and thereafter consistently raised relevant issues with CSC. His requests for documentation from CSC met with lengthy delays, and representatives from his office did not get to see the IERT video until late January 1995. On 14 February 1995 the correctional investigator sent a special report to the solicitor general, chronicling – among other matters – his concerns about the use of the IERT team, the use of segregation, and the failings of the Board of Investigation. The solicitor general announced that there would be an independent inquiry and, on the same day, the Canadian Broadcasting Corporation (CBC) transmitted a *Fifth Estate* program that contained substantial extracts from the IERT video. There was a largely horrified reaction across the country, despite a *Toronto Sun* editorial that issued "congratulations to the all-male emergency response team that so professionally put down the April riot at Kingston's infamous Prison for Women" (23 February 1995).[17] On 19 April 1995 Madame Justice Arbour was appointed to head an inquiry. Her eventual report castigated CSC for its "deplorable defensive culture" (Arbour 1996, 174) and showed, in forensic detail, how CSC chose to disregard "the Rule of Law" whenever it suited its purposes and had a "disturbing lack of commitment to the ideals of justice" (198).

Remembering how recently CSC had accepted *Creating Choices*, and

that it was in the midst of planning the proposed new prisons, one of
Madame Justice Arbour's comments appears to sound a particularly
relevant note of warning: "despite its recent initiative, the Correctional
Service resorts invariably to the view that women's prisons are or
should be, just like any other prison" (Arbour 1996, 178). In chapter
7 the disturbing parallels between what happened in April 1994 at the
Prison for Women, and what subsequently happened at one of the
newly opened prisons, Nova Institution for Women, is discussed. But
it is now time to turn to the new prisons themselves and to deal with
them in very general terms before focusing upon the Edmonton Institution for Women. It should be borne in mind that the Arbour Commission's hearings were taking place as the first of the prisons were
opening, and the publication of the subsequent report, with its
damning conclusions, led to the resignation of Commissioner of Corrections John Edwards. He was replaced by an interim commissioner,
John Tait, who was himself replaced by Ole Ingstrup, who had been
commissioner at the time of the task force.

A NEW STYLE OF PRISON?

The new prisons were eventually to be sited in Truro (Nova Scotia),
Joliette (Quebec), Kitchener (Ontario), Edmonton (Alberta), and
Maple Creek (Saskatchewan) and the first two were some distance
from the task force-specified localities. While it might have been anticipated that the Healing Lodge would have unique design features, it
could have been assumed that the others would have features in
common. Despite this, separate architects were commissioned for each
prison and plans were produced that specifically suited each site. The
one feature they had in common – apart from the Healing Lodge,
which did not have one – was the inclusion of enhanced units
(maximum security units) as an extension or integral part of the main
administration building. All the prisons had "cottage"-style accommodation, which was an attempt to introduce some semblance of community normality into the living arrangements. They were to incorporate "all environmental factors known to promote wellness ... natural
light, fresh air, colour, space, privacy and access to land" (TFFSW 1990,
115). The houses, apart from an eventual supported living unit at
Nova (Truro), were solely occupied by the women; staff visited to do
"head counts" but were not permanently placed in each house (which
was a surprising and complete departure from the task force model).
Overall, 285 regular and enhanced unit beds were provided for federally sentenced women. There were also a further seventeen segregation
cells, which, officially, were not classified as "beds."

Although the task force carefully considered the proposed physical layout of the new facilities, it was not prescriptive as to how each would look but had noted Axon's "speculative" findings that there was a "connection between styles of security and the atmosphere within the institutions." Axon (1989, 10) said that, while Shakopee prison (the exemplar for the new prisons) had no perimeter fence, it was fortunate in that it had the support of the local community, and she concluded that the "optimal arrangement" was for the new prisons to have "a perimeter fence to permit greater inmate freedom within its confines." With the exception of the Healing Lodge, which had none, all the new prisons had relatively low fences, conveying to the community the low risk federally sentenced women generally presented. Only around the exercise yards of the enhanced units were more substantial fences used, and these were generally not visible to the public.

Living conditions within each of these houses were radically different from anything previously available at either the Prison for Women or provincial prisons.[18] The women were expected to clean and cook for themselves, having budgeted for and ordered food, and could choose to cook communally or individually. They were expected, with the assistance of staff, to co-exist with women with disparate needs and from widely varying backgrounds. Disagreements were to be resolved through house meetings, and the ultimate sanction for infraction of the rules was removal to the enhanced unit. Each woman had her own room (cell) and within "her" house she had some degree of choice about how she might live. For its "ideal prison"[19] the task force had also idealized women and their individual capabilities.

FURTHER DEFINING
THE "DIFFICULT-TO-MANAGE" WOMAN

In planning these new prisons there was an assumption that most women would be capable of responding to the demands and responsibilities placed upon them. With hindsight, this seems a curiously naïve view to adopt, but it was linked to the task force's reluctance to label women. While it referred to *"all federally sentenced women"* as being "high needs" and requiring a "supportive environment" (TFFSW 1990, 90, emphasis added), these needs evidently did not preclude their being capable in other, supposedly "womanly," spheres. It was, once again, the rhetoric of the reformatory, which emphasized the femininity of both prisoners and the women charged with their guidance.

Creating Choices was predicated on the assumption that federally sentenced women presented "high needs/low risk," and the task force had concluded that a changed environment would make their management less challenging. Additionally, the task force had only reluctantly identified 5 percent of federally sentenced women as being in need of extra care and support. "Enhanced units" were not part of the vocabulary of the task force; it had only envisaged "cottages," with one being for women who were "especially high risk or high need ... requir[ing] high levels of staffing, support, counselling and other aspects of dynamic security" (TFFSW 1990, 116), while another was to be a separate "assessment cottage" for new arrivals.

It was not until June 1994 (two months after the events leading to the Arbour Commission) that CSC *officially* decided to increase the number of maximum security beds to 10 percent.[20] Yet this figure of 10 percent high-needs women had been decided much earlier, by July 1992, when the operational plan announced that "approximately 10 percent of the women will require accommodation that appropriately reflects their increased security needs" (CSC 1992, 69).[21] That 1992 document contradicted itself because it contained no evidence for such a leap; rather, the reverse. The operational plan discussed the classification of women and said:

Two separate methods [of classification used by CSC] ... both demonstrated that less than 5% of the women warranted a maximum security classification, the large majority being either minimum or low medium. In 1991, only 4.6% of the in residence Prison for Women population were classified as maximum security. (CSC 1992, 10)

In then going on to describe the envisaged enhanced units, the operational plan inaccurately cited the task force as being the source of the 10 percent figure (CSC 1992, 38). At no time did the task force commit itself to a figure of 10 percent. It would appear that CSC either had its own, unpublished, figures upon which it was relying – or it had its own plans. That initial 1992 operational plan suggested that "the presence of vigilant, interactive staff ... should preclude the need for escorts between the enhanced unit and the general program area" (CSC 1992, 38), something which did not happen once the Edmonton Institution for Women (EIFW) and Nova Institution for Women (Nova) opened. The plan also indicated that the enhanced unit would be solely for "difficult-to-manage" women, and that most women would be immediately assigned to a house rather than to "potentially inappropriate accommodation (e.g. enhanced security unit)" (30). By July 1995 CSC had changed tack, acknowledging that the units were by then intended to house "those who were acting out, serious escape risks ... and new admissions" and that the smallness of the new prisons precluded separate provision for these disparate groups (CSC 1995, 7). At the "brain-storming session" at which these comments were made, reservations were expressed about using enhanced units and the possibility that they would be "re-introducing and entrenching a 'jailhouse culture'" (13).

NEW PHILOSOPHY, NEW STAFF

"Jailhouse cultures" are not only encouraged by the type of prison building: the quality and commitment of staff plays a crucial role in promoting or forestalling such climates. The task force had been vague but recommended that staff should be recruited from "a wide variety of backgrounds and educational traditions" (TFFSW 1990, 116). The draft operational plan amplified this, stating: "staff must be creative, demonstrate understanding of and empathy toward [sic] women and multi-cultural groups" (CSC 1992, 16). In the event, the majority of staff recruited as primary workers (guards) for the new prisons had no previous experience of corrections – a policy deliberately pursued so as to avoid importing any of the old correctional attitudes into the new prisons. A large number of the new guards were very young and many had backgrounds in social work or equivalent spheres. They under-went the basic correctional training and had an additional period of training in "women-centred" issues. In line with the philosophy of *Creating Choices* there was a flat structure to the staffing hierarchy, with a warden (reporting to her regional deputy commissioner), deputy warden, team leaders, and primary workers as well as a number of other professionals and support workers.

In employing such staff it was anticipated that the new prisons would rely, to a great extent, on "dynamic security," "based upon active and meaningful staff/offender interaction [which would] be the primary means of ensuring safety and security" (CSC 1992, 69). In other words, direct and frequent contact between staff and women would facilitate the staff's understanding and prediction of the women's likely behaviour, and the need for static security, such as fences and electronic detection systems, would consequently be mini-mized. Although it might be assumed that attitudes have changed greatly from the days when a former governor of Holloway Prison could write "many prison officials begin by trying to treat ... prisoners as ordinary human beings, but are compelled by their experience to do otherwise" (Kelley 1967, 58), there is nevertheless a certain truth con-tained within that statement. Prison guards' attitudes to prisoners change, irrespective of what their training might have led them to expect. Their need for personal safety means that "some wariness (or even mistrust)" creeps into their relationships with prisoners (Liebling and Price 2001, 90). Yet their growing knowledge of some of the prisoners may also lead to a blurring of the professional barriers, and "they may come to like and respect certain of their charges ... sometimes more than they like and respect their own managers" (124). These changing relationships have an inevitable effect on the day-to-day management of a prison, and it could not be assumed that dynamic security at the new Canadian prisons would remain free of such influences. The concept of dynamic security also implied that the women would be responsive to, and trust, such interaction and would voluntarily wish to modify their own behaviour in the interests of the prison's security. Federally sentenced women were being asked to share responsibility for the security of the prison in which they were imprisoned (see Hannah-Moffat, 2001). What will now be examined is whether such theorizing survived the reality of the new prisons, using the Edmonton Institution for Women (EIFW) as the first example.

EDMONTON INSTITUTION FOR WOMEN

In the Prairies[22] many towns had sent unsolicited bids for the prison as soon as the task force was published, even though it had stipulated where the new prisons should be sited. Some of the submissions were united by a common thread: they claimed that their communities were dying as a consequence of recession and changing employment patterns. One town wrote: "it could mean the difference between growth and the death of our community. Our children are leaving upon high school graduation and we have nothing to offer to bring them back. Edmonton doesn't want this facility. They don't need it. We do!"[23] Other towns were keen to emphasize the savings that could be made, should the prison be built alongside other local correctional institutions, an argument that was also used in the Atlantic region.[24] Yet Edmonton won in the end, and on 23 November 1992 Solicitor General Doug Lewis announced that, despite hundreds of applications received from across Alberta, the city had been successful in its application. (The Atlantic and Ontario sites had been announced eleven months earlier.) Four months later the assistant warden for correctional programs at Saskatchewan Penitentiary, Jan Fox, was appointed warden of Edmonton Institution for Women.[25]

"A TOWN THAT DOESN'T WANT THE PRISON, NEVER WANTED THE PRISON"[26]

Edmonton's successful bid did not necessarily mean that local citizens backed the initiative, as soon became apparent. In choosing a locality for the new prison CSC were obliged to look at all available federally owned properties in the area. Seven properties were identified, with only one meeting the criteria, and in April 1993 it was announced that undeveloped military land would house the new prison. Public reaction was instantaneous and almost unanimously unfavourable. Local residents demanded that the facility should be moved to a non-residential area and that it should not "invade their community." The *Edmonton Sun*, not known for its liberal views, took the campaigners to task in an editorial headlined "Stop the whining": "They're ba-a-a-ck. That old NIMBY gang is once again in full cry ... [Castle Downs] has ... the Griesbach military base on which the proposed prison would be located. That's a real break for the taxpayer who for once isn't paying big bucks for expensive real estate."[27]

Despite a series of public meetings addressed by Fox, residents remained concerned about public safety and the effect of the new prison on property prices. Local opposition prevailed and the site selection process was expanded. From the beginning of her appointment Fox was the public face of the new prison, frequently being asked to defend and explain what was proposed. Decisions were made by correctional officials, yet she was held responsible, in the public mind, for any new developments. As much of the argument about where the prison should be sited took place through the media, the warden continued to speak for CSC, emphasizing that the prison would house "high-needs" rather than "high-risk" women and stressing the limits on the women's movements, saying, "It's not like we're opening up the doors every morning and saying 'Go for it ladies, have a good day at the Mall.' I'm accountable for what happens if one of them commits an offence. Guess who will lose her job?"[28]

The Prairie Region's deputy commissioner for corrections, declared: "the site that will be chosen after consulting with the involved communities will be the one that has the least local opposition."[29] CSC began a campaign of persuasion, spending $17,000 to distribute a newsletter about the proposed prison and the newly selected sites to 172,000 households, only to be further criticized by some community groups for "distorting" the facts.[30] In December 1993 CSC finally announced that the prison would be built on a 17.5 acre site in a light industrial area to the west of the city. Federally sentenced women were to be kept physically apart from any established community, hitherto seen as an essential support component by the task force.

A particularly tight building schedule envisaged the prison being ready for occupancy in November 1995 – and the local papers kept abreast of each stage. Jan Fox continued to speak on behalf of Corrections and in July the *Edmonton Journal*, highlighting the fears of local

Edmonton Institution for Women

residents, quoted her as saying that there would be rigorous security for the few high-risk inmates. A pre-opening audit of the prison was conducted by the National Headquarters' Audit Team in late September, and, at that stage, less than seven weeks before opening, none of the buildings was completed, so the team's comments were necessarily restricted.[31] However, some points, relevant to issues that later emerged were addressed, specifically: the number of women due to arrive at EIFW, and classified as medium and maximum security, exceeded those provided for when the prison was designed; the perimeter fencing did not reflect the security needs of that larger-than-anticipated group; contracts for the provision of programs were not agreed; the Health Care Centre was not built, nor the staff for it hired; and, standing orders[32] were incomplete (CSC 1996b, 26).

In mid-November the *Edmonton Journal* described preparations for the opening of the prison and Fox was quoted as saying "things are really shaping up. There may still be a few problems, but nothing life-shattering."[33] The opening ceremonies were held on 18 November 1995, and on 20 November the prison formally opened with the arrival of four women, who were followed by several small groups from the Regional Psychiatric Centre in Saskatoon during December, January, and February.

FROM CONCEPT TO PHYSICAL REALITY

What happened at EIFW during the first year of its opening is now explored, and, at this point, the prison's design needs clarification because it was fundamentally linked to subsequent events.

As initially constructed, with its two-metre high chain-link fence, the prison could easily have been mistaken for a light industrial or office complex. Seen from the road, there was a very large semi-circular facade to the prison, which contained all the administration areas as well as workshops, education rooms, a gymnasium, chapel, Aboriginal spirituality room, and health care centre. The frontage hid a large grassed and paved courtyard containing five double storey living units as well as a private visiting house,[34] all outwardly similar in style to much Canadian civilian housing. Each living unit could house eleven women, and some included provision for children's accommodation. A large, well-equipped kitchen was adjacent to the communal living area. Bedrooms were on both floors and each was fitted with standard Corcan[35] furniture, with the effect being that of well appointed student accommodation. The women had keys to their own rooms (cells) and each could purchase her own television. When the prison first opened all living unit doors and windows, although alarmed, could not be locked because of fire regulations. Staff were not permanently positioned within the houses, and the women were living in almost a reverse panopticon, where the continuous disciplinary surveillance of staff was absent and replaced by the self-surveillance of the women themselves.

The enhanced unit, attached to the administration building, was a maximum security unit and, when the institution first opened, was intended to house: new arrivals, those in segregation for purposes of discipline, those in crisis, vulnerable women (in need of protection from other prisoners), and those whose escape could possibly place the public in danger. The enhanced unit (then) consisted of two wings. One was more secure, and its six cells – the use of this word reflected the difference in appearance and style compared with the minimum/medium living units – had steel beds and integral lavatories. The other wing contained a kitchen, and all six cells had wooden furniture, with the women using a shared bathing facility. The only room available for programming was small and was used by both wings, with the added complication that it also provided the only access to the small exercise yard. The control post for the whole of the prison was also placed in the enhanced unit. From this post staff had to oversee all of the houses (alarms went off and had to be checked whenever house doors were opened) as well as monitor radio transmissions. Control staff could not concentrate solely on the women living in the enhanced unit and were not meant to.

The prison's official capacity was for fifty-eight women. Additionally, the enhanced unit had twelve cells, which were double-bunked, so could actually hold twenty-four women. Six of the enhanced unit cells were segregation cells and were not considered part of the prison's official capacity, yet, as will be seen, they were used when the prison opened. The prison therefore had an *unofficial* capacity of eighty-two. However, in September 1993, when the site of the prison was still undecided and CSC was anxious to allay fears about the proposed prison, the local *Mill Woods Newsletter* (publishing information provided by CSC) said: "if the prison were to open today a total of 44 women would be incarcerated ... *The larger number is intended to meet our needs well into the next millennium. There are no plans to expand the facility*" (emphasis added). As the newsletter made clear, these figures were "based on [the then] 74 Prairie Region offenders, 30 of whom will be incarcerated in an [sic] facility for Aboriginal offenders in Saskatchewan ... Only a small number of women are expected to need extra security measures." This "facility" for Aboriginal women was the Healing Lodge, originally planned as a multi-level facility but later to be restricted to minimum- and medium-security women (see chapter 9), which meant that EIFW would have to take all the Prairie maximum security women, as CSC already knew.

At the time the prison actually opened it was still far from complete. The administration building was unfinished so, instead, staff used both the private family visiting house and offices, which were some distance from the prison. The health care unit, workshops, gymnasium, chapel and Aboriginal spirituality room, education room, and library remained largely unavailable to the women. The enhanced unit, where all new arrivals were placed, irrespective of classification, had been completed just two days prior to opening and became the unintended focus of activity within the prison. Building debris cluttered the grounds and the particularly harsh Edmonton winter added to the difficulties all faced in coming to grips with the new prison. Programs were scheduled to be held within the administration building, but its incomplete state meant that all programs initially had to be held in the cramped enhanced unit, where the majority of the maximum security women were also living. (Pressure on space, occasioned by the disproportionate number of maximum security women, led to House D being temporarily designated as maximum security.) In order to prevent the passage of drugs, any woman taking a program was strip-searched every time she entered or left the enhanced unit, irrespective of her security classification.

AN UNMANAGEABLE PRISON?

By the end of February, with twenty-five women in the institution, there had been ten incidents of self-injury (with four requiring visits to hospital), one attempted suicide, and one attempt to swallow an unnamed substance. Only one of these incidents had taken place outside the enhanced unit. On 29 February 1996 Denise Fayant was found with a ligature around her neck in her cell in the enhanced unit, and she died on 2 March.

A national board of investigation was set up to investigate Ms Fayant's death and other incidents at the prison. Such investigations have: "three levels ...: local, regional and national. *The most serious incidents are the subject of national investigations.* In these cases, the Board of Investigation is appointed by the Commissioner. To ensure the objectivity of the investigations, all National Boards of Investigation have a community member as a full Member of the Board" (emphasis added).[36]

Before the investigation could begin three further incidents at the prison – separate assaults on a nurse and a doctor, and an attempted suicide – caused the terms of reference for the investigation to be enlarged. The Board of Investigation began work at the institution on 18 March 1996, and by then two further incidents had occurred, so the board finally investigated one suicide, two attempted suicides, two assaults on staff, and thirteen incidents of self-injury. These had all happened within a period of a little over three months, and the prison, at that stage, had been open for just under four months. (There had been another incident in December 1995, but this was outside the board's remit.) The board was also asked to comment on "underlying factors that may have played a role in these incidents" (CSC 1996b, 4). By the time the board submitted its official report it knew that the cause of Denise Fayant's death was murder rather than suicide, but it had not addressed it as such. Meanwhile, in February there had been another suicide at the still-functioning Prison for Women.

As outlined in the board's report, twenty-five women were held at the prison while the team was investigating: ten were in the minimum and medium security houses and fifteen were in the (temporarily maximum security) House D and enhanced unit. These fifteen maximum security women represented 60 percent of the then population of the prison. As has earlier been explained, the enhanced unit had multiple functions and was expected to house other than just maximum security women. Ten women were involved in the eighteen separate incidents, of whom eight of the women were known to have a history of self-injury prior to arriving at Edmonton. In total, seven were classified as maximum security and eight were Aboriginal. The overcrowding in the enhanced unit had an important part to play in events leading up to the death of Denise Fayant. Her death needs to be examined in some detail because the circumstances reflected the difficulties both women and staff faced at the incomplete prison. They also reflected the struggle to implement the actual philosophy of *Creating Choices* and the manner in which women reacted to their changed circumstances. In discussing this event the Board of Investigation's report, and the subsequent Fatality Inquiry,[37] will be referred to. Both provided retrospective views of events.

THE DEATH OF DENISE FAYANT

Denise Fayant arrived at Edmonton on 28 February 1996. She had made five suicide attempts since 1994 and had been involved in twenty-one violent incidents, many of which had targeted her rather than been instigated by her. Concern had been expressed at the prospect of her arrival at Edmonton because she was known to be "incompatible"[38] with a large number of women on the enhanced unit and was also due to testify in court against a prisoner held there. Not only was Ms Fayant incompatible with many of the women in the enhanced unit but some of those women were also incompatible with each other, a phenomenon unanticipated in the "supportive environment" of the new prisons (TFFSW 1990, 90). This left the staff at Edmonton with no clear alternatives; they could not separate everyone. Further, although House D had been redesignated to accommodate maximum security women, it was only available for those who had demonstrated their reliability, as fire regulations prevented the doors being locked. According to an exhibit presented at the Fatality Inquiry, Ms Fayant had written on the transfer form that she did not want to go to "inhance [sic]," preferring to be sent to House D. As she had not been formally assessed, and was considered a risk to the community, that was impossible.

In the new spirit of *Creating Choices*, whereby the imprisoned women were informed and consulted, three meetings were held with them to explain the difficulties posed by Ms Fayant's arrival and to obtain their cooperation. Not only were the women being asked to take responsibility for their own behaviour within the prison but they were also being asked to guarantee the safety of another prisoner. It was a further step in the "responsibilizing" of the women (see Hannah-Moffat 2001). At the last meeting – attended by all the women at Edmonton – they agreed, in the presence of an Elder and Warden Fox, to "take care" of Denise Fayant. As one woman present at the meeting said two and a half years later, this phrase was ambiguous – a point also made in the Inquiry Report.[39]

On arrival at the enhanced unit Denise Fayant was visibly frightened by her reception. She was later advised to remain in the view of staff if she was concerned for her safety, and she was given the choice of being locked up for the night, which she declined. Just prior to lock-up a staff member went into her wing to tell the women to return to their cells and noticed that Ms Fayant was not in her room. She was finally discovered lying between her bed and the wall, with a ligature around her neck. Artificial respiration could not begin immediately because the first aid bag did not contain a mouthpiece, and oxygen could not be supplied because keys were unlabelled and staff could not find the correct ones for the healthcare centre. Denise Fayant was eventually taken to hospital, where she died. The police, having been told by prison staff that Ms Fayant had been suicidal in the past, assumed that this was again the case and conducted no immediate interviews, nor did they collect evidence. Their theory was passed on to the hospital and to the medical examiner, who made the same assumption. Consequently, no forensic autopsy was conducted. There was simply an external examination of the body, following which Ms Fayant was cremated. As later emerged, a member of the prison's staff told police the night of the suspected suicide that she was unsure Denise Fayant had killed herself. A homicide inquiry was not launched until May, when an anonymous phone call to a local radio station suggested that her death was suspicious. Two prisoners (one of whom Ms Fayant was due to testify against) were later charged and convicted of her murder.

As Remi Gobeil, the deputy commissioner for the Prairies, testified at the Fatality Inquiry, there was no option for Ms Fayant but Edmonton. The whole thrust of federal correctional policy was that women should be moved to Edmonton from the Regional Psychiatric Centre (RPC) (where they had been detained in order to bring them closer to their homes rather than because of a need for psychiatric treatment). Following CSC's acceptance of the Emergency Measures accompanying *Creating Choices* it was not federal policy to move Ms Fayant to the still-functioning Prison for Women, and the prison in Burnaby, British Columbia, had declined to take her. Gobeil elaborated: "We were operating under a philosophy that we did not want to use those places. We were going to use our own facility in Edmonton ... It was a program that had been accepted by our Minister, had been accepted by Treasury Board; had been accepted by anybody who can say yea or nay to such a thing in our system. And that was the total thrust of our philosophy on how to manage women offenders in the Correctional Service of Canada" (Chrumka 2000, 68). Nevertheless, Ms Fayant was consulted about the move in a manner that suggested that she had choices. Gobeil clarified that position: "the review [of Ms Fayant's proposed move was] largely to fulfil the requirements of a paper world, you know. It was very clear to everyone that we were closing down the RPC with reference to a Women's Unit" (ibid.).

That decision-making process should be seen in the context of what had been happening elsewhere. As noted at the beginning of this chapter, Madame Justice Arbour had begun the public hearings into the April 1994 events at the Prison for Women in August 1995. These continued for some months, and she was expected to submit her findings no later than 31 March 1996. Because of what was emerging at the hearings CSC could not have failed to anticipate that Justice Arbour's conclusions might be unfavourable; CSC was under considerable pressure to open the new prisons and to demonstrate that it remained committed to the closure of the Prison for Women. Indeed, Arbour (1996, xvi) noted that her reporting deadline was constrained by the fact that "the two largest new regional facilities will open in the coming months," which implied that her report could be expected to have an impact on their running. It has been suggested that Arbour "scared, rushed and revealed" CSC, and it is not improbable that the pressure to open Edmonton on time was related.[40]

It is already clear that Edmonton had been asked to take a larger than anticipated number of maximum security women, that the prison was not designed to cope with such numbers, and that management had no choice in the matter. The difficulties were compounded by the fact that the prison was incomplete when the first women were transferred, which led to the institutionalizing of strip-searching for all the women, and that there was a great deal of pressure on the few amenities available. As the Fatality Inquiry into Denise Fayant's death revealed, one of the women already held in the enhanced unit had been involved in the 1994 incidents at the Prison for Women. Although many of the staff members at Edmonton were new to corrections, it is unlikely that they would have been left unaware of the woman's history – and the histories of other women classified as maximum and transferred to the prison. This knowledge would have added to the worries of new staff members as they struggled to apply a new philosophy of corrections, while lacking many of its components, such as adequate accommodation and the ability to provide consistent programming.

But Gobeil's statement was important in another sense, too, because it highlighted the limits of "choice" at that stage. Some five and a half years after the task force had completed its work CSC was unable, within a newly built prison, to provide "at-risk" or "vulnerable" women with safe accommodation. Protective custody was not part of the philosophy of *Creating Choices*. Previously, the constraints of choice had been illustrated by the dilemma facing federal women held provincially, who had to choose between location and programming. Women such as Denise Fayant faced a much starker choice – safety, through being confined to a cell for twenty-three hours each day in protective custody, or risk of physical harm. The dilemma was one shared by staff, as Warden Fox explained during the Fatality Inquiry:

Q: And when you were looking at some of these prisoners coming to your place, did you have another realistic option as to where they could go other than Edmonton?
Fox: I did not believe that I did.
Q: Could you go to Mr. Gobeil and present him with another realistic option?
Fox: I would not have been able to present him with a realistic option. (Chrumka 2000, 65)

At that point Edmonton was alone in being unable to refuse women. Both Nova and the Healing Lodge had exercised the right to do so.

FURTHER INCIDENTS

Incidents at the prison had not ceased with the death of Denise Fayant, and the media remained focused on the prison. On 12 April three medium security women escaped over the fence. One was at large for two days and two for a week. On 27 April another prisoner climbed out of a window in the maximum security house, scaled the fence, spent three hours outside, then phoned the police and asked them to come and get her. This was the first ever escape by a maximum security woman from a federal prison in Canada. During this period there were a number of calls for the resignation of Jan Fox, who still had the task of responding to the media. Fox wanted the public to know that a bigger fence did not guarantee there would be no future escapes, saying "I don't want people to think, 'well gee, we have a fence therefore this will never happen again.' That would be misleading."[41] As the public "face" of the prison Fox was now having to defend situations that the local community had been told were most unlikely to arise.

On 30 April three other maximum security women, including one later convicted of the murder of Denise Fayant, walked out of an unlocked door in the gymnasium but were caught almost immediately. With public concern continuing to mount, the pressure on officialdom finally proved too much, and on 1 May 1996 it was announced that the prison would be closed, but the women were not immediately informed. The women were sent from work back to their houses, accompanied by staff and members of the Citizens' Advisory Committee, and were told not to listen to the radio or watch television. They inevitably did so and heard the closure news, by which point the perimeter fence was surrounded by news teams. Jan Fox later visited the houses to say that she was doing all she could to ensure that the minimum security women would be allowed to stay. That evening the maximum and medium women, in the full glare of the television cameras, were removed from the prison and staff members were left to pack up their belongings and forward them. Ted Bailey, the chair of the Citizens' Advisory Committee, was quoted as saying that four inmates slashed themselves after they learned from news reports that nineteen women were to be removed from the prison. Bailey blamed the provincial correctional authorities for the self-harm, citing the inappropriate manner of making the announcement. Eight women remained at the prison during the closure period and were housed in the enhanced unit for much of that time, under constant supervision and with levels of security that their classification did not justify.

On 2 May Alberta's minister of justice, Brian Evans, said he had been asked by the federal justice minister, Herb Gray, to take charge of the more "dangerous" inmates until the prison renovation and a security review could be completed. It was also announced that csc would be spending $400,000 to make Edmonton more secure – and that maximum security women would return to the prison once the upgrade was completed.[42]

Fox continued to take the brunt of sustained media criticism, and the debate about EIFW spilled onto the floor of the House of Commons in Ottawa. But it was not only local and national politicians who were calling for Fox's departure. The *Edmonton Journal* vociferously called for Fox's resignation but also apportioned the blame more widely: "Fox shouldn't shoulder the whole blame for the women's prison fiasco. Everyone, from Corrections Canada to the prison staff, to the prisoners themselves, bears some responsibility."[43]

The staff of the prison found themselves in limbo, managing a prison reduced to holding eight minimum security women in a maximum security enhanced unit, while not knowing when the other women would be allowed back to the prison. Edmonton residents wanted to know just which categories of federally sentenced women would be returning once the prison was functioning again, and no one, publicly, knew what would happen to the women who had been removed from Edmonton. CAEFS' executive director, Kim Pate, wrote to Commissioner Ingstrup, having discovered that csc was once again withholding information from the society: "I ... find it most disturbing to have been advised on the afternoon of July 8, 1996 that the options for the Prairie women were not clearly elucidated, only to now have a document, dated July 9, 1996, which details said 'options,' including a draft press release and allusion to a strategy regarding the manner in which our organization should be dealt with." She wanted to know: "what other impact has or will the EIFW situation have upon the transitional planning, opening, programming, staff training and accountability mechanisms for the other women's prisons?"[44] – a question voluntary agencies from across Canada were also asking.

Individual CAEFS' groups added their voices: "the security and other institutional problems there [at EIFW] are the result, not of the implementation of a model based on *Creating Choices*, but rather are the result of failure to implement a model faithful to *Creating Choices*," wrote the director of the Ontario Region to Solicitor General Gray.[45] CAEFS' president, Susan Hendricks, also wrote to Gray: "despite all you have learned about the manner in which the senior managers of the Correctional Service of Canada have consistently and unabashedly misled you in the past [as revealed at the Arbour inquiry], you appear to be once again accepting their notions and exculpatory explanations of the configuration of events in Edmonton over the past six months."[46] Once again, CSC was imposing its own solutions. Once again, the lessons of history were being relearned (see Cohen 1985).

CHANGING THE IMAGE
OF FEDERALLY SENTENCED WOMEN

The focus of the official discourse was starting to change. Whereas the previous emphasis had been on the low risk of the women, whom the local community could welcome, by 23 July 1996 Ole Ingstrup was writing to Kim Pate: "internal and perimeter security enhancements [at Edmonton] are being put in place ... safeguarding the community from undue risk." Pate remained a consistent observer and critic of developments, and her interventions were not always welcomed, as is evident in this letter from Remi Gobeil: "if indeed you have new solutions, I would like to discuss them, but to simply reiterate that everyone should simply be returned to the EIFW, in my view, demonstrates the E. Fry Society's lack of appreciation for what occurred there over the winter months, an underestimation of the inmates we deal with and lack of responsibility vis-à-vis the safety of the public, the staff and inmates."[47] Just who was responsible for this "underestimation" – and whether it was "underestimation" rather than failure to plan adequately, or interpret faithfully, as CAEFS had alleged – was not addressed.

Nearly three months after the women were removed from Edmonton they still had not been told their final destination, but on 22 August the *Interim Instruction: Placement of FSW in the Prairie Region* (CD [Commissioner's Directive] 500) was issued: "placement of female inmates in the Prairie Region may ... be made to an institution other than a women's institution." This paved the way for placing federally sentenced women back inside men's prisons, an option that the task force had entirely rejected on the basis of federally sentenced women's histories of physical and sexual abuse at the hands of men.

The openings of Grand Valley Institution in Ontario and Etablissement Joliette in Quebec were delayed as a consequence of events at Edmonton. Ole Ingstrup wrote to Kim Pate, saying that a decision had been made that maximum women would not be transferred to EIFW "at this time" as EIFW would have enough to cope with in accommodating the approximately twenty medium and minimum women waiting to be transferred as well as new admissions. Ingstrup added: "The FSW [federally sentenced women's] population has increased significantly during the last two years. The three regional facilities do not have the capacity to house all the women in their respective region of residence."[48] Yet some three years earlier Edmonton residents had been told that the maximum bed occupancy of the prison would not be needed until "well into the next millennium." Again, predictions were being disproved.

In the same letter Ingstrup commented on the women's mental health needs, citing work undertaken by Dr. Margo Rivera during the first three months of 1996. She had interviewed twenty-six women imprisoned at Edmonton, Nova Institution for Women, and the Prison for Women because there had been concerns that: "a minority of federally sentenced women would not be able to participate constructively in such an environment [at the new prisons] without very specialized attention being paid to their need for an enhanced level of psychological support services" (Rivera 1996, 1). Ingstrup, in citing her work, was adding to the reconstruction of the image of some of the federally sentenced women. Moreover, he was pathologizing the women, and their alleged failure to cope at Edmonton was attributed solely to their own shortcomings rather than to the failure of CSC to be adequately prepared for their arrival. (See Sim 1990 for an account of similar medicalizing of women prisoners in the United Kingdom.) While it might be said that the origin of the failure lay in the task force's reluctance to define and label more women as being both "high needs" and "high risk" (TFFSW 1990, 116), by 1995 the final responsibility for the type of provision lay with CSC.

Almost four months passed between the prison's almost complete closure and its reopening on 29 August 1996. The staff underwent retraining, but this was not fully completed by the time the women returned.[49] The prison passed its security audit and had: a higher fence, topped with razor wire; motion sensors; video surveillance; a new master control room separate from the enhanced unit; and lockable doors in the living units which did not infringe fire regulations. Throughout, the minimum security women continued to reside at Edmonton, with some reaching parole eligibility and returning to the community. Pending the completion of a national study of the future of high-risk females, no maximum security women were allowed to return to the prison. They were placed in either Saskatchewan Penitentiary or the Regional Psychiatric Centre (RPC), both of which were male prisons and in Saskatchewan rather than in Alberta. Corrections spent $289,000 on upgrading facilities at the penitentiary and a further $220,000 at the RPC. A corrections' spokesman said: "We've learned from our mistakes. We know from the experiences at the Edmonton Institution for Women that we received too many maximum-security inmates and those with mental health needs at once."[50]

On 12 September 1996 the *Interim Instruction: Regional Women's Facilities Are Not Reception Centres* (CD 500) was issued: "the current policy of the Correctional Service of Canada is that no federally sentenced woman who is designated as a maximum security inmate will be accommodated at any of the new regional facilities." A single commissioner's directive swept away a central plank of *Creating Choices*: the idea that all federally sentenced women, irrespective of their security level, would – and could – live in the same prison, sharing the same facilities. On 19 September all maximum security women were removed from the only other prison to hold maximum security women, Nova Institution for Women (with consequences that are explored in the next chapter). All such classified women would remain in men's prisons until alternative plans could be formulated, with the consequent isolation and high levels of security.[51]

Kim Pate continued her correspondence with Ole Ingstrup: "We ... are aware of the millions of dollars you are spending on new security measures for the regional women's prisons, as well as the preparation of units for women in men's prisons ... CAEFS continues to urge you to focus upon readying the staff and ensuring the availability of appropriate programs and services ... rather than engage in the regression of women's corrections in this country" (24 September 1996).

Having returned to its advocacy role, CAEFS was unlikely to acknowledge that its own representatives had contributed to the task force's failure to countenance the possibility that more than 5 percent of federally sentenced women might need extra help and/or extra security in the new prisons. The organization could not even hint at repudiating the report – nor would it have wished to (because of the light *Creating Choices* shone on federally sentenced women) – as it well knew that a number of its own members had counselled against the initial enterprise on the grounds of the possible risk of incorporation.

CSC did not release the National Board of Investigation's report until 19 September 1997, and, for the first time since the temporary closure of the prison, Jan Fox was publicly interviewed. She admitted she had made mistakes, saying: "I've never denied that and I never will, but I still believe in the philosophy ... You can call it naïve if you want, but we – the Correctional Service of Canada – believe that all these women can successfully reintegrate into our society. That's our mission."[52] There were further calls for Fox's resignation. In October the Edmonton police confirmed they were investigating charges of criminal negligence causing death and failing to supply the necessities of life in connection with Denise Fayant's death.[53] Late that month a lawsuit was filed against Fox and CSC by Ms Fayant's mother, alleging negligence in that they "failed to provide extra security for her when they knew or ought to have known that her life was in severe jeopardy."[54]

The report of the Fatality Inquiry was not published until January 2000. It contained seven recommendations, one of which read: "Members of Correctional Service of Canada ought to be compelled to read the transcript of the Fayant Inquiry for its educational merit. The evidence demonstrates a lack of fore-thought, a lack of administrative accountability and a callous and cavalier approach within Correctional Service of Canada which cannot be condoned or tolerated" (Chrumka 2000, 73). It also referred to Denise Fayant as being "helpless, a victim of a process intent upon implementing an untested concept to manage federally sentenced female inmates. She was the test. The process failed tragically and inhumanly. Her death was avoidable" (71).

THE BURDEN OF EXPECTATION

This chapter has outlined the most prominent events during the first year of the prison's opening, and it is clear that none of these events happened in isolation. The situation is perhaps best summed up by a newspaper columnist, writing earlier but encapsulating what happened:

I have been reading about human sacrifices recently. ... We think of them as relics of the ancient world but really, they aren't ... If anything, today's human sacrifices are more cruel. We sacrifice the person publicly and then let them live to endure it all. Last week the recently opened Edmonton prison for women made the news again ... And this in a town that doesn't want the prison; never wanted the prison and shows no sign of ever thinking a prison for women in Edmonton is anything but a bad idea to be terminated soon ... But as the criticism of Canada's new policy grows, who do you think will go on the chopping block? Will it be the people who insisted on the policy? Those who put it in place? The government who awarded the new prison as a prize to Edmonton? The inmates? The people who designed a prison that can't hold prisoners? Or shall we sacrifice Jan Fox?[55]

Edmonton Institution for Women was the first of the new prisons to open. It had taken five and a half years for the vision of *Creating Choices* to take physical shape and, inevitably, Edmonton carried a huge burden of expectation. The events outlined here had a profound impact on all the other new prisons, if perhaps less visibly, certainly no less deeply, at the Healing Lodge. Why was the labour of five and a half years so precipitately derailed, judged, and found wanting as a result of the presumed failings of one prison, which had been open for only five and a half months? Further, why did this particular prison cause so many individual women to respond to it in such a distressed manner? These are questions that are explored in chapter 8, in considering both EIFW and Nova as examples of what will be termed "non-Aboriginal" prisons, even though Edmonton had a very large number of Aboriginal prisoners. This is done so that the Healing Lodge may then be separately assessed as an Aboriginal prison.

For the moment, it is clear that the traumatic early history of Edmonton shows that the task force's failure to provide prescriptively for the "difficult-to-manage women" had allowed CSC to determine its own solution. That this solution so signally failed can be laid at no other door than that of CSC, although it can also be suggested that federally sentenced women themselves shared responsibility for the outcome. So it is instructive to see how Nova Institution for Women, in Truro, fared during its first year of opening, a period of time roughly contemporaneous with that of Edmonton. Did any similar situations arise? Are there notable parallels? Did events at Edmonton influence policy at that distant prison? Above all, did the two prisons embody the vision of *Creating Choices*? The next chapter explores these questions.

CHAPTER SEVEN

Nova Institution for Women

Federal departments do not necessarily separate one province from another administratively, and, for correctional purposes, the "Atlantic Region" covers the smaller provinces of Nova Scotia (NS), New Brunswick (NB), Prince Edward Island (PEI), and Newfoundland (NF).[1] During the task force consultations in these provinces a great deal was heard about the inadequate prisons available for provincially sentenced women and the enormous distances between some communities. Federally sentenced women were even more disadvantaged, generally having little option but confinement at the Prison for Women for the major part of their sentence (and then, because of the limited regimes, finding an eventual return to provincial jurisdiction difficult to adapt to). As one presenter at the consultations said: "it was not just Aboriginal women who were dislodged from their culture [by imprisonment at the Prison for Women], but Maritime women as well."[2]

EVERYONE WANTS A PRISON?

The task force had identified a site "in or near Halifax" (TFFSW 1990, 114) as its preferred location for a new prison, reflecting the fact that most federally sentenced women from the Atlantic Region came from Nova Scotia. While the task force's recommendation would not lessen the geographic dislocation for many other women – St John's (NF), for example, was approximately 966 kilometres from Halifax – it would ensure that a greater proportion of women remained in their home province. However, by May 1991, some eight months after Ole Ingstrup had accepted the report, thirteen communities across Nova Scotia were already competing with each other to attract the proposed new prison. The Atlantic provinces had significant unemployment problems compared with other parts of Canada, and, because of the associated financial benefits, there was intense political lobbying for the prison to be sited in various areas. Communities that already had federal penitentiaries stressed the savings on administrative costs that the federal government could make were it to build in their areas, as did Prairie communities. There was an awareness of the benefits Kingston (ON) derived from the several prisons located in its vicinity and an assumption that some of those benefits could be enjoyed in the Maritimes.

Chapter 6 discusses CSC's secret decision to allow communities within a hundred kilometre radius of the task force-designated locations for the new prisons to be considered as possible sites. Once this became public knowledge towns in the Maritimes that had not already done so were encouraged to submit bids. The Halifax MP Mary Clancy immediately said that no further time should be wasted "listening to people ... from Truro or Bridgewater or whatever ... Let's start looking right away for sites within the metropolitan [Halifax] area that are close to the facilities these women need." She was echoed by Felicity Hawthorne, a co-chair of the task force, speaking on behalf of CAEFS, who said that if the government were truly addressing the criteria laid down in *Creating Choices*, then it had no option but to choose Halifax as the site as "we certainly don't want those facilities out in the sticks so that every time a woman wants to go to hospital or her counsellor or whatever it's a major performance to get her there."[3] Halifax became more vocal in its lobbying for the prison, and Dartmouth, Nova Scotia's second largest city (situated just across the harbour from Halifax), also decided to pursue its own case, with the city council's administrator speaking of the "multi-million dollar economic development opportunity for the city."[4] An irate resident countered, "no way ... It's going to blow our property prices to you know where! If you want to sell your house, you won't have a snowball's chance in hell if that prison comes in."[5]

In November 1991 Halifax City Council publicly released its bid for the new prison and revealed that it included a list of eight possible sites, some of which were residential and whose owners had not been consulted.[6] There was an immediate, negative response from residents, who feared that land might be expropriated. Shortly afterwards the council barred the prison from any residential sites, and Halifax's deputy mayor suggested that, by removing them from the list, "we might have sealed our own fate."[7] That same month CSC's evaluation team assessed the various submissions, and public expectation was that either Halifax or Dartmouth would readily fulfill the location criteria stipulated in *Creating Choices*. CSC's decision was not long in coming, and the small town of Truro, on the very edge of the extended search radius, had most unexpectedly won out over all the other Nova Scotia contenders. Solicitor General Doug Lewis travelled to Truro in December 1991 to confirm the news, telling townspeople of the economic benefits the prison would bring to their town.

Few in the Maritimes had considered isolated Truro a possible site for the prison. The director of the Halifax-Dartmouth branch of the Elizabeth Fry Society said they were "deeply disturbed" by the town's selection as it had no women-centred programs for healthcare, mental health, and substance abuse,[8] and she complained that Solicitor General Lewis and the Conservative (Tory) government of Brian Mulroney had put political favouritism ahead of women's rights. She noted that the Cumberland-Colchester (Truro) MP was a Tory, whereas the Halifax MP was a Liberal.[9] The Native Women's Association of Canada (NWAC) pointed out that the criteria specified in *Creating Choices* had been ignored and, fearing a similar disregard when it came to selecting the Prairies' site, urgently asked for the steering committee to be reconvened.[10] But by February 1992 CAEFS had reluctantly recognized that the decision would not be reversed, with CAEFS' executive director Kim Pate saying that the association (through its Halifax branch) would work with Truro in order to ensure that the best possible services would be available.[11] This position of cooperation – in a sense coerced because of the needs of federally sentenced women – survived the June 1992 decision by CAEFS (and its member societies) to withdraw from the External Advisory Committee (see chapter 6), and the Halifax Elizabeth Fry Society continued to work with those planning the new Truro prison.

There were behind-the-scenes negotiations during the summer months of 1992 in an attempt to locate and agree on a site, and in July an application for the rezoning of land east of Truro was made, without any prior public consultation. (This failure to consult with the local community before making decisions was repeated a year later in Edmonton, where CSC did not appear to have learned from the mistakes made in Truro.) After protests, the rezoning request was withdrawn, and in October 1992 CSC announced that a site in a suburban area, whose residents had expressed little opposition, would house the new prison. Thérèse LeBlanc was appointed warden on 17 March 1993, and throughout the site selection process she was the "face" of corrections, as was Jan Fox in Edmonton.

The local Conservative MP represented the solicitor general at the sod-turning ceremony in October 1993 but lost his seat in the election that followed later that month. His Liberal successor had to deal with rumours in December that the prison had been put "on hold" because of calls from Liberals in Dorchester (NB) that the prison should be resited there. Thérèse LeBlanc attempted to allay fears, explaining that there would be considerable costs should the prison be relocated because the design work was specific to the site already chosen.[12] This "hiccup" overcome, tenders were expected to be let by February 1994, but in March there was a further delay when the prison was again put "on hold," following allegations that Ottawa was considering locating the prison in the military base in Chatham (NB), the riding of the Liberal premier of New Brunswick. The matter was finally resolved when the new Solicitor General, Herb Gray, intervened, confirming that Truro would indeed house the prison.

In examining the way in which the prison site was selected, what becomes apparent is that the prison was much sought after. Although residents in Halifax and Dartmouth, as well as in Truro, voiced disquiet about certain aspects of the prison, it was largely perceived as a desirable acquisition for whichever community happened to win in the end. This was in stark contrast to what was rumbling on in Edmonton, a largely prosperous city, where the local community had huge misgivings about such a project. The extending of the search radius was an economic blessing for a small town like Truro, beset by recession and the drift to the cities. This also explains why other Maritime communities did not see the awarding of the "prize" to Truro as the end of the matter, and why members of Parliament continued to lobby for the prison to be assigned elsewhere. Had the smaller communities been bidding for a lumber mill the reaction would have been the same because any new businesses meant jobs; the prison was seen as benefiting the community. Whether the community had anything to offer in return, apart from a potentially willing workforce, was not part of the debate. Whether the federally sentenced women would benefit from being accommodated in their community seemed to be entirely lost from view, as was later admitted by a member of the local steering committee that had originally worked to bring the prison to Truro: "originally our focus for bringing the Correctional Centre to Truro was based solely on what it would mean for our town in employment opportunities and other spin-offs ... The balance quickly changed, however, as the community became more involved. Now there is no question the correctional facility will definitely realize benefits from being located in Truro."[13]

BUILDING BEGINS

Construction of the twenty-one bed prison commenced some three years after the planning for a new Atlantic facility began. In September 1994 Nova's warden, Thérèse LeBlanc (who had recently been a member of CSC's National Board of Investigation into the April 1994 events at the Prison for Women, as described in chapter 6)[14] left to take charge of the Prison for Women. An interim successor held the reins at Nova until Christine Manuge was appointed warden on 17 February 1995. At that stage some of the senior team members were already in place, but the bulk of staff were still to be appointed and the nine-week training program for those selected was not due to begin for some time.[15] In April 1995 Thérèse LeBlanc returned to Truro to address a meeting of the Nova Scotia Criminology and Corrections Association. She thought the women who would be arriving at the new prison might find it harder to be there than at the Prison for Women, saying "this will be very frightening for them. They'll be losing friendships, leaving what has been their home for several years." She added that "the first six months will make or break these new facilities ... If we fail it will have consequences on our communities."[16]

At the beginning of August the federal government officially took possession of the almost completed prison. A census of federal women prisoners had revealed the need for increased capacity for Atlantic federally sentenced women, so a fourth living unit, which had been dropped from the original plan for economic reasons, was added to the prison, increasing regular bed capacity to twenty-eight (with four "unfunded"[17] beds in the enhanced unit). Officials inspected Nova to ensure that it met federal standards, and a spokesperson said "it's now a matter of getting familiar with the surroundings and carrying out training onsite to ensure all staff know the facility and what to do in the event of an emergency." To assist the opening process, women were to be transferred from Kingston in small groups.[18] The Truro public was encouraged to tour the prison and reaction was divided, as was encapsulated in an article in the local paper: "Prison or country club? That's the question under discussion over coffee in many places around Truro as tours of the soon-to-open prison move into high-gear." Manuge said that, while some might see the facility as excessive, it was less costly to build a prison in a residential style.[19] This theme was expanded upon by Commissioner John Edwards at the prison's official opening on 27 October 1995: "It would be so much easier, perhaps, to build the more traditional type of penitentiary, with high fences, cell blocks full of steel and concrete surrounded by all the latest in high-tech security systems and hardware ... For a number of inmates such institutions are and will continue to be required. They are also very expensive to build and operate. These new units cost about two thirds of what it would normally cost to build a traditional prison."[20] But Nova already contained a small section "full of steel and concrete" for that group of women: an enhanced unit. Corrections had publicized the enhanced unit in a communiqué it produced to mark the opening of the prison, explaining that it would be used both to assess new arrivals and to house those who were a danger to themselves or others. Yet the fact that some women might be a danger to others had rarely been part of the public debate about the prison.

Nova opened shortly before Edmonton, but Truro had been identified as the site of a new prison a full year before Edmonton was named. Site selection caused delays to both projects, and construction at Nova started a little after construction at Edmonton. However, Nova was half the size of Edmonton, and the construction team did not have to contend with the ferocity of an Alberta winter, so Nova was completed on time and physically ready for the women when they first began arriving. But slowness to appoint staff meant that there was little time for the new, inexperienced team to become familiar with the prison. In moving now to examine the first year of Nova's opening, it is possible to see whether any of the difficulties experienced at Edmonton were in any sense replicated in Truro.

"NOT A HOME, BUT A PRISON"

The first three carefully selected women arrived at Nova on 9 December 1995. They had flown from Kingston and, as an observer commented: "were just in a state of shock [at seeing the style of the prison and having to grapple with the degree of autonomy offered them]."[21] Shortly afterwards CAEFS' Kim Pate was asked to comment on Nova. She hoped that the opening of the facility marked a new approach by CSC towards female offenders, but she "fear[ed] that the new plan for communal living ... could be jeopardized by a lack of planning and support for the transition the women [would] have to make." Warden Manuge countered by acknowledging that there was bound to be conflict in the living houses, saying "the residential housing mirrors community living. They will have to learn conflict-resolution so that they can solve their own problems and not end up screeching, swearing or smacking each other."[22]

The prison to which the women were transferring stood in stark contrast to the high-security Prison for Women. Nova was designed specifically to take advantage of its sloping, wooded site and was located at the end of a quiet residential street. The project brief provided a broadbrush outline of what was required but, beyond being specific about the number and type of rooms required in the living houses and the enhanced unit, left the architects with remarkable freedom to design the new facility.[23] As in Edmonton, the final design gave the initial impression of an office complex, which, indeed, the frontage was. The living units were not visible from the road and, even from within the prison, were partially hidden by the tree-filled central area, providing immediate problems of supervision for staff. Part of the administration area was to the left of the entrance, and, when the prison first opened, this was open-plan and easily accessible to the women, leaving administrative staff unable to work freely with confidential materials (a situation later amended by the addition of an extra wall). A corridor led around to the education, library, craft, and other areas and eventually to the gymnasium. The second floor of the administration building contained the multi-faith spirituality room (not easily accessible to the women), further office space, the health centre, and the enhanced unit. This was the only part of the prison that came close to resembling a traditional prison, but it had no bars and was furnished with conventional porcelain washbasins and toilets as well as mirrors (with the consequences being seen some months later). The unit contained four cells, one of which could be used for observation purposes. Its small, high-walled exercise yard was in vivid contrast to the greenery of the rest of the site, and when the pre-opening audit of the prison was carried out it took the audit team a very short while to scale the wall. Once the women were in situ, there was the added complication that the locks in the enhanced unit failed to function reliably.[24] For those few staff members who had correctional experience, the first view of the prison was a shock. As one said: "I thought, 'Oh my, what are we going to do with this?' Because the way the buildings were all in line I thought, 'How ever are you going to watch what's going on? It's going to be a security nightmare ... they could walk right out of the front door [of the administration building] or walk around the building' ... it was a little bit scary."[25]

The four living units and one family visiting house were in a semi-circle towards the rear of the site. Doors and windows were alarmed but, as at Edmonton, could not initially be locked because of fire regulations. The same Corcan furniture furnished the prison, and the bedrooms (cells) again had the feel of a student-type residence. Two of the houses could also accommodate a child. The prison had a minimal fence, which acted more as a boundary marker and, in the eyes of the staff, compromised security, with the consequence that women were escorted between the administration building and their own houses instead of being allowed to move freely, as had been anticipated by the task force. Staff were not resident in any of the living units, apart from the enhanced unit, and the houses were checked hourly, with a hand-held "dyster" electronically recording each visit. Male staff entering houses were meant to call out and alert the women, and formal counts took place four times a day.[26] Staff members were permanently posi-

Nova Institution for Women

tioned in the Structured Living House when it opened in March 1996, providing support for a group of women with diverse needs.

By mid-January 1996 there were eight women in the prison, and the local community was not beyond drawing unfavourable comparisons with the perceived privileged lifestyle of the women at Nova when economic difficulties forced cuts in local budgets, leaving the bus service for the disabled under threat. "People with disabilities in Colchester County will become prisoners in their own homes [if they lose their bus]," said the service coordinator. "The real prisoners at the new women's prison will enjoy a more interesting life, needing only to walk down the hall to access gym equipment, computer training and the pending swimming pool."[27]

But life at the prison was not as easy as the papers would have their readers believe. It had been apparent almost immediately the women began arriving that a number would find living in the houses difficult. Nova was the only one of the new prisons not to have its enhanced unit enlarged (the Healing Lodge had two "quiet rooms") and so was using its four-bed unit for reception and initial assessment, administrative segregation, and maximum security women. This left little leeway for dealing with others whose behaviour required at least temporary accommodation within the unit, and, consequently, some women in need of extra support were placed prematurely in houses, none of which had resident staff. As is already clear from events at Edmonton, the houses demanded many social skills of federally sentenced women. Unlike Edmonton, where the houses were initially under-used because of the unfinished state of the prison and the security classification of many of the women, the houses at Nova were almost immediately occupied.

The Atlantic Region had – and still has – a disproportionately high number of federally sentenced women with "special needs."[28] Indeed, some could not make the initial move to Nova because it was recognized that they did not "fit" the new model. While wardens did not have the right to decline prisoners (as was made clear by Jan Fox during the Fatality Inquiry into the death of Denise Fayant), anecdotally it is clear that Christine Manuge refused to accept at least one prisoner.[29] Before the prison opened CSC realized that special provision would have to be made for these women and commissioned a study of possible intervention strategies from Whitehall. An initial examination of records had identified ten women, out of the twenty-four due to move to Nova, who were "low functioning or [had] mental health problems" (Whitehall 1995, 1). There were deep concerns about the women's ability to cope with the communal living, particularly as some of them were serially incompatible with each other. Additionally, some had been known to set fires both in the community and in prison, which made kitchen safety an issue. Under the Corrections and Conditional Release Act, 1992, prisoners should be housed in the "least restrictive environment possible" (cited in Whitehall 1995, 7). Acting on Whitehall's advice, CSC decided that Nova would be provided with a structured living house (SLH), specifically for "special needs" women, who would be supported by resident staff and specially tailored programming. As Whitehall's report was unavailable until October 1995, the SLH was not ready until March 1996, so the "special needs" women who transferred earlier had a disproportionate impact on other women sharing their houses as well as on staff. Although most women in the houses were prepared to make allowances for other women's unpredictable behaviour, it could not be expected that the majority of prisoners would willingly assume the role of helper for an unlimited period. As was made clear in a subsequent report prepared by Alan Warner,[30] the prison had little time to prepare for the SLH: an occupational therapist was hired to coordinate the changeover in March 1996 and contract staff were hired to provide round-the-clock support.

Once the SLH was finally available it became home to three distinct groups of women: the mentally challenged, who needed extensive guidance in basic living skills; those with severe mental health difficulties, who exhibited self-destructive behaviour alongside very apparent emotional distress; and a small, but influential, group of women that was felt to have been manipulative in the other living units. A program coordinator was only hired on a part-time basis, making provision for each group even more difficult, and staff members were challenged by the need to provide a program that would adequately respond to such disparate needs. According to Shimmel[31] "the Prison for Women culture was ever-present" and "individuals who did attempt ... positive changes were taunted and/or threatened to conform by other inmates" (cited in Warner 1998, 18). Warner stated quite unequivocally that, "largely, the structured living house was the only available supervised setting and thus the admission criteria [sic] became the need for *supervision*, rather than the need for a particular living situation and type of programming" (19, emphasis added).

Creating Choices had anticipated that individual cottages might serve specific purposes, but it had not expected that one cottage would need to provide for such multifarious needs, or that the combination of such needs would eventually prove to be so combustible. The staff – and not just those assigned to the SLH – had to cope with the outcome. The primary workers were almost entirely new to corrections and, as part of their case management[32] tasks, had responsibility for individual women. Their inexperience, and what was beginning to appear to be a significant underestimation of how many staff would be required to run such a facility, eventually became manifest in tiredness and stress. The wisdom of having selected Truro as a site was also being tested because the rush to open on time, combined with the late training of staff, meant that programs had not been put in place as soon as had been expected; none was available locally and the women were under-occupied and, frequently, bored: "I was promised programs, that's why I came here. I took the substance abuse programme [elsewhere] but there's no NA [Narcotics Anonymous] here. I need help with drugs. That's why I'm here."[33] The women's inability to move freely around the prison, as they had anticipated, added to their frustration and they became increasingly disturbed by what they took to be inconsistency on the part of the staff: "They don't know what to do. They ask us. We tell *them* what to do."[34]

Although programs were to appear as the prison got into its stride, the women who first arrived felt that they were part of a puzzling experiment. Even those women with a broader experience of coping socially found that the new prison presented them with enormous personal challenges after the constraints of the Prison for Women. One said she spent the first weeks wishing that she could return to Kingston – not because she preferred the cramped, old building, but because she found the new one frightening. She had grown unaccustomed to being given choices, to being treated with consistent courtesy; she found that she was longing for the certainty of the old structure, which she might not have liked but within which she was at least able to understand the "rules."[35] So distinct groups began to emerge: women who wished for change (but were also fearful of it); women who resisted change because it undermined the power they had previously enjoyed; and staff members who wanted to effect change but were unsure of how they could do so consistently. These groups were functioning within a physical environment that did not always appear to provide security and safety. Indeed, it could be said that the new buildings were potentially more dangerous than the Prison for Women because of the lack of direct supervision and the ready availability of kitchen equipment, which could be used as weapons.

If developments at Nova are now compared with what was happening at Edmonton at about the same time, similarities can be seen. In the Edmonton enhanced unit there were problems with overcrowding and disparate groups being uneasily imprisoned together. The maximum security women took a disproportionate amount of staff time and energy, leaving other women with equally demanding needs feeling neglected and ignored. In those cramped quarters the women could not have "time out" from each other, and tensions were increased as some attempted to assert their authority by "muscling" others. Undue levels of security affected all of the women indiscriminately. This situation was partially replicated at Nova but in the SLH rather than in the enhanced unit. As the SLH had been adapted, instead of specially designed from the outset, its design faults made adequate supervision difficult. Being in the house "stigmatized" the women – the house became known as "the crazy house" – and gave them little sense of the possibility of being part of a larger community (Warner 1998, 20). Some of the women could scarcely cope with their own problems, let alone with those of the other women with whom they lived in such close proximity, and Nova was simply unable to offer the degree of separation provided at the Prison for Women, however inadequate that might have been. At Nova the enhanced unit was not a long-term option for anyone, so the houses were the last – and only – resort. In a sense, this replicated the situation at Edmonton, where, as has been noted, the newly designed prison was unable to offer a safe environment for women known to be incompatible with others.

It can be seen from this comparison that both prisons had specific groups of women providing management and accommodation problems; the accommodation was either not ready for the women or was unsuited to its purpose; and inexperienced staff had difficulties in dealing with women who were not conforming to the image of the federally sentenced women they had been trained to expect. Additionally, some federally sentenced women, who were themselves new prisoners, "were affected and 'infected' by the negativity"[36] of some of the women who had transferred from the Prison for Women.

DISTANT INFLUENCES, INSTANT REACTIONS

In May 1996 the escapes at distant Edmonton (see chapter 6) overtook
the other prisons, with the exception of the Healing Lodge. All the
fences at the new prisons were to be raised to three metres and
crowned by barbed wire. As Nova's warden said at the time, "a couple
of the women felt it was unfortunate that they all have to pay the price
for what happened in Edmonton."[37] By contrast with Edmonton, the
administration building at Nova was deemed to be part of the "fence,"
so the frontage did not look remarkably different once the alterations
had been made. These included enhanced electronic surveillance along
the front, with window, door, and roof alarms, plus infra-red cameras
for night-time surveillance.

When a prison security review was announced at the end of April
one of the Nova women was quoted in the local paper as saying, "We
... prefer not to be compared to Edmonton. What happened out there
is something that they are dealing with. What is going on here is something totally different and we would like to keep it like that."[38] But
some of the women thought the addition of the fence was a positive
development for Nova because it provided protection from possible
community aggression and lessened, in their eyes, the temptation to
escape. Some also hoped that the higher fence would allow them
greater freedom of movement, without the need for constant supervision as they moved from area to area.[39] These views were not necessarily shared, and CAEFS' Kim Pate was immediate in her condemna-
tion of the decision, saying that "despite a commitment to a more
open, community based approach to the rehabilitation of women
offenders, federal correctional staff are reverting to old solutions when
problems at the new facilities arise."[40] This was a presentiment of the
fear articulated by Madame Justice Arbour (1996, 178) that: "the Correctional Service resorts invariably to the view that women's prisons
are or should be, just like any other prison." In an editorial, the local
paper expressed disappointment that a high fence should be considered
necessary for the prison: "It is a visible denial of philosophies and policies which were strongly expressed when the prison was announced. It
has been suggested the fence will be made as inconspicuous as possible
but the fact it is felt necessary to do that further underscores the
anomaly of its construction. No matter how inconspicuous it may be
made to appear it clearly affirms to all who pass by that this is not a
home but a prison."[41]

The construction of a higher fence did much more. It was indeed a
"visible denial of philosophies and policies," but it also showed that
CSC viewed all the prisons as being non-autonomous entities and had

adopted a "one-size-fits-all" approach to them. It is not being suggested that CSC should have treated federally sentenced women differently from each other, depending upon the prison in which they happened to be confined. Rather, it is being suggested that CSC gave none
of the other prisons the chance to see whether the original model proposed by the task force worked for them – and, if it did, whether their
experience could benefit practice at Edmonton. At times the women
felt that there was a higher level of surveillance at Nova than had been
the case at the Prison for Women, where the high walls allowed some
freedom of movement, albeit within a confined space. Women were
once again being subjected by CSC to the arbitrariness that they had
hoped to leave behind upon returning to their home region.

While women at Nova found the inconsistency of the staff hard to
bear, at that point many were prepared to make allowances because
they thought they might benefit. To find that the larger organization,
CSC, was prepared to allow events at a prison some 4,800 kilometres
from Nova to determine what happened to them was entirely different.
The women's resentment was shared by the staff members, whose idealism had been tested as they struggled to provide for women for
whom they had been inadequately prepared. The women's unpredictable behaviour left many staff members exhausted and unsure of
their professionalism but still largely committed to the vision of *Creating Choices*. Staff members were "flying by the seat of their pants, creating policies as circumstances arose, and then changing them when
they did not work" (Rivera 1996, 21). The sudden appearance of much
more overt security was unwelcome evidence of the fragility of the new
philosophy they were meant to be pursuing. Additionally, the raised
fences signalled to the communities that *all* the women were "high
risk," completely contradicting public assurances given earlier by CSC.

Such official responses are not uncommon, as is evident in the
United Kingdom when escapes from male prisons (documented in both
the Woodcock and Learmont inquiries) led to an escalation of security
measures in women's prisons as well. (See Carlen 1998 for a discussion
of the most immediate impact of these decisions on women prisoners.)
To act unilaterally is the simplest way to implement policy, but when
such actions appear unjust they undermine the informal structures of
control within a prison. Within the Canadian context such a heavy
response undermined the "dynamic security" so fundamental to the
running of the new prisons. The relatively "good" behaviour of the
women at Nova was immaterial, and they faced tangible proof, in the
form of higher fences, that their cooperation was no longer essential to
the security of the prisons.

Staff members were increasingly under stress as their workload increased, and Warner later highlighted some of their difficulties. When the SLH was opened the contract staff brought in from outside the correctional service had little, or no, experience of security and mental health issues. While these new staff members were then spending up to eight hours each day with the women, and building up a knowledge of them, they were not always able to communicate what they had learned to the primary workers, who retained responsibility for individual women yet spent far less time with them than did others. The primary workers felt aggrieved that their direct contact with the women had been so minimized because they had come into their positions expecting to have responsibility for specific women; instead, they were preoccupied with security and form filling, and, as Warner (1998, 19) highlights, this gave some of the women in the SLH the opportunity to play staff off against each other.

ESCALATING DIFFICULTIES

It was against this backdrop that the situation in the SLH came to a head on 4 September 1996. Following an attempted knife attack on one of the women living in the SLH, an attempt was made to remove the assailant. Some of the other women tried to intervene on her behalf and this resulted in four women being removed to the enhanced unit, where they were double-bunked because of lack of space. The following day they damaged the two cells they were occupying, and that evening an all-women cell-extraction team (CET) entered the enhanced unit and removed the women. They were then strip searched and removed to a prison in St John, New Brunswick. The whole procedure was videotaped, and a member of the Citizen's Advisory Committee was present. A CSC spokesman announced that the rest of the prison had been largely unaffected, except for the fact that all the women were confined to their quarters until late Friday, by which time a prison-wide search had been completed.[42] As is already known, the houses were unlocked because of fire regulations and, had the other women chosen to leave their houses while the women were being extracted from the SLH, Nova's staff would conceivably have been unable to cope. That the women did not was never officially recognized. Nor was it recognized that some of the new staff were as frightened by the turn of events as were some of the women observing developments from their houses.[43] One later reflected on the incident: "With a little support and consideration things could have been different. Indeed, it didn't have to happen at all and in fact it wasn't THAT big a deal. I've seen men riot and this was a bump in comparison. And do we not expect the occasional upset? These are people –

and often disturbed people – enclosed in a space together, one feeding on the other. What did they think? That this was going to be a tea party?"[44]

Nova did not have a breathing space before national decisions, again stemming from previous events at Edmonton, affected the prison. It was announced that maximum security women would no longer be held at any of the new prisons. This only affected Nova since those at Edmonton had been removed, the Healing Lodge had never been allowed them, and the opening of both Joliette and Grand Valley had been postponed. The news was due to be relayed to the women on 19 September, when the deputy commissioner for women, Nancy Stableforth, and the regional deputy commissioner, Alphonse Cormier, were also due at the prison. A dinner was to be held in the prison's gymnasium, to which a number of local residents, members of both the Citizens' Advisory Committee and the Regional Advisory Committee, representatives from the Elizabeth Fry Society, and women from the prison were invited. The meal was to be a celebration; the prison had been open for almost a year and it was thought that its record compared favourably with Edmonton's, despite the recent incident. The Atlantic Region appeared, publicly, to be developing a prison with a style of its own, and the attempt to provide a structured living unit, while flawed, was seen as a creative attempt to find effective ways of dealing with women who had been insufficiently provided for by both the task force and, subsequently, the National Implementation Committee. Yet Nova was also a prison under stress, with staff and women having taken the full brunt of opening in a very short space of time, without many of the requisite tools to hand, such as sufficient programs and community contacts. Many of the high expectations had not been realized, and for all involved there had been a very steep – and painful – learning curve.

Once it was realized that the planned removal of the maximum security women would clash with the dinner there were attempts to have the dinner cancelled or at least postponed. Pressure from the regional correctional headquarters meant this was not possible, as was explained to me by a number of people on the actual day when, in the midst of fieldwork, I asked why the dinner should be going ahead in such circumstances.[45] The venue was moved to a local hotel, and the women were eventually provided with a "takeaway" ordered in as compensation for having been excluded from the meal. During that day the prison was in a lockdown situation, with all movement suspended and the women confined to their houses. They were told during the morning that the three maximum security women were to be removed to Springhill Institution, a male prison holding some 400 men.[46] The women were eventually removed from the prison and taken to Springhill late on the evening of the nineteenth, arriving at a unit that had been hastily prepared for them. csc's spokeswoman was later to say that "the announcement created some *minor reaction* among the general population, but not those women classified as maximum-security risks (emphasis added)." She stressed that the "three or four inmates" being sent to Springhill were not necessarily those involved in the incident two weeks previously.[47]

The dinner took place, and, as one observer noted, the guests were told: "'We're just going to update you on what we're doing and we're just going to move the maximum women out of Nova and send them to Springhill Institution.' I just couldn't speak ... I was just so angry. They have us there for what I thought was a nice little supper ... getting to know each other, kind of lighten the mood after the incident [on 4–5 September 1996], end on a positive note – and this is what it is. It surprised everybody."[48] What those at the dinner largely did not know was what had actually happened at the prison during the day.

Much of what follows has been documented in a report prepared for the Atlantic Region deputy commissioner, Alphonse Cormier.[49] By contrast with Edmonton's National Board of Investigation, this was a middle tier investigation, reflecting the assumption that the incidents were not at the same level of seriousness.[50] The initial Board of Investigation's report was later to have an addendum attached, signed by one of the members of a subsequent disciplinary board of investigation, wherein certain events had been reviewed and discrepancies noted. These combined findings are now incorporated into the general chronology of events that follows.

On the morning of 19 September 1996 the women were finally told of the removal of the maximum security women, and later that morning two women in the slh began to behave disruptively, to the extent that a cet was thought necessary to remove the women from the house. As the addendum to the Board of Investigation made clear, this decision was taken by the warden, in consultation with others. Once the cet entered the house, finding one inmate in her room and having managed to persuade the other to return to hers, the situation was thought to be "calm and under control." Further instructions were sought and it was decided that both women would be removed to segregation. One of the women agreed to go voluntarily and was removed without the use of force. The other woman was offered the same choice but reacted by breaking a picture frame, cutting herself, and finally barricading herself in her room. Once her door was forced open, she was pepper-sprayed then escorted to the enhanced unit in handcuffs and leg irons. Upon reaching the enhanced unit at midday the woman was strip-searched and, as noted in the report: "when staff leave the cell, inmate — is left handcuffed (behind her back) and in leg irons, lying on her stomach, on a bed frame without a mattress or blanket. She is naked with the exception of a towel that staff draped over her" (CSC 1997a, 5).

Within half an hour the woman had managed to remove her handcuffs and place them in the toilet, refusing to retrieve them when asked to do so by staff. Again, as noted: "When staff leave the cell, inmate — - is lying on the floor, naked, with flexicuffs applied to her wrists behind her back with leg irons still intact. The cell is devoid of any mattress or blankets" (6).

An hour later the woman managed to remove the flexicuffs, retrieve the handcuffs from the toilet, and break the sink with them. This led to the further use of pepper spray and the woman's removal to a camera cell, while still naked, but with a towel held in front of her. A brief attempt was made to wash areas of her body affected by the spray. The report noted: "In the camera cell, the CET removes the handcuffs from —, replacing them with a body chain (positions wrists at the sides). She is left naked, kneeling on the bed in the camera cell with leg irons secured to the foot of the bed. No mattress or blankets are given" (CSC 1997a, 7).

An attempt by the woman to remove the body chain led to staff removing it and reapplying handcuffs, but again: "at this point inmate — is still nude and left lying face down on the bed, handcuffed behind the back with leg irons attached to the bottom of the bed. There is no mattress or blanket in the cell" (CSC 1997a, 7).

The woman was eventually supplied with a gown at approximately 14:15 hours and a mattress by "at least" 15:00 hours (CSC 1997b, 1). It was not until nearly twelve hours after the original use of the pepper spray that the woman was fully (and forcibly) decontaminated by staff, who held her under a shower. The woman was eventually removed to Springhill Institution[51] at some time after 10:00 PM. Every procedure was videotaped, as is required by official regulations.

In the days that followed the newspapers kept abreast of the removal of the maximum security women without, at that stage, being aware of what had actually transpired. CSC continued to use a spokesperson from outside the prison, reflecting a policy change stemming from the events at Edmonton. In early October the four women involved in the first September incident were charged and eventually had extra time added to their sentences.

The Board of Investigation into the 19 September incident began its inquiries once the regional deputy commissioner had signed the convening order. Its report criticized aspects of the treatment of the woman involved and a disciplinary board of investigation was assembled as a consequence. The warden, Christine Manuge, was suspended on 19 January 1997 and eventually reassigned to other duties, as was a team leader. An official announcement was not made until 10 February 1997, when it was also announced that Jim Davidson would act as an interim warden. He became the third warden at the prison in the space of nearly four years (and there had been a temporary one to cover the gap between the departure of Therese LeBlanc and the arrival of Christine Manuge). The fourth warden, Mary Ennis, was appointed in May 1997. The prison staff members were demoralized and many felt badly let down by managers who, as they saw it, had attempted to shift responsibility for their own incompetence onto the staff.

REFLECTING ON THE INVESTIGATION

When the heavily vetted[52] Board of Investigation report on the 19 September 1996 events at the prison was eventually released by CSC,[53] the many deleted portions encouraged speculation as to whose names fitted the gaps, leaving staff members vulnerable to assumptions about their individual culpability. The Disciplinary Board of Investigation, generally dealing with management issues, was similarly vetted and consequently offered little explanation of why the warden and team leader operations subsequently did not return to the prison. The reports as published allow us to have a very general idea of what transpired, but what they do *not* do is provide context by mentioning what else was happening at Nova on that day. The disciplinary board "felt that some components of effective management leadership and direction were lacking at Nova Institution during and prior to this incident" (CSC 1997b, 1). Both reports failed to make clear that the regional commissioner and the deputy commissioner for women were both at the prison on the day when the events took place, which itself might be interpreted as CSC continuing to protect its more senior employees as it did during the Arbour inquiry (and for which it was castigated). The reports failed to clarify that a major event was planned at Nova for the evening of 19 September 1996. They did not follow the example of Edmonton's Board of Investigation and place events within the context of the specific difficulties staff at Nova faced in dealing with the disproportionate number of "lower-functioning" women. They did not reflect on the difficulties women had in coping with such a different prison and whether these might have contributed to the tensions within the prison. They did not point out that the warden had only been appointed eleven months prior to the opening of the prison; that most staff members had still not been selected at the time of her appointment; and that staff members then had to undergo training before they could familiarize themselves with the prison.

The disciplinary board also criticized the fact that "no comprehensive policies were available to staff on or before 96–09–19, regarding the operation and management of the Enhanced Housing Unit (EHU) or relating to the management of Use of Force or Cell Extraction situations. Staff working in the EHU learned the operational procedures for the area from other peers and improvised over time, but no formalized instructions were available" (CSC 1997b, 1). (This was a point also made in *Investigation of Minor Disturbance* [CSC 1997b].) The disciplinary board did not point out that Edmonton had also operated without revised standing orders during the months prior to its closure, information which should have then been available to senior corrections' employees, even if at the regional level. There were subsequent allegations of selective interviewing of staff at Nova, with the clear implication being that both boards heard what they wanted to hear.[54] Whatever the truth of that, in having such a narrow view of the wider enterprise – the opening of five new, radically different prisons – both reports allowed all the failings at Nova to become solely the responsibility of Nova's staff and the women. That CSC itself might have shared some of this responsibility was never the point at issue.

While discussion of the incident is important because of the questions raised about the general preparedness of the prison, perhaps the most important question to be asked is why, and how, such an event could have happened following the release of the Arbour Report in April 1996 (see chapter 6 for a fuller discussion of those April 1994 events). A woman had been left naked and manacled to a bed, without a mattress to lie on and without having been decontaminated following being pepper-sprayed. How could staff members on that unit possibly have thought such conduct acceptable, irrespective of whether or not they were being supervised by management? While it should be remembered that many of the staff members were young, so had had relatively little experience of coping with stressful situations wherever they occurred, it should also be borne in mind that many of them were totally new to corrections, and had only recently completed their training. It is unlikely that the training school would not have discussed the Arbour Report with them, particularly as Arbour had roundly criticized CSC for its failure to develop a "culture of rights" within its prisons (Arbour 1996, 179).

The board concluded, when examining each specific development during the 19 September 1996 incident, that the use of force had not been excessive. What it *did* find unjustifiable was the apparent lack of care in the treatment of the woman subsequent to each use of force. Arbour's examination of the strip-searching of the women at the Prison for Women is important to what has been related here because those April 1994 events showed CSC's complete disregard for the law. A similar disregard was shown at Nova – and by staff also largely new to corrections, as was the case with those primarily involved in the incidents at the Prison for Women. Would more experienced staff members have defused the original situation before it developed? Or would their employment have led to a replication of the Prison for Women's culture? Indeed, the event reflected that culture, which suggests that the training offered the new staff was not dissimilar from that previously offered. So, were the new staff ill-trained? The board failed to address this point.

Also pertinent to what is presently being discussed is Arbour's dissection of the original Board of Investigation report into the April incidents at the Prison for Women. She carefully showed how the report was edited at National Headquarters so that the most serious aspects of the April incidents disappeared from view. That original 1994 board had been composed solely of CSC personnel, and recommendation 10(a) of the Arbour Report was "that all National Boards of Investigation include a member from *outside* the Correctional Service" (Arbour 1996, 256, emphasis added). Arbour had also suggested that the list of incidents eligible for a national investigation should be extended to include "mistreatment of prisoners" (119). The investigation at Nova contained a community member – but it was *not* a national board; nearly six months after the publication of the Arbour Report the Atlantic regional commissioner, who was at the prison on the actual day, still thought it appropriate to investigate the Nova events as a "minor disturbance." It is not being suggested that there was any deliberate attempt to minimize the seriousness of what happened at Nova, but it remains a matter of conjecture, especially within the context of what had emerged during the Arbour Inquiry and the supposed spirit of *Creating Choices*, as to why Edmonton was dealt with one way and Nova another. And further, that no heed was paid to Arbour's recommendation that "the fact finding methods of Boards of Investigation be improved, and, more importantly, that the focus of investigations *include prominently the performance of the Service*" (Arbour 1996, 120, emphasis added). In the case of Nova and the "performance of the Service," two of the larger considerations are: (1) the quality of staff training and whose responsibility this might have been, and (2) the failure to have necessary programs and staff in place, immediately the prison opened, to provide for those women with "special needs."

All of this is equally relevant to the use CSC made of each warden as representative of the "public face" of each prison. The wardens were encouraged to explain and to justify these prisons to the local community, yet were unable to say what they knew from their own experience of working with prisoners: that the involuntary nature of co-existence meant that prisons were often places of stress and tension. The wardens' job was to smooth the passage of the new prisons into the local communities, and in order to do this they had to emphasize that the majority of federally sentenced women were "low risk." While this meant that the risk they posed to the community was low, their institutional behaviour was not always predictable and unproblematic, as was clearly shown at both Edmonton and Nova. In projecting this image, the wardens reflected the views expressed in *Creating Choices,* but the task force's initial failure to address how "difficult-to-manage" women should be provided for (beyond suggesting a separate house for them) was exposed by events at both prisons. Arguably, it can also be said that these events exposed the failings of both CSC and the regions as they were responsible for implementing the vision of the task force's plan. Although the warden at Nova had largely ceased to be the spokesperson for the prison by the time of the September incident (as a result of events at Edmonton), she was still "the face" of the prison to the community at large. Lacking an adequate explanation of what had actually happened at the prison, Truro's community could simply guess. The "reassignment" of the warden to other duties publicly implied culpability, but the complete story was never fully explained.

This discussion does not imply support for one side or the other; rather, it explores the wider role assigned to the wardens by CSC as *Creating Choices* was being implemented and the difficult position in which it potentially left these women once things began to go wrong. The role of the larger controlling organization (i.e., CSC) behind the wardens was not always apparent to the host communities – and was certainly not made explicit in the reports. In the context of what happened at both Nova and Edmonton one of the main questions is why two wardens were treated so differently. Had Nova's Board of Investigation followed Arbour's suggestion that "the performance of the service" should be scrutinized, then it is just possible that Nova's warden, despite being legally accountable for what happened in her prison, might have remained in place because responsibility for the event would have been seen as more widespread.

It is clear that many of the problems that arose at Nova and Edmonton could – and should – have been anticipated by both the task force and CSC. Ownership of the project had, however, largely been assumed by CSC. The next chapter assesses the consequence of CSC's ownership of these two "non-Aboriginal" prisons.

CHAPTER EIGHT

Shared Birth, Shared Problems

Two prisons, thousands of kilometres apart, shared a common history. As is clear, they also shared a common and very public birth. Edmonton and Nova bore the brunt of being the first of the "non-Aboriginal" prisons to open (although Edmonton did, of course, have a very large number of Aboriginal prisoners), and, at this point, it is useful to consider what differentiated them from each other. Nova was built in a town that actively solicited its arrival, whereas the city of Edmonton was suspicious of the new prison from the start. Nova was a small prison and physically complete when it opened, while Edmonton was (relatively) large and unfinished. Nova, to begin with, had few maximum security women, whereas Edmonton had many more than had been planned for or it could accommodate. Yet these differences mask what united both prisons, which was the failure to have all the components of the new scheme in place before it was put to the test; the plan envisaged in *Creating Choices* was never fully implemented at either prison. The Task Force on Federally Sentenced Women's vision was therefore immediately compromised.

There has been a public tendency to blame both the document itself and federally sentenced women for any implementation failures rather than csc. To understand that *Creating Choices* is a visionary document rather than a complete plan of action is not to ignore the fact that it has a fatal flaw at its heart, which is that it does not sufficiently and prescriptively enough provide for "difficult-to-manage" women. However, it should be remembered that csc had taken five years to plan and build the new penitentiaries and that it had already made it clear, when increasing bed provision for the difficult-to-manage women, that it disagreed with the task force's views. Even disregarding the preparedness or otherwise of both prisons during their first year, what cannot be avoided is that csc was largely familiar with the institutional histories of the women due to be sent to the new prisons; had planned multipurpose enhanced units; had trained the staff; and had been responsible for preparing the women for the different and demanding institutional environments. It is now time to examine several issues in more detail – issues that are common to both these prisons and that help explain why things unfolded as they did.

THE FENCE AS AN IMAGE OF RISK

Creating Choices, in rejecting traditional prison design, also rejected the public symbolism of high walls and visible static security. The low fences surrounding both of the prisons did more than nominally "contain" the women.[1] They sent a message to the local communities that the women were "low risk" and indicated that the prisons were normal parts of each locality. The fences were also part of the "choices" faced by the women and, for some, they presented a personal challenge: would they be able to resist walking away or not? They made others feel less safe because they were not high enough to deter potential intruders, so the messages conveyed by the fences, to both the communities and the women, were decidedly mixed. At Nova the staff thought the low fences compromised security so did not allow the women to walk unescorted around the prison, whereas for a few women at Edmonton, the fences were simply a challenge to be overcome once the winter ended, as these comments from two separate interviewees indicate: "The women thought the fence was a joke. I spoke to this very wise Aboriginal woman who said 'as soon as the weather gets warm' ... [so] the first nice warm day and ... the women were at the fence. It was a lark, it was no big deal, they didn't realize there would be consequences."[2] And: "One of the inmates who got recaptured, she said to me, 'I told you to put a fence up so I wouldn't do this! I wouldn't have escaped, I just wanted to show you that I could.'"[3] For women accustomed to being able to walk relatively freely within the ultra-secure Prison for Women, the low fences paradoxically imposed more restraint than did the huge wall to which they had been accustomed.

Once the fences were increased in height, and more overt security was installed, the message conveyed to the local communities also changed. All the women confined by the fences were now characterized as "high risk," whereas, with the removal of the maximum security women from the prisons, it might have been said that the women were even more "low risk" than they had previously been.

CONTAINING RISK BEHIND THE FENCES

While there was an ill-informed public perception of risky women, there was also the reality that CSC's planning strategy required distinct groups of women to be held together, irrespective of their risk. As a consequence, the enhanced units at Edmonton and Nova were almost immediately under pressure. Even had Edmonton been finished when it first opened, the enhanced unit could not adequately hold maximum security women, those being held in administrative segregation, and all new arrivals. Additionally, the large number of women compromised the protective element of containment, as was evident in the death of Denise Fayant. Nova's smaller enhanced unit had a similar function, yet was overwhelmed when a few women "acted out."

The enhanced units' inadequacy raises the question of why they were built in the first place. The task force did not envisage enhanced units, and even CSC's initial planning assumed a different style of enhanced unit from the ones eventually constructed. A detailed draft master plan for the Grand Valley Institution (in Ontario), already available in November 1992, described what was termed the "Enhanced Security House." It was clearly intended that its design should be similar to the other houses, except that it would have "containment capability in each bedroom and for the house envelope." Women would retain "the same responsibilities for food preparation, cleaning etc" as the rest of the houses (CSC 1992c, 50). The same master plan also clarified policy for newly admitted women; they were to "be assigned to a specific house" and "within 4 to 6 weeks a complete assessment of [their] needs [would] be made" (54). Yet by June 1994 the enhanced units had been "modified and enlarged," and it had also been decided that they would house "two different groups: inmates who behave[d] violently and inmates who require[d] a greater level of staff monitoring for a period of time, for example, new admissions and some special needs inmates" (CSC 1995b, 4–5). The curious point is that the June 1992 National Implementation Committee minutes suggest that the enhanced units should become extensions of the administration building rather than stand-alone houses with extra security, which suggests that those providing the blueprints were not being kept abreast of NIC decisions.

The size of the new prisons, relative to the Prison for Women and the overall size of the federally sentenced women population, ensured that provision could not be made for every group of women with distinct needs, and this basic fact eventually led to the concept of a multipurpose/multilevel enhanced unit (albeit one built to maximum security standards). What both prisons created was essentially the same: a prison within a prison, separating some women from the others. As one interviewee observed: "How do you think it would feel if you were a really difficult-to-manage woman anyway, and you really need healing, and you're locked in a cell in that enhanced unit, and you have a window and you get to look out ... and see all those other inmates tossing round a frisbee, planting a garden, interacting with staff, having visits ... How do you think you'd react to that? I might get a little violent myself, because I wouldn't see myself as getting there."[4] This was a point echoed by Rivera (1996, 31), who refers to the "status differential" of various women in the enhanced units, who "saw themselves in the enhanced unit for the foreseeable future." Prison managements have to make immediate, difficult decisions when admitting prisoners because they, and their needs, are sometimes unknown. However, had the prisons been allowed to follow the original plan outlined in *Creating Choices*, even in part, then a separate, staffed house could have been used for assessment purposes, and this separation of purpose might have made the management of the maximum security women at Edmonton somewhat easier than it was. But was the fact that this did not happen surprising? Bureaucracies often plan for their own convenience (see Rothman 1980; Cohen 1985), and it was conceivably easier, and less costly, to contain disparate groups together rather than to fund staffing of individual houses.

ADJUSTING TO LIFE BEHIND THE FENCES: THE WOMEN AND THE STAFF

This failure to provide adequate accommodation for specific groups of women contributed to the difficulties both prisons faced, but there were also underlying management problems, centred on the new philosophy of imprisonment. Hitherto, the women's prison lives had been highly structured and no amount of theorizing was able to prepare them for the communal living awaiting them at Edmonton and Nova. They had lived in small, sometimes barred, cells; had meals provided for them; had little choice of work or programs; and were supervised by guards who had a clear understanding of their role as correctional officers. Coming from such an environment, many women found the style of the new prisons unnerving and, at times, frightening.

At Edmonton it was estimated that it took an average of six weeks for a woman to complete her assessment and to move from the enhanced unit to her cottage. During that time she had to come to terms with living with a diverse group of women, then make the switch to a very different type of accommodation and another group of women. Despite assumptions that being "female" meant having an instinctive knowledge of how to cook, clean, and budget, and having the social assurance needed to live successfully with a group of strangers, many lacked some or all of these skills. The relatively few who had experienced a settled home-life found it hard coping with others who had no idea of how to maintain a house, let alone the concept of preparing and having meals at fixed times. The stress experienced by the women was compounded by the strip searching and the need to be escorted throughout the prison because of its unfinished state.

At the same time they were expected to work. Edmonton's management had decided that each day should reflect the most common working pattern on the "outside," so work eventually occupied much of the day. Programs essential to the women's successful parole applications, such as anger management, had to be fitted in after work had finished. Consequently, there was the initial spectacle of some staff being employed to work with the women during the very hours the women were unavailable to them.[5] As an observer at Edmonton reflected: "[The women said] their treatment needs were completely ignored. Work was so important and the work they needed to do on themselves was when they were tired ... There wasn't a single woman in the maximum security unit who had ever worked to this bizarre concept of 9 to 5, of eating meals at a particular time."[6]

The needs of the maximum security (and "low-functioning" women at Nova) took up a disproportionate amount of time, and staff members were unable to give sufficient support to *all* the women as they adapted to their new prison. The women were expected to conform to disciplines appropriate to life outside, such as time-keeping and appropriate decision making, without it being acknowledged that the absence of those disciplines from their non-prison lives might have contributed to their offending. To cite these "disciplines" is not to denigrate their importance – and they were certainly values nineteenth-century reformers were keen to impart to imprisoned women – but they could not always be acquired immediately, or easily, and needed to be delivered within a structured and gradual program. Without these skills many women could not take advantage of the changed environment, and their failure to do so was sometimes seen by staff as a *refusal* to do so. The staff did not always understand how much was being asked of the women (and how frightening some of the women found their changed circumstances). Conversely, the women had no idea that staff had been trained to expect different responses and were themselves sometimes frightened by the challenges presented.

Many of the women were further confused by the unaccustomed level of supervision to which they were subjected. At Nova, staff more comfortable in their own roles might have felt able to avoid escorting women everywhere. At Edmonton that was initially precluded by the state of the prison, yet the practice continued long after the prison was completed. However, there is a more important aspect to be considered: the fact that staff were not continuously present in the houses. The new prisons were a reversal of the panopticon, where prisoners could always be observed. Indeed, the design of each prison prevented staff from seeing the women from a central point. The new houses required the women to be responsible for their own surveillance as well as for the surveillance of those sharing their accommodation. Surveillance, within the context of prisons, is a form of discipline, and in these new federal prisons self-surveillance was part of the "responsibilizing strategy" imposed upon the women (see Hannah-Moffat 2001). It became an internalized discipline and part of the "choices" philosophy, whereby women could choose how they might act. If a woman chose to ignore the need for self-surveillance this could be interpreted as an act of indiscipline rather than as an act of resistance to control imposed upon an involuntary population (see Bosworth 1999 for a wider discussion of women's resistance within prisons).

"Reading" the staff

Beyond the difficulties posed by life in the houses and the enhanced units lay those posed by the new staff themselves. Guards at the Prison for Women had reflected the background of the women themselves. Staff members were generally not highly educated or necessarily "middle class," yet they had often achieved their positions despite social disadvantages that sometimes equalled those of the women. They had an understanding of the women that was tempered by their own experience. While this is not uncommon within correctional environments (see Liebling and Price 2001 for some discussion of this), the Task Force on Federally Sentenced Women hoped to create a new professional mould, and, in opting for young graduates, CSC set up a "cultural disparity between the guards and the prisoners" (Faith 1993, 165).[7]

Selecting inexperienced staff also led to an unanticipated role reversal: the women, whether they lived in ordinary cottages or in the secure units, became the correctional experts ("we told them what to do!").[8] Yet, having transferred from the Prison for Women or the Regional Psychiatric Centre, the women were "experts" in the old style of corrections and were often confused by the new, which seemed to have few recognizable rules. It did not take them long, however, to discover that some of the staff members were just as unsure of their own roles and the prisons' rules, and that primary workers could be overruled by their team leaders or the warden. This is commented on by Rivera (1996, 22) both within the context of the often irreconcilable dual role of the primary workers and the lack of coherent policy at both prisons. Some women chose to take advantage of the confusion by playing staff off against each other, while many of the staff lacked an instinctive response to situations and often had to seek guidance from others.

The ambivalence felt by many of the women towards the primary workers, who seemed more like social workers, had an additional impact on "dynamic security" because there appeared to be no clear lines of demarcation. According to Coyle (1994, 99), "prisons are never places of love and companionship ... but there is normally a sensation, at least at a superficial level, of mutual tolerance." The mutual tolerance and respect intended by the task force to underpin the dynamic security was undermined by the mixed messages the women received. The staff had been trained in a form of risk management that suggested that there should be a move from the idea of "risk/security" to "risk/support", which they would provide (TFFSW 1990, 91). The improved physical conditions of the prisons and the greater autonomy of the women were meant to create easier relationships between staff and women, a departure from the traditional correctional model of the "guard" and the "guarded." But this anomalous role baffled and upset the women: "They [staff] didn't realize that the women needed to debrief what it was like having a primary worker [guard] who wasn't a screw ... as a counsellor you maintain confidentiality; as a correctional officer you cannot maintain confidentiality. So the women were telling these people who were primary workers things that were very important and treating them as counsellors – and then they'd [staff] go and tell a supervisor and then there would perhaps be a kind of correctional disposition."[9]

Some staff were equally confounded by the behaviour of the women: "They'd [women] slash and the staff were crying and that was completely unnerving for them [the women]. They didn't see that as support at all."[10] Yet the staff *were* correctional officers, rather than social workers, and had to be prepared to perform the tasks traditionally expected of them: the strip searches, the room searches, and being members of cell extraction teams (see CSC 1995a; Faith 1993). These tasks did not sit well with the new image of the primary worker but became increasingly necessary as the prisons absorbed larger numbers of women. Relationships between staff and the women began to alter, and some of the staff members found it hard to be, as they saw it, rejected by the women. This was articulated by one observer at Edmonton: "They [women] were just like princesses for the first little while and then, as more and more staff were beginning to say 'no' to a few things, the women slashed a few times. And the first time a woman slashed the staff felt that they had been slapped across the face. 'I treated you with respect and you slash yourself?' ... And what they [staff] hadn't realized is that maybe these women hadn't lived with respect for their entire lives."[11]

But the difficulties both groups faced could also be ascribed to the pressures staff members encountered as they tried to make sense of prisons housing populations for which they were not properly designed. As another Edmonton interviewee said: "We weren't given a blueprint ... each institution is designed individually. You've got to figure it out, how it's going to work for your place and a lot of energy is consumed doing that, and if you don't have the right numbers of staff in the first place, your staff are really tired and you priorize [sic] ... You wouldn't believe the external pressure that was put on us ... from within the service, from the higher-ups. ... If you have staff that aren't used to working in that environment you frustrate them and burn them out very quickly."[12] Part of the physical model of the prisons, as exemplified by the enhanced units, did not fit the philosophical model. All were feeling their way and, as the number of difficult-to-manage-women increased, staff members were left reeling, and many ended up being reactive to events rather than proactive. Inevitably the women were affected: "Over and over we've told them, 'We're not used to you guys being nice to us.' It's like this concept, this new thing ... I don't know what to think of it."[13]

Most primary workers were initially clear about where their loyalties lay. However, in being asked to assume the status of "role model," to use their social work skills, and to be available to the women on a one-to-one basis, their whole position was less than clear to the women and, eventually, to the staff members themselves. Faith (1993) has suggested that the idealism of some staff members does not always withstand prolonged exposure to their work, and cynicism certainly began to affect how staff at the new prisons dealt with the women. Not that this was a new phenomenon. At the Mercer Reformatory in Toronto, in the late nineteenth century, staff found it difficult "tempering severity with feminine tenderness" (Strange 1985, 85), while in England Kelley (1967, 176) wrote that in "period[s] of transition" prison officers sometimes feel they have "the worst of both worlds, the old and the new."

Mathiesen (1990, 130) examines the role of staff in the light of Sykes' five "pains of imprisonment" and suggests that there ought to be a sixth, "the *power* which the prison wields in and over the lives of prisoners." He makes a particular point of the power exercised by staff over inmates and the manner in which it is used, an issue also explored by Sparks et al. (1996) and Liebling and Price (2001). The latter coined the phrase "the un-exercise" of power to describe the means by which staff carry out their duties, and they differ from Sparks et al. (who refer to much the same process as "accommodations") by asserting that the "un-exercise" of power constitutes "the best of prison officer work." In other words, judicious use of discretion helps to maintain good order within a prison rather than to undermine authority. Such discretion is not necessarily something that may be taught at staff training college but, rather, is acquired through practical experience. In the new prisons the women were generally not being exposed to judicious discretion because the staff members were too new to have acquired it, so the women were living under Mathiesen's sixth "pain": power. And it was an inconsistent power, making it all the more difficult for the women to endure the apparent goodwill of the staff.

Supporting the staff

At Nova the incidents occurred when staff members were feeling the effect of having worked at full stretch for almost a year, while still learning their own jobs. They were stressed and many were at "burn-out" point. Warner (1998, 19) alludes to this: "When the violent incidents finally occurred [at Nova], line staff felt blamed for their handling of the incidents when they believed they should have been acknowledged and supported for preventing them for such a long period, given the mix and explosiveness of the house." Following the September incidents some reacted by changing their working practices, feeling the need to look after themselves rather than their colleagues, because they were not confident that the larger organization would support them should another incident occur (see also Liebling and Price 2001). Filling in forms, getting the paperwork right, took on a new meaning as staff members endeavoured to protect themselves. As some at Nova made clear, they also had the example of what had happened to their warden, whom many felt had been unfairly "reassigned" to another position.[14]

Further complexity was added to the situation by the status of individual staff members at Nova. Those who were "indeterminate" (permanent) staff had a reasonable degree of job security, but those who were "casuals" and "term" employees had no such certainty.[15] Nevertheless, all casuals and term staff were given responsibilities commensurate with being a permanent staff member, suggesting that while CSC required loyalty, it was not always prepared to offer it in return.

At Edmonton the incidents happened much sooner than they did at Nova, with the staff members' situation exacerbated by the physical inadequacy of the prison and their own inexperience. Although they received debriefings after individual incidents, there was no follow-up provided, and the prison management seemed unaware of official procedures. Neither prison had a critical incident stress management (CISM) team in place, in contravention of CSC's own policy, as set out in CD 257. Edmonton's Board of Investigation said that, following the incidents, it had "interviewed a number of very enthusiastic, very dedicated employees who exhibited symptoms of burn-out and post-traumatic stress" (CSC 1996b, 173). At both these prisons the large proportion of new staff meant that there was no collective memory of how stressful incidents had been dealt with in the past, and staff could not necessarily see that some of the stress was inherent in being a correctional officer. They did not always know where "normal" prison stress ended and where the "abnormal" stress engendered by being part of an "untested concept," as Chrumka (2000, 71) termed it, began.

STANDING ORDERS

The staff's inconsistencies, which have already been discussed, could partly be attributed to the lack of up-to-date standing orders (see note 32 in chapter 6) and the failure of both prisons to have these ready by the time of opening. This was an astonishing oversight on the part of CSC, even though such orders are prepared locally rather than centrally. Whenever new prisons opened it had always been customary to adapt standing orders from other prisons, but the new women's prisons could not be dealt with so easily. Part of the rationale for *Creating Choices* was that women should not be discriminated against because they happened to be in different prisons from other federally sentenced women. It was essential that there should be uniformity in the overall administration of the prisons, with each standing order being measured against the *Creating Choices* model (in so far as it applied by the time the prisons opened). The Nova *Investigation of Minor Disturbance* report made it clear that "the security standing orders were not up to date" (CSC 1997a, 23), and the disciplinary board added that "no comprehensive institutional policies and procedures were available to staff" (CSC 1997b, 1). The same criticisms were levelled by the Edmonton Board of Investigation, which commented on "out of date" standing orders and the fact that directions to staff were liable to change "on a daily basis ... making it very difficult for primary workers to keep up to date" (CSC 1996b, 142–3). When faced with crisis situations staff members at both prisons had no formal written guidance at their disposal, and this oversight was entirely the responsibility of CSC, which had failed to ensure that the formal structures, essential to the running of each prison, were in place.

STRIP SEARCHING

The uneasy relationships between women and staff members were further tested at Edmonton. One of the immediate consequences of failing to have the prison completed on time was that, in an effort to prevent the passage of drugs into the enhanced unit, all women were routinely strip-searched each time they moved in or out of the unit. This meant as many as eight strip searches per day for some women, irrespective of their security rating. CAEFS' president wrote to Commissioner Edwards: "[We believe that the] notion of dynamic security did not contemplate regular and routine invasive searches: CAEFS regards the strip searches of the women in Edmonton as an illegal practice that is antithetical to the principles of *Creating Choices*. Given that the enhanced units are not classified as segregation units, the stripping of women in and out of those units contravenes your policy (CD #571) and the legislation governing this area (s.48 of the *CCRA*: s.7 of the *Canadian Charter of Rights and Freedoms*)."[16]

Edwards replied that "the interim practice of routine strip searches prior to entering the temporary program area in the enhanced unit was completely terminated on January 29, 1996." He also added that women on Security Management Levels One and Two were never stripped "as it was considered that their minimum security classification implied a level of trust and self-responsibility which should be recognised."[17] Further, CSC had decided that the definition of what constituted a "segregation unit" was flexible, and Edwards explained that the law did not reflect the reality of the multipurpose design of the new institutions. It appeared from his letter that CSC had adopted a policy of having a moveable segregation area, which meant that wherever a Level Five (Administrative Segregation) woman happened to be at a given time became, for that period, a segregation area,[18] an explanation that CAEFS later labelled "legal gymnastics."[19] Strip searching did not cease, and at the end of April all the Prairie Elizabeth Fry Societies jointly wrote to Jan Fox, commenting on how negatively this affected the women's relationships with staff.[20] These letters were ignored and the practice continued until the removal of the majority of the women from the prison. In its report into Denise Fayant's death, the Board of Investigation made it clear that all women *were* stripped and that "thus minimum security offenders were subjected routinely to procedures normally reserved for maximum security individuals" (CSC 1996b, 2).

Strip searching was particularly important, both because of the impact it had on the way women and staff related to each other and because of the way in which it diminished the influence of the new correctional philosophy. Irrespective of how strip searching is carried out, it involves the public display of parts of the body normally kept hidden from public gaze (see Newburn and Hayman 2002; Carlen 1998; Scraton et al. 1991). A strip search can never be carried out sensitively because the whole manner of exposing the body is fundamentally insensitive, denoting relations of power between those being stripped and those responsible for the stripping. The prisoner is in a position of abject humiliation, as was also very evident during the 19 September 1996 incident at Nova. Unsurprisingly, the women at Edmonton detested being stripped (as they saw it, unnecessarily) and were particularly resistant to being stripped by a correctional officer who was also their primary worker. The practice was out of step with what women had been led to expect at Edmonton and immediately affected their relationships with staff. Yet the situation was largely beyond the control of the guards, who felt themselves just as much affected by CSC's failure to provide them with a completed prison, and who were perturbed by being part of an exercise so far removed from the concept of dynamic security. Having resorted to stripping as a control measure because the prison was not finished, the instinct to check women was already inculcated in officers and management by the time the women finally returned to the prison. Although strip searching was then reserved for cases such as suspected harbouring of offensive weapons, the women at Edmonton continued to be frisked as they left the administration building at the end of each work session, and, unlike at the other prisons, this was still the practice in 1998.

PROGRAMS

Failure to have adequate programming available at a prison can lead to a woman not completing her sentence plan. Such failures can delay parole hearings and might be interpreted by the parole board as the woman's unwillingness to address the root causes of her "offending." The task force had selected the initial prison locations partly because they were linked to women's networks and larger educational facilities, which could ease re-entry to the community for released prisoners. Edmonton certainly had networks that could be tapped, but at the time the prison opened there were still large gaps in provision. The physical constraints of the unfinished prison then limited the delivery of those programs that had been arranged, as did the insistence that work should take priority during the day. In Truro networks had to be created, and there were considerable delays in arranging program contracts. There were also financial consequences to locating the prison in Truro as large sums of money were needed to send women to see specialists in Halifax. Similarly, extra money was needed to fund the temporary absence program, under which, for example, women make home visits (and generally require escorts). As most of the women did not live in or near Truro, this was a considerable drain on the prison's budget.

Funding limitations dictated the scale of the facilities provided in each prison, and education rooms, though well resourced, were small and unable to cope with more than a few women at a time. Apart from an eventual graphics workshop at Edmonton, which employed very few women, and a horticulture program at Nova, which struggled without a greenhouse, there were no workshops that would enable women to develop skills that might best be described as "non-gendered." While some innovative programs were eventually introduced at both prisons, the constraints under which they were delivered – lack of space, lack of funding to bring in more contract staff – had an impact on the women. The size of the prisons also meant that certain treatment programs would only be "bought in" when there were sufficient women to justify the expense, which again affected how quickly women progressed in their sentence plan. It had been anticipated that women would make "choices" regarding the programs best suited to them, but the reality was that, to begin with, relatively few choices were available. At both prisons the failure to make programs one of the first planning priorities rebounded on both the staff and the women. Bored women, living in either a cramped enhanced unit, or under the restrictions imposed on the houses, wondered just what the new prisons were offering them and could see little improvement upon the Prison for Women. As staff became more involved – particularly at Edmonton – in fire-fighting the spiralling incidents, they had less time to devote to getting to know individual women and encouraging them to participate in those programs that were available.

ROLE OF THE MEDIA

Both previous chapters considered the roles assigned the wardens. Such positioning of key players has always been a useful device for large organizations, which are then able to hide behind individuals while preserving the careers and reputations of others. With the opening of the prisons there was another complicating dimension added to the public debate: the voices of the women themselves. Under the commissioner's directive (CD) 022, prisoners have the right to talk to the press.[21] It was alleged that: "they [press] often manipulated what the women had to say,"[22] and at Edmonton the comments, appearing out of context, contributed to the public impression of a prison out of control. At Edmonton there were also unforeseen consequences: "In [a woman's] discussions with the press, other offenders in the population interpreted quite differently what she intended to say. So there was not only the public out there listening to this ... the women [in the prison] started to experience difficulty in living in this environment because of some of the things that were said."[23]

At Edmonton the level of outside observation was high, and the frequency of the media's attention left staff feeling undermined. Some later reflected on this and recounted what it felt like to arrive at work not knowing what would happen that day, or to arrive at work and realize, because of the assembled media, that something had already happened.[24] The overall effect of the persistent press attention was more noticeable at Edmonton because the prison had been contentious from the moment it was first announced and later became part of the "law-and-order" debate initiated by local politicians. Truro was some distance from the consistent gaze of the television cameras and did not present such an immediate target, but the underlying fact remained the same at both prisons: the wardens became the public face of CSC as soon as they assumed the role of advocates for the prisons. They remained the public face, even after they had been removed from the role of spokesperson, and carried much of the blame for events at their prisons, whereas the reality was that the wardens were employees of CSC and that CSC had final responsibility for what happened at Nova and Edmonton.

ABORIGINAL WOMEN

While chapter 9 focuses more fully on Aboriginal federally sentenced women, their position at Edmonton needs to be assessed separately. Edmonton was different from Nova in that it held a disproportionate number of Aboriginal prisoners, and most of those were accommodated in the enhanced unit when the prison first opened. Some had applied to be sent to the Healing Lodge and not been accepted, mainly because their security rating was above Management Level Three. The Board of Investigation made an important point in discussing this: "the proportion of medium- and maximum-security [Aboriginal] offenders at EIFW, relative to the whole population, will be larger [because of numbers of Aboriginal peoples in the Prairies]; [and] Aboriginal women who are not accepted by the Healing Lodge may feel less commitment to engage in the program at EIFW because they are 'stuck' there" (CSC 1996b, 141). This was supported by Rivera (1996, 28): "it is extremely important that the Edmonton Institution is not perceived of as a dumping ground by Aboriginal women who are not accepted into the Healing Lodge. If more integration is not effected between the Healing Lodge and the EI4W [Edmonton Institution for Women], some Aboriginal women ... will make little effort to buy into its philosophy or programming."

Edmonton was always going to have a disproportionate number of federally sentenced Aboriginal women once the unpublicized decision to bar maximum security women from the Healing Lodge was taken (see chapter 9). It was an inescapable demographic fact, but one insufficiently conveyed to the women as the new prisons reached completion. Many of the Aboriginal prisoners had assumed they would be eligible for the Healing Lodge, having seen that the security levels of some of their peers (including one who had been involved in the April 1994 incidents) had been reduced to facilitate transfers from Kingston's Prison for Women. For those who had been rejected, finding themselves subsequently accommodated in the small enhanced unit at Edmonton compounded their disappointment and gave them little incentive to participate in the new-style prison. To begin with, Edmonton offered little specifically Aboriginal programming and scarcely differed, in that respect, from the prisons the women had left behind. Once Edmonton reopened many of these Aboriginal women were barred even from Edmonton (because of their maximum security status) and became yet more isolated within the federal system. As Morin (1999) makes clear, CSC did not fulfill its own commissioner's directive on the treatment of imprisoned Aboriginal peoples, leaving them with insufficient services while enduring their isolation.

WHOSE FAILURE?

In summarizing events at both Nova and Edmonton it is possible to see several failures emerging from CSC's implementation of the task force's report. By way of subsequent justification, one theme was later rehearsed by CSC: that some federally sentenced women did not, and never would, fit the model. If the test was the women's reaction to the new prisons, as revealed in the last two chapters, then CSC was right to make this point: a number of women manifestly did not cope with what was offered. Some reacted most forcefully against the new model – and some of those were women who had responded in similar fashion when imprisoned in the Prison for Women or the Regional Psychiatric Centre.

This image of a separate group was further emphasized by the deputy commissioner for Women, Nancy Stableforth, during the Denise Fayant Fatality Inquiry, when she said "some theories in favour of kinder, gentler prisons were shattered by Fayant's slaying," and "we've learned in the last couple of years that we had to look at whether the women had the capacity for change ... we learned a small group of women don't have the capacity for change."[25] She was denying csc's mission statement Core Values One and Two, which recognized the "potential for human growth and development" and "that the offender has the potential to live as a law-abiding citizen." Stableforth, in saying "we've learned in the last couple of years," was also implying that *Creating Choices*, rather than csc, had got it wrong with a significant minority of women. What Stableforth did not speak about was whether the model presented at Edmonton and Nova was the model envisaged by the task force; she was blaming the women for failing to take advantage of a model that had never been fully or properly implemented at the time Ms Fayant was murdered at Edmonton. This failure could not, of course, ever excuse the violence that took place in the enhanced unit at Edmonton that February evening, but Stableforth's comments, being made some two and a half years after the event, ignored all that had preceded and followed Denise Fayant's death. It ignored the fact that the women were participants in an experiment for which they had been inadequately prepared. It ignored the fact that staff themselves were attempting to implement a model without all the necessary components. The consequences were profound. As an interviewee commented: "What about the maximum women who did nothing? They might have been able to function here. Did we ever really try this model? No. Has this model ever been evaluated? Absolutely not ... we are at various stages working towards it, but it sure as heck isn't implemented."[26]

While it is tempting to blame csc entirely for the failures of implementation at the two prisons, this would be a partial view of what transpired. The task force that produced *Creating Choices* has to bear some responsibility for the outcome. It was not just implementation that failed but also an aspect of *Creating Choices* itself, specifically the way in which the report reflected the task force's concerns about labelling women. In refusing to deal fully with the difficult-to-manage women, and in being reluctant to accept that women's violence was not always linked to their victimization, the task force presented csc with the opportunity to define the problem and to decide upon a solution. The consensus model under which the working group worked stilled the ambivalence of many voices. csc was familiar with producing a single response and, with an unerring eye for an opportunity, adopted the plan as its own.

What is perhaps not so apparent from this discussion is that much went well at these prisons. Some women benefited from a less restrictive environment and were able to make choices that allowed them to move beyond the prison to an eventual life outside. A number of staff found a means of balancing their competing, and often irreconcilable, roles and assisted this reformation. So the "vision" of *Creating Choices*, while diminished, never entirely disappeared.

Understanding the successes and failures of both Nova and Edmonton is important because their genesis was so very different from that of the Healing Lodge. They were largely the result of correctional officials' planning, divorced from the influence and scrutiny of the voluntary sector. The Healing Lodge, by contrast, was conceived and inspired by independent Aboriginal women during its entire transformation from concept to physical reality. csc officials facilitated the transformation but were not its total source. Potentially, then, if all three prisons are critically assessed, there is the possibility of two different correctional outcomes. The question now arises of whether the consistent influence of Aboriginal people upon planning for the Healing Lodge enabled a truly radical model of imprisonment to emerge from *Creating Choices*. Or could it be that the hand of corrections has had a longer reach than anyone might have anticipated?

CHAPTER NINE

Okimaw Ohci Healing Lodge: A Healing Prison?

We did this all on faith. We started without a vision of what it would look like and each step of the way, when we would maybe get a little anxious ... the Elders would say, "I want you to stop and I want you to look back. See how far you've come. Now look forward. We don't have that much further to go."[1]

The building of the Healing Lodge was an experiment unique to Canada and Aboriginal peoples, and the Correctional Service of Canada embarked upon a venture without precedent or guideline. The continuing presence of Aboriginal peoples as partners in the venture attested to what had been achieved by the Task Force on Federally Sentenced Women itself: recognition of Aboriginal peoples as a distinct group and one possessing an increasing political clout. The crucial importance of Aboriginal people to the story told so far has been the way in which they so unexpectedly influenced the planning of the task force and the language of its report, *Creating Choices*. This chapter now explores the way in which *Creating Choices'* tentative description of the Healing Lodge was expanded upon and transformed. Unlike the four "non-Aboriginal" prisons, which were built by CSC without voluntary-sector guidance, planning for the Healing Lodge was largely devolved to a subcommittee of the National Implementation Committee (NIC), which was finally known as the Healing Lodge Planning Circle (HLPC). The HLPC's work was undertaken with the active support of Aboriginal women, two of whom had played a major role in influencing the content of *Creating Choices*. The report's assertion that "control over our [Aboriginal] future ... must rest within Aboriginal communities" (TFFSW 1990, 15) was to be tested in a very practical sense.

This chapter might have been a simple recounting of the practical details of what was achieved; indeed, there are no major "incidents" to relate. But the story of the development of the lodge transcends practicalities because of the questions posed by this unparalleled combination of culture and spirituality within a prison – questions that few might have anticipated at the time of the task force. This chapter differs from the others in that it covers a longer period of time because the issues that eventually surfaced at the Healing Lodge were not so immediately apparent. At times it is necessary to refer to Aboriginal ceremonies in order to explain the day to day style of the Healing Lodge; this is done cautiously, in the knowledge that Aboriginal custom is for things to be spoken rather than written.

PLANNING AN ABORIGINAL PRISON

Part of the difficulty faced by Aboriginal women on the task force was the fear that their participation might confer legitimacy on Euro-Canadian law. Participating was also difficult on other levels, as articulated by this observer: "When you have the people who are involved in CAEFS, they're all interested in women in prison. We don't have that luxury or privilege of that experience as Aboriginal people because ... this [imprisonment] is a big picture in our families that we experience on a daily basis – and it's not an experience that's separated by gender."[2] The Aboriginal chapter in *Creating Choices* amplifies this: "Aboriginal culture teaches connection and not separation. Our nations do not separate men from women, although we do recognize that each has its own unique roles and responsibilities" (TFFSW 1990, 18). It was not culturally appropriate to view imprisonment through the prism of gender, yet this was what the Aboriginal women agreed to do by virtue of becoming members of the task force. In the same way that CAEFS felt it could not ignore the plight of federally sentenced women, on a point of principle, these Aboriginal women felt a similar responsibility to the arguably even more disadvantaged Aboriginal federally sentenced women.

The Healing Lodge required an exceptional approach, yet, to begin with, only an Aboriginal advisory committee (AAC), with a function similar to that of the steering committee, was envisaged. The first meeting took place in February 1991, shortly after another Aboriginal woman had committed suicide at the Prison for Women, and for the two task force members who had joined that committee the death would have been a singularly painful reminder of the earlier suicides during the life of the task force. They, together with the other Aboriginal representatives, resorted to direct action. Rather than pass a formal motion to send to the commissioner, as had the task force on that earlier occasion, they instead pressed for a more "hands on involvement in the development of the Healing Lodge." This meant altering their role so that "Native women/Elders [would] join with CSC to form a combined committee [to] develop the Healing Lodge."[3] Again, Aboriginal women were insisting that they be placed in a position where they would have direct influence over planning for Aboriginal federally sentenced women. Again, CSC acquiesced.[4]

Creating Choices had stipulated that the Healing Lodge should be in an unspecified "prairie location" (TFFSW 1990, 115), whereas the working group had earlier suggested that Saskatchewan was the logical choice. The selection of the Prairies as a location was unsurprising, given that the majority of federally sentenced Aboriginal women originated from there; but narrowing the field to a site in either Alberta, Manitoba, or Saskatchewan was less easy. The considerations leading to the task force's having selected Halifax, Montreal, and Edmonton as the preferred sites – that a network of well-placed support organizations should be readily available – no longer fully applied. The task force had plainly said that connection to an Aboriginal community was "essential [for the Healing Lodge's] survival" (TFFSW 1990, 115).

Although the location criteria[5] for the Healing Lodge were decided relatively quickly by the committee, they were not immediately published as they first had to be approved by Solicitor General Doug Lewis – and he had yet to decide upon a province. Even as the extension of the search radius for the other prisons to 100 kilometres was announced in July 1991, his decision was delayed, leaving CSC fearful that many communities, without realistic chances of success, would submit bids to have the Healing Lodge in their localities. It has been suggested that there might have been a political reason for the delay. As has already been noted, it was believed that the decision to locate the Maritimes' prison in Truro was linked to the political affiliation of the sitting MP. In looking at the decisions made regarding the siting of the rest of the prisons a pattern can be seen. In Quebec, Montreal (largely Liberal) was ignored in favour of Joliette, which had a Progressive Conservative MP, whereas in Ontario, where the (Liberal) Hamilton corridor had been favoured by the task force, the town of Kitchener (with a Progressive Conservative MP) was chosen instead. In Alberta, Edmonton had six MPs, five of whom were Progressive Conservatives, and the city survived the 100–kilometre extended-search radius to be selected for a prison. The Reform Party was beginning to make political inroads across the Prairies, but particularly in Alberta and parts of southern Saskatchewan, and in the 1993 federal election the Progressive Conservatives lost all but two of their 169 seats across the country. The Progressive Conservatives would have been aware of the threat to their hegemony in the Prairies, and, based on these trends, it is not unreasonable to suggest that the selection of sites for the new prisons, at times in clear disregard of the task force's wishes, had a party-political dimension to them.

It took until 10 December 1991 for Solicitor General Lewis to announce that the Healing Lodge would indeed be located in Saskatchewan, but by then a number of communities had already declared an interest. The delay in deciding on an actual province allowed for a very brief response time, and applicants had six weeks in which to complete their submissions and return them to csc.

BIDDING FOR THE HEALING LODGE

Maple Creek, a town of 2,500 (with a further 3,400 in outlying areas) in the southwest of Saskatchewan, had been one of the many prairie communities to bid for the new regional prison, which was eventually awarded to Edmonton. When the town council was told that its application had been unsuccessful it was also asked if it might be interested in hosting the Healing Lodge. As with other small prairie towns, unemployment was a concern, and the council thought the proposition worth pursuing. Some twenty-nine kilometres to the south of Maple Creek, in the Cypress Hills, the 250–person Nekaneet Band (of the Cree Nation) lived on its reserve and had also received information about the proposed lodge. As a (then) band councillor explained, his reaction was "that some of these bigger reserves should probably apply for this and politics would be involved and ... they would probably get it and we shouldn't even bother applying. So I left it at that, but then the Economic Development worker [from Maple Creek] ... phoned me and asked if I had seen this ... and wanted to know if we wanted to jointly submit the proposal. I told her about my reservations about doing that ... but then I thought, we were on this mode of working together and getting along with the community in Maple Creek so that this would be a good thing to practise with, you know, putting this proposal together."[6]

A small committee was set up to take the proposal further. Underlining the lack of professional expertise of the Maple Creek group, as opposed to the commercial organizations hired by some other areas to put their proposals together, the band councillor explained: "We scheduled a meeting and it just so happened that I was taking my son to skating and there was a girl there from the University of Saskatchewan ... and she was wanting to do some work on Aboriginal communities ... I said, 'well I'm actually going to a meeting right now and we're going to talk about this thing and you can come and sit in and see how we work with the town.'"[7] As a consequence of this unexpected meeting, the student agreed to put the proposal together, using infor-

mation supplied by the rest of the committee. The finished submission
was not large, and a great deal of emphasis was placed on the willingness of the two communities to work together. The history of the
Nekaneet was briefly touched upon: "When the Plains Cree inhabiting
these hills were ordered to move out ... in the early 1880s they refused.
The [Nekaneet] Band was forcibly shipped out of the area but they
moved back and hid in the hills. Because of their refusal to move, this
small Band was cut off from any government assistance and left to fend
for itself ... For over eighty years, they lived without reserve[8] or status,
providing for themselves by hunting, trapping, selling fence posts, and
working for ranchers. The Nekaneet Band lives on its ancestral territory, *remaining true to its traditions*" (emphasis added).[9]

To the Nekaneet, this last was of particular importance because they
saw their traditions as being undiluted by outside influences. As was
explained: "You drive around here [reserve] you won't see any semblance of a church or anything like that. We've never been watered
down in that sense ... What I find in different communities, some
people did get the right teachings, or the teachings that coincide with
the Nekaneet teachings, but the problem with them is that they take it
a step further and they try to parallel it with Christianity. We don't
bother with that. We're secure with the fact that this is the way our
Elders were taught by their Elders ... and that's good enough for us."[10]
The Nekaneet felt that they could offer imprisoned Aboriginal women
a culturally appropriate and safe environment as they began their
"healing" journey. In particular, the Nekaneet believed that they had a
cultural environment largely unadulterated by Euro-Canadian mores.
In applying to CSC the band showed remarkable trust in a federal
organization, given the history of government betrayal of the Nekaneet.[11] In offering the assistance of their Elders and medicine people
the Nekaneet clarified their position: "the Indian teachings and practices are orally taught and preserved, therefore, it would be inappropriate to write about how the Native women attending a Healing
Lodge would be healed."[12] The assumption was that Nekaneet Elders
would be involved with the women should the Healing Lodge be
awarded to their community.

The proposal emphasized the beauty of the location and the
"healing" nature of the landscape. In terms of what the town could
offer, much was made of its location vis-à-vis the main cities in Alberta
and Saskatchewan; the local services available in Maple Creek; and,
above all, the fact that both Nekaneet and the local council had cooperated enthusiastically in putting together the proposal. As the band
councillor said: "I think what they [CSC] wanted at the time was a non-
Aboriginal/Aboriginal proposal that had already specified that they do

get along as opposed to they're going to get along."[13] Nevertheless, not all of the Nekaneet and residents of Maple Creek were happy with the suggestion that the Healing Lodge should be sited in their community, but few thought it likely that the proposal would be accepted, and there was no organized opposition. The proposal was submitted and the committee waited for a decision to be made. One committee member recalled: "We worked at it, like we really did this in a time frame of about two weeks I think. I remember [another committee member] tossed it across the table and said, 'What do we do if we get this?' I'll never forget that."[14]

Despite the earlier suggestion that party-political considerations contributed to the site selection of each prison, an official selection process was undergone in each area. The process for the Healing Lodge was the same as it was elsewhere, and a group of evaluators scrutinized each proposal. As one assessor said:

Each of us went through all the proposals [beforehand] and then we all came together in Saskatoon. We had set aside a week where we could go through each proposal ... We had our Elders with us ... We were into our third day and we had all of our sheets up, each of them scored and we weren't quite finished. We had a stack of the proposals on the table and they [Elders] came in and said, "Well, how is it going?" [We said] "Well, we're about half way there and we anticipate being done maybe tomorrow night." ... There were three of them [Elders] ... They went over to the table and Mary [Elder] took one [proposal] and she passed it on [to the other Elders] and they did this to all twenty-eight [of the proposals]. And there were three [proposals] they put in a pile and then they did it again [handled the three proposals], and [Mary] looked at them [Elders] and she said, "What do you think? I think it's this one here." And they both said, "Yes, that's the one." So they said, "Well, this is the one here," and we all looked at each other, because we still had our process to finish. So we said, "Okay, but in order for corrections to be able to defend the decision we've got to finish the process."[15]

The Elders had chosen Maple Creek. Upon being asked during an interview if the official process also selected Maple Creek, the assessor continued: "Yes. Head and shoulders above the rest as a matter of fact. It was interesting because the Maple Creek proposal had already been evaluated [before the Elders handled them], so we finished them off, being very diligent, and we didn't know what the scores were, because they hadn't been compiled. And when we finally had them compiled the score [for Maple Creek] was half again as much as the [next ones] and those next ones were the other two [selected by the Elders]."[16]

In mid-May Maple Creek's committee was asked to assemble a group of local representatives to meet the solicitor general, who was coming to the town on 22 May 1992. Prior to that, both the band office and the mayor had received a call asking how much land was being offered for the Healing Lodge, and csc's property management group was astonished to discover that it was a quarter section. (In ranching country, such as at Maple Creek, land is traditionally reckoned in quarter sections, which comprise 160 acres.) It was a far larger amount than had been anticipated, but the band thought this amount of land necessary for spiritual ceremonies. Solicitor General Lewis arrived, together with Commissioner Ole Ingstrup, and announced that Maple Creek had been selected, emphasizing, as in Truro, the economic gains for the community.

GUIDING THE PLANNING CIRCLE

Unlike the other prisons, the planning of the Healing Lodge involved a great deal of local input, and representatives of both the band and the town were invited to join the Healing Lodge Planning Circle. Town and country had collaborated with little expectation of success, and the reality of the hard work involved was soon to become apparent. From May 1992 the enlarged HLPC initially met at least once a month, for a period of two to three days, with members flying in from across Canada and being accommodated in Maple Creek. The immense cost of this, between $17,000 and $19,000 per meeting, was borne by csc. The meetings were no ordinary civil service meetings; each day began with ceremonies and prayers, and the end of the day's work was often marked by further prayer and "talking circles," which sometimes extended into the evening. The protocol attached to such ceremonies meant that agendas were not always adhered to as speakers could not be interrupted and the size of the HLPC, with an average of twenty-five attendees, meant that business proceeded slowly.

The HLPC was helped in its deliberations by two documents that had been prepared by the earlier, smaller committee: the *Role Statement*,[17] which amplified the bare description of a Healing Lodge contained in *Creating Choices*; and the *Healing Lodge Vision Statement* (NWAC 1991, 3), devised by the Aboriginal members but also signed by the csc representatives, which was intended to provide a spiritual rationale for the Healing Lodge and, by extension, for the HLPC as it deliberated. The *Vision* had immense significance because it both continued the political discourse begun during the task force and broke with oral tradition by writing down the principles underpinning Aboriginal culture and spirituality. It was an essential means of educating the Euro-Canadians.[18] The *Vision* briefly emphasized the political reality that: "as long as our people can remember, the Aboriginal people of Turtle Island [North America] ... lived here long before history was written ... We were sovereign." It showed how Aboriginal understanding of the world was explained by the teachings of the "Circle of Life"[19] and how the practical application of those beliefs enabled Aboriginal nations to live in harmony with themselves and others. Without explicitly saying so, the *Vision* thus became a model of Aboriginal justice, and therein lies its other importance, because CSC accepted that the HLPC would be influenced by the *Vision* as it planned the Healing Lodge.

The HLPC itself then produced the "Healing Lodge Operational Plan,"[20] a "blueprint" covering most aspects of the day-to-day running of the lodge, defining (among other things), the management model, the living arrangements, the physical care of the women, and the programming. It also prepared the "Planning Parameters: Healing Lodge," which fleshed out the physical details of the proposed lodge, while emphasizing that the design had to be "culturally aware" and reflective of the *Vision*. CSC was allowing a non-CSC-defined philosophy to be the guiding rationale for one of its new prisons, and the Operational Plan was an important reference point throughout the HLPC's deliberations.

PROVIDING THE LAND

A site for the Healing Lodge had to be selected, but it was not simply a question of looking for the place that appeared, from a construction perspective, to be most suitable. The Healing Lodge had to be in a place with spiritual qualities and close to a source of water, and a vision quest was the traditional means of locating such sites. Mary Louie, the Elder instrumental in originally selecting the Nekaneet/ Maple Creek proposal, led the quest, having been given details of a few locations that band members thought might be suitable. Two descriptions of the event unite in one major respect. First: "They went right to that hill. I thought maybe they would choose the other side as there was more open spots and a road could be built in. As far as construction and all that, they probably chose the spot that was most difficult!"[21] Second: "They had a group of Elders who were meeting in the Planning Circle and they went out this one afternoon to the reserve and actually walked through the bush ... and they tracked these hillsides and they said when they came to this spot that that was it, they knew that was it ... It's been questioned since. It was a very difficult place to build, I tell you ... right on the side hill and the rocks, it's solid rock out there."[22] The architects struggled to find solutions to the difficult, steeply sloping terrain as the buildings needed to reflect the Four Directions (as explained by the Circle of Life), yet also had to "fit" the land on which they were to be constructed.

The amount of land to be handed over by the band was a further complication. CSC was extremely reluctant to accept a quarter section because of the cost implications and the fear that the Treasury Board would not authorize the expenditure. Legally, CSC was not allowed to take on more land than was actually required for a new prison, so the quarter section was justified by a document entitled *Healing Lodge Land Rationale* (1991),[23] which provided a justification for the number of acres. The *Rationale* explained that many nations would be present at the lodge, each with conceivably different needs. The preamble elaborated: "For ceremonial purposes, Aboriginal people require large areas of land. This is to allow for the natural state of the land to provide cleansing and healing for its people. Aboriginal people do not take from the land without giving back to the land; therefore, the replenishment of the land is critical."[24]

This relationship with the land was fundamental to the planning of the Healing Lodge and a different – and difficult – concept for CSC to accept. Some of the difficulty lay in accepting that CSC might be party to constructing a prison that, theoretically, permitted women to walk alone to isolated places in order to "greet the new day,"[25] instead of restricting them to houses set behind fences, where their movements would be more easily monitored. CSC also had to accept the logic of the site selection, the rocky nature of which presented enormous structural difficulties; yet the Aboriginal members could point to the *Vision* for explanation: "At Creation, we were given four Sacred Gifts of Life: From the East, the gift of Fire; from the South, the gift of Rock; from the West, the gift of Water; and from the North, the gift of Wind." CSC was in uncharted territory, and the logic of the "dominant culture" was challenged, as the HLPC's minutes showed in May: "perhaps it is better that the Planning Circle meet with the Treasury Board ... as other people don't always understand the [land] rationale no matter how it is explained on paper, primarily due to the fact that spirituality cannot be explained in detail or with Justice (sic) on paper."[26]

FISCAL REALITY, MISMATCHED EXPECTATIONS

The original estimates for the prison had failed to take fully into account the cost of supplying utilities to the lodge, and the specific difficulties occasioned by the site itself added considerably to costs. As delays in the project occurred, and costs continued to rise, there was continual pressure from CSC that the HLPC should reduce the size of the prison. In February 1993 the HLPC deferred the gymnasium, reduced the size of the administration area, and deleted a work room from the plans, yet CSC continued to press for more savings and greater speed in planning. Despite this, the HLPC increased the size of the Cedar Tipi (spiritual lodge) because of the need to incorporate the Aboriginal concept of "all my relations" (i.e., the extended family) and the fact that the local community would also be participating in ceremonies at the lodge. CSC was insisting on budgetary restraint, while conceding "Aboriginal" additions to the plan, but the consequence of this bargaining was that basic facilities such as a gymnasium were denied to Aboriginal women but were permitted in the other prisons, where spiritual needs were also provided for. The importance of having buildings reflect Aboriginal beliefs complicated the design process at every stage. The HLPC was later told that the other wardens questioned the necessity for having two-bedroom living units (thought by the Elders to be essential to the "healing" of the women) and that these might be thought unfair when other facilities were making do with much larger cottages.[27] The scale of the day-care centre seemed excessive, but to remove children from the plan would have been entirely unacceptable to the Aboriginal planners. Counter-balancing these successes was the removal of the second Private Family Visiting House from the plans (on the grounds of excessive cost), leading to women having fewer means of retaining family ties than they would have had if they had been in the "non-Aboriginal" prisons. CSC was allowing the construction of an Aboriginal-influenced prison, yet it seemed to be assuming that costs would – and should – be proportionately no greater than elsewhere.

The commissioner began expressing concerns about delays as the Healing Lodge's disrupted schedule was affecting the closure date of the Prison for Women. The lodge was already considerably over budget; there was no possibility of persuading the Treasury Board to provide more federal money; and a CSC member of the HLPC was asking that the circle provide "true" figures rather than "figures from the sky."[28] A good proportion of the HLPC members were involved because of their connection with the Nekaneet Band or Maple Creek rather than because of their financial acumen, so they were unaccustomed to presenting detail in the manner essential to procuring both federal dollars and support – and by May the costs of the Healing Lodge were then some $3.2 million over budget. To complicate matters further, agreement had still not been reached with the Nekaneet for the land transfer.[29]

By September 1993 the HLPC had been meeting for seventeen months and CSC was deeply unhappy with progress. There was a clear divergence in operating manner between the Aboriginal and Maple Creek representatives, on the one hand, and those of csc, on the other. Even the style of the minutes would have exasperated the civil servants because they contained the barest details of discussions, with little indication of precisely what had been agreed upon. A senior representative from csc had attended the meeting and later sent a list of "actions which we agreed to take," while being careful to reassure HLPC members that the minutes were not being superseded.[30] There was a distinct air of "let's get on with this" attached to the letter, despite the diplomacy of the language. HLPC representatives were due to attend an ExCom (Executive Committee of csc) meeting, and a civil servant was asked to draft the presentation because the wording of the Land Rationale, among other things, needed to be transformed into "bureaucratic language" for it to be acceptable to ExCom. It was being made clear that the HLPC needed to adopt what csc considered to be a more professional approach to its work.

By November 1993 csc already knew that the closing date for the Prison for Women would have to be deferred because of the late opening of all of the new prisons, and a further letter was sent to the HLPC, stressing "the importance of the upcoming events such as the land designation, the hiring process of the Kikawinaw ... [as] these events impact directly on the selection process for the candidates to be trained [and] any modifications in our plan will demand that we readjust the other planned starting dates."[31] The Kikawinaw (director)[32] of the Healing Lodge was eventually appointed in December 1993, although the formal announcement that Norma Green was to hold this position was not made until March 1994. The Competition Board[33] comprised two representatives from csc, an Elder and an executive member of the Native Women's Association of Canada. The chief of the Nekaneet Band and his son, a band councillor, attended as observers but were not permitted to ask questions, which was an unfortunate breach of Aboriginal protocol. With hindsight, this was something of an indication of the future role to be played by the Nekaneet at the Healing Lodge.

In January 1994 the circle signed off on the conceptual design of the lodge, with csc's design representative indicating that the budget was in "reasonable order" and that savings could be made in the materials used, without impinging on the overall quality of the prison. The budget for the circle meetings was not, however, similarly under control, and the HLPC was told that there was "no money available for the continuation of the large Circle, Sub-Committees and frequent meetings, nor could [these] be justified."[34] The minutes showed resistance to the idea, stating: "The reorganization of the Circle could be detrimental to the entire vision as it appears it would become a Circle without any decision making power but rather a rubber stamp for what happens, to praise when things are going well or voice concerns when not, but really have no power to make decisions ... the vision cannot be carried out by individuals who have not been an integral part of the vision."[35]

Land clearing for the Healing Lodge did not begin until May 1994, and the Blessing of the Land Ceremony was held on 8 June 1994, when a small group of Elders and members of the Planning Circle joined together for the ritual. On the same day the *Memorandum of Understanding*, covering the lease of the land, was finally signed by both the Nekaneet and CSC. The memorandum provided the Nekaneet with an initial $21,000 per year,[36] and in return the band "surrendered" the land to CSC for a period of twenty-five years and allowed CSC an option to renew for a further twenty-five years. It took a further year for the Healing Lodge to reach completion, and its formal opening took place on 23–24 August 1995.

What this much abbreviated discussion of the planning for the lodge demonstrates is that Aboriginal perspectives did not necessarily sit happily within the formal structures of a government department. Aboriginal understanding of justice was also disjunctive from that of the "dominant culture," and the Aboriginal groups involved in the HLPC were helping to provide a system of punishment for Aboriginal women that had no cultural foundation in Aboriginal practices. As has already been explained, at the time these groups – like CAEFS – felt they had no other option and, within those constraints, they fought hard to instill Aboriginal influences at the lodge. Central to their endeavours were three beliefs: that the Nekaneet and their Elders should be fully involved; that Aboriginal staff needed to be employed at the heart of the lodge; and that Aboriginal governance needed to be maintained, with the result that CSC could not be the ultimate philosophical influence, even though it remained the paymaster. This requires an assessment of parts of the *Memorandum of Understanding* between the Nekaneet and CSC, and how it was interpreted by both parties.

THE KE-KUN-WEM-KON-A-WUK
(KEEPERS OF THE VISION)

It had always been intended by CSC's Aboriginal "partners" that Aboriginal influence would be paramount at the lodge, despite the fiscal reality of CSC's paying entirely for its running. The HLPC wanted to ensure that the highest placed Aboriginal member of staff (the Kikawinaw) would be locked into a system of accountability to other Aboriginal people. When the 1993 Operational Plan (see above) was

devised, it clearly delineated the management structure. The Kikawinaw was to "support, assist and guide" the women and was also
specifically "accountable" to two tiers of management: the regional
deputy commissioner and the Ke-kun-wem-kon-a-wuk (comprising
national Elders, local Elders, and members of the HLPC). The Ke-kun-
wem-kon-a-wuk's role was to provide "guidance, support and assistance" to the women and the Kikawinaw, but it was *not* "accountable"
to the Kikawinaw (CSC 1993a, 4–5).

By the time the lodge opened this position had been reversed and
was made quite specific in the *Memorandum of Understanding* signed
by the Nekaneet Band in June 1994. Schedule B 3(a) reads: "the operation of the Healing Lodge will be the responsibility of the Kikawinaw
(Director) who is appointed by CSC. CSC will establish a national committee, the Ke-kun-wem-kon-a-wuk ... to provide guidance, support
and assistance to the Kikawinaw and CSC." The memorandum made
no mention of the Kikawinaw being *accountable* to the Ke-kun-wem-
kon-a-wuk, which meant that her decision making was only accountable to the regional deputy commissioner and the national commissioner, leaving the checks and balances fractured. The band had been
required, as part of its undertaking, to seek advice from a solicitor
regarding the memorandum before it signed it, but it is doubtful
whether anyone who had not been part of the HLPC decision making
would have recognized the significance of that section of Schedule B. It
also appeared to nullify part of the intention of Section 1(d) of Schedule B, which acknowledged that the band had entered into the agreement based upon consideration of: "the ability of the Band to participate in the *management* of the Healing Lodge through the
Ke-kun-wem-kon-a-wuk" (emphasis added). The word "management"
could not be equated with "guidance, support and assistance." The
interpretation of the HLPC's intentions was central to the issue of who
had responsibility for the Healing Lodge because the *Memorandum of
Understanding* consigned final authority to CSC. Moreover, the (Aboriginal) Kikawinaw was solely accountable to CSC, and the (largely
Aboriginal) Ke-kun-wem-kon-a-wuk was left with little authority. The
effect was twofold: Aboriginal, including Nekaneet, influence was
restricted, and the Kikawinaw became a warden, just as much as any
of the other new wardens, with CSC being the ultimate authority to
which she must answer.

This development was unsurprising, given the reality that CSC was
statutorily responsible both for the administration of the prison and its
financing. However, the failure to honour the earlier agreement – that
the Kikawinaw should be answerable to the Ke-kun-wem-kon-a-wuk –
raises the possibility that CSC knowingly used the Aboriginal represen-

tatives to legitimate a venture over which it had no intention of relinquishing final control. The same allegations were earlier made in relation to CAEFS' involvement in the task force, and the way in which the organization was omitted from the key implementation committee, the NIC. It is already clear that CSC had far exceeded any previous arrangements in agreeing to the Aboriginal members having such a central role on the HLPC and that CSC had agreed to the construction of a prison radically different from the other new federal prisons for women. But in altering the lines of accountability, CSC bound the Kikawinaw into its own structures and ensured that the Nekaneet would be sidestepped.

NEW PHILOSOPHY, NEW STAFF

It was not just the Kikawinaw who was thought essential to the Aboriginal environment of the lodge. The *Memorandum of Understanding* contained a number of "Specific Undertakings of the Solicitor General." Section 14.3 agreed to: "a) implementing a staffing and training plan for the operation of the Healing Lodge designed to be inclusive of the Nekaneet Band members with respect to eligibility for consideration; [and], b) implementing a staffing process for available positions at the Healing Lodge ... by open competition until 50% of the Healing Lodge staff positions are occupied by Nekaneet Band members."[37]

The HLPC knew from the beginning that it wanted to employ a large number of Aboriginal women at the lodge. While the members could not provide for all the nations who might be represented by the federally sentenced women at the Healing Lodge, they could work towards an environment reflecting essential Aboriginal beliefs, and this could only be achieved with a high proportion of Aboriginal staff. Nekaneet women were the obvious first choice, not least because the band had made much of its commitment to working with the women. But employing Nekaneet women was not straightforward as many had not remained at school long enough to complete their Grade 12, an essential requirement for correctional staff, so it was arranged that a number of women would attend upgrading classes in Maple Creek. Many people applied for posts at the lodge, and the HLPC finally selected forty candidates, including eighteen Nekaneet women, for training (even though only 26.5 posts were actually available) to ensure that others could be called upon once further vacancies arose. Four phases of training were planned. The first, and arguably the most important, lasted almost a month and took place at two non-correctional treatment centres. With this strategy, the Healing Lodge set out on its own path. As explained by one circle

Cedar Tipi at the Healing Lodge

member: "What we thought we could provide for the workers was for them to be able to start at a place where they weren't superior to the women. So that was one of the rationales for sending them off for treatment as clients, as opposed to just shadowing someone and learning how to do it."[38] The staff needed to develop an understanding of what it was like to battle addiction and/or to cope with the aftermath of abuse before they could support other women. Staff members became *participants* in the program rather than observers, and they took that knowledge back with them to the Healing Lodge.

Thereafter, all training took place in Maple Creek, so that local women could more easily take part, and it covered areas such as cultural/Aboriginal awareness, counselling, co-dependency, and the Corrections Training Program (CTP) – a component common to all staff at the new institutions. The latter introduced staff to the formal role of correctional officer, a role perhaps belied by the term "Kimisinaw," or "older sister," and which was the equivalent of that of a primary worker in the other prisons. (More senior staff members were known as Kikawisinaw, or "aunt.") The Kikawinaw, despite the initial expectations of the HLPC and the hiring committee, did not participate in any phase of the training.[39]

The significance of the training program should not be underestimated, particularly its length and the "treatment" component. The first phase was demanding of all the participants, not least the Aborig-

Living lodges at the Healing Lodge

inal trainees, who were confronting issues that had played a large part in the destruction of Aboriginal communities across Canada, if not necessarily their own. Additionally, although the bid for the Healing Lodge had been a joint undertaking by the band and the town of Maple Creek, it did not mean that the two communities generally mixed, and both the Nekaneet and Euro-Canadian women had to adjust their perceptions of each other. The end result was that the women emerged from their training with a cohesion that staff at other prisons could not match. Yet knowledge of Aboriginal culture, although an essential part of the training, could not be sufficiently imparted to the Euro-Canadians within such a short period. Nor could the disparities in levels of education be overcome, and this meant that mostly non-Aboriginal women were appointed to senior positions once hiring began. Section 14.3 (c) of the *Memorandum of Understanding* explicitly committed CSC to identifying "potential management candidates," and some form of affirmative hiring strategy could have been implemented. Had this happened, Aboriginal influence at the lodge would have been more secure as the years passed.

AN ABORIGINAL PRISON?

The pursuit of both the task force's and the HLPC's vision led inexorably to the Healing Lodge itself. This section begins with a brief description of how the lodge functions as a prison and is followed by a critical assessment of the emerging issues.

The Nekaneet Reserve, in the Cypress Hills, is some 1,200 metres above the surrounding countryside, which extends below in a seemingly endless vista of plains. The only road from Maple Creek is unsealed and single-tracked, and there is no public transport available to either the reserve or the prison. Apart from a monitored gate on the side road to the Healing Lodge, there is little visible security as the prison is approached, and, unlike the other new prisons, the Healing Lodge was exempt from the later requirement that a fence should be constructed. The lodge is visually striking among the dense stands of aspen that surround it, with vivid use of colour in all the buildings providing a stark contrast to the grey stone austerity of the Prison for Women. The administration building is circular, reflecting the Circle of Life, and is the centre of daily activities. Around its small inner courtyard lie offices, the healthcare unit, education and library rooms, a large children's nursery, and the communal eating and cooking area. A large deck extends from the dining area, providing a panoramic view of the countryside and overlooking the Cedar Tipi (Spiritual Lodge) and adjacent living lodges. The steep terrain means that the lower floor of the main building only extends part-way underneath, and this contains – among other rooms – a small ceramics workshop. Some four years after the lodge opened further rooms were erected because budget constraints at the planning stage had meant insufficient space was available for education, workshops, and programming.[40]

Although the administration building is the functional heart of the prison, it is the Cedar Tipi that provides its spiritual and philosophical heart. Designed to be entered from the Four Directions,[41] it is also circular, with its roof rising steeply to reflect the shape of a traditional tipi. The interior immediately draws the eye to the centrally positioned fire, with its chimney extending through the great height of the roof. The fire is surrounded by a circular seating platform, which in turn is surrounded by a further circle of seats attached to the wooden walls. The Cedar Tipi is a place for reflection, instruction, and celebration; it is also the heart of a prison.

The living lodges each accommodate two women. There are single bedrooms and a shared living and dining area, where the women prepare their evening meals. Some of the lodges are designed to accommodate children, and one is used by visiting Elders. One lodge is more secure (the lodge's approximation of an enhanced unit) and can be monitored by CCTV (reluctantly agreed to by the HLPC) when a woman is thought to be in need of a more protected environment. A series of beaver dams lie below the living lodges, and, depending on the season, women may collect and braid the sweetgrass – essential to the ceremonies within the Cedar Tipi – from the surrounding land. The sweat lodge moves as required. Freedom to move about the land was never allowed in the manner envisaged by the *Land Rationale*, and women must be accompanied by a staff member or an Elder when outside the narrow envelope of the Healing Lodge buildings.

The pattern of each day was decided in consultation with the Elders. Women are now expected to begin their day in the Cedar Tipi, whereas attendance was initially optional.[42] The following description of the Cedar Tipi is necessary in order to highlight the different focus of this prison, and it is given while acknowledging that cultural and spiritual values are normally communicated verbally. Each morning the fire is lit and an offering of tobacco is made to the Elder or person leading the day's ceremony.[43] This is followed by the burning of sweetgrass and herbs, prayer, and perhaps a "teaching" for the day. Each member of the circle is then invited to speak; "good morning" suffices, but it is also an opportunity for some to say more, should they so choose. They will not be interrupted and there is a quiet sense of formality and courtesy. Staff also may participate in the circle.

The women then attend various activities, with the emphasis being on education, while maintenance and catering is also partly carried out by the women. Lunch is taken communally, with staff joining the women, which does not happen in the other new prisons. From the start, the wider expectation at the Healing Lodge was that barriers between staff and the women would be lowered as they jointly experienced everyday activities in more natural circumstances. The barriers between the local community and the women are also expected to be permeable, and there are occasional evening activities, such as a round-dance, involving members of the Nekaneet Band. Children are cared for by a trained nursery nurse during the day but become solely their mother's responsibility at night and over the weekend. (Although Etablissement Joliette, in Quebec, has a very well equipped nursery, the Healing Lodge was the only one of the prisons initially allowed to house children.)[44] The primary concern is that children not be exposed to any risky or distressing situations. All the women know that they will be removed from the lodge should their behaviour have an adverse impact upon a child.

For all new arrivals at the Healing Lodge the shock of change began immediately they left their previous prison as they were not required to wear handcuffs or shackles while being transferred.[45] For those federally sentenced women who arrived direct from the confines of the Prison for Women, or a similarly enclosed prison, one of the most immediate challenges was presented by the change in physical environment. After the ceaseless noise of the ranges at the Prison for Women the quietness was alarming. One woman spoke of how difficult the transition had been and that it had taken her months to settle into the lodge. She was fearful of coming out of her house in case alarms went off; was initially frightened by the voices coming out of the walls because she had failed to notice the intercom system; and was astonished to be given keys to her house, room, and mailbox.[46] The ability to walk freely between the living units and the administration building, without waiting for staff to unlock cells and gates, challenged the women's perceptions of imprisonment and required a degree of confidence that, for many, took some time to emerge.

A DIFFERENT PRISON: AN "ABORIGINAL" PRISON?

From the beginning there were particular expectations of the Healing Lodge: it would be supported by the local Aboriginal community; Aboriginal staff would be employed to the fullest extent possible; all Aboriginal federally sentenced women would be eligible for admission; and Aboriginal culture, healing, and spirituality would inform its day-to-day running. These points will now be examined.

Embedding the prison

For all its outward appearance belying the reality of its being a prison, the Healing Lodge is governed by rules that separate it from the local community. Paradoxically, that community does not feel it is altogether set apart because the Healing Lodge is a prison it helped create. Without the active solicitation of both the Nekaneet Band and residents of Maple Creek, the prison would not have been built in the Cypress Hills. It is striking that the Healing Lodge did not generate anything like the press coverage received by both Nova and Edmonton, and this was largely because there were no "incidents" (with one exception) that initially found their way into the public domain. But it was also to do with the remoteness of Maple Creek, the size of the local community, and the way information about the Healing Lodge was initially provided for the local newspaper by a member of the HLPC and then by the Kikawinaw herself. With hindsight, this was a clever device that kept the local community informed, solicited help, and, above all, located responsibility for the lodge within the community rather than solely with CSC. It represented a continuation of the cooperation that had initially brought the prison to the Cypress Hills. Any major incidents would immediately have been known to residents, and the local citizens were never part of an angry crowd, questioning the reason for having a prison in their area. The Kikawinaw, while still the "public face" of CSC, was never forced to defend her prison, as had been Jan Fox and Christine Manuge. Generally, there was little sense of a community keeping close watch while waiting for things to go wrong, and press interest largely focused on the uniqueness of the whole endeavour, often featuring the same women as representatives of the others. The Healing Lodge was permitted a rare degree of freedom to develop its own style.

Community and culture as a resource

Creating Choices emphasizes that "the connection of the Lodge to an Aboriginal community [would] be essential to its survival" (TFFSW 1990, 123). Schedule B 1(a) of the *Memorandum of Understanding* acknowledges the Nekaneet Band's wish to "make available the experience of its members in Aboriginal healing." This makes explicit what had been written in the original letter of support by the Nekaneet chief, who viewed the lodge as an opportunity to "share these gifts and our home with women who are looking for a place to be healed" (24 February 1992).

When the prison first opened the Nekaneet Elders were a very visible part of everyday life. They led the Spiritual Circles, conducted sweats, and were available to counsel the women. From the beginning, Elders from outside the area were also brought in on a rotational basis so that the teachings were not always those of the Nekaneet. As a visiting Elder commented: "You have the system to work with, people who come from different levels of understanding. So the system said we will hire some Elders ... we'll have a holistic approach and that means other nations coming here as teachers. But, to me, anybody who knows about the culture should never forget where they are and should have respect. It's like me coming into your house and trying to take over your house, disregarding your own background."[47]

From the Nekaneet perspective the situation was less than satisfactory, irrespective of how respectful visiting Elders might have been. Their assumption had been that as providers of the land they would have the main responsibility for the spiritual and cultural teaching of the women, as articulated here by a member of the band: "I guess I automatically assumed that we would be directly involved, because it was on Nekaneet land. That's where the difference of opinion occurred with Corrections ... it's the Aboriginal people who worked in Corrections who wanted to spell out that this was a national facility, therefore the Aboriginal program should be national in scope, whereas my thinking is that this is a Healing Lodge and it's located on Nekaneet [land] so therefore you should use traditional protocol and utilize Nekaneet's Aboriginal teachings first and foremost ... We've kind of been shunted aside."[48] The consequence has been that the Nekaneet Elders now play a reduced role at the lodge, and two Aboriginal women skilled at "facilitating" were later hired to do some of the work usually undertaken by Elders.[49] Whether "facilitating" is an Aboriginal concept might be debatable, but the underlying point is that Elders are not created by decree of an outside authority. Their wisdom is recognized by those around them, by their bands, and by their nations. They are the keepers of history, the link with the land and, thus, with the Creator. It is not the job of CSC to define who might fill that role, as is made explicit in CD 702 (1995-09-06), which defines an Elder as "a person recognized by an *external* Aboriginal community as having knowledge and understanding of the traditional culture of the community ... Elders may be identified as such *by Aboriginal communities only*" (emphasis added).

While this is a worrying instance, from an Aboriginal perspective, of CSC exercising control in an area over which it should have no authority, the underlying question is whether it is unsurprising from a penological perspective. The answer to this must be that it is not. In Harding et al.'s (1985) terms, prisons are seen to be "reactive" both to public demands and to their own internal needs, and CSC's need would have been to retain control over those who worked within its institutions. The need to establish an Aboriginal prison would have been circumscribed by the need to maintain control over possibly independent staff. There is a further dimension to this, in that Elders (like priests) working within a prison must themselves abide by the prison's rules and so have their independence compromised. This very soon becomes apparent to the prisoners, with consequences that will shortly be discussed.

PASSING THE VISION TO THE STAFF

Aboriginal values were also expected to be inculcated by staff. During the first months of opening immense care and effort went into settling the women into the new prison. Staff members were highly visible and accessible, joining the Spiritual Circle, eating with the women at meal times, and being available to talk. Despite the disparity between Aboriginal and non-Aboriginal staff, with the more senior positions being filled by Euro-Canadians, all were equally involved, and this can be explained by the quality of the training they had received. Unusually, a non-Aboriginal male held the position of assistant Kikawinaw (although how a male could be an assistant "mother" was never satisfactorily explained), and it was generally assumed by other staff that he was CSC's particular "representative" at the prison, thanks to his previous correctional experience. (His appointment was also replicated at Edmonton when it reopened.)

By late 1998 the environment had changed and was visible immediately to anyone who entered the Healing Lodge (as noted by Monture-Angus 2000). Staff screened visitors to the lodge with a hand-held scanner as well as women returning from outside visits or work. In most prisons such a security function is the norm, and thus unremarkable, but during its first years of opening the Healing Lodge had managed to incorporate more fully than the other new prisons the concept of "dynamic security," and such searches did not occur. The change emphasized the official relationship of the women and the staff, and also its inequality, a fact that had been somewhat masked by the sharing of the morning Spiritual Circles. Staff members were finding that they could not easily surmount, or cope with, their "status differential" (Rivera 1996, 31), which was made worse by the expectation that they should be both mentor and guard (see chapter 8 for a discussion of these conflicting roles). By 1998 staff numbers had increased, and there were fifty staff members employed for a maximum number of thirty prisoners (which may partly be explained by the extra difficulties posed by the isolation of the prison). Staff members were conspicuous by their absence and were generally to be found in their offices, with doors shut; the demands of bureaucracy appeared to have overtaken them. The majority no longer sat with the women at mealtimes, and there were few signs of the casual chat that had previously been so visible (see also Hannah-Moffat and Shaw 2001, 35). There was also evidence of the changing relationships between staff and their managers, with distinct groups having been formed among them, and an underlying unhappiness with what some staff perceived to be the changing style of the Healing Lodge. It was not uncommon to be told – by both women and staff – that the Healing Lodge was turning into a conventional prison, wherein staff could not focus adequately on the needs of the women, and the women had less time to concentrate on that which made the Healing Lodge unique: its Aboriginal dimension.

There was another reason for the change. A number of staff left and their replacements were not exposed to the intense training of that first group. They came to the Healing Lodge with more traditional correctional approaches and contributed to altering the balance between the women and the staff. Additionally, the top tier of management remained largely, with the exception of the Kikawinaw, non-Aboriginal. While it was never expected that the staffing of the lodge would quickly reach a full complement of Aboriginal staff – there were too few in the system at large, and certainly too few with the requisite qualifications available locally – there was a barrier to promotion because

CSC seemed reluctant to change the rules so that capable local staff could be promoted, despite its commitment in the *Memorandum of Understanding* to doing so.

A multilevel prison?

Of course, the Healing Lodge was dealing with women who had lower security ratings than those who were located elsewhere. Unlike both Edmonton and Nova, the Healing Lodge never accommodated maximum security women, although it was originally expected to do so. The 1992 CD 006, *Classification of Institutions*,[50] shows that *all* the new regional women's prisons were classed as "multilevel." The "Healing Lodge Operational Plan" specified that: "the Healing Lodge will accommodate Federally Sentenced Aboriginal women for all or part of their sentence, *regardless of their security classification,* therefore women may be admitted directly upon sentencing" (CSC 1993a, 8, emphasis added). November 1993's HLPC minutes, written eight months after the Operational Plan was published, clearly indicated that the prison was intended to be a multilevel one as, in the absence of any fence, security bracelets were being explored as a possible means of allowing "multilevel women" more freedom "in the 160 acres." However, the June 1994 HLPC minutes state that a member "had been alerted by the RPC [Regional Psychiatric Centre] staff in Saskatoon that only minimum security women would be able to get to the Healing Lodge ... [and that this] ... apparent CSC position had also been heard by other Planning Circle members as well as the women." This was the first hint that the multilevel nature of the facility might be altered. The meeting was told that "women would apply for placement at the Healing Lodge" and that the Kikawinaw would decide whether or not to accept a woman, clearly breaching the Operational Plan's expectation that women could be admitted "directly upon sentencing."

Even now, there is no CD referring to the barring of maximum security women from the Healing Lodge. The 1992 CD 006, classifying all the new prisons as multilevel (meaning that they could be any combination of security level), was not superseded until 22 August 1996, when the interim CD 500 declared that Prairie-region maximum security women were barred solely from Edmonton. A further interim CD 500, issued on 12 September 1996 and referring specifically to Grand Valley, Nova, and Joliette, barred maximum security women from those prisons as well. None of these CDs applied to the Healing Lodge, and the situation has been made no clearer since then.

Based on anecdotal evidence,[51] it seems that the decision to bar maximum security women from the Healing Lodge was confirmed in

June 1994, when the HLPC was first alerted to the possibility. During that meeting the HLPC decided that the Healing Lodge would not have an enhanced unit but would, instead, have a "safe lodge." This did not meet the security standards of an enhanced unit, and officials from CSC then announced that maximum security women would consequently be barred from the lodge. CSC's position was made more explicit during land transfer negotiations with the Nekaneet, when it was already clear that some band members were concerned about the ability of the lodge to function as a place of "healing" if it had to cope with women with multiple problems. There is also another factor to be considered, and this relates to the numbers of women the lodge can accommodate. It is limited to twenty-eight women, and the numbers of Aboriginal federally sentenced women hugely exceed that total. While it can easily be argued that maximum security Aboriginal women are possibly in greater need of what the lodge offers, that argument can be countered by the fact that some also pose greater risks to the stability of any prison. It is possible that CSC, having invested so much in the credibility of an Aboriginal prison, was not prepared to jeopardize the outcome. Incidents similar to those seen at both Nova and Edmonton would have shattered the carefully prepared image of a peaceful place of "healing." Consequently, a substantial group of Aboriginal women have never been able to move to the Healing Lodge – and the concept of a multilevel *Aboriginal* prison has never been tested.

This is yet another aspect of the overall task force plan that has not been implemented. However, it should also be acknowledged that the Kikawinaw, guided by the Elders, initially exercised considerable discretion in deciding which women should have their security classification reviewed, based on her conclusion that individual women were potentially suited to the ethos of the Healing Lodge. One of the first arrivals at the lodge was a woman who had been involved in the April 1994 incidents at the Prison for Women and had been labelled one of Canada's most dangerous women. Her eventual release from the lodge on parole some eighteen months later was to earn her a quarter page spread in the *Maple Creek News*,[52] including a photo of her being given a farewell hug by the Kikawinaw.

Aboriginal culture and spirituality within a prison

The draft Operational Plan had envisaged the Healing Lodge having a "non-denominational chapel" (CSC 1992b, 29), but in February 1993 the HLPC decided against this, which meant that Aboriginal women preferring to have a Christian or alternative option would have to forego the Healing Lodge. An Elder explained that the "women at the

Prison for Women did not want religious denominations at the Healing Lodge [as] there remain[ed] a lot of pain to heal from the wounds inflicted by religious institutions."[53] This decision facilitated the Healing Lodge's resolute focus on Aboriginal spirituality. There are always risks involved in new ventures, but the particular risk in the opening of the Healing Lodge resided not in questions of security but, rather, in the use of Aboriginal culture and spirituality within a penal setting. As Faith (1995, 80) notes: "spirituality, the central force of traditional healing, is the antithesis of a prison regime." While Faith is referring to the voluntary nature of spiritual beliefs, it is important to understand that the Aboriginal planners were also offering, if not imposing, a spiritual standpoint in much the same way that early prison reformers offered the principles of Christianity as a moral exemplar (see Ignatieff 1978; Rafter 1985; Hannah-Moffat 2001). However, the crucial difference in the Canadian case is that spirituality cannot be divorced from culture and, together, they contribute to an essentially Aboriginal perspective being offered within a prison setting. For the Aboriginal planners this combination was essential to the environment they were working to create, but the Healing Lodge's architecture blurred the message the women received. The prison initially gave little outward sign of being a prison: the overt physical discipline of the old penitentiary in Kingston had disappeared and been replaced by more subtle forms of self-discipline, or self-surveillance. The Healing Lodge was an understated extension of the reverse-panopticon evident at the "non-Aboriginal" prisons, with the extra dimension of culture adding to the burden of reponsibilization imposed upon women charged with their own surveillance.

Many of the women who first arrived at the prison made the choice because they wanted to be in an Aboriginal environment while serving their sentences. However, a woman's decision to go to the Healing Lodge did not necessarily mean that she felt a specific need to explore her own culture; rather, it meant that she wished to be away from the "dominant culture" of Euro-Canada and to be surrounded by other Aboriginal people. Such a decision, however, left the women unexpectedly answerable to two sets of rules: the official correctional ones and implicit Aboriginal ones. In choosing to go to a prison where there would be a number of Aboriginal staff and a partially Aboriginal daily routine, women were also agreeing to participate in the spiritual and cultural life of the prison. While for many this was a welcome choice, it is not the point being made here, which is that the issue of choice for other federally sentenced women was never predicated on their agreeing to participate in a particular spiritual worldview. For Aboriginal women, their choice was between a total package of environment *and spirituality and culture*, on the one hand, or a prison with relatively few Aboriginal inmates, on the other.

There are three issues that are of particular importance here. The first relates to the aspect of compulsion and whether this is compatible with participation in what are spiritual ceremonies. This element was clearly evident some two years after the lodge first opened, when attendance at the morning ceremonies had become compulsory (see also Monture-Angus 2000). Some of the women resented this coercion of spirituality because it related to something fundamental to their lives. Other women, who were perhaps discovering this aspect of Aboriginal culture for the first time, similarly resented the coercion because it took away any element of choice. In the wider environment of what the task force hoped to achieve, "choice" was of particular importance as it conferred a degree of autonomy on imprisoned women.

The second issue relates to staff members and their relationship with the women while participating in spiritual ceremonies. This is most visible in the Cedar Tipi, where staff members are expected to join the women for the morning ceremonies (although few actually did by the time of the second fieldtrip, and even fewer by the third and fourth). The circle is meant to be a place of safety and confidentiality, where women can speak and not be judged. While women are likely to reserve certain matters for private discussions with Elders, the circle in its intimacy invites relaxation of a woman's guard. Should a woman inadvertently reveal something during the circle that might be thought relevant to her correctional record, staff members are then brought face-to-face with the reality of their own positions: they are correctional officers and should record the information. The women privately expressed concerns about the changed nature of the circle and said that they were extremely careful about how they joined in.[54] The ultimate concern was that information unintentionally disclosed during the spiritual circle might end up on a woman's official record and harm her future release prospects. This incorporation of Aboriginal spirituality for correctional purposes compromised the sanctity of the circle. In such circumstances the Cedar Tipi could *never* assert its authority over the prison because it had become part of it.

Kendall (1993, 84) suggests that those working in prisons should "truthfully inform" prisoners of "the realities associated with confidentiality and other related factors"; however, at the Healing Lodge these issues were blurred by the Aboriginal dimension. Aboriginal members of staff were expected to participate in, and respect, religious ceremonies – and, in effect, to be equal to their Aboriginal prisoners – yet were simultaneously compromising Aboriginal spirituality by the possibility of having to breach confidentiality. This meant that they

were in the invidious position of potentially betraying both their Aboriginal "sisters" and their Aboriginal culture. Their role as correctional
officers was undoubtedly made harder by their ethnicity. Non-Aboriginal staff members were not placed in such doubly difficult situations
(although they still had to inform, when necessary) but contributed to
the compromising of Aboriginal culture by attending ceremonies that
they only superficially understood. The tensions were unlike anything
that staff members at the other new prisons faced, although they, too,
had to balance being guards with being quasi-counsellors and role
models.

The term "staff" can also be applied loosely to the Elders, even
though they might resist such terminology. Here the issue of confidentiality is of particular importance because their role sometimes encom-
passes counseling as well as imparting knowledge of culture and spirituality. Should they be forced to make a decision based on correctional,
rather than strictly Aboriginal, needs they risk compromising not just
their own standing but also the way in which their wider message is
perceived by the women.

This leads to the third issue: that the "success" of the prison will
inevitably be judged by the "success" of its prisoners once they return
to the outside world. What is "success"? Is it the ability to stay out of
prison completely? Or to stay out for twice as long as previously? Or
to return with a lesser charge because certain behaviour has been modified? Or will anything less than avoiding all conflict with the law be
adjudged failure? If the judgment is failure, who or what will be
blamed? Will it be the prison for failing to provide women with the
tools of the "dominant culture," so necessary for survival in the
outside world? Will it be the women themselves for having failed to
take advantage of what the prison offered them? Will it be csc for
having established an "Aboriginal" prison over which Aboriginal
peoples had no final authority? Might it conceivably be the actual
culture and spirituality of the Aboriginal nations themselves that is
found wanting? Will *they* be blamed for failure? And what of the
women themselves? Having been exposed to this "Aboriginal" prison,
how will they react to having "failed" as Aboriginal women? Is it possible that another form of prison discipline is emerging, whereby
women are regulated through a combination of ethnicity, culture, and
spirituality? And, if that is so, who should be held accountable if the
discipline should fail – csc or those Aboriginal members of the task
force who fought so hard for Aboriginal voices to be heard?

The isolation of the lodge further complicates possible outcomes.
Women serving very long sentences, of whom there are a disproportionate number at the Healing Lodge, will face considerable difficulties

living in such a small community once they have exhausted program possibilities, and it is not anticipated that they will serve their entire sentence at the lodge. Will they have been sufficiently well equipped to cope should they choose to move to one of the other prisons?

It is important that these questions be considered because they lead back to the point raised earlier: the extra responsibilities assumed by women who elected to transfer to the Healing Lodge. If they are thought of within the context of Hannah-Moffat's "responsible woman," who is drawn into accepting responsibility for her own self-governance and, by extension, the good order of the prison wherein she resides, then it can be seen that Aboriginal women are being asked to shoulder extra burdens. Comack (1996, 15) suggests that the word "prisoning" should be used "to get at the process of confinement and individuals' experiences of that process." The word seems apt here, in that the process to which Aboriginal women are exposed has extra layers, one of which has clear connections to cultural and spiritual responsibilities.

"SELLING" CULTURE

Alongside these points it is also important to consider the importance of the Healing Lodge to CSC's overall strategy, in the sense that the whole task force initiative has been followed internationally – and some would say promoted – as a possible blueprint for women's imprisonment. It cannot be assumed that what is appropriate for women in one country will necessarily be appropriate for women in another. This is even more the case when it comes to dealing with cultural elements of a plan. Madame Justice Arbour (1996, 218) considered the Healing Lodge in some detail in her report, suggesting that "qualitative program reforms of this kind [implementation of *Creating Choices*], if taken to their mature potential, could revolutionize correctional care for women prisoners ... Eventually, the success of program initiatives in women's corrections ... may serve as a blueprint for initiatives adapted to male offenders." This belief that programs specific to a particular group of women are transferable – and translatable – needs to be treated with caution. It appears to be the reverse of what has traditionally happened to women prisoners, who have been offered what is appropriate for men rather than for themselves. When Aboriginal-influenced programs are offered as part of a correctional package by a non-Aboriginal authority, the question of ownership becomes murky and there is considerable risk of cultural expropriation.

It would be wrong, however, to assume that the Healing Lodge had nothing to teach the other Canadian prisons or, indeed, other countries. The very fact that the lodge remained so free of trouble during its opening years suggests that much could be learned from it. One aspect stands out: to begin with, women at the Healing Lodge were not charged because charging was known to have an adverse effect on parole applications. Rather, mediation was used to solve problems. As charging has an impact on all imprisoned women, mediation could be much more widely applied, with the proviso that it is understood to be a "dominant culture" interpretation of the original concept rather than an incorporation of Aboriginal cultural practices. Other sanctions have been applied at the Healing Lodge. On New Year's Eve 1998 four women were found to be under the influence of prescription drugs, and one assaulted another woman: all four were removed from the lodge.

There have also been allegations of sexual abuse at the lodge, details of which may not be discussed because of provisions of the Privacy Act, 1985.[55] Following consultations with the female Elders, it has been decided that male Elders may no longer be alone with any of the women, which offers protection to both the Elders and the women. Yet, whatever happened during the alleged incident, there is the historical dimension of physical and sexual abuse within residential schools, and its subsequent extension into Aboriginal communities, to be taken into account. Many of the women imprisoned at the lodge have experienced sustained abuse during their non-prison lives (as have many other federally sentenced women). For Aboriginal women to be, or feel, exposed to further abuse while at the Healing Lodge lessens its authority as an Aboriginal-influenced institution. Yet prisons are places where acts of abuse and intimidation are common, and it is this reality that collides with the visionary nature of what is aspired to at the Healing Lodge: to be a place where Aboriginal women may safely begin the "healing" journey back to their communities. However, even that aspiration needs to be closely dissected because prisons are not places of "healing"; rather, they are places of involuntary confinement, where punishment is administered through the deprivation of liberty and autonomy. Perhaps the very name "Healing Lodge" adds to the complexity of that expectation, with the gentleness of the wording implying support and comfort. Had the lodge been named the Okimaw Ohci (Thunder Hills) Prison, would expectations have been lessened? The contradiction of prisons punishing in order to heal is explored in the final chapter.

Questions have been raised that need further consideration, alongside the wish of the Nekaneet Band to assume responsibility for the Healing Lodge under Section 81(1) of the Corrections and Conditional Release Act. And the question posed at the end of chapter 5 also needs to be reviewed: did the continuing influence of the Aboriginal representatives during the planning of the Healing Lodge enable a truly radical model of imprisonment to emerge? Were the Aboriginal members of the task force the great "winners"?

But the dominant question remains. Are women at the Healing Lodge being required to show a degree of involvement in their own imprisonment – unparalleled elsewhere – precisely because they are answerable to two disparate cultures: a correctional culture and an Aboriginal culture? Are they being regulated through their ethnicity and their implicit culture? In asking this, the light is once more shone upon the task force, whose Aboriginal members, through sheer strength of character and argument, forced the Healing Lodge on to the correctional agenda. It forces an assessment of the consequences of their pivotal role: were they right to overcome scruples about "imprisoning their sisters" and to become partners in the planning of a new prison? Might not there be personal consequences for them, too, should the original dream of a place where Aboriginal women could truly "heal" turns out to be just another prison? Or, in the light of Aboriginal history, an adult residential school? These questions are addressed in the concluding chapter.

CHAPTER TEN

The Lessons Learned?

Creating Choices: The Report of the Task Force on Federally Sentenced Women was accepted by the Government of Canada in 1990; the first of the new prisons opened in November 1995; and, on 6 July 2000 Kingston's Prison for Women finally shut. These three events encapsulate the achievement of the task force. Individually, they are formidable, in the light of previous attempts to close the prison. Yet they disguise the underlying failures of the task force and the fact that the price of failure has been paid by federally sentenced women, who are now labelled as being infinitely more "difficult to manage"[1] than most on the task force ever imagined possible. Many of the voluntary sector representatives who joined the task force did so, despite an inherent distrust of "the prison," because they feared that *failure* to participate would harm the women. They now know that their participation contributed to further harm and, for some members of the task force, the outcome has been profoundly troubling.

Although this book focuses on the first three prisons to open, two other prisons were included in the task force's plan and these were eventually sited in Kitchener and Joliette.[2] Events at Edmonton and Nova delayed their opening until 1997, and, once women were admitted, it would have seemed to an ill-informed public that the implementation of *Creating Choices* had been achieved (Kingston's Prison for Women remained open at that stage). This was far from the case, because the maximum security women were by then barred from all of the new prisons and accommodated in annexes within men's prisons. Further, *Creating Choices'* projected community element had not been funded by CSC to the extent envisaged, removing a central component of the task force's planning and ensuring a resolute focus upon imprisonment. With the difficult-to-manage maximum security women removed from the central equation, the new prisons held a presumably less risky group, yet the minimum and medium security women – with the exception of those held at the Healing Lodge – were still confined[3] behind new fences commensurate to the risk of maximum security women. Additionally, all federally sentenced women imprisoned in British Columbia remained, at that point, in their technological panopticon in Burnaby. To those familiar with *Creating Choices*, it was clear that implementation had benefited only a proportion of federally sentenced women, whereas the task force had resolutely planned for them all. Since then the situation has, if anything, deteriorated, and most federally sentenced women continue to live with disproportionate security, especially those classified as minimum risk (Moffat 1991; Hannah-Moffat and Shaw 2000; Hannah-Moffat 2001). Some of the maximum security women, having been characterized by the deputy commissioner for women as being "without the capacity for change,"[4] appear to have been abandoned, as is best illustrated with reference to the new secure units.

FINALLY PROVIDING FOR THE DIFFICULT-TO-MANAGE WOMEN

Chapter 6 assesses the development of the initial enhanced units and establishes that they were not planned by the task force. It also shows that CSC inflated the proportion of women thought to be in need of extra supervision to 10 percent, from the task force's figure of 5 percent. Most of the new enhanced units were consequently doubled in size. The reasons for the task force's unwillingness to quantify the problem have been explained earlier but, following CSC's unblushing adjustment of the numbers alleged to be in need of extra levels of security, it cannot be said too forcefully that the task force's refusal to plan prescriptively for this group enabled CSC to determine its own solution. At this juncture, it is useful to assess more comprehensively the importance and consequence of the task force's failure.

As the new prisons began to receive the first groups of women, and events, particularly at Edmonton, impinged on national consciousness, it seemed that significantly higher numbers of women indeed did not "fit" the new "theories" of imprisonment, as Deputy Commissioner for Women Nancy Stableforth suggested at the fatality inquiry into the death of Denise Fayant. Nor did it seem that the prisons were adequately designed to cope with these women. The public did not know that the *Creating Choices* model was never fully tried at Edmonton and that the prison's unfinished state played a major part in contributing to the unravelling of its supposed dynamic security. There had been immense pressure to close the Prison for Women, and there was the demographic fact that large numbers of Aboriginal women lived in the Prairies. A disproportionate number were classified as maximum security and so were ineligible for the Healing Lodge, which led to a large group of maximum security women being sent to Edmonton within a very brief period.[5] Once the incidents began, it appeared to the public that more federally sentenced women were "high risk" than had been indicated when the prisons first opened, and CSC faced increasing political pressure to act. CSC finally capitulated but, having removed most of the women from Edmonton to separate units in male prisons, it later had to decide whether or not the most problematic women should ever return to the new prisons.

The Intensive Intervention Strategy

In September 1999 CSC announced its Intensive Intervention Strategy for the high risk/high needs women, which was for the creation of secure units and structured living environment (SLE) houses at Nova, Edmonton, Joliette, and Grand Valley (the Healing Lodge was exempt from the plan). The existing enhanced units were to be upgraded and to become totally separate secure units within the perimeter fences of the prisons. Maximum security women would be kept apart from other federally sentenced women but have "the opportunity and flexibility for integration into the less secure part of the prison" by virtue of being accommodated in the prison. Minimum or medium security women, with mental health and/or special needs, had the option of moving to the new SLEs, where there would be twenty-four-hour staff supervision and support. A woman could refuse to enter an SLE but faced the possibility that she might be confined in maximum security if she failed to cope with life in one of the unstructured houses. It was estimated that "approximately thirty women" would be in the secure units and "approximately thirty-five women" (within the then federally sentenced women population) would be in the SLEs (CSC 1999).

Enhanced units accommodate maximum security women and those (from any security categorization) who are in administrative segregation. All life-sentenced prisoners now have to spend two years under maximum security conditions, although this is under review. Cells classified as being for purposes of segregation are *not* counted as part of the official capacity of each prison as it is assumed that they will be occupied intermittently by women who will shortly return to the general population. However, chapter 6 shows that at Edmonton the existing enhanced unit was double-bunked and so was capable of holding twenty-four women (see also Chrumka 2000, 55), yet it officially only added six beds to the rated capacity of the prison.[6] The new secure units contain single cells but might again be used for double bunking in *exceptional* circumstances if a warden obtained permission from her regional deputy commissioner. (The national commissioner normally controls exceptional changes.) It is difficult to obtain totally accurate figures for what the "regular" capacity of the prisons themselves was first intended to be. csc's publications give slightly differing figures, but they are not significantly at odds with each other. For the purposes of this chapter the figures published in 1995 are used (see csc 1995b). Using the 1995 figures for regular beds, and adding the enhanced unit beds, the following can be seen:

Table 10.1 Bed capacity of new prisons, 1995

	Regular beds	*Enhanced unit beds*	*Total*
Nova	28	3	31
Edmonton	56	6	62
Grand Valley	70	8	78
Joliette	76	8	84
Healing Lodge	28	–	28
	258 (91%)	25 (9%)	283

These figures show that csc originally provided space in the enhanced units for slightly fewer than the projected 10 percent of women labelled "difficult to manage" in their 1992 Operational Plan. By adding the prisons' seventeen segregation cells to these figures, the capacity is increased by a further 6 percent, making a total of 15 percent of all beds available for those women. This is done in the knowledge that segregation cells are *not* part of a prison's official capacity but that they were used as such at Edmonton and *theoretically* could be again (see Chrumka 2000, 55). In normal practice, a woman is removed to segregation and her regular bed remains empty. The above table does not include beds available at the psychiatric hospitals/prisons or at Isabel McNeil House as they were not part of the task force's planning. (The omission of the psychiatric units obscures the full extent of the women's supervision at that stage.)

At the same time it was planning to expand the secure and sle provision at each of the prisons, csc also added further regular houses at Nova, Edmonton, and Grand Valley. The following table gives the capacity, in March 2005, of the five new prisons.

Table 10.2   Bed capacity of new prisons, March 2005

	Regular beds	Secure unit beds	SLEs/mental health units	Total
Nova	53	10	8	71
Edmonton	90	15	8	113
Grand Valley	80	15	8	103
Joliette	81	10	8	99
Healing Lodge	28	–	–	28
	332 (80%)	50 (12%)	32 (8%)	414

This shows that bed capacity at just these five prisons has increased by 46 percent since 1995. Twenty percent of the beds now allow for extra levels of intervention and security, compared with 9 percent when they first opened.

Table 10.3 shows the *entire* bed capacity for federally sentenced women as of March 2005. It includes the newly converted Fraser Valley Institution for Women in British Columbia, the two psychiatric hospitals/prisons, and the minimum security Isabel McNeill House.

Table 10.3   Entire bed capacity for federally sentenced women, March 2005

	Regular beds	Secure unit beds	SLEs/mental health units	Total
Nova	53	10	8	71
Edmonton	90	15	8	113
Grand Valley	80	15	8	103
Joliette	81	10	8	99
Healing Lodge	28	–	–	28
Fraser Valley	45	–	8	53
RPC	–	–	12	12
Pinel	–	–	15	15
IMH (minimum)	10	–	–	10
	387 (77%)	50 (10%)	67 (13%)	504

This last set of figures shows that provision has been made for 23 percent of total bed capacity to be available for women thought to be in need of the Intensive Intervention Strategy, with secure unit beds increased from 1999's projected figure of thirty to an actual figure of fifty. The secure unit at Fraser Valley will be completed by March 2006 and will add a further ten beds, bringing the total to sixty. These will contribute to 25 percent of all federally sentenced women *normally* being under some form of extra intervention. If the present nineteen segregation cells are added to these figures a further 4 percent of beds become available, bringing the total number of beds available for intensive supervision to 29 percent. With the repeated caveat that it is *not* CSC's practice to include these beds as official capacity, based on past precedent it is impossible to be confident that segregation cells will never again be used to accommodate women on a more permanent basis should inmate figures increase even more rapidly than anticipated.

It must not be forgotten that, although the Healing Lodge appears to have been largely unaffected by these changes, this is not the case. With more women being sentenced to federal terms, and with 29 percent of all federally sentenced women now being Aboriginal, it can be deduced that a very large group of women should *theoretically* be eligible for the Healing Lodge, even though it is known that there have always been restrictions on who would be admitted. The outcome of these changes in bed provision will have an excessive impact on Aboriginal women and leave them further isolated from the general inmate population. Aboriginal women are disproportionately likely to be classified as maximum security or to be assessed as in need of help with mental health problems. In 2003 the Canadian Human Rights Commission recommended that maximum security Aboriginal federally sentenced women should be admitted to the Healing Lodge. CSC again declined to permit this, as it had after Justice Arbour made the same request in 1996 in her report into the April 1994 incidents at Kingston's Prison for Women. CSC committed itself to reviewing annually the security rating of these Aboriginal women (who in July 2003 comprised 46 percent of all women classified as maximum security),[7] but there are continuing concerns about the validity of the risk prediction scales and the particular impact they have on Aboriginal women.

These calculations should also be seen within the context of the increasing numbers of women sentenced to federal terms of imprisonment since the new prisons opened. Of course the courts determine who will receive a federal sentence, and CSC's task is to manage those prisoners. Some, or perhaps all, of this increase could be due to the increased seriousness of offences committed by women. However, there was always a concern that judges would be more willing to impose federal sentences upon women precisely because the new prisons appeared to offer a means of dealing with the reasons for their offending. The Prison for Women provided a disincentive for imposing a federal term, and further research might reveal interesting reasons for the increase.

The most alarming and contradictory aspect of the present situation, in terms of the intentions of *Creating Choices*, is that at least 25 percent of federally sentenced women will, under normal circumstances, be subjected to increased levels of intervention and supervision within prisons that were meant to offer them choices and autonomy. The possibility, under these circumstances, of empowering women to take responsibility for their own lives (as well as to accept responsibility for the dynamic security of the prison itself) appears remote. Yet csc would counter this by saying that if, as an organization, it was unconcerned with the needs of these women, then it would not have commissioned extensive research into their needs. Nor would they have incurred the vast expenditure necessitated by the implementation of the strategy. Indeed, if the perceived failure of implementation had been solely the fault of the women – a point that has earlier been raised – a more traditional correctional approach could have been adopted by csc. It should be acknowledged that plans may be introduced by correctional authorities because they, too, are concerned about the prisoners.

The Management Protocol

Yet the Intensive Intervention Strategy has not been csc's last word on the subject of difficult-to-manage women. A management protocol (CSC 2004a) for maximum security women involved in major incidents, which cause harm to others or jeopardize the safety of others, is now in place. This consists of three stages, which are much abbreviated in the following summary:

- *Step 1: Segregation* The woman concerned will be subject to an "emergency involuntary inter-regional transfer" from her current prison to a segregation unit, within a secure unit, in another prison. She may have no contact with other prisoners and is to be "in restraints" when outside her cell, with these being fitted through the food slot. Her door may only be opened by two officers and, depending upon her assumed risk, one officer *may* be carrying oc (oleoresin capsicum, i.e., pepper) spray. If she has to leave the unit, for whatever reason, she must be in restraints (handcuffed and in leg irons);
- *Step 2: Partial Reintegration* The woman will continue to reside in the segregation unit and will gradually be permitted access to programs available within the secure unit. She will have some contact with other prisoners in segregation but, should she have to leave the unit, will also be in restraints, dependent upon her assumed risk;
- *Step 3: Transition* The woman will gradually be reintegrated into the unit but will have no activities outside the unit.

The Management Protocol suggests that "once the inmate has maintained positive participation for a period of three months in the *Tran-*

sition Step, and if her risk is considered assumable, she can then be discharged from the Protocol," and her return to her original prison will be considered (CSC 2004, 10). Initial decisions regarding placing a woman on the protocol are made by each warden, after consultation with her/his regional deputy commissioner (RDC), and the warden and RDC of the receiving prison. The deputy commissioner for women is also kept informed. If the woman's behaviour deteriorates to the extent that administrative segregation is justified, she can be returned to Step 1.

The implementation of the Management Protocol is a complete denial of all that *Creating Choices* hoped to achieve for federally sentenced women. Moreover, it appears to be in contravention of the clear intention of Section 31 of the Corrections and Conditional Release Act, 1992, that prisoners should not normally be kept in segregation for more than thirty days at a time (although this may be increased to forty-five days if multiple convictions are involved; see Arbour 1996, 185). It also contravenes the existing CD 590 regarding the length of time prisoners may be kept segregated; this is because women placed on the Management Protocol may be returned to Step 1 whenever their behaviour seems to require it. In practical terms, this means that a woman might, theoretically, be liable to unlimited periods of segregation.

Arbour (1996) was particularly concerned about CSC's "frequent violation of the rules and regulations governing detention in segregation" (187) and quoted the correctional investigator's concern that past practices might re-emerge in the new prisons (191). The Management Protocol will have exceeded Arbour's worst imaginings, although it does not – yet – reproduce the conditions of a special handling unit, with its attendant implications (see Pizarro and Stenius 2004). Arbour documented the long-term damage segregation caused to prisoners' mental health, points that were later reinforced by Martel (1999, 105), who suggested that "confinement in such conditions produces severe effects often detrimental to their [women's] attempts at rehabilitation or, as the more recent correctional discourse intends it, at *healing*" (emphasis in original). The degree of staff surveillance and supervision necessary for the monitoring of any woman subject to the protocol, combined with the isolation from her peers, would be an extraordinary about turn. In practice, it would be producing segregation conditions worse than those that prevailed at the Prison for Women. Moreover, the design of the new segregation cells at Grand Valley Institution for Women is unsafe, in that the barred windows provide easily accessible ligature points and the stainless steel sanitary fittings offer ready opportunities for self harm.[8] CSC might counter that it is presently faced with a very small group of women who disproportionately, and chaotically, disrupt the regimes of the existing secure units. But to provide specifically for them offers a vista of providing, ever more rigorously, for a subgroup within that small group. Where does maximum security end?

This resort to "emergency involuntary inter-regional transfer[s]" takes federally sentenced women back to the situation so painfully highlighted during the life of the task force, when Sandy Sayer, an involuntarily transferred provincial prisoner, committed suicide. One of the main reasons for the closure of the Prison for Women was that women should be held in their own provinces. This was highlighted in the motion sent to Ole Ingstrup following the death of Sandy Sayer and in the *Emergency Measures* issued at the same time as *Creating Choices*. Ingstrup conceded that issue when he immediately arranged for interprovincial transfers to cease on the day that *Creating Choices* was first published. The return of such a correctional option is a devastating blow to the credibility of *Creating Choices*.

However, it is sometimes easier to criticize than it is to face the reality of some of the difficult-to-manage women. Undoubtedly, a minority pose very difficult problems for the correctional authorities as their institutional behaviour often makes them a danger, both to themselves and, increasingly, to other prisoners and staff. While such behaviour can be linked to the women's lives outside prison, and may be exacerbated by years of imprisonment itself, provision still has to be made for them while they are serving a sentence. It is challenging to provide for them the "least restrictive measures consistent with the protection of the public, staff members and offenders" (CCRA 1992, 4[d]). This is why the implementation of the Management Protocol is so important. For some women the loss of hope it could engender will ensure that they resist staff members rather than cooperate with them. Their resistance will be a means of reminding themselves that, in some small way, they retain control, even if that resistance should, paradoxically, lead to their having less control.

AGENCY AND DISCIPLINED CHOICES

Enabling women to make choices was at the heart of *Creating Choices*, and the context within which women have subsequently exercised choice has proved to be one of the most troubling issues. CSC remains publicly committed to the report's principles, even though they have been substantially reinterpreted in later CSC publications. While reformers often have little option but to articulate an alternative vision of imprisonment, even as they hope for its eventual demise, they face the risk that their language will be incorporated, redefined, taken out of context, and used to legitimate official penal discourse. The languages of feminism and Aboriginal culture and spirituality, as used in *Creating Choices*, have been subjected to all of these processes.

CSC took the opportunity presented to it by *Creating Choices*. In using feminist terminology, such as "empowering" women to make "responsible choices," in an official correctional document, the task force unwittingly permitted CSC first to adopt and then to determine the language's subsequent interpretation. It specifically allowed CSC to emphasize the responsibilities federally sentenced women had for their individual rehabilitation, and the security of the whole prison, rather than CSC's own responsibilities. *Creating Choices* ignored the reality that most choices in prison are constrained by loss of freedom, made in consideration of the possible consequences of decision making, and underscored by the discipline affecting every aspect of a prisoner's life.

A coercive environment limits the possibility of free choice and individual agency. The situation is further complicated when women are required to make "responsible" choices because what constitutes "responsible" is so rarely defined by the women themselves. Hudson (2002, 43) suggests that agency and choice are frequently conflated, becoming a "synonym for will, [assuming] an either/or character, such that persons have (freedom of) choice or they do not." She continues, "some people have far more choices than others," and this is particularly true when comparisons are drawn between the imprisoned and the free. The specific difficulty emerges when women are required to make choices about programming.

Prison is frequently seen as the site wherein offending women's needs may best be addressed and resolved. Such a presupposition ignores the fact that prisons are often unsafe places in which to begin exploring issues that have contributed to a woman's offending. CSC is legally mandated to work towards the rehabilitation of prisoners and, in many instances, programs such as those dealing with addiction might provide immediate assistance to prisoners. But in suggesting that each prison should be "program-driven" (TFFSW 1990, 118), the task force did not seriously challenge the orthodoxy that women should be "treated" while in prison.

Taking *Creating Choices* literally, CSC set about providing programs, with a core group being compulsory. While acknowledging that structural inequality might have contributed to a woman's offending, these programs largely emphasized the need for prisoners to rectify perceived defects within themselves through the acquisition of cognitive skills. Each woman became responsible for her own reformation, and the "responsible choices" she made also contributed to the good order of the prison. Kendall and Pollack (2005) explore the way in which an adapted form of dialectical behaviour therapy (DBT), used within the prisons, contribute to the pathologizing of women's offending behaviour, although this outcome was denied by CSC. They contend that the program "function[s] as a technology for the responsibilization" of the women (77). This "responsibilization" did not – and still does not – come with a concomitant degree of autonomy. It was a strategy that ensured, first, that prisoners largely shouldered the blame for their offending, then obliged them to use their newly acquired skills for the greater good of the prison. Individual need, and the freedom to make choices that truly empowered each woman, were secondary to the main aim of governing the prison.

The 2004 *Program Strategy for Women Offenders* continues the emphasis on programs, even as it claims that program participation is "voluntary and based on informed consent [and that] participants [are] given the opportunity to accept, decline or withdraw" (CSC 2004b, 4). Yet if specific programs are included in a woman's correctional plan, and she refuses to participate, her non-participation might also count against her at a parole board hearing. The crucial point is that the women themselves are much more likely than are staff members to know the extent of their ability to cope with programs that require close examination of their pre-prison lives, yet their decisions will not always be recognized as being in their own best interests. "Choice" is hedged by constraints and, when prisoners are further required to be "responsible," it is important to ask, "to whom?"

Yet choice, even outside the constraints of programming, cannot be avoided, and imprisonment frequently requires prisoners to choose from equally uninviting options. The authority of the prison makes it likely that the "responsible" prisoner will chose the option best guaranteed to contribute to early release. The power of the prison finally ensures that the prisoner's needs are secondary. While this might partially replicate the demands placed upon people living outside the prison, the distinction is that choice is then being exercised freely. Prisoners, in that sense, are never free (see Hannah-Moffat 2001; Kendall 2002).

The additional expectation that these Canadian prisoners should also make "responsible" choices, in order to contribute to the dynamic security of an institution in which they are involuntarily detained, further complicates their situation. They are not simply being asked to take responsibility for their own actions and to maintain self-surveillance; they are being drawn into the net of control surrounding all federally sentenced women. Agency and choice are thus conflated with responsibility, while the underlying discipline is hidden within the CSC-interpreted language of second-wave feminism.

A number of women will find resistance to such demands an essential strategy for coping with the loss of self that imprisonment entails, seeing such strategies as a means of asserting their own identity. Resistance within the larger (male) prison environment might take the form of disorder or violence against others. In women's prisons resistance most commonly centres on the self and, at its most extreme, is manifest in self-harm or, increasingly, in violence towards others. More commonly, resistance is apparent in quiet strategies of survival that test the authority of the prison (see Bosworth 1999). Correctional authorities might nevertheless interpret such strategies as a failure to make responsible choices rather than as rational choices made in irrational conditions. The final authority of the prison is never, ultimately, capable of being challenged.

CONCLUSION: THE LESSONS LEARNED

This Canadian story embraces various strands, but central to them all is the Task Force on Federally Sentenced Women, whose work raises various questions: have federally sentenced women benefited? Should the voluntary sector have cooperated? Should Aboriginal peoples, in particular, have participated?

In beginning to answer these points it can initially be tempting to blame the bureaucrats entirely for the outcome as they were ultimately responsible for implementation. That would be wrong. The task force itself presented a report that unfailingly glossed over the difficult issues. The language of *Creating Choices* distorted the reality that it was a document about imprisonment: that it was concerned with the building of new prisons rather than of places where women would simply "heal"; and that it was concerned with *offending* women rather than women with multiple problems. When the language of victimization prevailed it became almost inevitable that the task force would not – and could not – plan specifically for the difficult-to-manage women, in part because the image of the homogeneous federally sentenced "woman" had already been constructed. In transforming federally sentenced women into an idealized "woman," the task force determined the nature of the rest of its planning, leaving that "woman" the touchstone for all that ensued. The cottages, so often devoid of staff, reflected her low risk, as did the absence of fences and the small enhanced units. The range of accommodation was inevitably limited by the apparent lack of diversity between one "woman" and another. The new staff members, responding to her low-risk (but high-needs) profile, had a brief more akin to that of social workers than actual guards – and were then bewildered by her unanticipated reality. Having stripped this "woman" of her diversity, the task force ensured that she could not then re-emerge as possibly violent or disturbed, at least in so far as prescriptive planning was concerned, because that would have shaken the foundations of the task force's original conception.

In denying the multiplicity of women, the task force inadvertently set federally sentenced women up for failure once they transferred to the new prisons. These diverse women could not collectively respond in the calculated, rational manner essential to the realization of the plan, and the more they reacted (inappropriately, as it seemed) to the new regime, the more restraint was imposed. The subsequent question should not have been simply whether extra restraint was necessary but, rather, why did some women at Edmonton and Nova respond in such a way? The initial social demands of both prisons, and the physical limitations of the unfinished Edmonton prison, overwhelmed a proportion of the women but, in interpreting what was known about events at these prisons, the public assumption was that it was only the *women's* failure rather than the task force's or csc's failure. These misconceptions can be directly linked to the imprecise language of *Creating Choices*, which in turn emerged from the task force's failure to grapple with the difficult issues, such as possibly violent women, because of consensus being adopted in order to reconcile the divergent views of task force members. The authors of *Creating Choices*, with typical linguistic obfuscation, did not refer to these women as "prisoners" and thus obscured the reality of their situation. Nevertheless, although the task force, through *Creating Choices*, set the scene for such an outcome, the civil servants and the correctional authorities bear final responsibility for what transpired. They allowed Edmonton to open before it was physically complete and then transferred a disproportionate number of maximum security women to its inadequate enhanced unit, with both decisions subsequently having a profound effect on all the other prisons. The bureaucrats were also responsible for the training that failed to prevent some staff at Nova, post-Arbour, from treating a woman with flagrant lack of care (see csc 1997a). Once the prisons opened, the spirit of the task force was unable to survive either the pressures of planning or the pressures of politicians, despite the fact that some of the task force's civil service members were involved in much of the implementation. Rothman (1980, 9) succinctly summarizes such outcomes, in connection with early American attempts to reform "the prison": "progressive innovations may well have done less to upgrade dismal conditions than they did to create nightmares of their own." The creation of the new secure units has indeed reflected those fears, and it is possible that the Healing Lodge may come to be similarly viewed.

Expropriating Aboriginal culture

While this story is about the consequences of the reforms for all federally sentenced women, it is also very specifically about the consequences for the disproportionate number of Aboriginal federally sentenced women. The initial failure to recognize their needs, and thus to include their representatives on the task force, was historically unsurprising. Aboriginal nations have been the backdrop to Euro-Canadian history since colonization began – a group of nations displaced from their own lands, removed from their cultures, and never seen as being at the forefront of their country's history. The Native Women's Association of Canada (NWAC) challenged this neglect and insistently pushed for Aboriginal representation on the task force. These Aboriginal women ultimately succeeded in an unprecedented manner, politicizing the task force's deliberations, imbuing the final report with Aboriginal "language" and perspectives, and finally becoming influential partners in the planning of the Healing Lodge.

Prisons are the rawest expression of the state's delegated power to discipline its citizens and, unsurprisingly, prisons become sites of political action as both prisoners and reformers question and resist that power (Kidman 1947; Sullivan 1990; Culhane 1991; Adams 1992). The Aboriginal members saw a government-sponsored task force on imprisonment as a vehicle both for expressing their own resistance to Euro-Canadian authority and for assisting Aboriginal federally sentenced women. This meant, paradoxically, that they were using what was for them an illegitimate Euro-Canadian legal body ("Our Peoples ... have never consented to the application of Euro-Canadian legal systems" [TFFSW 1990, 17]) to demonstrate their rejection of Euro-Canadian law. The irony was that some then continued the relationship and shared responsibility for the planning of an Aboriginal prison with CSC, one of many government agencies to have harmed their people. Prisons were not part of Aboriginal justice, so these Aboriginal women were again adopting Euro-Canadian constructs in order to achieve greater separation from the dominant culture and their own means of "healing" imprisoned Aboriginal women. This was a deliberate, yet perilous calculation. In partnering CSC the Aboriginal members again risked the possibility of incorporation as both they and the Canadian Association of Elizabeth Fry Societies (CAEFS) had done when the task force was first undertaken. In a narrower sense, they had already begun the journey towards incorporation, having enabled CSC to use Aboriginal language and perspectives, alongside the language of feminism, once *Creating Choices* became a public document.

The Aboriginal Healing Lodge Planning Circle (HLPC) members showed considerable ingenuity in challenging CSC while the Healing Lodge was being planned and were generally successful in imposing their views. Nevertheless, having contributed to planning a prison that reflects Aboriginal principles, they presently face a situation where senior management lies firmly in the hands of Euro-Canadians (with the exception of the Kikawinaw). As is made clear in chapter 9, the *Memorandum of Agreement* signed by CSC and the Nekaneet restricted the influence of the band, because of the restructuring of the Ke-kun-wem-kon-a-wuk, and the story unveiled so far has charted the steady decline of local Aboriginal influence within the prison (see also Monture-Angus 2000). This is not to suggest that Aboriginal beliefs are ignored or entirely absent from the new prison but, rather, to make the point that Aboriginal influence is mediated through the authority of both CSC and its Euro-Canadian employees. Whether this should have been anticipated will be explored, but it is important to assess other aspects of the Healing Lodge before reaching any conclusions.

Healing versus discipline   The Healing Lodge is a prison: no soft terminology can alter that basic fact – and prison is an involuntary institution. Women might choose to go there (providing their security classification makes them eligible), but their choice is between one prison and another. Few, if any, women would elect to undertake "healing" in a prison if a community option should be available. Aboriginal women electing to be transferred to the Healing Lodge have to accept that the symbols of Aboriginal culture and spirituality, such as the use of sweetgrass ceremonies and the sweatlodge, will be part of any "healing" they might choose to undertake – and part of their imprisonment. Some women will accept the symbols at face value and find them a means of support as they attempt to evaluate their own lives. Others will accept them as a "contemporary identity that is a reaction to oppression ... supported by age old traditions ... recast as answers to contemporary problems" (Waldram 1997, 217). They will have decided to cloak themselves in the symbols of their Aboriginal identity and participate in ceremonies, while not necessarily accepting the beliefs that underpin them. And some will accept these symbols as the price they must pay to be with other Aboriginal women, even though they would not choose to accept them outside the prison.

Having made their individual decisions there is little doubt that some women derive a healing strength from these symbols. As Waldram (1997, 73) contends, "symbolic healing [may be] more concerned with social aspects of illness, and teaching people to cope with trauma and dysfunction, than it is with achieving a 'cure.'" But, as Kendall (1993b) demonstrates regarding the Prison for Women, prisons are unsafe environments for women attempting to unravel the complexities of their lives. Prisons can be extraordinarily dangerous places because they isolate, rather than consistently support, prisoners undertaking a "healing" journey. The presence of counsellors – or Elders – is no guarantee that the prisoner will be undamaged by the journey. The Healing Lodge offers more than conventional prisons in that it is not hemmed in by walls; there is a sense of space and potential freedom as well as access to the Elders. But if the "healing" is seen as being imposed, as being part of the condition of imprisonment, then it can never be anything other than a form of discipline (Bruckert 1985).

While this was unforeseen, the Elders contribute to this discipline as their ultimate responsibility is to the correctional authorities. Just as the Kimisinaw (guards) must breach the confidentiality of the healing circle should certain information be revealed, so the Elders face similar constraints. The safety of the wider prison becomes their concern because of their relationship with csc, a position faced by all priests and counsellors working within corrections. They become part of the network of control, and the needs of individual women can never take precedence. Waldram (1997) cites instances of Elders working within male prisons being obliged to try to fit ceremonies and counselling into the correctional timetable, and the reluctance of management to accept that such events differ greatly from those common in, for example, the Christian tradition. The difficulty for Aboriginal people working alongside corrections is that they have no choice but to collaborate if they are to be allowed to assist Aboriginal prisoners subject to Euro-Canadian law and punishment. This uneasy relationship specifically compromises the Elders' traditional role of priest/counsellor/healer and brings them into conflict with their own Aboriginal traditions, forcing them to become more Euro-Canadian in their strategies in order to avoid outright conflict (also see Ross 1996).

There is a wider dilemma here, which links this Aboriginal-inspired prison to the extended prison network. The debate about the extent to which Aboriginal culture and spirituality should be part of penal discourse reflects the older question of providing therapy within prisons. The wish to transform prisoners can be traced to the early reformers, such as Elizabeth Fry, who saw that prisons might have a function other than a punitive one. It survives in the use of the word "corrections," with the implication that prisoners may be "corrected" or, by extension, "cured" of their offending behaviour (see Duguid 2000, 33).

The model most explicit at the lodge is one of healing, and it encapsulates, despite the fact that it is taking place within an Aboriginal prison, the dilemmas posed by the bifurcated tensions of the therapeutic model. This is centred on the dual roles expected to be played by staff, whose difficulties have been rehearsed at the other prisons, where they frequently found the competing demands irreconcilable. The Healing Lodge faces similar problems, which are exacerbated by the dimensions of culture and spirituality. The Healing Lodge is in many respects another version of a therapeutic community (with "culture" and "spirituality" being interchangeable with the term "therapy"), and both women and staff are expected to be "mutually responsible" while experiencing "intensive social interaction" (Rotman 1995, 170). While a few prisons, such as HMP Grendon in the United Kingdom, have partially overcome the problem of reconciling authority with treatment, "the externally imposed requirement that the treatment-oriented prison restrain and punish the inmates who are being treated also creates *internal* conditions that make transformation of the organisation into a true treatment centre extremely difficult" (Cressey 1960, 505). Mutual responsibility is largely unattainable in any coercive environment, and at the Healing Lodge the staff members are responsible to CSC rather than to the women. This means the subordination of culture and spirituality to the correctional enterprise, and it imposes separate strains on Aboriginal staff, additional to the ones experienced by non-Aboriginal staff.

The consequences of cooperation Although the integrity and desperation that inspired the development of the Healing Lodge are beyond doubt, there have been significant consequent losses in terms of Aboriginal identity and independence. While a new model of confinement might have been developed for Aboriginal women, it was still imprisonment and, therefore, a non-Aboriginal construct. In the hands of CSC Aboriginal culture and spirituality became concepts upon which to hang another style of imprisonment, despite CSC's initial acceptance of the legitimacy of an Aboriginal prison. They also became concepts that could be "sold" to other jurisdictions by corrections.

As was earlier suggested (see chapter 9), the consequences of this development for Aboriginal federally sentenced women have been very specific. In a coercive environment they have become part of a doubly responsibilizing strategy, whereby they are now answerable to two authorities: CSC and their own Nations, as represented by the Elders and, initially, the Ke-kun-wem-kon-a-wuk. The women might be inclined towards Aboriginal authority, but the reality remains that the Healing Lodge is a Euro-Canadian operated prison. In order to overcome the hurdles imposed by Euro-Canadian laws, and reach their parole eligibility date, Aboriginal federally sentenced women must primarily abide by the demands of the dominant culture. Aboriginal women, their Elders, and the Aboriginal staff working alongside them, are being asked to compromise their Aboriginal heritage by a correctional organization that has only a superficial grasp of what this might mean. And when women fail outside prison, as some inevitably will, it is likely that it will be an Aboriginal vision of a prison that is blamed rather than the actual source of discipline – CSC.

The prime concern must be for the women themselves. Those who begin this healing journey and initially "fail" (by Euro-Canadian standards) might also feel that they have failed those doing most to assist them: the Elders. This doubly responsibilizing strategy has the potential to increase the burden of inadequacy borne by many Aboriginal federally sentenced women, who have already been labelled inadequate for most of their pre-prison lives.

With these points having been made, were the Aboriginal members right to join the task force and then to fight so hard for the primacy of their views and for the Healing Lodge itself? Should they have foreseen any of the consequences of their cooperation with CSC? What cannot be ignored is the fact that most of the women dying in the Prison for Women were Aboriginal, and on that basis alone NWAC could justify its decision to participate in the task force. Whether they should have taken the next step and become involved in planning a Healing Lodge is harder to answer. Waldram's conclusion that Aboriginal culture and spirituality have a part to play in the healing of Aboriginal prisoners does not mean that an Aboriginal prison is the logical extension of such provision. If there are any lessons to be learned from penal history, the prime one is that "the prison" has an extraordinary ability to adopt practices and then to subvert them. The incorporation of Aboriginal beliefs into penal discourse can only weaken the authority of Aboriginal culture once prisoners see that it has no final power over the dominant Euro-Canadian penal system.

This powerlessness is soon apparent to prisoners, who realize that they are being offered an "Aboriginal-lite" environment and that even this can be reduced by the demands of bureaucracy and security. The significance of these compromises relate to what they say about Aboriginal culture and spirituality, in that they imply Aboriginal values are negotiable. For the Elders to be involved in such negotiation, as their relationship with the correctional authorities ensures happens, devalues any role they might play and lessens their own authority as well as that of their culture. An "Aboriginal" prison concerned with "healing" relies on the integrity of its message, and at the Healing Lodge the message is that Aboriginal culture and spirituality are inextricably linked to penality.

This was always the understood risk for the Aboriginal members of the task force and the HLPC. That they were prepared to take it was a measure of the desperate situation faced by Aboriginal federally sentenced women, but their hope that this penal venture might be the one to succeed ahead of others has not necessarily been vindicated. The Aboriginal members of the task force might now be in a less distressing position had they simply pushed for the employment of more Aboriginal staff within the new conventional prisons rather than for a so-called Aboriginal prison now run by Euro-Canadians. By this means Elders could have continued to work at each prison, while acknowledging the limitations imposed upon them by their relationship with CSC. Aboriginal federally sentenced women would then be in a position to make informed choices regarding their participation in Aboriginal practices at each prison.

Whether these women should have anticipated any of these consequences is a separate question. They were not necessarily aware of the history of penal reform, but they were aware of the history of Euro-Canada's involvement with Aboriginal peoples and its contribution to the disproportionate criminalization of their families and communities. They were also aware of the contempt that had historically been showered upon their culture and spirituality, and this should have alerted them to the possibility that the dominant culture would continue to undermine any attempts made by Aboriginal groups to reverse this process. This is not to imply that individual civil servants were involved in a deliberate policy of undermining the planning of the Aboriginal members of the task force and HLPC. The suggestion is that imprisonment itself, being the dominant culture's means of social control, would assert itself against any person or group attempting to challenge its authority.

Having been actively involved in first proposing, and then planning, the Healing Lodge the Aboriginal members of the task force and HLPC cannot now avoid being linked to its outcome. As suggested in chapter 9, failure at the Healing Lodge could lead to its becoming an Aboriginal-inspired and sanctioned version of the despised and discredited residential schools, wherein Aboriginal women are subjected to discipline in order to make them "good" Aboriginal people, as opposed to "good" Canadians. The Aboriginal members of the task force and of the HLPC have all taken a tremendous risk.

And yet, and yet ... it remains hard to be largely critical of the enterprise. The position taken is, in many respects, based upon a careful examination of the compromises required of those Aboriginal

members of the task force, flowing from their participation in the planning of the Healing Lodge. The position itself can be subject to criticism
because it concentrates on what might have been lost by the enterprise
rather than on what might have been gained. While it is important that
the consequences of the incorporation of culture and spirituality into
penal discourse should be examined, in order to understand the way in
which bureaucracies warp intentions, that perspective is also distorted
if what is gained by the process of reform is not included.

What cannot be denied is that some Aboriginal federally sentenced
women have derived considerable support and comfort from the
Healing Lodge. They are not necessarily concerned about some of the
issues explored in this book and have found at the Healing Lodge the
personal space in which to reconnect with who they are as Aboriginal
women. They might not all have succeeded in avoiding a return to
prison, but they have begun a journey that might finally enable them
to achieve that. The Aboriginal members of the task force would take
comfort from that possibility because few of their "sisters" would have
found such strength within the Prison for Women.

Which leaves to be answered the question raised in chapter 5: were
the Aboriginal members of the task force the "great winners" of this
enterprise? It is too early to give a definitive answer, but a tentative one
may be proposed. They were not. And the reason they were not is that
they have been drawn into a net of social control that may compromise
the very cultural values they hoped would lead to the "healing" of
Aboriginal federally sentenced women.

The way forward for the Healing Lodge?   It is possibly a false assumption to suppose that prisons might have a part to play in the restoration
of Aboriginal people to their own communities as prisons are largely
places to which those failed by their communities are consigned (and
are not part of Aboriginal justice). However, the advent of Section 81(1)
of the Corrections and Conditional Release Act, 1992, whereby Aboriginal communities can apply to "provide correctional services for
Aboriginal offenders," offers a means for Aboriginal communities to
take responsibility for Aboriginal offenders, albeit still under the
authority of Euro-Canadian law. It will be instructive to see what solutions Aboriginal peoples eventually find solely for themselves.

THE LESSONS LEARNED

One of the main fears of the task force was that its work might lead to
the creation of five mini-Prisons for Women, and the new secure units
suggest that four of the new prisons are perilously close to realizing

that fear. The prisons face enormous challenges as they enter a new phase. All have new wardens and, with other staff also leaving, the vision of *Creating Choices* is now dependent upon the skill and commitment of those who have assumed these roles. The woman-centred training, so essential when the first staff members were being recruited, was subsequently reduced by half, and some new workers transferring from other prisons received none at all.[9] Although this has implications for all the prisons, especially as more men are hired,[10] it has a particular importance for the Healing Lodge, where staff underwent training of a quality and depth that could have been the exemplar for the rest of the prisons.

What happens next is of crucial importance. Meanwhile, many in the voluntary sector feel compromised, incorporated, and betrayed by their association with CSC and now question the wisdom of having participated in the task force. CAEFS in particular, having learned the lesson of being neutralized by CSC, has returned to its former role and again become a vigilant advocate for federally sentenced women.

The risks of reform   The consequences of involvement in the task force have been various for the four distinct groups represented. The civil servants have seen their working estate increase and achieve a higher profile. The non-Aboriginal voluntary sector is inextricably linked to a plan it helped devise but played no part in implementing, and which it can only criticize from the sidelines. The Aboriginal participants have an allegedly Aboriginal prison that denies entry to a significant number of Aboriginal women, who are now even more isolated from the rest of the federally sentenced women's population because of their security classification. A good proportion of federally sentenced women continue to live in conditions of security disproportionate to their actual risk, as they did in the Prison for Women. Furthermore, they appear to have been blamed by CSC for many of the problems that emerged at the new prisons, despite the fact that CSC itself bore considerable responsibility (and acknowledged this in an internal presentation entitled "The Lessons Learned" in June 1996). Should any, or all, of this have been anticipated by the voluntary sector, and particularly by CAEFS, when it decided to join the task force?

Being captured by Canadian history   To begin answering the preceding question, it is necessary to recall those intense months during which the task force – and, specifically, the working group – edged towards the completion of *Creating Choices*. The working group did not necessarily have a comprehensive knowledge of the consequences of attempted penal reform in other jurisdictions, had insufficient time to read thoroughly all the background material provided for it, and wanted a *Canadian* solution to the problems posed by the Prison for Women. Moreover, the working group members' diverse backgrounds and competing perspectives could only be reconciled by adopting consensus as an operating tool. Consensus led to the working group's construct of the homogeneous, passive, victimized "woman" and to its final failure – or refusal – to plan definitively for the few difficult-to-manage women whom they reluctantly identified. The unusual aspect was that the civil servants, whose anticipated function was to influence and steer the tripartite working group, were part of that consensus as well. With few exceptions, they accepted the characterization of "federally sentenced woman as victim," partly because they acknowledged the strength of the argument when applied to Aboriginal women and partly out of pragmatism and the need to complete their task.

While the original impetus towards this could accurately be described as politically driven, in that the Aboriginal members of the task force were using the task force to focus upon historic reasons for Aboriginal offending, the task force's eventual perspective was not one of simply excusing deviant behaviour. Rather, as has previously been explored, it wanted to situate the offending of all – not just Aboriginal – federally sentenced women within its socio-economic context and to show that such women transcended the stereotype of the "bad" or "mad" offender. Aboriginal history could not be divorced from this process. The initial means of assembling the task force was a shared conscience regarding the safety of women within the Prison for Women. An unanticipated shared conscience regarding the treatment of Canada's Aboriginal peoples became the reason for finally seeing federally sentenced women as "victims" in their own right. This did not mean that the task force failed to accept that federally sentenced women had themselves created victims, nor did it mean that federally sentenced women should be unregulated by the discipline of the prison. It meant that the solution they sought had to recognize the *Canadian* dimension of their enterprise, which eventually involved acknowledging their colonial history.

It was this understanding, rather than the broader historical narrative of penal reform, that captured them all and enabled many to discount the possibility that their carefully devised plan might later be captured by a less sympathetic implementation team. To a certain extent, the task force dared hope that *this* particular project would be the exception to those littering the wayside of penal reform. It was absorbed by what was appropriate for the Canadian federally sentenced women it had come to assume it knew, and the women's eventual shared identity incorporated the socio-economic dysfunction common to many Aboriginal women prisoners. Within that context the lessons of penal reform from elsewhere seemed remote and irrelevant: the task force felt it was breaking new ground.

Shared consciences However, it is what brought two of these three disparate groups – CAEFS and NWAC – to the task force that provides perhaps the clearest answer to whether they should have anticipated the derailment of their project. Those organizations had suspended their instinctive distrust of "the prison" because of the stark fact that the Prison for Women was a life-threatening institution (as are most prisons). They were troubled by the responsibilities they shouldered and the possibility that their work might lead to further "oppression"[11] of federally sentenced women. Yet neither group could fully allow itself to contemplate the eventual failure of the task force because that would almost certainly mean that more women would die should the Prison for Women remain open. Simply continuing to call for the prison's closure was no longer an option for CAEFS and NWAC. The civil servants, on the other hand, needed no such rationalization as the task force was an extension of their professional lives; they *had* to provide a realizable plan for the commissioner.

In the final December 1989 steering committee meeting, during which the almost completed report was discussed, an Aboriginal member queried *Creating Choices*' failure to discuss the fact that there were "two schools of thought" on the task force (the abolitionists and the reformers) and suggested that the omission might leave readers puzzled by the seeming lack of consensus on some matters. While the task force was united by a shared conscience regarding the safety of those in the Prison for Women, addressing what *divided* them – those "two schools of thought" – offered the very real prospect of the task force collapsing around them. Any acknowledgment by CAEFS and NWAC of possible failure of the task force would have removed any justification for their participation.

So the important underlying question is whether the voluntary sector members were right to set aside their individual reservations about the enterprise and actively join with the civil servants in the planning of new prisons. On the simple grounds of humanity, they were: they could not, having finally been offered the chance to effect change, stand on principle and watch more women die within the Prison for Women. Yet to participate – for the best of reasons – was also to accept responsibility for the possible consequences, and the closure of one dangerous prison did not mean that their solution would necessarily be a safer one.

In accepting the challenge and the risk the task force firmly allied itself with the long tradition of benevolent reformers. While both Rothman (1971, 1980) and Cohen (1985) suggest that the outcome of penal reformers' good intentions should be distrusted, this is not to say that benevolence itself should universally be treated sceptically. Without benevolence and without identification with those oppressed by the state, or by conglomerates, or by individuals, there would be stasis. In the sphere of criminal justice there would not have been the rising influence of the victims' movement; there would not have been the changed attitudes towards domestic violence, or abuse of children, with concomitant changes in legislation. However, Rothman and Cohen are right to warn of the unintended consequences of benevolence within the specific sphere of prison reform and to alert us to the historic parallels that demonstrate that the correctional enterprise has an astonishing power to subvert and reinterpret "good intentions." Bureaucratic institutions resist attempts to change them from the outside because of the consequent diminution of their power and authority. It is the incorporation and distortion of benevolence within the larger correctional agenda that should be resisted.

So, should the voluntary sector members have joined the task force? They were right *then* to participate but were wrong to assume that the influence of their painfully devised plan would be lasting. Even the most cursory reading of the history of penal reform would have prepared them for this, if not for the scale of their lost influence.

In this Canadian story the names and language of the voluntary sector have been incorporated into the larger correctional agenda. Those groups' participation in the task force has contributed to the worsening situation now faced by those labelled "difficult to manage," including a disproportionate number of Aboriginal women. They helped legitimate the institution of imprisonment, which many instinctively felt was illegitimate to begin with. As Shaw (1996b, 195) rightly suggests, *Creating Choices* diverts attention from "rethinking the use of imprisonment" in that it does not challenge its utility and the stigma it imposes on those finally released into the community. Had the task force done that, it is conceivable that fewer prisons might have been built.

Yet a proportion of federally sentenced women have benefited from the work of the task force, so this Canadian venture cannot be said to have failed completely. The word "failed" is used advisedly in assessing the work of the task force and the implementation of *Creating Choices* because the outcome is being judged by the high standards the task force set itself. Its work became tightly focused upon a vision of providing all imprisoned federally sentenced women with greater autonomy in a less oppressive physical setting and this has, largely, not been achieved.

Interpreting the task force's vision of what "success" might have been does not suggest that offending women should never be subjected to regulation. It does, however, presuppose that women's patterns of offending, by comparison with those of men, should be taken into account when determining the extent and manner of the regulation. Federally sentenced women are, by definition, at the most serious end of the offending spectrum, yet their crimes are often situated in a history of extended abuse during their pre-prison lives. Research has shown that they are "often not at risk of re-offending violently against the general public" (Hannah-Moffat and Shaw 2001, 15), and csc's own research shows that those serving long-term sentences of over ten years' duration[12] are among the most stable of the federal population (see Luciani 2000; Grant and Johnson 2000). This suggests that the task force's reluctance to label women as "difficult to manage" was largely justified, despite acknowledging that stability within prison is not necessarily a prediction of stability outside.

csc has now decided that 25 percent of the federally sentenced women are in need of "intensive intervention," with 15 percent of these to be housed in the new secure units. At the other end of the spectrum, the type of accommodation available for just ten minimum security women at Isabel McNeill House (located in distant Kingston and itself under threat of closure) has not been replicated at the new prisons. Approximately 35 percent of all federally sentenced women are classified as minimum security. While the regional prisons have relatively little of the claustrophobic atmosphere of the old prison in Kingston (although this might be disputed by those held in the new secure units), it is still only the medium security women who now have a greater degree of physical freedom. The positioning of the secure units as separate entities within the larger, and now fenced, prisons highlights the disparities between the various groups of imprisoned women.

Creating Choices is premised on the notion that federally sentenced women, despite their offences, generally present a low risk within prison or to the public and that they need support rather than excessive security. A point to be emphasized is that, for many of the women, their present regulation is once again heavily dependent upon levels of security disproportionate to their anticipated risk within the prison. Moreover, their "responsible" choice of programs is an additional form of regulation, denying women the autonomy envisaged by the task force, which anticipated that women would make choices relevant to their own needs rather than those of the prison. As articulated in *Creating Choices*, the dynamic security of each prison was always unrealistically dependent upon the correctness of those choices and ignored the coercive context within which such choices were being made. "The prison" has always depended upon implicit power regulating prisoners.

Yet complete failure of the task force would have meant the Prison for Women still functioning as a prison. It has been closed, but there are those who now suggest that the Prison for Women was not as bad as claimed and that insufficient heed was paid to the problems women brought inside with them. The implication now is that the *women* were the problem rather than the prison itself (see Hayman 2000). What should never be forgotten is the sheer physical inadequacy of the old prison. In the short period between December 1988 and February 1991 six women committed suicide inside the Prison for Women, and another woman took her life, a short distance from the prison, within days of being released on parole. In the seven years since the new prisons opened in 1995 there have been three suicides, two at Établissement Joliette and one at Grand Valley Institution. A woman committed suicide in the co-located maximum security unit at Saskatchewan Penitentiary, and a woman also took her life in the Burnaby Correctional Centre. These figures demonstrate that the new prisons have an infinitely better record than did the Prison for Women, and on that basis alone the task force has fully justified its work.

But the corollary of the task force's "success" has been an increase in capacity for federally sentenced women and conditions for maximum security women that are certainly, in terms of the degree of restraint imposed, the equivalent of anything the old Kingston prison offered. Summarizing the Fatality Inquiry into the death of Denise Fayant at Edmonton, Judge Chrumka (2000) characterized the new style of the prisons as an "untested concept." In the sense that Denise Fayant's death was *Creating Choices*' particular "test," he was right. But, as penal history makes clear – and as this story has charted – the Canadian undertaking was not untested. It had its roots in the work of the first women prison reformers, who wanted to improve both prison conditions and the women themselves, without necessarily challenging the need for imprisonment itself. The task force hoped that federally sentenced women, in a physically freer environment, would be enabled to make choices leading to their personal reformation. In *Creating Choices* they articulated this vision, using the language of feminism to suggest that personal change was feasible within the confines of an "institution." The reality of the prison itself disappeared under the weight of the illusory language adopted by the task force, and members could not bring themselves to say bluntly that change was to be effected through the use of punishment.

Carlen (2002b, 221) analyzes what she terms "carceral clawback," a process that she sees, in one respect, as being "powered by the common-sense ideologies of optimistic campaigners" and "the prisons' continuing need for legitimacy." The prison can never succeed fully (as this would mean its self-destruction), yet it must always be seen to be working towards success because its efforts legitimate its existence. In these terms, the prison's very failure ensures its continuance as there is never a point reached where reformers feel it is safe for them to disengage from attempts to ameliorate the harm inflicted by imprisonment. Yet failure to disengage means that the rationale for the prison – punishment – is inconsistently examined and is even less likely to become part of public debate. Carlen (2002a, 120) refers to "those who might be disheartened by the *unexpected* turn of events in the Canadian federal prisons for women" (emphasis added). Events in Canada have been entirely consonant with other attempts at penal reform in that they demonstrate the unfailing ability of the prison to reassert its supremacy over those attempting its reformation. The present outcome should not have been unexpected.

Punishment is fundamental to the prison experience, but this does not mean that it should go hand in hand with a nihilism that suggests that no good may emerge from imprisonment. So the provision of varied programs should also be part of the prison, in the hope that personal change may be facilitated. Such assistance can be – and is – provided outside the prison walls, and, if the aim were simply to make offending women lead safer, non-criminal lives, then many of those not a danger to others or themselves could be kept in the community.

But offending women (and men) are not sent to prison simply for improving programs. Where much of the reform enterprise comes spectacularly adrift is in its resolute refusal to publicize the central fact that reform occurs in tandem with existing and continuing punishment. It can be surmised that the task force, in the understandable wish to close the Prison for Women, lost sight of this as its members began to hope that their projected model prisons might actually do good. *Creating Choices* contributed to this masking of the real meaning of imprisonment through its refusal to make explicit such hard issues. But while imprisonment remains central to the control of aberrant populations, the commitment and integrity of those prepared to engage in the political act of trying to lessen some of the inequities of the prison should also be acknowledged. The Task Force on Federally Sentenced Women can look back at the signal achievement of having closed the Prison for Women.

Creating Choices has significance beyond Canada because of its focus solely on imprisoned women and their needs. The rigour with which the task force pursued its program of research into federally sentenced women has ensured that those women will never again be so anonymous to those responsible for their care. The report has become part of that history of penal reform that Canadians generally ignored as they tried to find Canadian solutions to a Canadian problem. The lessons of implementation have moved beyond gender and show the continuing power of the prison to survive and subvert its redefinition. The prison's essential discipline cannot be masked by spacious grounds, attractive architecture, and seemingly benevolent programming. As Rothman, Cohen, and others have consistently demonstrated, prisons are always in a state of being transformed, or re-formed, in the hope that an adjustment here, or rebuilding there, will provide the solution to the intractable problem of why prisons do not work. Prisons are not places of healing: they are sites of coercion, repression, and pain.

It is almost inevitable that there will be a future task force on federally sentenced women because these new prisons will continue the historic pattern of triumphing over and subverting reform. Subsequent reformers will face the dilemmas that confronted this task force and will similarly agonize over the extent of any collaboration they might undertake. Community dispositions will, in all likelihood, still seem as unattainable as they did in 1990, so conscience will again tempt new reformers to suspend their distrust of the prison and to participate because of the difficulties in ignoring the immediate harm caused by imprisonment. The new task force will, unsurprisingly, include substantial numbers of civil servants, and most will be as committed to the ideals of reform as were those on the 1990 task force. Their fiscal and legislative hegemony will also ensure that they retain responsibility for, and control over, implementation of any new plan, leading to an outcome similar to the story related in this book. It is conceivable that the composition of the new task force will reflect the changing demographics of Canada and that its focus will not be so resolutely upon Aboriginal women. There is also the possibility that the Healing Lodge will by then be seen as just another prison for federally sentenced women. Perhaps the politics of Canadian federalism will have altered the entire picture, and the distinction between provincial and federal prisoners will no longer exist.

What seems inconceivable is that imprisonment, as the main means of disciplining the unruly in Canada, will have disappeared, which is why the lessons of this particular venture are so crucial. It is essential that potential reformers remember the history of prison reform and resist the siren lure of working alongside an institution that has no intention of relinquishing its power. Their role is to publicize the fact

that "the prison" damages more people than it assists – and that the
damage is not confined to the prisoner but extends through the prisoner's family and into the wider community. They should remain advocates for prisoners, pressing for community dispositions rather than
legitimate imprisonment through their participation.

The members of the Task Force on Federally Sentenced Women were
but the latest in a long line of reformers hoping to find the grail of
penal reform. Their failure to do so cannot be blamed on an imperfect
realization of their plan or, entirely, on those responsible for its flawed
implementation, or on the women themselves. The lesson to be derived
from what has happened in Canada is that the task force's venture is
simply another footnote in the history of trying to repair what is fundamentally irreparable. The task force's failure was inevitable because
the basic premise of imprisonment – that you can coerce people into
being good by depriving them of their liberty and imposing change
upon them – is fatally flawed.

Notes

INTRODUCTION

1 Interview 30

CHAPTER ONE

1 Brown, who accused Warden Smith of "financial maladministration and profligacy," thought of the penitentiary as an "enterprise that wasted public funds" (Oliver 1998, 147). The prison could not earn enough from convict labour to finance it, and the construction costs exceeded receipts from those sources and the government.

2 Unless otherwise indicated, I have relied on Margaret Shaw's *The Federal Female Offender* (1991), companion vol. 3 to *Creating Choices* (TFFSW 1990) for much of the historical background.

3 The term "multi-level" indicates that women of all security classifications may be held within the same prison.

4 Exchange of service agreements were first negotiated in 1973, and they enabled provinces to assume responsibility for some federally sentenced women, especially francophones. By this means, some women were able to be imprisoned closer to their homes, but there were significant penalties. "An offender transferred to another Canadian jurisdiction is subject to all the statutes, regulations and rules applicable in the receiving jurisdiction. In other words, a federal inmate transferred to a provincial jurisdiction becomes a 'provincial prisoner' " (TFFSW 1990, 63).

5 Agnes Macphail was the first woman to be elected to the Canadian House of Commons and Kidman (1947, 48) credits her with being instrumental in achieving the establishment of the Archambault Commission. Hannah-Moffat (2001, 110) gives a full description of Macphail's developing interest in penal affairs, which changed from

being primarily concerned with male prisoners to encouraging the formation
of the Toronto branch of the Elizabeth Fry Society in the 1950s.

6 CAEFS is a "federation of autonomous societies which works with, and on
behalf of, women involved with the justice system, particularly women in
conflict with the law" (taken from the CAEFS's Mission Statement). CAEFS is
recognized within Canada as being the pre-eminent advocacy organization for
imprisoned women.

7 Freedman (1981, 68) expanded on their design. Writing of the Massachusetts
Reformatory Prison for Women, she said: "instead of cells, the reformatory
had 'private rooms' which ranged from 50 to 90 square feet, slightly larger
than most men's prison quarters. Iron bedsteads and white linen, not the
typical bare cot, adorned each room. Well behaved inmates could decorate
their quarters, enjoy unbarred windows and have wood slats instead of grat-
ings on their doors. Room size and location was determined by a merit
system." Similarly, the Hudson House in New York State had "cottages fitted
up as nearly as possible like an average family house."

8 Berzins and Hayes detailed their sacking, after being hired by the Ministry of
the Solicitor General to follow up the recommendations of the Clark Committee (1977). They were the first to work "exclusively on the needs of
women," and they prepared a review of programs for women offenders that
incurred the "wrath" of the then commissioner of corrections. Shortly thereafter they were told that their contracts would be terminated. In a telling
section, echoing Rothman (1980), they wrote: "it appears that a powerful
system which did not hesitate to compromise the interests of women in its
charge for convenience's sake, also dealt unscrupulously with women hired to
correct those inequities" (Berzins and Hayes 1987, 169).

9 As later becomes evident, when the role played by Aboriginal women in the
TFFSW is discussed, the debates centred on the patriation of the Constitution
and the Canadian Charter of Rights and Freedoms were of fundamental
importance to culturally distinct groups as well. A meeting of First Ministers
in 1981 agreed (without the assent of the premier of Quebec) to the insertion
of Section 33 in the Charter, which gave any provincial government the right
to ignore sections of the Charter (including those deemed so important by
women, Sections 15 and 28) if they were thought to be in conflict with
provincial interests. Additionally, Section 27 protected multiculturalism
within Canada. Interpretations of the meaning of "culture" have been used
within Canada (and elsewhere) as a means of defining and restricting the
freedom and autonomy of women. Some Aboriginal women believed that
some Aboriginal men might claim that cultural practices and traditions
required that women should be treated differently from men. Aboriginal
women needed the reassurance that Section 28 would be applied equally to
themselves and to other culturally distinct groups because the law had signally failed them when they had sought redress under the Canadian Bill of

Rights. The "notwithstanding" clause, Section 33, caused women to protest vehemently because it was feared that it could be adversely applied to Section 28, which guaranteed rights and freedoms equally to men and to women. This was finally acknowledged when Section 28 was specifically declared exempt from the "notwithstanding" clause. See Krosenbrink-Gelissen 1993; Brodsky and Day 1989; and Razack 1991.

10 The Women's Legal Education and Action Fund (LEAF) was founded in 1984 by "a small group of influential Canadian women, almost all lawyers" (Hannah-Moffat 2001, 136). LEAF had been "impressed by the record of the ... National Association for the Advancement of Coloured People (NAACP), in particular their strategy of pursuing incremental gains in specific areas [and had] concluded that Canadian women could best secure their legal rights in a similar way" (Razack 1991, 52). For a fuller discussion of the importance of LEAF see Razack 1991.

11 The challenge remained dormant until 2002, when it was finally settled. Details remain confidential.

12 Interview 18.

13 Interview 27.

14 October/November 1988 CAEFS' Executive Director's Report.

15 The closest comparison is derived from figures for "on-register" prisoners (federal prisoners in provincial or federal prisons, and provincial prisoners in federal prisons, including those on day parole) in 1990–91. Aboriginal men comprised nearly 13 percent of "on-register" male prisoners. Figures presented in the same table showed women to be 2 percent of the *total* "on-register" prisoners, but they do not give a breakdown for Aboriginal women (Boe 1992, 14). We know from Shaw et al. (1991b) that Aboriginal women comprised 23 percent of the federally sentenced women's population, but there is not an exact correlation because those figures do not include all "on-register" Aboriginal women or provincial women serving sentences in federal prisons.

16 October/November 1988 CAEFS' Executive Director's Report.

17 Memorandum, 1 February 1989.

18 Interview 27.

19 Personal notes, 1996.

20 The fact that sustaining grants are funded by the Secretariat means that there is a degree of independence between CSC and the Secretariat. Even if CSC were to cancel service contracts with organizations such as CAEFS, the sustaining grants would not be affected. CAEFS currently receives a grant of approximately $500,000 annually.

21 An exchange of service agreement, concluded in 1988, covering federally sentenced women in British Columbia.

22 Letter from Bonnie Diamond to Joseph Stanford, 13 February 1989.

23 Ibid.

24 Memorandum 23 March 1989.
25 Proposal for a Task Force on Federally Sentenced Women (unamended version)
26 All government departments are subject to the Financial Administration Act, 1985, and Ingstrup would have been unable to delegate any authority for financial matters.
27 Interview 19.
28 Responsibility for some of this work, such as parole supervision, has now been reclaimed by csc.
29 Ryan (1983) details similar dilemmas faced by a British abolitionist group, Radical Alternatives to Prison (RAP), whose very outspoken view that prisons "could not rehabilitate" antagonized the Home Office, leaving RAP unable to influence official policy in the way that more pragmatic organizations, such as the Howard League and the National Association for the Care and Resettlement of Offenders (NACRO), did. CAEFS had always taken a less confrontational path, partly, it might be suggested, because of its financial relationship with government.
30 A term coined by Australian feminists to cover feminists working in a government bureaucracy (see Stetson and Mazur 1995).

CHAPTER TWO

1 Memorandum, 14 March 1989.
2 The Task Force on Federally Sentenced Women chose to adopt the word "Aboriginal" for its report because it was the term used in the Constitution Act, 1982.
3 Treaties were originally made through the Crown but, post-Confederation, were made through the Canadian Government. The treaties, in taking control of Aboriginal-held land to facilitate European immigration, created reserves and provided small annuities for individual Aboriginal peoples. At the time these treaties were signed by the Aboriginal nations, various verbal assurances (such as assistance with agriculture) were given by those negotiating on behalf of the government. Aboriginal nations, being accustomed to oral transactions, assumed that the Government would honour them and the failure to do so, and to clarify entitlement to land, has led to protracted claims from individual Bands. (See Frideres 1993; RCAP 1996).
4 "Status," in this context, refers to those who were legally entitled to call themselves Indian. "The terms 'legal,' 'registered' and 'status' are generally used interchangeably to denote an Indian who is of federal concern ... 'Indian' refers to a person who, pursuant to the *Indian Act*, is registered as an Indian, or is entitled to be registered as an Indian" (Frideres 1993, 28). At no time were Aboriginal peoples permitted to self-identify as Indians. For a fuller discussion of the many ways in which the Indian Act determined who

might be classified as a "status" Indian – and those whom the act excluded –
see RCAP 1996 and Frideres 1993.

5 Chapter 11 of RCAP, vol. 1, provides an extensive review of many of these
relocations and the consequences for the communities involved. These relocations continued until well into the 1960s.

6 This is a reference to an 1879 report compiled by Nicholas Flood Davin, MP,
who had been asked to report on the industrial schools.

7 There is a growing literature on the history of the residential schools. RCAP
(1996) received extensive testimony in both written and oral form, some of
which found its way into the final report. Miller (1996) gives a particularly
broad view of the history and the consequences of the residential school
experiment. As well as singling out the various churches for their roles in
running the schools, Miller also makes it clear that the federal government
had – and continues to have – responsibility for what happened. Chrisjohn
and Young (1997, 3) take issue with what they term the "standard account"
of the rationale for residential schools and offer an alternative "irregular
account," which begins: "residential schools were one of many attempts at
the genocide of the Aboriginal people."

8 A phrase coined by Patrick Johnston to cover the period, which began in
1959, when large numbers of Aboriginal children were removed from their
homes and placed in (frequently non-Aboriginal) foster care on the grounds
of "child protection." The phrase is cited in Fournier and Crey (1997, 9,
who describe the "damage done to the generations of people who narrowly
escaped residential schools only to wind up in foster homes."

9 Memorandum, 14 March 1989.

10 For administrative convenience CSC has five correctional regions: Atlantic,
covering the Maritimes and Newfoundland; Québec; Ontario; Prairies, covering Manitoba, Saskatchewan, Alberta, and the Northwest Territories; and
Pacific, covering British Columbia. As has been discussed in Chapter 1, the
federal government is responsible for those sentenced to terms of more than
two years' imprisonment.

11 "Sovereignty-association" was part of the political discourse of the Parti
Quebecois prior to its election win in 1976, but its official position on the
matter was not outlined until 1979, in the White Paper *Quebec – Canada: A
New Deal*. It was proposed that Quebec would become a sovereign state but
that there would be a very high degree of economic continuity and cooperation with the rest of Canada. See Bothwell 1998; McRoberts 1993.

12 Elijah Harper daily sat in the Manitoba Legislature, holding an eagle feather,
and saying "no" whenever the Speaker asked if the Meech Lake Accord
could be considered. The accord eventually failed because it was not ratified
within the necessary time limit. Harper was later to say: "We blocked the
accord because it posed a threat to aboriginal people. Aboriginal people have
no quarrel with Quebec. But we're a distinct society too, and we've fought

for many years for the basic rights that Quebec takes for granted, such as
participating in constitutional talks" (cited in Miller 2000, 377).

13 See, for example, Hamilton and Sinclair (1991) *The Justice System and
Aboriginal People: Report of the Aboriginal Justice Inquiry of Manitoba*;
and Nova Scotia (1989) *Royal Commission on the Donald Marshall Jr.
Prosecution*.

14 NWAC "represents Aboriginal women who base their identity on self-identify-
ing criteria and includes non-status and status Indian women" (Krosenbrink
1993, 344). Its constitution dates from 1973, and its activities cover most
areas impinging on the welfare of Aboriginal women. Like CAEFS, it has an
executive board composed of representatives from regional/provincial associ-
ations across Canada. Although not predicated on the issue of sexual equality, NWAC was heavily involved in campaigning for "Indian rights for Indian
women" following the initial failure of the *Lavell* and *Bedard* cases, which
challenged the discrimination Indian women experienced under the Indian
Act when they married non-status males or Aboriginal peoples from other
bands. See also Razack (1991) for further discussion of the *Lavell* case. See
Behiels (2000) for a comprehensive overview of the role of NWAC in challenging both the government and male Aboriginal organizations over their treatment of Aboriginal women.

15 In 1989 Aboriginal women comprised 45 percent of all female admissions to
provincial institutions (La Prairie 1993).

16 La Prairie (1992) explores Braithwaite's theory of reintegrative shaming
within the context of Canada's Aboriginal population, showing that shaming
was "a standard response to deviance in traditional, communal aboriginal
communities" in Canada, but that its impact had been lessened by the "rup-
turing of traditional institutions of social control."

17 Interview 20.

18 CAEFS, in its written proposals submitted to James Phelps in December 1988,
had asked that the task force "actively seek out and incorporate the views
and ideas of federally incarcerated women," but it had not suggested they
should actually be on the task force. In March 1989 a meeting took place
between Bonnie Diamond and a CSC representative, during which the composition of both the steering committee and the working group was reviewed,
and it was then that Diamond suggested that an Aboriginal woman should
be on each.

19 Working Group Minutes, 13 April 1989. The "particular oppression" can
best be explained as the extra burden carried into prison by Aboriginal
women who, having experienced both socio-economic and racial discrimination on the outside, often found themselves exposed to racism on the inside.

20 Minutes of Working Group, 13–14 April 1989, Appendix B.

21 Interview 18.

22 Interview 17.

CHAPTER THREE

1 Steering Committee Minutes, 3 April 1989.
2 Working Group Minutes, 13– 4 April 1989.
3 Working Group Minutes, 13– 4 April 1989. These principles should not be confused with the Working Principles, allied to the mandate, which set out the "ground rules" guiding the task force (see TFFSW 1990, 72).
4 Memorandum, 2 May 1989.
5 Notes of conversation, November 1999.
6 Interview 28.
7 Interview 27.
8 Interview 19.
9 Interview 19.
10 Working Group Minutes, 10–12 May 1989.
11 Interview 19.
12 Ibid.
13 Memorandum, 28 April 1989.
14 Letter from John Edwards to Ole Ingstrup, 22 September 1988.
15 I am grateful for Margaret Shaw's assistance in clarifying the issues in these two paragraphs.
16 Faith (1993, 58) relates how, during the 1980s, "women's groups succeeded in persuading criminal justice agencies, including CSC, to refer to convicted female lawbreakers as 'women in conflict with the law' [which] comes closer to a non-judgmental description in that it doesn't denigrate or permanently label the woman in question. It doesn't presume that she is a criminal 'type' but rather that she is in an adversarial position vis-à-vis the law." She continues: "The key problem with the phrase ... is that it denies the fundamental inequality of the relationship ... one simply cannot be 'in conflict' with power to which one is subordinate" (Faith 1993, 58). In a personal letter Faith amplified her view, saying that "the change grew out of the grassroots, initiated by prisoners objecting to 'female offender' " (August 2001).
17 This lack of prison-based expertise on the working group did not indicate a disregard for the knowledge of individual wardens; rather, it reflected the fact that there was only one federal prison for women and that, consequently, the pool of specific expertise was restricted. The steering committee included the director of a Quebec provincial facility, but the needs of a provincial prison, with its transient population, do not always translate into a federal model.
18 Interview 29.
19 Interviews 27 and 31.
20 Minutes of meeting of Sub-Committee on Consultations, 21 April 1989.
21 Guideline Questions for Consultations, 21 April 1989.
22 Memorandum, 17 May 1989.
23 Steering Committee Minutes, 19 June 1989.

24 A distinction needs to be made between those who were francophones (i.e., French-speaking) and those who were francophone Quebecois (both culturally and linguistically of that province).

25 Working Group Minutes 10–12 May 1989. There were provincial difficulties once the regional consultations began (Minutes of Consultations Sub-Group, 6 June 1989). The francophones expected that French would be used during the Quebec consultations because, to do otherwise in a largely French-speaking province, would be politically insensitive, but few on the working group were fluent French speakers. Additionally, as with all the task force's documentation, the need to translate documents delayed the distribution of information in Quebec, and organizations and individuals who might contribute to the consultations in that province were not contacted as quickly as were others across the country.

26 Interview 19.

27 BCCW was newly built, and the decision was later made that it would not be replaced by one of the institutions subsequently recommended by the task force. This was an uncanny echo of the reasons for not closing the Prison for Women in 1938 – that it would be fiscally irresponsible to close a prison so recently built.

28 Working group members were each assigned to a proportion of the consultations. It would have been an impossibility, within the time scale, for all to attend every consultation meeting.

29 Progress Report on Consultations, September 1989, 3.

30 Claire Culhane occupies a special place in the history of Canadian penal reform, noted for (among many things) her resolute advocacy of prisoners' rights and the books detailing removal of her visiting rights at provincial and federal men's prisons in British Columbia. See Culhane (1979, 1985, and 1991).

31 Working Group Minutes, 15–16 August 1989.

32 Memorandum, 2 August 1989.

33 For Aboriginal peoples, Elders have the same function as priests and chaplains. They are valued for their wisdom, insight, and knowledge, and are considered to have special spiritual gifts. They are valued by their communities for their ability to guide others, both by example and through teachings.

34 Paper presented at the Aboriginal Women's Caucus, 30 August 1989.

35 Working Group Minutes, 21–22 September 1989.

36 Interview 32.

37 Detailed Notes of Steering Committee Meeting, 19 September 1989.

38 The task force was right to be concerned about events at the Prison for Women. A minor assault led to a "lockdown" on A and B ranges and tight restrictions on all prisoner movement. Shortly afterwards three protective custody inmates were assaulted, which led to a lockdown of the entire institution for a day and a half. Restrictions were gradually eased, but the prison-

ers were very resentful of what they saw as an overly harsh response. The situation deteriorated, and the chair of the Inmate Committee called the press to protest about what was happening. The ensuing publicity focused on the supposed violence of the women in the prison rather than on institutional policy.

39 Steering Committee Minutes, 19 September 1989.

40 Detailed Notes of Steering Committee Meeting, 19 September 1989.

41 Working Group Minutes, 21–22 September 1989.

42 Steering Committee Minutes, 3 April 1989.

43 Working Group Minutes, 6–7 July 1989.

44 Working Group Minutes, 6–7 July 1989.

45 Interviews 28 and 27.

46 Detailed Notes of Steering Committee Meeting, 19 September 1989.

47 The community-needs interviews of non-Aboriginal women were also being carried out at the same time, and both pieces of research were to become separate companion volumes to the final report.

48 Steering Committee Minutes, 19 September 1989.

49 Working Group Minutes, 21–22 September 1989.

50 Ibid.

51 Ibid.

CHAPTER FOUR

1 As Horii (2001) makes clear, the use of the term "involuntarily transferred" obscures the fact that prisoners are being *forcibly* transferred.

2 The word "associated" is used because one of the women who died in the period leading up to the death of Sandy Sayer took her life across the road from the prison, very shortly after having been released on parole.

3 Interview 20.

4 Interview 28.

5 Steering Committee Minutes, 16 October 1989.

6 Motion from the Task Force on Federally Sentenced Women, 16 October 1989.

7 Interview 31.

8 Interview, 2000.

9 Heney (1990, 30) noted that "a good deal of the counselling/emotional support that takes place in ... prison is provided by the prisoners themselves." She suggested that prisoners should be trained as "support counsellors," and her recommendation led to the first "peer-support" team being formed at the Prison for Women in 1990. All of the new regional prisons for federally sentenced women have similar teams of trained prisoners able to offer help to fellow inmates during times of personal crisis.

10 *The Survey of Federally Sentenced Women* was to be published as a compan-

ion volume to the task force's eventual report, and it concentrated on those federal women actually in custody. *The Release Study: Survey of Federally Sentenced Women in the Community* and the *Survey of Federally Sentenced Aboriginal Women in the Community* provided another view of these women and their lives.

11 All this information is taken from *The Survey of Federally Sentenced Women* (Shaw et al. 1991b).

12 Working Group Minutes, 25–27 October 1989.

13 Canada has embraced the principles of restorative justice in a correctional context, and victim-offender mediation has been in use for nearly twenty-five years. Community conferencing, based on the New Zealand model of family group conferencing, is now being used more widely. Community sentencing panels are also being set up. The Restorative Justice and Dispute Resolution Unit of CSC produced a lengthy list of projects, either ongoing or about to be implemented, in 1998. Much of the emphasis appeared to be on Aboriginal-style projects, which is not to say that they are necessarily faithful to Aboriginal principles of justice. The new Aboriginal healing lodges are based on Aboriginal principles of justice, which also happen to be restorative.

14 However, the Corrections and Conditional Release Act (CCRA),1992, replaced previous legislation controlling the work of CSC. The CCRA reflected the rights obtained under the Canadian Charter of Rights and Freedoms (see Chapter 1), while also providing specifically for imprisoned Aboriginals and women. This suggests that the need for legislation was not entirely the impediment the task force assumed it to be, and it raises questions about whether the civil servants should have been – or were – better informed. I am grateful to Kelly Hannah-Moffat for having drawn my attention to some of these points.

15 Working Group Minutes, 25–27 October 1989.

16 Interview 31.

17 A distinction should be made between the co-corrections or "mixing" model, and "shared-site detention," wherein men and women are housed totally separately on the same site, while sharing program and recreation facilities at different times (see Faith 1993; Hayman 1996). With the co-corrections model, most activities may be jointly undertaken but accommodation is generally separate.

18 Steering Committee Minutes, 19 September 1989.

19 The minutes are contradictory, at first referring to twelve women in protective custody and later to ten. I have calculated on the basis of twelve being in protective custody.

20 The 1993 conviction of Karla Homolka in connection with the murder of her sister and two other young women received enormous publicity in Canada. The controversy surrounding her trial, and plea-bargain with officials, focused attention on women's capacity for violence. However, part of the

plea-bargaining centred on the abuse allegedly suffered by Homolka at the hands of her husband and her reduced culpability. The graphic facts of the case, preserved on video by both Homolka and her husband, and only fully available after the plea-bargaining, have unsurprisingly coloured subsequent public debate on women's propensity for violence. These crimes were exceptional and occurred after the task force had completed its report. In 1989/90 much of the academic discussion of women offenders focused on the context of their offending behaviour, and this was often seen to be socio-economic and abusive.

21 Interview 31.
22 Interview 28.
23 Interview 27.
24 Interview 31.
25 Detailed Notes were provided for the September steering committee meeting. The steering committee subsequently decided that Detailed Notes would not be provided and that all recordings and notes would be destroyed once the minutes had been drawn up. In the light of the repeated complaints by the Aboriginal participants that their comments were frequently omitted from the official record, this was a bizarre decision, even if it continued the consensus model agreed upon by the working group.
26 Interview 30.
27 Some communities managed to find their own solutions, but only after years of struggle. Alkali Lake is perhaps one of the most famous examples because of the way in which it managed to find a collective way back to sobriety. (See Warry 1998; Morrison and Wilson 1986.)
28 TFFSW 1990, 69.
29 Section 81(1) of the CCRA was eventually to make this possible. See Chapter 9.
30 A prisoner's entitlement to private family visits is dealt with in the Commissioner's Directive (CD) 770. Prisoners may no longer have a private family visit with another prisoner as, under the CCRA, a "visitor" is "any person other than an inmate or staff member." See, *Gilles Laliberté v. Commissioner of Corrections and Attorney General of Canada*, 27 April 2000.
31 Working Group Minutes, 25–27 October 1989.
32 Ibid.
33 In all of the minutes there was relatively little discussion of staff members, which is an interesting omission, bearing in mind their important role within a prison. The May 1989 working group minutes indicated that members of the group were to meet union members at the Prison for Women, so staff views would have been heard then, but, overall, their knowledge of the women was not called upon. This can partly be related to the group's wish to avoid importing any of the old staff culture into the new prisons. Staff members at the Prison for Women were later told that they would not "fit" the new prisons.

34 Madam Justice Arbour (1996, 252–3) recommended that a cross gender staffing monitor should be appointed to deal with the issue of whether or not men should be front-line workers at the new prisons. Additionally, Arbour suggested that women should have the option of serving their sentence in a prison that had no men working as front-line correctional officers (217). CSC designated Edmonton Institution for Women free of men and, through the Public Service Commission, obtained a three-year exclusion order, which was then extended for a further year (see CSC 1995b.) The Cross Gender Monitoring Project's Third Annual Report (September 2000) recommended that *all* males should be barred from front-line positions because CSC had failed to implement four recommendations regarding the deployment of male staff, which had been made in its Second Annual Report (Lajeunesse and Jefferson 2000, 4). Both Edmonton and the Healing Lodge initially decided against hiring male primary workers, whereas Joliette and Nova took a small proportion.

35 This derives from the "potlatch" and refers to a gift given to mark an event. It was originally used to denote the status of the giver, with gifts of different value being conferred according to the rank of the recipient. Historically, the potlatch became more and more extravagant and the alleged excesses associated with it were used as an excuse for its being banned in 1884 under the Indian Act. This prohibition was only removed in 1951, when the Indian Act was rewritten. See McMillan (1995) for a fuller discussion.

36 Working Group Minutes, 25–27 October 1989.

37 Ibid.

38 1 November 1989.

39 Taken from undated chapter comments, submitted to editors of TFFSW.

CHAPTER FIVE

1 Until otherwise indicated, all quotations that follow are from the Steering Committee Minutes, 20 November 1989.

2 Interview 19.

3 The principles have been alluded to on a number of occasions and are an important philosophical part of the final report. They are discussed more fully at the end of this chapter.

4 Interview 30.

5 The outside assistance of Linda McLeod as the final co-ordinator/editor of the transcript had already been agreed.

6 Subsequent quotations are taken from the Steering Committee Minutes, 18 December 1989, unless otherwise indicated.

7 Interview 30.

8 Steering Committee Minutes 20 November 1989.

9 Interview 28.

10 To an extent, this did happen at the Burnaby Correctional Centre for Women, where the federal government shared responsibility with the provincial authorities. The crucial difference was that the federal government paid the provincial government to provide programs and services equal to those available to federally sentenced women in the new prisons.

11 In 1996 Madam Justice Arbour recommended the appointment of a deputy commissioner for women, and Nancy Stableforth was appointed later that year. However, the wardens of the new prisons reported directly to their regional deputy commissioners rather than directly to Stableforth, so women still remained at a remove from the top level of correctional administration.

12 Note to author, 20 September 1999.

13 For an alternative view see Chrisjohn and Young, with Maraun (1997) who present what they term the "irregular account" of "Indian" residential schools, suggesting that genocide does not always involve killing. Forced assimilation can also be seen as a form of genocide, with the Residential Schools' policy being seen by some as an example of this.

14 Personal letter, 12 March 1990.

15 The front cover of the first edition of *Creating Choices* carried a hazy photograph of all the working group, and Nuffield is seen standing among them. However, as the members were not individually identified, many readers of *Creating Choices* would have had no idea who any of those women were. Additionally, because the number of women in the photo exceeded those listed in the report as belonging to the working group, the connection would not necessarily have been made.

16 Undated draft of what was then Chapter 6.

17 Letter to author, 1999.

18 Although the task force had accepted that the Burnaby Correctional Centre for Women would not be replaced, it still recommended that a fifth prison should be in "the lower mainland of British Columbia" (TFFSW 1990, 114).

19 C-SPAC Minutes, 16 September 1988.

20 Interview 32.

21 Private notes 2000.

22 Interview 28.

23 Interview 32.

24 This distrust was to explode disastrously during the standoff, lasting seventy-eight days, between Mohawks and the army at Oka in 1990. The conflict centred on thirty-nine hectares of land, claimed by the Mohawks as historically theirs, and which the local municipality wanted to develop as a golf course. See Frideres (1993) for a chronology and discussion of the event. See also Wagamese (1996) for a more personal view of what happened.

25 Interview 32.

26 As earlier noted, an external editor, Linda McLeod, was also employed for the final draft.

27 Memorandum 28 April 1989.
28 Personal letter, August 2001.
29 Interview 30.
30 Interview 27.
31 Interview 32.

CHAPTER SIX

1 Both Margaret Shaw (1991a) and Lee Axon (1989) provided comprehensive reviews of international trends and practices for the task force.
2 Personal notes, 2001.
3 Briefing Paper, July 1991.
4 The deliberate withholding of relevant information was already suspected by the EAC and later became part of the reason for the withdrawal of CAEFS from the committee and the implementation process.
5 CAEFS Report January/February 1992.
6 CAEFS Board Minutes 23 February 1992.
7 Private letter, 2002.
8 CAEFS Board Minutes, June 1992.
9 Dawn Fleming, 18 June 1992.
10 Personal letter, 2002.
11 Personal notes, 1996. However, it is government policy that staff members should reapply for jobs when the work description is significantly altered, as was the case following the acceptance of *Creating Choices*. Additionally, some of the staff members preferred not to move away from Kingston as their partners were working in nearby prisons.
12 Lockdowns must be authorized by the head of each prison. They are then scrutinized by CSC headquarters for reasonable grounds before being implemented.
13 Madame Justice Louise Arbour was appointed to head the Commission of Inquiry into Certain Events at the Prison for Women in Kingston in April 1995. Her report, of the same name, was published in March 1996.
14 The "ranges" are described in chapter 1.
15 "The purpose of [a] cell extraction is to remove and strip search an unwilling inmate and then to place the inmate in segregation if the prisoner is in the prison's general population, or to return him or her to a stripped cell if the inmate is already in segregation" (Arbour 1996, 67).
16 "It is the function of the Correctional Investigator to conduct investigations into the problems of offenders related to decisions, recommendations, acts or omissions of the Commissioner or any person under the control and management of, or performing services for, or on behalf of, the Commissioner that affect offenders either individually or as a group" (CCRA 1992, Statute 167[1]). For a full explanation of his/her role, see Arbour (1996, 20–1, 162–71).

17 See Shaw (1999) for an extensive discussion of the public impact of the tapes and the way in which the media responded.

18 While such changes in living conditions were radical, in so far as Canadian prisons were concerned, the communal living did not differ greatly from what was sometimes available in other jurisdictions, if only with limited frequency. See, for example, Coyle's (1994) description of the Barlinnie Special Unit in Scotland. The major difference lay in the fact that such changes were expected to be made available to *all* federally sentenced women rather than to a selected few, and the physical specification of each prison was linked to community standards of accommodation.

19 See Hannah-Moffat and Shaw (2000).

20 *Board of Investigation Report into a Suicide in February 1996, and other Major Incidents at Edmonton Institution for Women* (CSC 1996b, 3). Additionally, CSC was concerned that the maximum security women should be separated from those with mental health needs.

21 *Regional Facilities for Federally Sentenced Women,* Construction Policy and Services/National Implementation Committee, July 1992.

22 The Prairies, as a Correctional region, cover Manitoba, Saskatchewan, Alberta, and the Northwest Territories.

23 4 June 1991.

24 Taken from a transcript of *Wild Rose Country*, a program broadcast on CBC Radio Calgary on 26 November 1991.

25 Fox was appointed on 17 March 1993, as were the wardens for Nova, Joliette, and Grand Valley.

26 Connie Sampson, untitled column, *Edmonton Journal*, March 1996.

27 Unsigned Editorial, *Edmonton Sun* 14 March 1993, 10.

28 Kathy Kohut, "Barring the Prison," *Alberta Report* (The Law), 16 July, 26.

29 Mike Sadava, "Separation of Homes, Prison Sites May Ease Opposition," *Edmonton Journal,* 6 August 1993.

30 Author unknown, "What You Should Know about a Federal Correctional Institution for Women," *Mill Woods Newsletter,* September 1993, 46.

31 *Board of Investigation into a Suicide on February 29, 1996, and other Major Incidents at Edmonton Institution for Women 1996* (CSC 1996b).

32 Prisons are governed by a series of measures: Corrections and Conditional Release Act (CCRA 1992) statutes and regulations; Commissioner's Directives (CDs), which apply universally to all prisons operated by the Correctional Service of Canada and are issued under the authority of Section 98(1) of the CCRA, 1992; Regional Instructions (RIs), which may enlarge on CDs or be specific to regional issues; Standing Orders (SOs), which are specific to a particular prison, and; Post Orders, which are specific to a "post" within a particular prison. Additionally, there are policy manuals dealing with issues in even greater detail. For a fuller explanation see Arbour (1996, 3–4).

33 Diane Coulter, *Edmonton Journal* 15 November 1995.

34 The private visiting house was used by women with the right to a (largely) unsupervised private visit from family or from people acknowledged as having close ties with them. Visits could last up to seventy-two hours. At Edmonton women needed to be on Management Levels One to Three to qualify. Those on Level Four were taken to Edmonton Institution for Men for private visits, and those on Level Five were not entitled to visits. The right is defined in the CCRA, 1992, under Sections 59, 60, and 71. CD 700 applies to private family visits.

35 Corcan is the trading name of Correctional Service of Canada's industrial arm.

36 Appendix A, Convening order and terms of reference, signed 13 March 1996. *Board of Investigation Report into a Suicide in February 1996, and Other Major Incidents at Edmonton Institution for Women* (CSC 1996b). Unlike the report provided by the Board of Investigation (CSC 1994a) into the April 1994 incidents at the Prison for Women, which prominently displayed the offending histories of the women concerned, this 1996 report largely blacked out all information relating to the women involved in the incidents at Edmonton.

37 *Report to the Attorney General: Public Inquiry into the Death of Denise Fayant* 14 January 2000. The Inquiry was conducted by Judge A. Chrumka, of the Provincial Court of Alberta. Although it was held in September 1998, the Report took seventeen months to appear and was composed largely of direct quotations taken from the transcript of the Inquiry. Its strength lay in the fact that it clearly set out what had happened during the days preceding and following the death of Ms Fayant, showing the ill-prepared state of the prison and the inability of its staff to provide adequately for the women in the Enhanced Unit.

38 This term is used by CSC to indicate that a prisoner cannot easily live alongside, or has clashed with, another prisoner or prisoners.

39 Personal notes, October 1998.

40 Private letter, 2002.

41 Tony Blais, "Warden Touts Tough Security," *Edmonton Sun*, 25 April 1996.

42 Heather Hill and Paula Simons, "Alarmed Fence Big Part of Jail Refit,"*Edmonton Journal*, 2 May 1996.

43 Unsigned editorial, "The Warden Should Step Down," *Edmonton Journal*, 17 May 1996, 18.

44 16 July 1996.

45 28 May 1996.

46 10 June 1996.

47 9 August 1996.

48 29 August 1996.

49 Training schedule provided for CAEFS on 12 September 1996.

50 Tony Blais, "Prison Errors Admitted," *Edmonton Sun*, 29 August 1996, 5.

51 These units were discrete units within the larger men's prisons. They were separately managed and had their own program staff.

52 *Board of Investigation into a Suicide on February 29, 1996, and other Major Incidents at Edmonton Institution for Women* (CSC 1996b).

53 Ashley Geddes, "Police Investigate Negligence Charges in Inmate's Death,"*Edmonton Journal,* 9 October 1997. These charges were dropped in April 1998. The case had been thought so sensitive that, unusually, four senior prosecutors were involved in the decision not to proceed.

54 Tom Barrett, "Mother of Slain Inmate Sues Prison Warden," *Edmonton Journal,* 23 October 1997.

55 Connie Sampson, untitled column, *Edmonton Journal,* March 1996.

CHAPTER SEVEN

1 At times the women from this region will be referred to as being from the Maritimes, which is an area covering the first three of the Atlantic Region provinces. Newfoundland is not part of the Maritimes but, for the purposes of this chapter, can be assumed to be included when the term is used.

2 August 1989. The principles espoused by the Task Force on Federally Sentenced Women (TFFSW) were later adopted in *Blueprint for Change: Report of the Solicitor General's Special Committee on Provincially Incarcerated Women* (1992). The Committee acknowledged the ground-breaking role of the Task Force and "found [its] work made easier by these pioneers in systemic change" (1992, ii). While being an examination of *provincial* provision for remanded and sentenced women, the conclusions reached by *Blueprint for Change* revealed that many of the problems encountered by provincially incarcerated women were similar to those of federally sentenced women. Importantly, the report highlighted the plight of black women within the correctional system, pointing out the neglect of their needs in correctional planning. (The TFFSW was criticized for failing to consider this group separately in *Creating Choices.*) Although there was a fairly sizeable Aboriginal population living in the Atlantic region, the sentenced population did not reflect the Canada-wide trend of disproportionate Aboriginal representation in the prisons. The Maritimes also has a distinct group of Acadians, with different cultural needs. Little in *Blueprint for Change* was subsequently implemented.

3 Kathy Krawchuk, "Prison Selection Process Rapped," *Chronicle Herald,* 1 August 1991.

4 Gloria Kelly, "Dartmouth Council Backs Prison Bid," *Chronicle Herald,* 22 August 1991.

5 Peter McLaughlin, "Woodsiders Don't Want Prison in Their Backyard," *Daily News,* 26 August 1991, 4.

6 Rob Roberts, "Halifax Lists Potential Sites for Women's Prison," *Daily News,* 20 November 1991, 3.

7 Marla Cranston, "Metro Municipalities Await Word on Jail," *Daily News*, November 1991.

8 Rob Roberts, "Truro Wins Women's Prison: Support Services Questioned," *Daily News*, 17 December 1991.

9 Randy Jones, "Fry Society Renews Metro Bid for Prison," *Chronicle Herald*, 13 January 1992.

10 Letter from Gail Stacey-Moore to The Honourable Doug Lewis, 16 January 1992.

11 Author unknown, title unknown, *Daily News*, 8 February 1992.

12 Alan Elliott, "Women's Prison Proceeding," *Daily News*, 15 December 1993.

13 csc *Communiqué*, 27 October 1995.

14 See *Commission of Inquiry into Certain Events at the Prison for Women in Kingston* (1996), particularly chapter 2:7.2–7.9.

15 It was subsequently suggested that the hiring authorities rejected any applicant at the outset if they did not have a university education, thus losing the potential talents and life experiences of those who had pursued other career paths and ignoring the wishes of *Creating Choices* (Manzer 1996).

16 Todd Hyslop, "LeBlanc Supplies Prison Background," *Daily News*, 24 April 1995.

17 Beds in the segregation cells were not "funded" as regular living spaces for the women. The assumption was that they would be used, intermittently, by women who were normally accommodated in the houses. They were not considered to be part of the total capacity of the prison, even when they were used as such at Edmonton.

18 Steve Proctor, "New Truro Prison Tries New Approach," *Chronicle Herald*, 3 August 1995.

19 Steve Proctor, "Reaction to New Prison Mostly Favourable," *Chronicle Herald*, 21 October 1995, 10.

20 Speaking notes for John Edwards at the official opening of the Truro (sic) Institution for Women.

21 Interview 11.

22 Kevin Cox, "Women's Prison Has Commitment to Provide Inmate Community Living,"*Daily News*, 8 November 1995.

23 Correctional Service Canada, Construction Policy and Services, 11 September 1992.

24 Interview 11.

25 Ibid.

26 Unlike Edmonton, which abided by the task force recommendation that men should not be employed on "front-line" duties, Nova employed a few men when it first opened. They were permitted to work directly with the women as primary workers (guards). Refer to the three *Cross Gender Monitoring Reports* for further information on csc policy.

27 Brian Rau, "Colchester Disabled Could Lose Bus Service," *Chronicle Herald*, 15 March 1996.
28 In a later report commissioned by CSC, Warner (1998, 6) categorized these as covering: "those with basic skills and cognitive challenges ... those with emotional distress needs ... [those who] in maximum security environments may require intensive programming to assist them in changing anti-social attitudes and behaviour." The term "low functioning" is used interchangeably with "mentally challenged" in official documents to describe women with low intellectual capabilities who lack the social and educational skills necessary for many everyday tasks.
29 Personal letter to author, 25 May 2004.
30 See Warner 1998.
31 L. Shimmel, *The Structured Living House Program: Nova Institution for Women* CSC (1996). Not obtained by author.
32 In Commissioner's Directive (CD) 701, Section 2 reads: "The case management process shall provide for the proper assessment, classification, counselling, programme planning and supervision of offenders throughout their sentence." And, in Section 7, it says: "A team approach to case work shall be co-ordinated by the appropriate case management officer in the institution or the community."
33 Personal notes, 1996.
34 Ibid.
35 Ibid.
36 Personal letter to author, 2001.
37 Author unknown, "Chain Fence Going up Round Nova Institution," *Daily News*, 30 May 1996.
38 Andrew Thompson, "Worse than Kingston Says Inmate," *The Record* 7 May 1996.
39 Personal notes, 1996.
40 Steve Proctor, "Fencing Truro Prison No Solution – Advocate," *Chronicle Herald*, 31 May 1996.
41 Author unknown, "Erecting Walls," *Chronicle Herald*, 31 May 1996.
42 Steve Proctor, "No Quick Answers in Fracas at Prison," *Chronicle Herald*, 7 September 1996.
43 Personal notes, 1996.
44 Personal communication, 2001.
45 Personal notes, 1996.
46 The *Interim Instruction* "Annexe 'A' 006" was issued on 19 September 1996. It reclassified that portion of Springhill accommodating women as "multi-level," which meant that any troublesome woman could be transferred from Nova, irrespective of her security classification.
47 Cathy Nicholl, "High-Risk Women Moved," *Daily News*, 21 September 1996, 3.

48 Interview 2.
49 *Investigation of Minor Disturbance – Use of Force*, Administrative Investigation, Nova Institution, 96–09–19.
50 It is csc's policy to hold either national or regional investigations into incidents that might have a bearing on policy and/or legal compliance. The decision is based on an assessment of the seriousness of the incident. Investigations must be national if serious bodily harm, or a death, has occurred.
51 The unit was next to the men's segregation unit and could hold up to ten women. Women-centred training was not provided for the staff until a year after the unit first started operating. There were also problems in providing sufficient female staff so that the women would not be seen by male staff when in the observation cells. Fluctuating numbers meant that consistent programming was impossible. Men and women could shout to each other when in their (separate) exercise yards, and during the time the women were held at Springhill there were "serious acting out behaviours" (Warner 1998, 23).
52 All such reports are vetted under the Access to Information Act, 1985, and the Privacy Act, 1985.
53 The board's report, *Investigation of Minor Disturbance – Use of Force*, was initially obtained and made public under the Access to Information Act by the local Truro newspaper, the *Daily News*. The paper published its account of the report on the 25 June 1997.
54 Personal notes, 1998.

CHAPTER EIGHT

1 The draft master plan for Kitchener stated that the "boundary" was to "create an identifiable edge that will discourage *un*intentional movement on to the site. No containment capability is required" (1992c, 34).
2 Interview 10.
3 Interview 8.
4 Ibid.
5 Personal notes, 1996
6 Interview 10
7 There was a deliberate attempt to avoid importing any of the "old" corrections into the new prisons, and staff at the Prison for Women were told quite bluntly that most of them would not be offered jobs in the new system. (Personal notes, 1996).
8 Personal notes, 1996.
9 Interview 10.
10 Ibid.
11 Ibid.
12 Interview 8.

13 *Eyewitness News,* CFRN (TV). Taken from transcript, 19 March 1996.

14 Jackie Fitton, "Nova Warden Gets Axe," *Daily News,* 11 February 1997.

15 "Casuals" were trained correctional staff but could not work more than 125 days a year. They could be offered "term" positions, which were of at least three months duration, but again there was no certainty that the "term" would be translated into "indeterminate" status.

16 Letter from Susan Hendricks, CAEFS' president, to Commissioner John Edwards, 21 February 1996.

17 Edwards to Hendricks, 27 February 1996.

18 Ibid.

19 Kim Pate, Executive Director CAEFS, to John Edwards, 1 March 1996.

20 Letter sent by Michelle Clarke on behalf of Elizabeth Fry Societies of Calgary, Edmonton, Manitoba, and Saskatchewan, 30 April 1996.

21 CD 022 covers "Media Relations." Sections 14 to 20 cover when and how "offenders" may be interviewed by the media. Interviews may be in person or by phone and are dependent upon permission being granted by the "Operational Unit Head." Permission may be refused if an interview is thought to be "contrary to the objectives of the offender's Correctional Treatment Plan."

22 Interview 9.

23 Ibid.

24 Personal notes, 1998.

25 Tom Barrett, "Warden Says Danger Was Unforeseen," *Edmonton Journal,* 9 September 1998. Statement made at Fatality Inquiry into the death of Denise Fayant.

26 Interview 8.

CHAPTER NINE

1 Interview 29.

2 Interview 20.

3 Healing Lodge Sub-Committee Progress Report, 14 March 1991.

4 *Creating Choices* had tacitly conceded that the establishing of the Healing Lodge would not be solely an Aboriginal endeavour when it said: "the development of the Healing Lodge will draw on the expertise of Aboriginal women" (TFFSW 1990, 115). Sharon McIvor and Fran Sugar were the sole Aboriginal members of the task force included on that initial twelve-strong subcommittee, and they were joined by three Aboriginal Elders and three other Aboriginal women as well as by four CSC representatives. The subcommittee was eventually renamed the Healing Lodge Planning Circle (HLPC) and, at that point, was much enlarged.

5 These listed specific requirements, such as proximity to the home communities of the majority of federally sentenced women, being near a supportive Aboriginal community, and proximity to women's support networks.

6 Interview 15.
7 Ibid.
8 This is not strictly accurate. The band was granted its reserve in 1913 but did not receive benefits until 1975. See Hildebrandt and Hubner (1994, 111).
9 "Federally Sentenced Women Initiative: Healing Lodge Facility," Nekaneet Band/Maple Creek Proposal.
10 Interview 15.
11 Chief Nekaneet signed Treaty Four in 1874, yet the Canadian authorities failed to provide a reserve for the Nekaneet until 1913 and the band received no treaty benefits until 1975. On 23 September 1992 the Nekaneet Band signed an agreement finally settling its land claim, receiving $8.3 million in compensation. Under the terms of the agreement they were obliged to buy 16,160 acres of land, which was equal to the acreage Chief Nekaneet failed to receive when he signed Treaty Four. For a fuller exploration of the history of the Nekaneet, see Hildebrandt and Hubner (1994).
12 "Federally Sentenced Women Initiative: Healing Lodge Facility," Nekaneet Band/Maple Creek Proposal.
13 Interview 15.
14 Interview 16.
15 Interview 21.
16 Ibid.
17 December 1991.
18 The arrival of the first Christian missionaries on Turtle Island (North America) heralded a sustained campaign to rid the continent of supposedly pagan beliefs. As explained in chapter 2, in Canada many Aboriginal spiritual ceremonies were banned and the passing on of traditional Aboriginal prac- tices was disrupted by the removal of children from their families and their placement in (largely Christian) residential schools. As Aboriginal peoples have begun to reclaim the right to practise their own spirituality, there has been a tendency among some Euro-Canadians to assert that the expression of such beliefs has more to do with making a political statement than it does with actual cultural traditions. While this is incorrect – even if, as Waldram (1997) shows, spirituality within prisons has of necessity needed to empha- size its pan-Aboriginal aspects rather than those of individual nations – it is also offensive. McGaa (1990, 6) puts it bluntly: "We have been told over and over by Christian missionaries that a man, born of a virgin, died, rose again three days after his death, pushed a big stone back from his tomb, and then ascended into the spiritual world. An Indian would consider it poor manners to make fun of this spiritual story, especially if it is part of a people's spiritual history." The renaissance of interest in Aboriginal spirituality and culture is a consequence of, and interlinked with, Aboriginal peoples reconnecting with their ethnic identity. As Aboriginal peoples' own oral histories have taught them, they have always had a unique responsibility for the stewardship of

Notes to pages 207–11   281

what they see as "their land." That this stewardship should be expressed in stories is entirely consonant with the practices of other nations who might, for example, term their faiths Christian, Muslim, or Jewish. Faiths rely on storytelling as a means of explication; faiths are subjected to criticism from non-believers; and faiths have played a part in the creating of distinct cultures within nations. The *Vision*, provided by the HLPC, should be understood in the light of its attempt to make rational, for a sometimes sceptical audience, core Aboriginal beliefs.

19 The "Circle of Life" reflects Aboriginal peoples' relationship with the Creator, the earth, and everything and everybody inhabiting the earth. It charts an individual's progress through infancy, childhood, adulthood, and old age. It delineates the responsibilities they assume for the continuation of an unbroken "Circle of Life." Nothing may be seen in isolation; everything is interlinked.

20 February 1993.

21 Interview 15.

22 Interview 16.

23 *Healing Lodge Land Rationale*, 1993.

24 Ibid.

25 Ibid.

26 HLPC Minutes, 26 May 1993.

27 Ibid., 17 November 1993.

28 Ibid., 20 April 1993.

29 Formal permission had to be obtained from all members of the band, by means of a referendum, for land to be leased to CSC. The band needed to achieve a "majority of the majority" (*HLPC Minutes* 17–19 November 1993) vote to pass the referendum (i.e., 160 eligible, 81 required to vote, 41 to vote yes).

30 Letter from Denis Méthé, Director General Correctional Programs, to HLPC, 28 September 1993.

31 Letter from Méthé to HLPC, 2 December 1993.

32 The HLPC wanted to make a distinction between the more traditional role assigned to the wardens at the other prisons and that of the Kikawinaw. The term "director" was therefore used whenever an English translation was required.

33 A competition board is used within government departments for interviewing candidates for positions.

34 HLPC Minutes, 12 January 1994.

35 Ibid.

36 This figure was agreed following calculations as to what the band could realize for the land if it were used for pasture, the most common use of land in that part of Saskatchewan. An annual percentage adjustment relative to the Consumer Price Index was made each year

37 *Memorandum of Understanding* between the Nekaneet Band, the minister of Indian affairs and northern development, and the solicitor general of Canada.

38 Interview 16.

39 HLPC Minutes, 7 July 1993.

40 To begin with, whenever a program such as substance abuse was "bought-in," all programming was suspended and every woman would participate. All were at the same starting point, and it was assumed that all would benefit. As more women arrived, and others began to leave, this rationale could not be sustained, and the question of cost-effectiveness became more important. Completion of programming is vital to the success of a woman's sentence plan.

41 North, south, east, and west.

42 Women may not enter the Spiritual Lodge when it is their monthly cycle.

43 Tobacco is fundamental to most Aboriginal ceremonies. It represents the "unity of humans and the Creator ... Tobacco is one way the humans can touch the Creator. The smoke from burning tobacco naturally rises and can touch the spirits of the sun and wind. The smoke carries one's prayers to the Creator" (Waldram 1997, 97).

44 This was one issue about which some in the local community felt very strongly. The children were a welcome addition to the Healing Lodge, but their nursery attracted adverse criticism because of the lavishness of its provision. Many of the HLPC's minutes referred to the "Indian Auctions" held at the conclusion of each monthly meeting and that raised a considerable sum. As one observer said: "When I walked in [to the nursery] I just stood there with my mouth open. I could not believe how it was equipped ... When we were having our monthly meetings the government told us that we could have a day care centre, but there'd be no money to equip [it] so we'd have to raise the money locally to do that ... I tell you that there's $6,000 sitting in a bank account down there and that money was to go to equip the day care. I agree with the day care centre, I think that's a good idea, but where do you draw the line? Where's the fiscal responsibility?" (Interview 16).

45 Historically, this was not a new tactic, although it was unprecedented in more recent times. Freedman (1981, 89) wrote of a woman arriving at an Indianapolis reformatory in manacles, whereupon the superintendent asked for them to be removed, saying to those delivering her, "She is my prisoner, not yours," before embracing the woman and taking her to her room.

46 Personal notes, 1998.

47 Interview 14.

48 Interview 15.

49 Personal notes, 1998.

50 11 September 1992.

51 Personal notes, 2002.

52 21 January 1997.

53 HLPC Minutes, 24 February 1993.
54 Personal notes, 1998.
55 Ibid.

CHAPTER TEN

1 In this chapter the term "difficult to manage" is used collectively to cover both maximum security women and those with mental health needs. CSC does not view them as a single group.
2 Burnaby Correctional Centre for Women closed in 2004 and the women were transferred to the newly renovated Fraser Valley Institution.
3 The fences are commensurate with the level of security provided for medium security men, with the difference being that there is no vehicle patrol. It should be acknowledged that medium security federally sentenced men do not have the degree of physical freedom provided for similarly classified federally sentenced women.
4 Tom Barrett, "Warden Says Danger Was Unforeseen," *Edmonton Journal*, 9 September 1998.
5 A number were already being held in a co-located unit at the male Regional Psychiatric Unit (RPC) in Saskatoon, where they were held under an exchange of service agreement (ESA). The secure-hospital style of the RPC, as well as its focus upon males, was unsuitable for the women, which added to the pressure to move them to Edmonton.
6 Double-bunking has to be approved by the commissioner of corrections under CD 550.
7 See Canadian Human Rights Commission (2003).
8 The same design is used in segregation cells for both men and women. The installation of such cells in the new women's prisons demonstrates that the task force's steering committee was prescient in its 20 November 1989 minutes, which read: "areas [of] security and staffing should be clearly discussed [so as] to direct the implementation committee, and to avoid undesirable traditional responses."
9 The women-centred training has now been reinstated as a ten-day course.
10 The cross gender monitor was appointed by CSC following a recommendation of Mme Justice Arbour. The Third Cross Gender Monitoring Report (2000) recommends that males should no longer be hired as front-line primary workers because CSC has failed to pay attention to the project's earlier recommendations regarding how men might be deployed.
11 Working Group Minutes, 13–14 April 1989.
12 Based on figures from 1999, when eighty-two women were in this category, representing a little less than 20 percent of the total federally sentenced women's population.

References

Adams, R. 1994. *Prison Riots in Britain and the USA*. London: Macmillan.

Adelburgh, E., and C. Currie, eds. 1987. *Too Few to Count*. Vancouver: Press Gang Publishers.

– 1993. *In Conflict with the Law*. Vancouver: Press Gang Publishers.

Adler, F. 1975. *Sisters in Crime*. New York: McGraw Hill.

Allen, H. 1987. "Rendering Them Harmless: The Professional Portrayal of Women Charged with Serious Violent Crimes." In *Gender, Crime and Justice*, ed. P. Carlen and A. Worrall, 81–94. Milton Keynes: Open University Press.

Arbour, Hon. L. 1996. *Commission of Inquiry into Certain Events at the Prison for Women*. Ottawa: Public Works and Government Services.

Axon, L. 1989. *Model and Exemplary Programs for Female Inmates: An Internal Review*. Vol. 1: *Report*. Ottawa: Ministry of the Solicitor General of Canada.

Behiels, M., ed. 1989. *The Meech Lake Primer: Conflicting Views of the 1987 Constitutional Accord*. Ottawa: University of Ottawa Press.

– 2000. "Native Feminism vs. Aboriginal Nationalism: The Native Women's Association of Canada's Quest for Gender Equality, 1983–94." In *Nation, Ideas, Identities: Essays in Honour of Ramsay Cook*, ed. M. Behiels and M. Martel, 212–27. Oxford: Oxford University Press.

Berzins, L., and B. Hayes. 1987. "The Diaries of Two Change Agents." In *Too Few to Count*, ed. E. Adelburgh and C. Currie, 163–79. Vancouver: Press Gang Publishers.

Boe, R. 1992. *CSC Offender Population Forecast: Models, Data and Requirements – with Provisional Forecasts for 1998–2007*. Ottawa: Research Branch, Correctional Service of Canada.

Bosworth, M. 1999. *Engendering Resistance: Agency and Power in Women's Prisons*. Aldershot: Dartmouth.

Bothwell, R. 1998. *Canada and Québec: One Country – Two Identities*. Vancouver: UBC Press.

Box, S. 1983. *Power, Crime and Mystification.* London: Tavistock.

Brodsky, G., and S. Day. 1989. *Canadian Charter Equality Rights for Women: One Step Forward or Two Steps Back?* Ottawa: Canadian Advisory Council on the Status of Women.

Bruckert, C. 1993. *Creating Choices: The Report of the Task Force on Federally Sentenced Women – A Critical Analysis.* Ottawa: University of Ottawa.

Canada. 1914. *Report of the Royal Commission on Penitentiaries (MacDonnell Report).* Ottawa: King's Printer.

– 1921. *Report on the State and Management of the Female Prison at Kingston Penitentiary (Nickle Commission).* Ottawa: King's Printer.

– 1977a. *Report of the National Advisory Committee on the Female Offender (Clark Report).* Ottawa: Ministry of the Solicitor General

– 1977b. *Report of the Sub-Committee on the Penitentiary System in Canada (MacGuigan Report).* Ottawa: Supply and Services.

– Royal Commission on Aboriginal Peoples. 1996. *Report of the Royal Commission on Aboriginal Peoples.* Vols. 1–4. Ottawa: Supply and Services.

– 1994. *Memorandum of Understanding between the Minister of Indian Affairs and Northern Development, the Solicitor General and the Nekaneet Band of Indians.* Ottawa: Public Works and Government Services.

Canadian Human Rights Commission. 2003. *Protecting Their Rights: A Systemic Review of Human Rights in Correctional Services for Federally Sentenced Women.* Ottawa: Public Works and Government Services.

Carlen, P. 1998. *Sledgehammer.* Basingstoke: Macmillan Press.

– 2002a. "New Discourses of Justification and Reform for Women's Imprisonment in England." In *Women and Punishment: The Struggle for Justice,* 220–36. Devon: Willan.

– ed. 2002b. *Women and Punishment: The Struggle for Justice.* Devon: Willan.

Chodos, R., R. Murphy, and E. Hamovitch. 1991. *The Unmaking of Canada.* Toronto: James Lorimer and Co.

Chrisjohn, R., S. Young, and M. Maraun. 1997. *The Circle Game.* Penticton: Theytus Books Ltd.

Chrumka, A.G. 2000. *Report to the Attorney General: Public Inquiry into the Death of Denise Fayant.* Alberta: Department of Justice.

Cohen, S. 1989. "Social-Control Talk: Telling Stories about Correctional Change." In *The Power to Punish: Contemporary Penality and Social Analysis,* ed. D. Garland and P. Young, 101–29. Aldershot: Gower Publishing.

– 1985. *Visions of Social Control.* Oxford: Blackwell.

Comack, E. 1996. *Women in Trouble.* Halifax: Fernwood Publishing.

Cook, R. 1986. *Canada, Québec and the Uses of Nationalism.* Toronto: McClelland and Stewart.

Cook, S. and S. Davies. 1999. *Harsh Punishment: International Experiences of Women's Imprisonment.* Boston: Northeastern University Press.

Cooper, S. 1993. "The Evolution of the Federal Women's Prison." In *In Con-*

flict with the Law, ed. E. Adelburgh and C. Currie, 33–49. Vancouver: Press Gang Publishers.

Correctional Service of Canada (CSC). 1992a. *Federally Sentenced Women Draft Master Plan.* Ottawa: Correctional Service of Canada.

– 1992b *The Healing Lodge Operational Plan December Draft 3.* Ottawa: Correctional Service of Canada.

– 1992c. *Regional Facilities for Federally Sentenced Women Draft 4 Operational Plan.* Ottawa: Correctional Service of Canada.

– 1993a. *Healing Lodge Final Operating Plan.* Ottawa: Correctional Service of Canada.

– 1993b. *Planning Parameters: Healing Lodge.* Ottawa: Correctional Service of Canada.

– 1994a. *Board of Investigation: Major Disturbance and Other Related Incidents – Prison for Women from Friday April 22 to Tuesday April 26, 1994.* Ottawa: Correctional Service of Canada.

– 1995a. *Brainstorming Session: Understanding Violence by Women and Dealing with Women's Anger.* Ottawa: Correctional Service of Canada.

– 1995b. *Regional Facilities for Federally Sentenced Women.* Ottawa: Correctional Service of Canada.

– 1996a. *Board of Investigation Report into a Suicide in February 1996, and Other Major Incidents at Edmonton Institution for Women.* Ottawa: Correctional Service of Canada.

– 1996b. *Lessons Learned for the Future: Federally Sentenced Women's Program.* Ottawa: Correctional Service of Canada.

– 1997a. *Disciplinary Board of Investigation: Segregation and Use of Force.* Ottawa: Correctional Service of Canada.

– 1997b. *Investigation of Minor Disturbance: Use of Force Nova Institution, 96–09–19.* Ottawa: Correctional Service of Canada.

– 1999. *Backgrounder: Intensive Intervention Strategy.* Ottawa: Correctional Service of Canada.

– 2004a. *Management Protocol.* Ottawa: Correctional Service of Canada.

– 2004b. *Program Strategy for Women Offenders.* Ottawa: Correctional Service of Canada.

Coyle, A. 1994. *The Prisons We Deserve.* London: HarperCollins.

Cressey, D. 1962. "Limits of Treatment." In *The Sociology of Punishment and Correction*, ed. N. Johnston, L. Savitz, and M. Wolfgang, 501–8. New York: John Wiley and Sons, Inc.

Culhane, C. 1979. *Barred from Prison: A Personal Account.* Vancouver: Pulp Press

– 1985. *Still Barred from Prison.* Montreal: Black Rose Books.

– 1991. *No Longer Barred from Prison.* Montreal/New York: Black Rose Books.

DiIulio, J. 1991. *No Escape: The Future of American Corrections.* New York: Basic Books.

Dobash, R., R. Dobash, and S. Gutteridge. 1986. *The Imprisonment of Women.* Oxford: Blackwell.

Doern, G.B., and P. Aucoin. 1971. *The Structures of Policy Making in Canada.* London: Macmillan.

Duguid, S. 2000. *Can Prisons Work? The Prisoner as Object and Subject in Modern Corrections.* Toronto: University of Toronto Press.

Eaton, M. 1993. *Women after Prison.* Buckingham: Open University Press.

Ekstedt, J., and C. Griffiths. 1988. *Corrections in Canada: Policy and Practice.* Vancouver: Butterworths.

Faith, K. 1993. *Unruly Women: The Politics of Confinement and Resistance.* Vancouver: Press Gang Publishers.

– 1995. "Aboriginal Women's Healing Lodge: Challenge to Penal Correctionalism?" *Journal of Human Justice* 6, 2: 79–104.

Fournier, S., and E. Crey. 1997. *Stolen from Our Embrace: The Abduction of First Nations Children and the Restoration of Aboriginal Communities.* Vancouver: Douglas and MacIntyre Ltd.

Freedman, E. 1981. *Their Sisters' Keepers: Women's Prison Reform in America, 1830–1930.* Ann Arbor: University of Michigan Press.

Frideres, J. 1993. *Native Peoples in Canada: Contemporary Conflicts.* Scarborough: Prentice Hall Canada Inc.

Garland, D., and P. Young, eds. 1989. *The Power to Punish: Contemporary Penality and Social Analysis.* Aldershot: Gower Publishing.

Gavigan, S. 1987. "Women's Crime: New Perspectives and Old Theories." In *Too Few to Count*, ed. E. Adelburgh and C. Currie, 47–66. Vancouver: Press Gang Publishers.

Geller-Schwartz, L. 1995. "Feminism and the State in Canada." In *Comparative State Feminism*, ed. D.M. Stetson and A. Mazur, 40–58. London: Sage.

Hall, A. 1989. "What Are We? Chopped Liver? Aboriginal Affairs in the Constitutional Politics of Canada in the 1980s." In *The Meech Lake Primer*, ed. M. Behiels, 423–56. Ottawa: University of Ottawa Press.

Hamilton, A.C., and M. Sinclair. 1991. *The Justice System and Aboriginal People: Report of the Aboriginal Justice Inquiry of Manitoba.* Winnipeg: Queen's Printer.

Hannah-Moffat, K. 1994. "Feminine Fortresses: Women-Centred Prisons?" In *Prison Journal* 75, 2: 135–64.

– 2000. "Reforming the Prison: Rethinking our Ideals." In *An Ideal Prison? Critical Essays on Women's Imprisonment in Canada,* ed. K. Hannah-Moffat and M. Shaw, 30–40. Halifax: Fernwood Publishing.

– 2001. *Punishment in Disguise: Penal Governance and Canadian Women's Imprisonment.* Toronto: University of Toronto Press.

Hannah-Moffat, K., and M. Shaw, eds. 2000. *An Ideal Prison? Critical Essays on Women's Imprisonment in Canada.* Halifax: Fernwood Publishing.

– 2001. *Taking Risks: Incorporating Gender and Culture into the Classifica-*

tion and Assessment of Federally Sentenced Women in Canada. Ottawa: Status of Women Canada.

Harding, C., B. Hines, R. Ireland, and P. Rawlings. 1985. *Imprisonment in England and Wales: A Concise History*. London: Croom Helm.

Hayman, S. 1996. *Community Prisons for Women: A Comparative Study of Practice in England and the Netherlands*. London: Prison Reform Trust.

– 2000. "Prison Reform and Incorporation." In *An Ideal Prison? Critical Essays on Women's Imprisonment in Canada*, ed. K. Hannah-Moffat and M. Shaw, 41–51. Halifax: Fernwood Publishing.

Heidensohn, F. 1985. *Women and Crime*. Basingstoke: MacMillan.

– 1987. "Women and Crime: Questions for Criminology." In *Gender, Crime and Justice*, ed. P. Carlen and A. Worrall, 16–27. Milton Keynes: Open University Press.

– 1994. "Gender and Crime." In *The Oxford Handbook of Criminology*, ed. R. Reiner, R. Morgan and M. Maguire, 997–1040. Oxford: Oxford University Press.

Heney, J. 1990. *Report on Self-Injurious Behaviour in the Kingston Prison for Women*. Ottawa: Correctional Service of Canada.

Hildebrandt, W., and B. Hubner. 1994. *The Cypress Hills: The Land and Its People*. Saskatoon: Purich Publishing.

Horii, G. 2001. "Women's Imprisonment and the State: The Praxis of Power." In *[Ab]Using Power: The Canadian Experience*, ed. S. Boyd, D. Chunn and R. Menzies, 236–52. Halifax: Fernwood Publishing.

Hudson, B. 2002. "Gender Issues in Penal Policy and Penal Theory." In *Women and Punishment: The Struggle for Justice*, ed. P. Carlen, 21–46. Devon: Willan.

Ignatieff, M. 1978. *A Just Measure of Pain*. London: Penguin.

Jackson, M. 1988. *The Maori and the Criminal Justice System: A New Perspective – He Whaipaanga Hou Part 2*. Wellington: Department of Justice.

Johnson, B. 1984. "Women behind Bars." In *Equinox*, March/April.

Johnson, H. 1987. "Getting the Facts Straight: A Statistical Overview." In *Too Few to Count,* ed. E. Adelburgh and C. Currie, 11–22. Vancouver: Press Gang Publishers.

Johnson, H., and K. Rodgers. 1993. "A Statistical Overview of Women and Crime in Canada." In *In Conflict with the Law*, ed. E. Adelburgh and C. Currie, 95–116. Vancouver: Press Gang Publishers.

Johnson, S.L., and B.A. Grant. 2000. "Women Offenders Serving Long Sentences in Custody." *Forum on Corrections Research* 12, 3: 16–20.

Kelley, J. 1967. *When the Gates Shut*. London: Longman.

Kendall, K. 1993a. *Program Evaluation of Therapeutic Services at the Prison for Women*. Ottawa: Correctional Service of Canada.

– 1993b. *Companion Volume I to Program Evaluation of Therapeutic Services at the Prison for Women*. Ottawa: Correctional Service of Canada.

– 1993c. *Supporting Documents, Companion Vol. 11, to Program Evaluation of Therapeutic Services at the Prison for Women.* Ottawa: Correctional Service of Canada.
– 1994b. "The Discipline and Control of Women." *Journal of Human Justice* 6, 1: 111–19.
– 1994c. "Therapy behind Walls: A Contradiction in Terms?." *Prison Service Journal* 96: 2–11.
– 1998. "Evaluation of Programmes for Female Offenders." In *Female Offenders: Critical Perspectives and Effective Interventions*, ed. R. Zaplin, 361–79. Gaithersburg: Aspen Publishing.
– 2000. "Psy-ence Fiction: Governing Female Prisons through the Psychological Sciences." In *An Ideal Prison? Critical Essays on Women's Imprisonment in Canada*, ed. K. Hannah-Moffat and M. Shaw, 82–93. Halifax: Fernwood Publishing.
Kendall, K., and S. Pollack. 2005. "Taming the Shrew: Regulating Prisoners through Women-Centered Mental Health Programming." *Critical Criminology* 13: 71–87.
Kidman, J. 1947. *The Canadian Prison: The Story of a Tragedy.* Toronto: Ryerson Press.
Krosenbrink-Gelissen, L.E. 1993. "The Native Women's Association of Canada." In J. Frideres, *Native Peoples in Canada: Contemporary Conflicts*, 335–64. Scarborough: Prentice Hall Canada Inc.
Lajeunesse, T., C. Jefferson, J. Nuffield, and D. Majury. 2000. *The Cross Gender Monitoring Project Third Annual Report.* Ottawa: Federally Sentenced Women Programme – CSC.
La Prairie, C. 1993. "Aboriginal Women and Crime in Canada: Identifying the Issues." In *In Conflict with the Law*, ed. E. Adelburgh and C. Currie, 235–46. Vancouver: Press Gang Publishers.
Liebling, A., and D. Price. 2001. *The Prison Officer.* Aylesbury: Prison Service Journal.
Luciani, F. 2000. "Classifying Offenders Serving Life Sentences." *Forum on Corrections Research* 12, 3: 21–4.
McGaa, E. 1990. *Mother Earth Spirituality: Native American Paths to Healing Ourselves and Our World.* San Francisco: HarperSanFrancisco.
McRoberts, K. 1993. *Québec: Social Change and Political Crisis.* Toronto: Oxford University Press.
Manzer, Y. 1996. "Centre for Federally Sentenced Women." Unpublished paper, prepared for Maritime School of Social Work.
Maracle, B. 1993. *Crazy Water: Native Voices on Addiction and Recovery.* Toronto: Penguin.
Martel, J. 1999. *Solitude and Cold Storage: Women's Journeys of Endurance in Segregation.* Edmonton: Elizabeth Fry Society of Edmonton.
Mathiesen, T. 1989. "The Future of Control Systems: The Case of Norway."

In *The Power to Punish: Contemporary Penalty and Social Analysis,* ed. D. Garland and P. Young, 130–45. Aldershot: Gower Publishing

Mercredi, O., and M.E. Turpel. 1994. *In the Rapids: Investigating the Future of First Nations.* Toronto: Penguin.

Miller, J.R. 1996. *Shingwauk's Vision: A History of Native Residential Schools.* Toronto: University of Toronto Press.

– 2000. *Skyscrapers Hide the Heavens: A History of Indian-White Relations in Canada.* Toronto: University of Toronto Press.

Ministerial Committee of Inquiry into the Prisons System in New Zealand. 1989. *Te Ara Hou: The New Way.* New Zealand: Government Printing Office.

Ministry of Justice. 1992. *Proceedings of the International Seminar on Women In Detention: Perspectives for Change.* The Hague: Ministry of Justice.

Moffat, K. 1991. "Creating Choices or Repeating History: Canadian Female Offenders and Correctional Reform." *Social Justice* 83: 184–203.

Monture, P. 1989–90. Abstract prefacing, "Nistum Peyako Séht'wawin Iskwewak: Breaking Chains." *Canadian Journal of Women and the Law* 6, 1: 119–23.

Monture-Angus, P. 1995. *Thunder in My Soul: A Mohawk Woman Speaks.* Halifax: Fernwood Publishing.

– 2000. "Aboriginal Women and Correctional Practice." In *An Ideal Prison? Critical Essays on Women's Imprisonment in Canada,* ed. K. Hannah-Moffat and M. Shaw, 52–60. Halifax: Fernwood Publishing.

Morin, SkyBlue. 1991. *Healing Lodge Land Rationale.* Ottawa: Correctional Service of Canada.

Morrison, R., and C.R. Wilson, eds. 1995. *Native Peoples: The Canadian Experience.* Toronto: Oxford University Press.

Native Women's Association of Canada. 1991. *Healing Lodge Vision.* Ottawa: NWAC.

Nova Scotia. 1989. The Report of the Royal Commission on the Donald Marshall, Jr. Prosecution. Halifax: Province of Nova Scotia.

Oliver, P. 1998. *Terror to Evildoers: Prisons and Punishment in Nineteenth-Century Ontario.* Toronto: University of Toronto Press.

Pate, K. 1999. "csc and the 2 Percent Solution: The P4W Inquiry." *Women and Justice* 19, 1 and 2: 145–53.

Player, E., and M. Jenkins, eds. 1994. *Prisons after Woolf: Reform through Riot.* London: Routledge.

Proudfoot, P. 1978. *Report of the British Columbia Royal Commission on the Incarceration of Female Offenders.* Vancouver: Royal Commission on the Incarceration of Female Offenders.

Rafter, N.H. 1995. *Partial Justice: Women in State Prisons 1800–1935,* 2nd ed. Boston: Northeastern University Press.

Razack, S. 1991. *Canadian Feminism and the Law.* Toronto: Second Story Press.

Reiner, R., R. Morgan, and M. Maguire eds. 1994. *The Oxford Handbook of Criminology*. Oxford: Oxford University Press.

Rivera, M. 1996. *Giving Us a Chance: Needs Assessment – Mental Health Resources for Federally Sentenced Women in the Regional Facilities*. Ottawa: Correctional Service of Canada.

Rock, P. 1986. *A View from the Shadows*. Oxford: Oxford University Press.

– 1996. *Reconstructing a Women's Prison: The Holloway Redevelopment Project 1968–88*. Oxford: Oxford University Press.

Ross, L. 1998. *Inventing the Savage: The Social Construction of Native Deviance*. Austin: University of Texas Press.

Ross, R. 1992. *Dancing with a Ghost: Exploring Indian Reality*. Toronto: Reed Books Canada.

– 1996. *Returning to the Teachings: Exploring Aboriginal Teachings*. Toronto: Penguin.

Rothman, D. 1971. *The Discovery of the Asylum: Social Order and Disorder in the New Republic*. Boston: Little, Brown and Company.

– 1980. *Conscience and Convenience: The Asylum and Its Alternatives in Progressive America*. Boston: Little, Brown and Company.

Rotman, E. 1995. "The Failure of Reform." In *The Oxford History of the Prison*, ed. N. Morris and D. Rothman, 157–77. Oxford: Oxford University Press.

Ryan, M. 1983. *The Politics of Penal Reform*. London: Longman.

Scull, A. 1984 *Decarceration : Community Treatment and the Deviant : A Radical View,* 2nd ed. Cambridge: Polity Press

Shaw, M. 1991. *The Federal Female Offender: Report on a Preliminary Study*. Ottawa: Solicitor General of Canada.

– 1993. "Reforming Federal Women's Imprisonment." In *In Conflict with the Law*, ed. E. Adelburgh and C. Currie, 50–75. Vancouver: Press Gang Publishers.

– 1996a. "Is There a Feminist Future for Women's Prisons?" In *Prisons 2000*, ed. R. Matthews and P. Francis, 179–200. London: Macmillan Press Ltd.

– 1996b. "Knowledge without Acknowledgement: Violent Women, the Prison and the Cottage." Paper presented at the 48th annual meeting of the American Society of Criminology, 1996, at Chicago.

– 1997. "Conflicting Agendas: Evaluating Feminist Programs for Women Offenders." PhD diss., University of Nottingham.

– 1999. "A Video Camera Can Change Your Life." In *Harsh Punishment: International Experiences of Women's Imprisonment*, ed. S. Cook and S. Davies, 250–71. Boston: Northeastern University Press.

Shaw, M., K. Rodgers, J. Blanchette, T. Hattem, L. Seto Thomas, and L. Tamarack. 1991a. *Paying the Price: Federally Sentenced Women in Context*. Ottawa: Solicitor General of Canada.

- 1991b. *Survey of Federally Sentenced Women: Report to the Task Force on Federally Sentenced Women on the Prison Survey*. Ottawa: Solicitor General of Canada.

Solicitor General of Canada and Attorney General of British Columbia. 1976. *Bilateral Discussions on the Division of Correctional Responsibilities Between the Federal Government and Province of British Columbia*. Victoria: Ministry of the Attorney General.

Solicitor General's Special Committee on Provincially Incarcerated Women. 1992. *Blueprint for Change* Halifax: Nova Scotia Correctional Services.

Sparks, R., A. Bottoms, and W. Hay. 1996. *Prisons and the Problem of Order*. Oxford: Clarendon.

Stern, V. 1994. "The Future of the Voluntary Sector and the Pressure Groups." In *Prisons after Woolf: Reform through Riot*, ed. E. Player and M. Jenkins, 243–54. London: Routledge.

Stetson, D.M., and A. Mazur, eds. 1995. *Comparative State Feminism*. London: Sage.

Strange, C. 1985. "The Criminal and the Fallen of Their Sex: The Establishment of Canada's First Women's Prison 1874–1901." *Canadian Journal of Women and the Law* 1: 79–92.

Sugar, F., and L. Fox. 1990. *Survey of Federally Sentenced Aboriginal Women in the Community*. Ottawa: Correctional Service of Canada.

Sullivan, L.E. 1990. *The Prison Reform Movement: Forlorn Hope*. Boston: Twayne Publishers.

Task Force on Aboriginal Peoples in Federal Corrections. 1988. *Final Report: Task Force on Aboriginal Peoples in Federal Corrections*. Ottawa: Department of the Solicitor General.

Task Force on Federally Sentenced Women (TFFSW). 1990. *Creating Choices: The Report of the Task Force on Federally Sentenced Women*. Ottawa: Correctional Service of Canada.

Waldram, J. 1997. *The Way of the Pipe*. Peterborough, Ontario: Broadview Press.

Wagamese, R. 1996. *The Terrible Summer*. Toronto: Warwick Publishing.

Warner, A. 1998. *Implementing Choices at Regional Facilities: Programme Proposals for Women Offenders with Special Needs*. Ottawa: Correctional Service of Canada.

Warry, W. 1998. *Unfinished Dreams: Community Healing and the Reality of Aboriginal Self-Government*. Toronto: University of Toronto Press.

Wilson, V.S. 1971. "The Role of Royal Commissions and Task Forces." In *The Structures of Policy Making in Canada*, ed. G.B.Doern and P. Aucoin, 113–29, Toronto: Macmillan.

Wines, E.C., and T.W. Dwight. 1867. *Report on the Prisons and Reformatories of the United States and Canada*. Albany: van Benthuysen's Steam Printing House.

Woolf, Lord Justice 1991. *Prison Disturbances April 1990: Report of an Inquiry by the Rt. Hon Lord Justice Woolf (Parts I and II) and His Hon. Judge Stephen Tumim Part II).* London: HMSO.

Zedner, L. 1991. *Women, Crime and Custody in Victorian England.* Oxford: Clarendon Press.

– 1995. "Wayward Sisters: The Prison for Women." In *The Oxford History of the Prison,* ed. N. Morris and D. Rothman, 295–324. Oxford: Oxford University Press.

COLLECTED PAPERS

Canadian Association of Elizabeth Fry Societies
Correctional Service of Canada
Anonymous member of task force

PRESS CUTTINGS

Canadian Press
Chronicle Herald (Truro)
Daily News (Truro)
Edmonton Examiner
Edmonton Journal
Edmonton Sun
Kingston Whig Standard
The Law
Mill Woods Newsletter (Edmonton)
The Record (Truro)
Toronto Star

VIDEO TRANSCRIPT

CBC 5th Estate. 1995. *The Ultimate Response,* 22 February.

Index

Maple Creek, 203–5. *See also* Okimaw Ohci Healing Lodge
maternal logics: and structural relations of power, 64
McIvor, Sharon, 52, 72
McLeod, Linda, 271n26
McNeill, Isabel, 17
media, role of, 195–6; at Healing Lodge, 218–19
Meech Lake Accord, 47, 49–50
Mercrede, Ovide, 49
Miller-Ashton, Jane, 27, 55, 66, 71, 134
Ministry of the Solicitor General, 25
Minnesota Correctional Facility – Shakopee, 22, 104, 141
Monture, Patricia, 52, 53, 66, 71, 72, 106

National Implementation Committee (NIC), 134–7
National Indian Brotherhood, 48, 51
National Planning Committee on the Female Offender, 19
Native Women's Association of Canada (NWAC), 30, 42–3, 51–4, 163, 243, 264n14
Needham Report, 19
Nekaneet Band, 203–5, 219–20, 228; and reserve, 280n11. *See also* Okimaw Ohci Healing Lodge
Nickle Commission, 15
Northwest Territories: Task Force and, 102
Nova Institution for Women, 161–82; design of, 166–8; *Disciplinary Board of Investigation*, 177–80; *Disciplinary Board of Investigation* and comparisons with Arbour Commission, 179–81; disturbances at, 174–8; enhanced unit, 185–6; impact of events at Edmonton, 172–3, 175; siting of, 161–4; staff, 173–4; staff and the women, 187–92; static security, 184; Task Force and siting of, 101
Nuffield, Joan, 116

Okimaw Ohci Healing Lodge: 200–29, 243–9; children and, 282n44; design of, 216–18; Healing Lodge Planning Circle (HLPC), 200, 206–11; incorpora-
tion of culture and spirituality, 223–6; and increased responsibilities for women, 226–7; Ke-kun-wem-kon-a-wuk and, 211–13, 244; maximum security women and, 222–3; *Memorandum of Understanding*, 212–13, 215, 244; role of Elders and, 244–7; siting of, 202–3, 205, 207–8; staff, 213–15, 220–22; Task Force and siting of, 101; Task Force's planning of, 96–9, 110–11
Ouimet Committee, 13, 18

Papineau, Louis-Josèph, 44
Pate, Kim, 154–5, 156, 157, 163, 166, 172
peer support, 267n9
Penitentiary Act, 13
Phelps, James, 27, 29, 34, 55, 66, 69, 82, 109
potlatch, 37, 270n35
principles. *See Creating Choices*
Prison for Women, 15, 18, 24–6, 109, 266n38; closure, 230; construction, 15; design of, 15–17; LSD experiments, 95; male prisoners and, 15; staff, 269n33, 272n11; suicides 81–2, 255, 267n2. *See also* Arbour Commission
prison reform, risks of, 250–8
private family visits, 269n30, 274n34
Proudfoot Commission, 20
prudentialism, 121

Quebec, 42–3, 67–8, 77–8, 127–32; Bill 22, 46; history, 44–7; imprisoned federally sentenced women's population and, 43; Official Languages Act, 46; "Quiet Revolution", 45, 46; Royal Commission on Bilingualism and Biculturism, 45; Task Force and siting of new prison, 101, 115; War Measures Act, 46;

reformatory movement, 63; USA and, 20–1, 260n7. *See also* Andrew Mercer Reformatory for Women; Minnesota Correctional Facility for Women-Shakopee
regional prisons: design of, 103; 140–1; enhanced units, 140; locations, 100–2, 134–5; programs, 194–5, 239–41;